The Open Book

A Practical Perspective on OSI

Marshall T. Rose
The Wollongong Group, Inc.

Prentice Hall
Englewood Cliffs, New Jersey 07632

Library of Congress Cataloging-in-Publication Data

Rose, Marshall T.
    The open book : a practical perspective on OSI / Marshall T. Rose.
        p.   cm.
    Includes bibliographical references.
    ISBN 0-13-643016-3
    1. Computer networks. 2. Computer network protocols. 3. Computer
network architectures.   I. Title.
    TK5105.5.R67   1989
    004.6--dc20   67437   89-37756
                                                              CIP

Editorial/production supervision: *Jacqueline A. Jeglinski*
Cover design: *Lundgren Graphics*
Manufacturing buyer: *Ray Sintel*

 © 1990 by Prentice-Hall, Inc.
A division of Simon & Schuster
Englewood Cliffs, New Jersey 07632

The publisher offers discounts on this book when ordered
in bulk quantities. For more information, write:
    Special Sales/College Marketing
    Prentice-Hall, Inc.
    College Technical and Reference Division
    Englewood Cliffs, NJ 07632

Printed in the United States of America
10 9 8 7 6 5 4

ISBN 0-13-643016-3

For information about our audio products, write us at:
Newbridge Book Clubs, 3000 Cindel Drive, Delran, NJ 08370

Prentice-Hall International (UK) Limited, *London*
Prentice-Hall of Australia Pty. Limited, *Sydney*
Prentice-Hall Canada Inc., *Toronto*
Prentice-Hall Hispanoamericana, S.A., *Mexico*
Prentice-Hall of India Private Limited, *New Delhi*
Prentice-Hall of Japan, Inc., *Tokyo*
Simon & Schuster Asia Pte. Ltd., *Singapore*
Editora Prentice-Hall do Brasil, Ltda., *Rio de Janeiro*

for Bangles
(who still might get back together)

Contents

III   Application Services   123

6   Introduction to Application Services   125

List of Tables

List of Figures

Foreword

The Open Book is an extraordinary volume by an extraordinary author. Marshall Rose is one of the most productive engineers I have ever had the pleasure to work with. In this volume, he has poured not only his understanding of the details of the Open Systems Interconnection Protocols, but his personal experience implementing them, leavened by his personal experience in the TCP/IP Internet environment. The point I want to stress is that Marshall's observations and often blunt opinions are based on *implementation experience*, not merely paper review of published specifications. Even if one disagrees with an opinion or two, these views must be taken seriously, because of their basis in the real world.

This book is an important contribution to the networking literature for two reasons. First, it is one of the clearest expositions of the OSI architecture and protocols, and it deals with concrete issues, including implementation matters. Second, it seeks to explicate ways in which the TCP/IP Internet community may accommodate the phased introduction of OSI protocols. This latter contribution is of prime importance if this large and rapidly growing community is to benefit from the heavy vendor community investment in OSI software and services.

Vint Cerf
Camelot
Annandale, Virginia

Preface

This book is about Open Systems Interconnection (OSI). In particular, this book focuses on the pragmatic aspects of OSI: what OSI is, how OSI is implemented, and how OSI is integrated with existing networks.

Unfortunately, the phrase "open systems" has become rather all-encompassing these days, just as many terms take on all meanings, and therefore no meaning, when they become popular. This book is about computer networking. Computers communicate with each other using a set of rules, called a *protocol*, which make meaningful exchanges possible. A group of protocols, all related to a common model, is a called a *protocol suite*. This book is about one particular suite, which contains protocols based on the OSI Reference Model as promulgated by the International Organization for Standardization and International Electrotechnical Committee (ISO/IEC). The OSI protocol suite is particularly exciting as it has a rather unique promise: it has the potential to provide both a political and technical solution to world-wide networking. Computers from supers, to workstations, and to personals; from the executive suite, to the laboratory, and to the factory floor; from Palo Alto, to London, to Melbourne, all *can* share a common set of rules for communicating. Of course, it needn't be the case that *can implies shall*: administrative policies may prohibit one company's computers from talking to those of a competitor, even though it is technically possible for the machines to communicate.

There is often confusion about the term Open Systems Interconnection. A colleague, Einar Stefferud, suggests that it might be helpful to change the capitalization to OsI. The intent is to emphasize that the ISO/IEC effort is on Open Interconnection of arbitrary systems, as opposed to opening heretofore closed systems. That is, the exchange mechanisms *between* systems are open, rather than the internal behavior of any single system.

This book was written with a particular scenario in mind: OSI is becoming a popular technology. Although there are very few OSI systems deployed today, it is widely predicted that OSI will become the networking solution of choice within the next several years. However, there is little experience with OSI: the implementations that exist are few and largely skeletal; important considerations, such as performance and scaling, have had scant attention paid to them; and few have given serious consideration as to how the large installed base of computers, all performing perfectly useful computing, but using various non-OSI protocol suites, may transit to OSI. This book intends to examine those complex questions. To be sure, there are no simple answers, but there is a wide range of experience with implementing other similar protocol suites, on which we can draw as we seek those answers.

Earlier discussions of these topics (and indeed, OSI of itself) have been hampered by major changes in OSI over the last two years. OSI is an evolving technology, and many concepts will undergo change in the years to come. However, given the recent stabilization of the upper layers of OSI in March and December of 1988, now is the ideal time to consider both OSI and these issues. Although work continues, the author and the reader can both be assured of having a stable reference point upon which to base discussion.

Having said what this book is about, I should now say what this book is not about. This book is not *intentionally* of a political or partisan nature. I am constantly amazed at the tremendously high noise-to-signal ratio whenever two arguably rational professionals discuss OSI. This phenomenon is quite evident when one professional favors OSI and the other favors some other protocol suite. As a consequence, this book is concerned with the nuts and bolts details of the so-called *bleeding edge*. It is not the charter of this book to make glowing statements as to how wonderful everything will be once we simply "get everything implemented." (You can read such statements in the trade magazines on a daily basis.) Similarly, this book won't make predictions of disaster as to how "none of this stuff works." (You can also read such statements in the same trade magazines.) Regrettably, the technology of OSI is inseparable from the politics of OSI. This book will express non-technical perspectives from time to time, but will label them as such, namely as *soapboxes*. Look for text bracketed between the symbols $\boxed{\text{soap...}}$ and $\boxed{\text{...soap}}$, which appear in the margin. Further, the book will try to present a balanced set of perspectives.

The guiding rule will be one of fairness: when a concept in OSI lacks coherence, this will be pointed out, along with a discussion as to what a correct solution might be. Similarly, when a concept in OSI has elegance and style, this too will be emphasized as being superior to other approaches. This stance is a compromise that is unfortunately not very common. Let me explain with a personal story that highlights the perspective I'm advancing.

I first became involved with OSI back in 1981 when I started reading the draft documents that were to become the 1984 CCITT Recommendations on Message Handling Systems (commonly known as X.400). I was working on an electronic mail system then known as the Rand Message Handling System (MH). This system was based on the electronic mail services in the TCP/IP protocol suite (more properly known as the U.S. Department of Defense Internet Suite of Protocols — we'll be hearing a lot about the Internet suite of protocols throughout this book). Bluntly put, I was shocked when I read the X.400 documents. The nomenclature was foreign, the text was unreadable, and some of the concepts were, well, *alien* in comparison to the system that I was working on.

In defense of my naiveté, I hasten to explain that the electronic mail services in the Internet suite have two interesting properties: they are text-based, and they are ubiquitous. With few exceptions, the electronic mail protocol in the Internet suite, described in a document called RFC822, is used to exchange text-based messages from computers of all kinds over media of all kinds (telephone lines, local area networks, wide area networks, etc.). Of all the network applications, electronic mail is the most popular, and of all the mail protocols, RFC822 is the most widely used or imitated. In contrast, the X.400 recommendations describe a multi-media system, including images and voice in addition to text, and is only beginning to enjoy what might be taken for widespread use.

So, imagine my surprise when I was confronted with these OSI documents: here I was, processing 200 messages a day with my RFC822–based mail system (and progressing towards my doctorate), while this committee, using the most unintelligible language possible, was telling me how to do electronic mail! I promptly dismissed OSI (and X.400) as some quack plot and went back to my obscure dissertation area.

Of course, OSI did not just disappear from my life. In January of 1986, at the Northrop Research and Technology Center, the Automation Sciences Laboratory was interested in solving certain problems in the factory automation area. At that time, the Manufacturing Automation Protocol (MAP) was being suggested as the solution for networking on the factory floor. MAP is based heavily on OSI protocols. Use of OSI to build factory applications interested the Automation Sciences Laboratory, but they had one small problem: all of the networks we used at the Center were based on the Internet suite of protocols.

A colleague, Dwight E. Cass, and I collaborated on an after-hours OSI project. Our interest was to see whether we could add the richness of the OSI application environment to the robustness of the Internet end-to-end service environment. This really seemed like a great idea: the OSI application environment is very powerful and incorporates a number of interesting concepts. In contrast, the Internet application environment was much simpler. For example, one could build powerful applications, but there was no unifying theme to encourage either the reuse of components (e.g., each application tended to have its own way of representing data on the network, even though a common format would have sufficed), or the use of automatic tools in building applications. Similarly, the Internet end-to-end services were mature and ran everywhere; in contrast, the OSI end-to-end services were largely unusable because of poor performance and lack of deployment.

The technical work was simple, though it actually took us thirteen months finally to understand what we were doing and how to explain it succinctly. However, the response from fellow professionals was almost entirely unexpected: universal anger. Dwight would talk with the OSI camp, which thought that we were "committing the terrible crime of diluting the momentum of OSI by doing anything with TCP/IP." I would talk to the Internet camp, which thought that we were "foolish for doing anything with something that clearly will never work" (OSI). These are actual quotations. Because virtually everyone was against us (except senior management at Northrop — Dr. Stephen J. Lukasik, Vice President, Technology — was very supportive), Dwight and I *knew* we were on the right track, so we pushed forward.

After implementing the technology to run OSI applications in a network using TCP/IP, the only things we were missing were OSI applications, so we set out to implement a few. Before we could do this, we had to build the OSI upper-layer infrastructure. We consulted with several vendors of OSI software to see what of theirs we could use. None was interested in pursuing our approach, although all were willing to sell us their software at truly outrageous prices! So, Dwight and I thought, "How difficult and time-consuming could it be to write this stuff?" Ah, the folly of youthful enthusiasm!

Thus began a project called The ISO Development Environment (ISODE). The ISODE is an openly available implementation of the upper-layers of OSI. Openly available means that anyone can acquire, for a minimal distribution fee, a copy of the source code from any of the five distribution centers worldwide. I've been working on the ISODE, part-time, for nearly three years now, first at the Northrop Corporation, and now at The Wollongong Group, Inc. Dwight conveniently moved to another project right after he talked me into doing the work.

As work on ISODE progressed, something of a metamorphosis occurred: my leanings towards mixing the best parts of the OSI and Internet protocol suites strengthened considerably. For example, the ISODE now has an interesting package called *The Applications Cookbook*, which automates a lot of the tasks (code writing) involved in implementing a network application in the OSI environment. This was something that I never would have considered building in an Internet applications environment simply because it lacks the rich concepts used by OSI applications. However, I prefer to run my network applications on TCP/IP-based networks simply because TCP/IP networks tend to have better performance and reliability. In time, the OSI end-to-end services will mature, gaining much, one hopes, from the Internet suite of protocols. At present however, the OSI end-to-end services are woefully inadequate for a large class of useful networking situations. These experiences are integral with the central theme of this book: OSI must be tempered pragmatically with learning and experience with other protocol suites.

How to Use this Book

This book is intended to serve both as a graduate-level text and also as a professional reference. It is helpful to consider each of the four parts in the order in which they are presented, although a reader with a modest background in networking should be able to understand any of the four parts independently of the others.

The first part, *An Introduction to OSI*, presents the basic architecture and philosophy of OSI. Readers interested in gaining an understanding of the basics should start here, at the beginning. Knowledgeable practitioners may also wish to review this part, as they might encounter some alternative perspectives and interpretations of OSI technology.

The second part, *End-to-End Services*, concerns itself with the current OSI network and transport technologies. The emphasis here is on complexity, management, and performance. One problem that is examined and for which solutions are proposed is that the current dichotomy in OSI between connection-oriented and connectionless-mode networking services may prevent two conformant OSI systems from communicating with each other. This part also introduces the notion of providing an emulation of OSI transport services using other protocols, such as TCP. Emulation provides a way to field OSI applications in networks that are not based on OSI, whereby early experience may be gained.

The third part, *Application Services*, emphasizes the OSI upper-layer infrastructure as the basis for building network applications. In addition to introducing this rich infrastructure along with key OSI applications, programmatic tools for building these applications are discussed. This focuses on a critical aspect of the OSI upper-layers: re-use of components along with the use of automatic tools can speed the development process.

The fourth part, *Transition to OSI*, takes a step back and evaluates several approaches to the problems of transition and co-existence. This part, which many may find controversial, is motivated by a difficult real-world problem: given that the Internet suite of protocols is the long-standing solution of choice for non-proprietary networking, and considering that OSI might be several more years away as a worthwhile alternative, what can be done to ease the transition to OSI?

Instructors can easily build a one- or two-year course on this text, depending on the depth in which they wish to cover the material It is recommended that a laboratory accompany the course. When a laboratory corresponding to Part III is given, it will be useful to acquire the ISODE (see Appendix A for availability information). The ISODE will provide an excellent basis for the students to perform experiments.

One curriculum, which the author favors, is a two-year course: the first year devoted to the Second Edition of Tanenbaum's *Computer Networks* (ISBN 0–13–162959–X) and Part II of this text, the second year devoted to Parts III and IV of this text. *Computer Networks* is an excellent work that provides a solid grounding in all aspects of computer-computer communications, whilst *The Open Book* focuses on the OSI approach to networking. If only a one year course is desired, then the first semester might use *Computer Networks* for an in-depth treatment of end-to-end services, and the second semester might use this text for the application services.

Acknowledgements

Much of the information presented in this book can be found in the open literature in the form of standards, papers, and research notes. The perspectives presented here came about largely through professional and personal interaction with my colleagues. Since these interactions "didn't just happen overnight," it is impossible to acknowledge all of the individuals who have helped, directly or indirectly, with this book. However, some organizations and individuals stand out.

The one thread of continuity in my studies has been my colleague and university mentor, Einar Stefferud of Network Management Associates. It was he who first interested me in networking back in 1981, and to this day we continue many amusing arguments as to what is going wrong in networking and why. This book would not have been written without him.

It is fair to say that the basis for the third part of this book, *Application Services* came largely out of my experiences at the Northrop Research and Technology Center and with the ISODE both at Northrop and at Wollongong. At the Northrop Corporation, I credit Dwight E. Cass and Stephen J. Lukasik for providing both technical stimulation and support. As regards the ISODE, the contributors are too numerous to mention, although the Preface to *The ISO Development Environment: User's Manual* mentions as many as possible. Again, three names stand out: Stephen E. Kille of the University College London is easily the Deputy Architect of the ISODE, providing the most elegant and powerful abstractions found in the system. Similarly, Julian P. Onions of Nottingham University provided true power-coding of many fine concepts and certainly qualifies as the First Engineer of the ISODE. Finally, Christopher W. Moore of The Wollongong Group, Inc., has also had quite an impact on my understanding of the upper layers, in particular with the OSI Directory; section 11.1 is largely based on talks he has given in the past.

The fourth part of this book, *Transition to OSI*, is heavily based on a working paper, *Transition and Coexistence Strategies for TCP/IP to OSI*, which was developed whilst I was at Wollongong throughout 1988. Just as Northrop provided an environment to experiment with the ISODE, Wollongong provided the environment for me to study transition strategies (and also to write this book). David H. Crocker, formerly Vice President of Engineering at Wollongong, has had the most profound impact on my thinking in this area. In addition to Stef, Dave, and Chris, Norman Lombino of 3–COM and Robert Slaski of NetWorks One provided useful comments on the working paper. A small section of the working paper appeared as an article in the September, 1988 issue of the industry newletter *ConneXions* (ISSN 0894–5926) published by Advanced Computing Environments (ACE) in Mountain View, California.

Finally, there have been many reviewers who have spent considerable time pouring over countless manuscripts to help me produce the snappy prose contained herein: Vinton G. Cerf of The Corporation for National Research Initiatives; David H. Crocker; Geoffrey S. Goodfellow of Anterior Technology; Stephen E. Kille of University College London; Herb J. Martin, Keith McCloghrie, and Christopher W. Moore, of The Wollongong Group, Inc.; Julian P. Onions of Nottingham University; Craig Partridge of the U.S. NSF Network Service Center at BBN Systems and Technology Corporation; and Einar A. Stefferud of Network Management Associates. Jerry N. Sweet was kind enough to perform the copy-editing on *The Open Book*. His intense efforts brought this work to print six months earlier than I had thought possible!

And, of course, I should thank my cat, Cheetah, for tirelessly waking me up at 5:00 am each morning so I could work on this book!

/mtr

Mountain View, California

Part I

An Introduction to OSI

Chapter 1

Introduction to Open Systems

In the *Information Age,* information is as important to any organization as its employees, equipment, or buildings. To be useful, information must be both structured and mobile. If information is structured, then it can be processed: to verify facts, analyze trends, and synthesize ideas. The value of information is directly tied to the entity (person or program) that accesses it. One can increase the value of information simply by moving it to a place where some entity can make use of it. Mobility makes information valuable. The *structure* and *transfer* of information are of key importance to successful organizations.

Historically, information has been neither structured nor mobile. Although writing and clay tablets were probably a step in the right direction, they are generally viewed as sub-optimal. Until computers became indigenous to organizations, there were few ways to structure information. Before computers, processing information was slow and tedious. After computers became commonplace, the problem became how to make information mobile, easily and conveniently transferable between systems. Networks, which interconnect computers, are the movers of information.

Physically connecting computers isn't enough to achieve mobility of information. The computers must adhere to a common set of rules for defining their interactions, i.e., how they talk to one another. How computers talk to one another is termed a *protocol.* Protocols defined in terms of a common framework and administered by a common body form a *protocol suite.*

Concepts of computer communication are well understood by both computer vendors and users of computers. Each vendor began by developing its own protocol suite so that its own computers could communicate meaningfully amongst themselves. Such protocol suites are termed "proprietary" because they are controlled by a single entity: the vendor. Although publishing the protocol definitions is a step in the right direction, it is insufficient. With a proprietary protocol suite, the vendor is free to change the definitions at whim. It soon became clear that proprietary protocols were also sub-optimal as there is little value in having information that is mobile only between computers manufactured by a single vendor.

A single, non-proprietary protocol suite was required to achieve information mobility. To ensure that all computers belonging to an organization could communicate with each other (regardless of their manufacture), there had to be exactly one protocol suite. The protocol suite had to be open so that no one vendor would have an unfair competitive advantage in the market. Information mobility seemed imminent!

Then, *two* non-proprietary protocol suites emerged. One, termed the Internet suite of protocols, was sponsored by the U.S. Department of Defense (DoD), a user, not a vendor, of computers. The other, termed the OSI suite of protocols, was sponsored by the International community.

Although they started development at roughly the same time (the late-70's), unlike OSI, the Internet suite of protocols has seen extensive deployment — not only in the DoD community, but world-wide across the entire spectrum of user organizations. The Internet suite might be thought of as the property of the U.S. military, but this is an entirely pedantic view. The protocol suite is administered not by the U.S. military, but by researchers sponsored by many areas of the U.S. government. All computer users, regardless of nationality or profession, have benefited tremendously from the Internet suite.

The best term to use when describing the Internet protocols is *focused.* There was a problem to solve, that of allowing a collection of heterogeneous computers and networks to communicate. Solving the internetworking communications gap required a good deal of cutting edge research. The Internet researchers made open systems a reality by limiting the problem, gauging the technology, and, by and large, making a set of well thought out engineering decisions.

The OSI suite, on the other hand, had a tremendous disadvantage. By its very nature, it wasn't *allowed* to achieve focus. By opening the process to international comment, experts from every continent contributed to the standards process. Each expert had a private (provincial) vision, and few of these visions were in concert.

In 1988, ten years after official "birth" of the OSI suite, there were pilot projects, nothing more. In contrast, Internet technology was becoming a commodity market.

Despite this amusing turn of events, the Internet suite has a limited future. The long-term favorite is the OSI suite, although it is anyone's guess as to when the long term actually starts.

The preceding discussion has touched briefly upon the general benefits of open systems. These arguments may best be summarized as this point:

Open systems maximize leverage.

Open Systems force the communications aspects of computers to be viewed as a commodity. For users this is attractive because they no longer need to worry about whether the equipment they purchase will be able to communicate with the rest of their network. Planning and competition is enhanced, thereby increasing cost-effectiveness. For vendors this is attractive because communications development can be focused on a single set of protocols (at least in theory), making more effective use of engineering, marketing, and sales resources.

1.1   The Players of Open Systems

OSI stands for *Open Systems Interconnection*. Superficially, its sole purpose is to facilitate communications between computers. In practical terms, OSI represents a massive undertaking involving technologists, politicians, and users from the International community.

OSI is defined in terms of *standards*. A standard is a document that carries behind it the force of the sponsoring entity. This naturally leads to a discussion of who produces OSI standards.

1.1.1   Standards Organizations

Depending on the International community to which one belongs, there are two organizations that are viewed as having International authority. The International standards groups, it should be noted, have no force of law, per se. Each national government must determine which standards are mandated for a particular application.

ISO/IEC

The ISO/IEC is an abbreviation for the *International Organization for Standardization and International Electrotechnical Committee*. The members of the ISO/IEC are the national standards bodies, including the U.S.'s ANSI (the American National Standards Institute) and the U.K.'s BSI (the British Standards Institution). The ISO/IEC also maintains liaison with other multi-national standards organizations such as the Institute of Electrical and Electronic Engineers (IEEE) and the European Computer Manufacturers' Association (ECMA). Historically, ECMA has provided considerable input to the ISO/IEC on matters relating to OSI.

The ISO/IEC does a lot more than producing OSI standards. There are two sub-committees that are responsible for OSI:

- JTC1/SC6, Telecommunications and Information Exchange between Systems; and,

- JTC1/SC21, Information Retrieval, Transfer, and Management.

These are respectively sub-committees 6 and 21 of joint technical committee 1. In the context of the introductory discussion, JTC1/SC6 is in charge of data mobility and JTC1/SC21 is responsible for information structure.

The documents produced by the ISO/IEC are termed *International Standards*. The process of creating an international standard is a long and involved one, beginning with a proposal being submitted by a member body. The introductory proposal is termed a *Working Document* (WD), and is assigned a standards number and a sub-committee that is responsible for progressing the document to its final status. The standards number is retained by the document as it progresses through its various stages of development.

When consensus is reached that a WD should advance, the document is promoted to *Draft Proposal* (DP) status, and a date is set, typically six months forward, for a vote on the document's further promotion. DPs are given wide circulation for comment. After the months of discussion pass, the vote is taken. A member may vote in one of four ways:

- *no for reasons given*;

- *no with comments*, which means that if the attached comments were incorporated into the document, the member would instead vote yes;

- *yes with comments*, which means that the member prefers some changes to be made, but that a yes vote is still given; or,

- *yes.*

After the ballots return, it is up to the editor(s) of the document to see if they can convert the *no with comments* votes into *yes* votes. Because more than one member may vote *no with comments*, it may be impossible to reconcile conflicting comments and arrive at a yes consensus. However, the editor(s) work as best they can to modify the document so that it receives the widest support from the voting members.

If the ballot passes, then the document becomes a *Draft International Standard* (DIS), and a date six months forward is set for the next vote. Otherwise, the document remains a Draft Proposal, called the 2nd DP. A new date for a vote is set, and more meetings and discussion are held until that time. The same voting procedures are used. If consensus is reached, the document becomes a DIS. Otherwise, the document is considered unworkable; if there is still sufficient interest, a new document will be circulated, starting as a Working Draft.

Draft International Standards are considered to be technically stable, and the only changes allowed (in theory) are those fixing non-technical problems, such as typographical errors and textual descriptions. After the usual period of meetings and discussions, the voting procedures are invoked. If consensus is reached, the document then becomes an *International Standard* (IS). Otherwise, the document remains a Draft International Standard, being called the $2^{\underline{nd}}$ DIS. A new date for a vote is set, and more meetings and discussion are held until that time. The same voting procedures are used. If consensus is reached, the document becomes an IS. Otherwise, the document is demoted back to DP status. This effectively means that the document is considered unworkable.

When referring to a document in a particular state, a concise notation is used:

```
ISO/IEC <<state>> <<number>>
```

For example, if a document was assigned number 8648, it might be known through its journey to IS status as:

```
ISO/IEC WD 8648
ISO/IEC DP 8648
ISO/IEC DP2 8648    -- first DIS vote failed
ISO/IEC DIS 8648
ISO/IEC IS 8648
```

Since reaching International Standard status signifies the end of the process, the expression

```
ISO/IEC <<number>>
```

is commonly used for the last step, as in ISO 8648.

A standard that has achieved IS status is considered to be stable for quite some time. If it is necessary to amend a standard, there is an addendum process: first a *Proposed Draft Addendum* (PDAD), then a *Draft Addendum* (DAD), and finally an *Addendum* (AD) is produced. These are numbered in a similar fashion.

For example, these designations refer to the first Addendum to International Standard 8473 as the Addendum progressed through the standards process:

```
ISO/IEC 8473 PDAD1
ISO/IEC 8473 DAD1
ISO/IEC 8473 AD1
```

CCITT

The CCITT is an abbreviation for the *International Telephone and Telegraph Consultative Committee*. The members of the CCITT are the national Post, Telephone, and Telegraph (PTT) administrations. In countries where a single entity does not provide this function, an agency of the national government leads the delegation to the CCITT. The CCITT is a division of the *International Telecommunications Union* (ITU) which is under the United Nations.

Documents produced by the CCITT are termed *Recommendations*. This term is used because the CCITT recommends to its member bodies that they implement these documents. The CCITT is a cooperative process, and because the members of the CCITT effectively have global coverage, the recommendations have, in practice, much more impact than the standards produced by the ISO/IEC.

Unlike the ISO/IEC, the CCITT works in four year study periods. At the end of the fourth year, a new series of recommendations is published that supersedes the output from any previous study period. For example, the study period completed in 1988 produced recommendations that supersede those produced in 1984. All recommendations produced in the same study period are bound in books of the same color. In 1984, there were the "red books," whilst in 1988, there were the "blue books."

The naming convention for CCITT recommendations consists of a letter identifying a recommendation series and a number within that series, optionally followed by the year ending the study period:

```
<<series>>.<<number>> (<<period>>)
```

For example, X.25(80) refers to recommendation number 25 produced in the data network services series ("X") in the study period that ended in 1980. When referring to recommendations from the latest study period, the year is simply left off, as the latest recommendations purposefully obsolete all previous recommendations.

As might be expected, the ISO/IEC and the CCITT have joined forces to produce much of OSI. The respective sub-committees and study groups usually meet jointly to produce standards and recommendations that are technically aligned on matters of common interest.

Finally, it should be noted that there are many organizations devoted to producing standards at all levels of international and national participation. *The Open Book* has briefly introduced two. For a more thoughtful exposition and analysis, the reader should consult [CCarg89].

1.1.2   Functional Profiles

A standard often contains many more options than can be implemented altogether. If each vendor implements only a subset of options, there is no guarantee that any two vendors will implement the same subset. The result is systems that are interoperable in theory, but not in practice!

An important pragmatic step is to identify a common subset of options and related practices that can be used effectively. This is the purpose of groups that promulgate functional profiles.

In the United States, the National Institute of Standards and Technology (NIST) hosts the *OSI Implementors' Workshop* which meets quarterly to produce functional profiles on OSI. Once a year, the Workshop produces a set of *Stable Implementors' Agreements*, e.g., [NIST88]. The Workshops are largely driven by the output of the standards process.

Other national organizations exist to produce the functional profiles for their respective countries. Various collective communities of nations also have their own standards profiling organizations.

1.1.3   Standard Profiles

Functional profiles carry no force of law. Each vendor has sole discretion as to whether its products are aligned with the functional profiles.

The final step necessary to achieve the leverage of open systems is a national policy that mandates the use of functional profiles. In the United States, the U.S. Government OSI Profile (GOSIP) [USGOS88] provides the focus for Federal users of OSI. The GOSIP document, a U.S. Federal Information Processing Standard (FIPS), carries with it the force of law for Federal users. After a grace period of a few years, newly purchased computer equipment must conform to the GOSIP.

GOSIP has no direct standing with non-Federal entities such as regional and local agencies, and non-public organizations. However, many agencies and organizations in early 1989 were moving towards using the GOSIP as their lever into open systems.

As might be expected, other national governments have elevated some of their respective functional profiles to have the force of law. Most notable is the United Kingdom with its U.K. GOSIP [UKGOS88].

1.1.4 Internet Standards

It is important to appreciate that despite its multi-vendor support, widespread success, and numerous technical accomplishments, the Internet suite of protocols is *not* OSI. Proponents of both protocol suites agree that this is a good thing.

In the discussion that follows, the term *Internet Community* refers to all parties, world-wide, that use the Internet suite of protocols.

Internet Activities Board

The Internet suite of protocols was sponsored by the U.S. DoD and grew out of early research into survivable multi-media packet networking sponsored by the Defense Advanced Research Projects Agency (DARPA). At the time, there was only one network, called the ARPANET, which connected a few dozen computer systems around the country. With the advent of different networking technologies, such as Ethernet[1], Packet Radio, and Satellite, a method was needed for reliable transmission of information over media that do not guarantee reliable, error free delivery of information. (Information transmitted using these technologies can be lost or corrupted as the result of radio propagation or collision). Thus, the Internet suite of protocols was born.

---

[1]Ethernet is a trademark of the Xerox Corporation.

In addition to providing reliable delivery of information over possibly unreliable methods of transmission, the Internet suite of protocols offered inter-network interoperability, the ability for computer systems to communicate over one or more networks. Previously all communication had been within a single net, the ARPANET.

The technical body that oversees the development of the Internet suite of protocols is termed the *Internet Activity Board* (IAB). The IAB is composed of senior researchers who, for the most part, are the designers and original implementors of the Internet suite.

The IAB, per se, produces very few documents. Any member of the Internet community can design, document, implement, and test a protocol for use in the Internet suite. The IAB requires that protocols be documented in the *Request for Comments* (RFCs) series.   The RFC document series is a convenient place for the dissemination of ideas. Protocol authors are encouraged to use the RFC mechanism regardless of whether they expect their protocol to become an Internet standard.

If standardization is to be attempted, the protocol is first termed a *proposed protocol*. It is expected that several groups will independently implement and test the proposed protocol. This orthogonal development process results in an improved version of the protocol being designed and implemented.

When stability is achieved, the protocol must find a sponsor, a member of the IAB willing to champion the protocol in the IAB. When a sponsor is found and the case for standardization is made, the IAB reaches consensus and the protocol becomes a *Draft Internet Standard*. A new RFC is published indicating this status. The Internet community is typically given six months to review, implement, and test the protocol. Unless serious objections are raised or flaws are exposed, the IAB acts to declare the protocol an official *Internet Standard*.

Each RFC has two attributes: a *state*, which indicates the document's level of standardization, and a *status*, which indicates the level of support the Internet community must accord the document. The densities of RFCs falling into the combinations of these attributes are summarized in the following sparse matrix:

State	Status			
	Required	Recommended	Elective	Not Recommended
Internet Standard	√√√	√√	√	
Draft Standard		√	√√	
Proposed Standard			√√√	√
Experimental Protocol			√	√√√
Historical Protocol				√√√

The more √'s in a table category above, the greater the number of RFCs fitting into that category.

Each RFC is assigned a number by the RFC editor. If the text of the RFC is revised, a new number is assigned (in contrast to the ISO/IEC scheme of retaining the same number). In order to prevent confusion, if an RFC supercedes any previous RFCs, this is clearly stated on the cover of the newer RFC.

There are four RFCs that define the status of documents in the RFC series. These are:

Assigned Numbers: lists the assigned values used for the parameters in the Internet suite of protocols;

Official Protocols: lists all official protocols; and,

Gateway Requirements: lists all protocols and practices that relate to network nodes; and,

Host Requirements: lists all protocols and practices that relate to host nodes.

These RFCs are periodically updated. As with the rest of the RFC series, the most recent document always takes precedence. The key document that relates these RFCs is the Official Protocols RFC. This RFC is issued quarterly by the IAB with a strong warning to retrieve the next version when the current document reaches its expiration date. As of this writing, the latest version was [IAB89]. As of this reading, that version is obsolete.

1.2 Roadmap

For the remainder of *The Open Book*, the discussion focuses on four aspects of OSI.

The next chapter introduces the OSI model and related terminology. All OSI concepts are viewed in the context of this ubiquitous model. Models are useful for organizing concepts and mechanisms in order to explain some effect. In the OSI sense, the model provides the framework for explaining how computer systems interoperate.

Part II of this book focuses on the OSI end-to-end services. End-to-end mechanisms are used to transfer unsemanticized data from one computer to another. In defining end-to-end services, OSI has tried to accommodate two fundamentally different viewpoints. This has led to numerous problems. In describing the OSI end-to-end services, the author plays the role of the *angry young scientist*: the lack of workable end-to-end services will prove to be a major stumbling block for OSI.

Part III of this book focuses on the OSI application services. Application services are used to transfer semanticized information from one computer to another. OSI offers a rich set of services in this regard. These services are particularly attractive both to network users and applications programmers. In describing the OSI application services, the author plays the role of the *Pied Piper of OSI*, a title bestowed by Robert Braden, Executive Director of the IAB.

Part IV of this book focuses on transition to OSI. Networking was not invented by OSI, so it shouldn't be surprising that there are numerous non-OSI networks deployed today. How can network users and administrators transit from their existing network infrastructure to OSI? In describing transition technology, the author plays the role of the *elder statesman of networking*: after examining all the options, it will be noted that perhaps the best way to achieve transition is to enter a long period of coexistence.

Part V of this book presents a soapbox that "opens up the cover" on how Open Systems are *really* produced. After reading Parts I through IV of *The Open Book*, Part V will explain how things got the way they are. Of all the various honorific and derisive titles that have been bestowed upon the author, the one he prefers most is the *Cynic of OSI*. It is an easy job: with OSI, there is so much material to work with! After all, OSI is ambitious. It shouldn't be surprising to find that there are numerous problems to be solved.

The discussion that follows attempts to de-focus the formalisms of OSI. Although the concise terminology used in the standards documents is necessary to minimize confusion, it does very little for making the documents comprehensible. The goal of *The Open Book* is not to recite the standards, but rather to give the reader an intuitive feel for and a solid grasp of OSI and related technology.

Chapter 2

Models, Conventions, and Notation

A model is simply a way of organizing knowledge to explain the way things work.

In OSI, a reference model is used to describe computer communications. The Model is inherently abstract. It does not specify:

- programming language bindings,

- operating system bindings,

- application interface issues, or

- user interface issues.

The Model is intended solely to describe the external behavior of systems, independent of their internal constructions. From a communications standpoint, OSI says what goes on the wire and when, but not how computers are built to exhibit the mandated behavior.

As such, OSI standards are grouped into pairs: one defines the *service* offered by some entity, and the other specifies the *protocol* used by that entity to offer that service. This is a well understood concept of abstraction. It allows individual entities to be constructed with little knowledge of other entities. There are two advantages to an architecture that localizes knowledge:

- undesirable interactions caused by side-effects are avoided, because the external behavior of an entity is well defined; and

- the internal construction of a entity may vary without affecting other entities — providing the former maintains its same external behavior.

The discussion now proceeds to consider how OSI services and protocols are described.

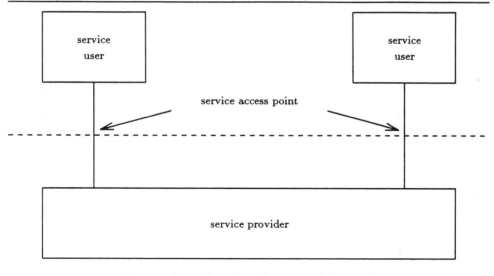

Figure 2.1: Service Users and Provider

2.1 Services

An ISO/IEC technical report, [OSI87b], defines the conventions used when describing OSI services.

A *service* represents a set of functions offered to a user by a provider. As shown here in Figure 2.1, the service is made available through *service access points* (SAPs). From the user perspective, all of the qualities of the service are completely defined by the interface at the SAP. Thus, the provider may be viewed entirely as an abstract entity.

This particular example shows a two-user service. Although this is by far the most common kind of service in OSI, there are other possible services. For example, a multicast service involves multiple receivers for data sent by one user.

It is not hard to imagine that the service provider itself might be composed of smaller entities, which in turn use the service immediate below as shown in Figure 2.2. In addition to introducing a new underlying service provider, this figure also explains how two entities combine to offer a new service: they use the services from below and they communicate using a protocol.

This is the fundamental concept known as *layering*: a relatively simple service may be augmented to offer more powerful services at

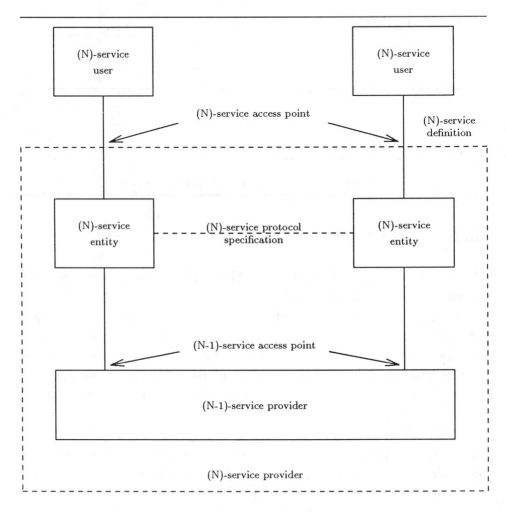

Figure 2.2: Service Layering

the layer immediately above. This process may continue indefinitely, until the desired level of abstraction and power is reached.

In OSI, layers are numbered from the bottom up, starting with level-1. The term "layer-(N)" is used to refer to a generic layer. Similarly, "layer-(N-1)" refers to the layer immediately below, and "layer-(N+1)" refers to the layer immediately above.

Thus, the (N)-service provider consists of two (N)-service entities. These are also (N-1)-service users.

2.1.1 Service Primitives

Each service offered by a provider can be characterized as describing one of three kinds of interactions. In OSI, *time sequence* diagrams are used to denote the relationship between the primitives that form a service and the order in which they occur.

A service may consists of one to four primitives. Each primitive consists of the name of the service, and a suffix that indicates at what point in the interaction the service occurs.

A *confirmed* service is one that involves a handshake between the user that requests the service, termed the *requesting* user, and the user that is informed that the service has been requested, termed the *accepting* user:

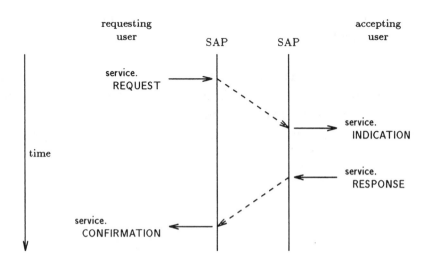

All confirmed services consist of four primitives:

- service.REQUEST, which is invoked by the requesting user;

- service.INDICATION, which is given to the accepting user by the service provider;

- service.RESPONSE, which is invoked by the accepting user; and,

- service.CONFIRMATION, which is given to the requesting user by the service provider;

In contrast, an *unconfirmed* service involves no handshake:

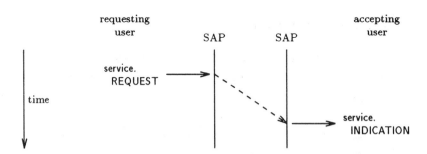

All unconfirmed services consist of two primitives:

- service.REQUEST, which is invoked by the requesting user; and,

- service.INDICATION, which is given to the accepting user by the service provider.

Hidden in these diagrams is the concept of asynchrony, e.g., the service.INDICATION primitive occurs some time after the service.RE-QUEST primitive.

The lack of confirmation has to do with a lack of synchronization, not a lack of *reliability*. If some failure occurs, the service provider will notify the users of this. Of course, the users will still have to coordinate between themselves to determine exactly what data was lost.

Finally, a *provider-initiated* service is, as the name implies, generated by the service provider in response to some internal condition:

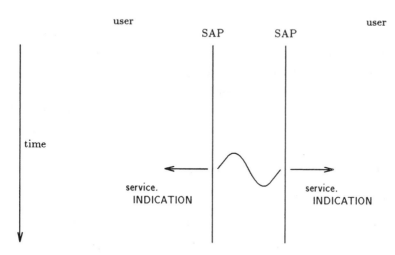

All provider-initiated services consist of one primitive:

- service.INDICATION, which is given to both users by the service provider.

Inherent to the service model is the notion of *queuing*. When a user-initiated service is invoked via the .REQUEST or .RESPONSE primitive, the corresponding .INDICATION and .CONFIRMATION service primitives arrive in the same order. Thus, it is possible for several services to be initiated in rapid sequence by a user, without the user having to wait between each initiation. The corresponding service primitives will be delivered to the other user in the same order that they were invoked.

There are two queues that carry these primitives, one in each direction. There is no explicit relationship between the two queues. However, a confirmed service, because it involves a handshake between the users, places a time ordering between the interactions of the two queues.

There are two exceptions to queuing in the service model. The first exception consists of any primitives that may be termed *expedited*. Conceptually, expedited primitives are ordered, but in a second queue. When a primitive is placed in the expedited queue, it has a special property. Anything placed in the second queue *may* arrive prior to primitives placed in the normal queue, even if the primitives were sent later. Thus, expedited primitives may overtake non-expedited primitives. However, expedited primitives may not overtake other expedited primitives — they are always queued in order, with identical priority to each other.

The second exception to the notion of queuing is that of *disruptive* services, which arbitrarily empty the queue(s) of any service primitives that might be delivered. Typically, each OSI service provides at least two disruptive services: a user-initiated service to terminate all activity in the layer immediately, and a provider-initiated service that serves the same purpose. These are usually called the user-initiated and provider-initiated **ABORT** services, respectively.

In OSI, each service is named using a simple convention:

```
<<layer>>-<<verb>>
```

where `<<layer>>` refers to an abbreviation for an OSI layer and `<<verb>>` denotes the kind of service. Consider a hypothetical layer, L, which might have a service that provides data transfer called **DATA**. If this was an unconfirmed service, there would be two primitives:

L-DATA.REQUEST

L-DATA.INDICATION

Each primitive has associated with it zero or more parameters. The service definition describes each parameter and uses a concise table to define the status of each parameter for the primitives that compose its service. A parameter is marked with one of these annotations:

M: the parameter is mandatory;

C: the parameter is conditional, depending on some rule described in the service definition;

(=): the value of the parameter is identical to value given in the preceding service primitive; and,

U: the parameter is optional, at the discretion of the service user.

Consider a user-initiated service with one parameter:

Parameter	L-DATA service	
	REQUEST	INDICATION
user-data	M	M(=)

In addition, a *blank* is sometimes used to indicate when a particular
parameter is not present for a given primitive (obviously, at least *one*
primitive in the table must use it). For example,

Parameter	L-DATA service	
	REQUEST	INDICATION
source		M
user-data	M	M(=)

would indicate that the "source" parameter is not present on the L-
DATA.REQUEST primitive, and that the provider generates it on the
L-DATA.INDICATION primitive.

2.1.2   Service Interfaces

Finally, the discussion considers the OSI formalism used to describe
the interaction occuring when a service primitive causes information
to pass from one layer to the next.

Suppose a service provider is asked to transfer some data to the
remote service user. This user-data is termed a *service data unit*
(SDU). The service provider attaches a small header to the user-data,
termed the *protocol control information* (PCI). The PCI identifies the
data that is to be transferred.

The resulting object is termed a *protocol data unit* (PDU). This
is the unit of information that is exchanged by peers, implementing a
protocol to offer a service.

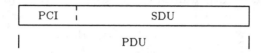

Next, it is necessary to invoke the (N-1)-service provider to cause
the data to be transmitted. To do this, *interface control information*
(ICI) is (conceptually) attached to the PDU. The ICI identifies the
service primitive that is to be invoked from the (N-1)-service.

The resulting object is termed an *interface data unit* (IDU). The
(N)-service provider now passes the IDU through the (N-1)-SAP.

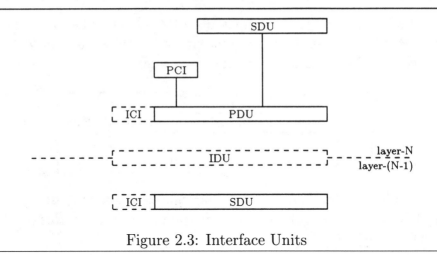

Figure 2.3: Interface Units

The (N-1)-service provider receives the IDU and breaks it apart into the ICI and an (N-1)-SDU. It then invokes the desired primitive based on the ICI. Note that from the perspective of the (N-1)-service provider, an (N)-PDU is precisely an (N-1)-SDU. All of these relationships are summarized in Figure 2.3.

Once the data is transferred, the remote (N-1)-service provider passes an IDU up to the remote (N)-service provider. This is broken into the ICI and PDU, which in turn is broken into the PCI and SDU. Finally, the SDU is delivered to the (N)-service user.

Of course, this is an excruciatingly abstract way to describe how primitives cross service boundaries. The distinction between protocol control information and user-data in a PDU is a well-known technique called *encapsulation*. This allows user-data to be transparently transmitted. More familiar terms from other protocol suites might be:

$$
\begin{aligned}
\text{SDU} &= \text{data} \\
\text{PCI} &= \text{header} \\
\text{PDU} &= \text{packet}
\end{aligned}
$$

The introductions of ICI and IDU are used simply to make the notion of the SAP work; they are formalisms that permit a service provider to offer multiple services and still have a single point of interaction. Indeed, many do not particular care for the notion of an IDU. They prefer to think of the interface information existing in parallel with the data unit, but not attached. That is, they prefer to keep the control and data aspects of the model separated.

It must be stressed that these service conventions are not intended to have any impact on implementations. For example, the IDU mechanism for layer communication is essentially a message passing scheme. Each message (the IDU) carries with it typing information (the ICI) and data (the PDU).

However, there is nothing to prevent an implementor from using a procedure call model instead. Each .REQUEST and .RESPONSE primitive might map to a procedure call in some programming language. In order to map the .INDICATION and .CONFIRMATION primitives, there are at least two different approaches. First, an *upcall* mechanism might be used (e.g., [DClar85]). In essence, when the service provider generates a service primitive, it calls a user-specified procedure. This is an example of an *asynchronous* interface policy.

The second approach would be to provide another procedure call that simply waits some specified amount of time for a service primitive to be generated. Once this happens, the procedure returns with information about what just happened. This is an example of a *synchronous* interface policy. A sophisticated policy might allow the user choose between *polling* (check if anything is ready to report, and return immediately if not), or *blocking* (wait forever until something is ready to report).

Of course, a synchronous interface policy can be implemented on top of an asynchronous policy. It's "just a simple matter of coding."

It is important to understand that OSI, per se, never specifies the notion of conformance to a service. That is, it is always the responsibility (and freedom) of an designer to implement a service faithfully. However, OSI makes no constraints as to how that service is implemented.

2.2 Protocols

OSI service providers are described as *finite state machines* (FSMs).

The protocol machine for a particular service starts in an initial state. Events, which are service primitives received from the user above or the provider below, as they occur, trigger activity on the part of the FSM. As a part of this activity, actions may be required (service primitives issued to the user and/or the underlying provider), and possibly a new state is entered. Eventually the SAP becomes inactive and the FSM returns to the initial state.

Thus, when examining any OSI protocol, there are three things to be discussed:

- how the underlying service is used;

- the elements of procedure for the protocol, which define the behavior of the FSM; and,

- how PDUs are encoded.

Each OSI protocol specification defines these activities. In addition, each usually contains an annex that contains a state table to describe formally the FSM composing the protocol machine.

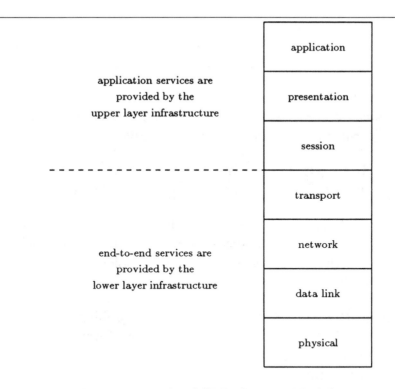

Figure 2.4: The OSI Reference Model

2.3 The 7 Layers

Finally, with the necessary notational conventions out of the way, the discussion looks at the OSI reference model as defined in [OSI84]. The Model divides the task of computer communications into seven functional layers.

There is no mystique to the choice of the number seven. Other protocol architectures have numbers of similar magnitude. The reader is strongly encouraged to read [DCohe83] for an insightful discussion on why the actual number of layers is not fixed and is largely unimportant.

The first four OSI layers form the lower-layer infrastructure of the OSI model. These provide the end-to-end services responsible for data transfer. The remaining three OSI layers form the upper-layer infrastructure of the OSI model. These provide the application services responsible for information transfer. The relation between these is shown in Figure 2.4.

The discussion now considers the individual layers that compose the reference model. The descriptions will be brief — all but the lowest two layers are examined in considerable detail in *The Open Book*.

physical layer (Ph): responsible for the electro-mechanical interface to the communications media.

data link layer (Dl): responsible for transmission, framing, and error control over a single communications link.

network layer (N): responsible for data transfer across the network, independent of both the media comprising the underlying subnetworks and the topology of those subnetworks.

transport layer (T): responsible for reliability and multiplexing of data transfer across the network (over and above that provided by the network layer) to the level required by the application.

session layer (S): responsible for adding control mechanisms to the data exchange.

presentation layer (P): responsible for adding structure to the units of data that are exchanged.

application layer: ultimately responsible for managing the communications between applications.

2.3.1   Services Revisited

In OSI, the service offered by a layer is either *connection-oriented* or *connectionless*.

A connection-oriented mode (CO-mode) service goes through three distinct phases:

connection establishment: in which the service users and the service provider negotiate the way in which the service will be used. If successful, this results in a *connection* being established. Once a connection is established, this is an explicit binding between the two service users. All other service primitives occur in the context of this binding.

Typically, each OSI layer provides a single connection establishment service, using the verb CONNECT.

data transfer: in which the service users exchange data.

connection release: in which the binding between users is discarded.

Typically, each OSI layer provides three connection release services. The first service, using the verb RELEASE, provides for a graceful release of the connection. This means that any service primitives queued for delivery are drained prior to the binding being destroyed. This is a confirmed service.

The second service, using the verb ABORT, provides for a user-initiated immediate release of the connection. This means that any service primitives queued for delivery may or may not be drained prior to the binding being destroyed. This is an unconfirmed service.

The final service, typically using the verb P-ABORT, is a provider-initiated service that also results in an immediate release of the connection. This is usually triggered by an underlying failure.

In contrast, a connectionless mode (CL-mode) service has one phase: data transfer. Any and all options must be supplied for each and every primitive as there is no explicit ongoing relationship established between service users.

Typically, each OSI layer provides a single CL-mode service using the verb UNITDATA. This is an unconfirmed service.

The OSI model is inherently connection-oriented. However, the first Addendum to the International Standard, [OSI87a], augments the model for connectionless-mode (CL-mode) transmission.

For historical reasons, OSI has been primarily interested only in connection-oriented services and protocols. Originally, only CO-mode versions of the services and protocols were defined. Then, the CL-mode lower-layers were defined. Finally, as of the end of 1988, CL-mode versions of the presentation, session, and transport services existed, but no OSI applications made use of them.

In contrast, both CO-mode and CL-mode versions of the data link and network service exist. The transport service may use either the CO-mode network service or the CL-mode network service in order to provide a connection-oriented transport service. Furthermore, either network service may use either data link service. The gist of this is simply stated: OSI application services are connection-oriented. The underlying end-to-end services presently offer a connection-oriented service, but may be internally composed of connectionless-mode protocols.

Part II

End-to-End Services

Chapter 3

Introduction to End-to-End Services

End-to-end services are concerned with *data transfer*. Unlike the application services, which are concerned with *information transfer*, end-to-services are interested solely in moving octets (eight-bit values) from one system to another. The syntax and semantics of those octets are unimportant: bits are bits.

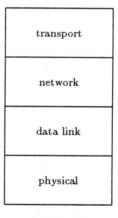

end-to-end services are
provided by the
lower layer infrastructure

From the perspective of these layers, the most significant achievement of OSI has been to provide a flexible framework for describing the diverse transmission media and protocols that combine to form end-to-end services. It should be noted that there is really very little "new" with the OSI perspective on end-to-end services; as a whole this technology was mature prior to OSI standardization. To be sure, OSI has introduced terminology and notation for discussing end-to-end services in a consistent fashion. Nevertheless, in terms of technical advancement, the *lower-layer infrastructure* of OSI is uninteresting. Interested readers will do well to consult the Second Edition of Tanenbaum's *Computer Networks* [ATane88] for the "raw" technology of end-to-end services, independent of the OSI perspective.

When describing the lower-layer infrastructure, it is always difficult to separate the functionality of the two key layers involved, the network and transport layers. This is because of the unfortunate history of the OSI end-to-end services: there have been two techno-political camps with very different views of the lower-layer infrastructure. This has resulted in the OSI end-to-end services becoming generalized to the point of strain, for flexibility doesn't always imply consistency. Throughout the discussion in Part II, the limitations of OSI end-to-end services will be examined along with various solutions proposed to circumvent these limitations.

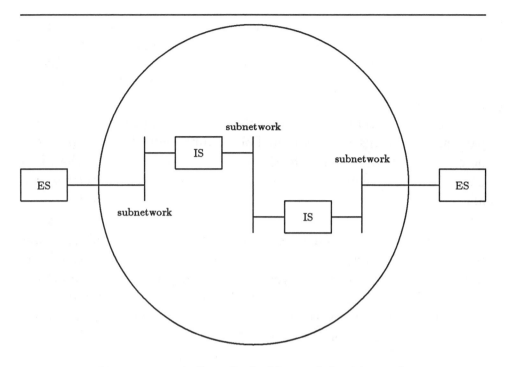

Figure 3.1: A Simplistic View of the Network

3.1 Concepts

At the simplest level, a *network* consists of:

- a collection of *subnetworks*,

- connected by *intermediate-systems* (ISs),

- and populated by *end-systems* (ESs).

Figure 3.1 shows a simplified view of a network. The reader should note that it is relatively pointless to present anything other than a stylized representation of a network topology; in practice, there is no such thing as a "representative" example.

3.1.1 Subnetworks

In OSI, a subnetwork is that which was previously considered to be a single network, e.g., several nodes connected together on a single (virtual) transmission medium. The properties of the medium largely determine the characteristics of the subnetwork. For example, a sub-network based on a point-to-point medium consists of a "wire" connected between exactly two nodes. In contrast, a subnetwork based on a broadcast medium consists of a "wire" connected to potentially many nodes.

There are myriad trade-offs involved in selecting a technology for a particular transmission medium. For example, whilst broadcast technologies might seem more effective because they allow more than two nodes to be connected, the subnetwork access protocols must worry about contention. This simply isn't a problem with a subnetwork based on a full-duplex point-to-point technology.

The full range of transmission media is evolving too quickly and is entirely too diverse to be discussed here. In fact, because of this diversity, the OSI network layer is particularly useful: it completely masks the underlying subnetwork technology. The topology of many interconnected subnetworks appears as a single homogeneous entity, from the perspective of a user of end-to-end services.

3.1.2   Intermediate-Systems

An intermediate-system (IS) is simply a single node, connected to more than one subnetwork, which is allowed to forward data from one subnetwork to another. A node performing this task need only have a subset of the OSI end-to-end services resident.[1] An intermediate-system performs two tasks: first, it forwards data from one subnetwork to another; and, second, in order to make the forwarding decision, it usually participates in a distributed routing algorithm. The forwarding decision requires the IS to decide where to send data next.

Routing is a Problem

It turns out that, in general, routing is an unsolved problem; although lots of problems have been solved, more keep popping up. In the early days of networking, it was quite a task to achieve a stable routing al-

---

[1]The OSI application services need not be present. However, since the OSI network management protocol resides at the application layer, and since it is a good idea to manage intermediate-systems, in practice an intermediate-system will need to contain the OSI application services to facilitate network management. However, this is incidental to the main purpose of an intermediate-system.

gorithm in a network composed of homogeneous subnetwork technologies under one administration. Fortunately, that problem was solved a long time ago.

Next, there was a need to perform routing among subnetworks under different administrations but still using a common framework. This was necessary as different organizations began connecting their collections of subnetworks together, as they didn't want bad routing information to escape into other collections of subnetworks. Once that was solved, it became a problem to just keep track of all the subnetworks connected together, because every intermediate-system in every subnetwork had a routing entry for every subnetwork. Thus, routing had to become hierarchical.

By the end of 1988, the solution to this problem was reaching consensus. The newest problem on the block is *policy-based* routing. Once several subnetworks, run by different organizations, are connected together, there may be requirements to overlay an administrative policy onto the routing algorithms. The list of administrative concerns is hard to bound. One simple example is that some administrations might want to restrict use of third-party forwarding in their collection of subnetworks. Ironically, it is much simpler to disable third-party forwarding altogether than merely to restrict its use; once a list of authorized traffic is generated, there must be a way of authenticating the traffic for each network transaction.

The author has every confidence that once policy-based routing is solved, some new problem with routing will arise.

3.1.3   End-Systems

An end-system (ES) is a node in the network containing both the end-to-end services necessary for data transfer along with the application services necessary for information transfer. Perhaps the best definition for an end-system is: "where the applications live."

The reason for this simplistic definition is that a node in the network may function both as an intermediate-system and as an end-system. As such, care must be taken to distinguish the role being played by a particular node at a given instant. As a rule, if forwarding is involved, then the node is performing as an intermediate-system.

Note that although performing both functions is no great problem technically, it can lead to administrative problems, since the operational aspects of being an IS tend to differ from those of an ES. In general, mixing modes is fine in networking experiments, but usually a poor idea in operational networks.

The participation of an end-system in providing end-to-end services to an application varies tremendously based on the services offered by the network. In some cases, an end-system is little more than a spectator with regard to use of the protocols that make up the end-to-end services. In other cases, an end-system is actually the most important player, as it has the final responsibility for robust communication.

3.2 Network Services

The *network service* is responsible for moving data from one end-system to another. Primarily, this involves *switching* and *routing*. The network service provides the powerful abstractions that hide the underlying subnetwork technology. Unfortunately, in OSI, there are *two* network services that are largely incompatible.

Earlier it was noted that there are two schools of thought as to the nature of the OSI end-to-end services. It is here, at the network service, where this schism first becomes visible.

CO-mode Network Service

One camp favors a *connection-oriented* (CO) network service. A CO-mode network service (CONS) is based on the notion of *reservation*. When data transfer is to occur between two end-systems, a connection request is given to the network. If the request is granted, then the resources needed to maintain that connection are reserved over the entire duration of the network connection. As might be guessed, the connection request, as it passes through each intermediate-system, results in resources being allocated for the network connection. The path taken by data transferred between the two end-systems becomes fixed for the entire connection.

This has several good qualities:

- because the path taken by the data is fixed, there is very little processing overheading for forwarding — all of the hard decisions were made during network connection establishment;

- because the resources, termed the *quality of service* for the connection, are reserved during network connection establishment, when a connection request is honored, the end-systems are relatively isolated from other network traffic loads; and,

- because the cost of network connection establishment is paid only once, it is a small cost to add accounting mechanisms to the connection establishment process.

Of course, the reservation philosophy also has some bad qualities:

- because of all the work done during network connection establishment, this is relatively slow and expensive — some applications will find this penalty unacceptable, particularly when only a small burst of data need be sent;

- because the path taken by the data is fixed during network connection establishment, a failure of one of the supporting intermediate-systems or subnetworks will result in the network connection being lost — even if alternative paths between the end-systems exist; and,

- if a network connection is established but not in use, then the resources associated with that connection are unavailable to others — even though they could be applied to other network connections.

Of course, proponents of the CONS philosophy have devised solutions to these deficiencies. It should be noted however, that these solutions are largely realized by circumventing the reservation process. Thus, additional complexity is added to the system when these methods are employed.

CL-mode Network Service

The other camp favors a *connectionless-mode* (CL) network service. A CL-mode network service (CLNS) is based on the notion of "come as you are." When data transfer is to occur between two end-systems, no connection request is made of the network service; instead, the data is just sent. It is the responsibility of the network service to make a best effort delivery, whilst it is the responsibility of the transport service to ensure reliability. As might be guessed, the data sent in each network transaction might take a different path to the destination end-system, and potentially the ordering of the data sent might be changed. Further, some of the data might be discarded along the way because of a lack of resources (e.g., no buffer space). The transport protocol using the CL-mode network service must resolve all of these issues.

In comparison to the CO-mode network service, there are several advantages:

- because there is no resource reservation at intermediate-systems during connection establishment, initial data transit may occur with less delay;

- because there is no fixed path for the network traffic, the transport connection is potentially more robust in the face of network failure (alternative paths may be used); and,

- because intermediate-systems do not keep track of reserved resources, more efficient use of network resources may be realized.

Of course, there are disadvantages as well:

- because the path is not fixed, each intermediate-system must compute the next hop in the path for *each* network transaction;

- the transport protocols must be well-behaved when network resources reach saturation (otherwise the network suffers *congestion collapse*); and,

- it may be impossible to realize accurate accounting mechanisms unless a single provider owns the entire network.

As can be inferred, for a CL-mode network service to be effective, the transport protocols residing above must be considerably sophisticated. Further, because each network transaction is theoretically independent from other network transactions, an intermediate-system must be able to perform the next hop computation quickly.

A Problem in the Making

As divergent as the CONS and CLNS philosophies seem, they are both completely reasonable, rational, and well thought-out approaches. Unfortunately, when it came time to standardize on the OSI network service, neither side could demonstrate a decisive superiority. Thus, the "correct" *political* compromise was made: the OSI network service would honor both philosophies.

Unfortunately, the "correct" *technical* solution was not forthcoming. How can two end-systems, one using a CONS and the other using a CLNS, talk to each other? The problem is quite complex, as in practice, it spans both the network and transport layers. (The relationship between the network and transport layers is not as distinct as the OSI model might suggest.) As might be expected, different network services imply different transport protocols. At the present time, OSI has a dearth of solutions for this problem. In fact, towards the end of Part II, it will be shown that, in general, only non-OSI approaches can currently be used to solve this problem!

soap...

Put in simplest terms: the CONS and CLNS camps fought a battle, and the loser was OSI.

Thanks to the unyielding efforts of the CONS and CLNS camps, we can all rest assured that systems using the OSI network service will be of a technically inferior nature for quite some time. Frankly, it would have been better to decide the matter with a coin-toss: either the CO-mode or CL-mode style of network service can be made to work well: but making the two of them work together has proven to

...soap

be simply too painful!

3.3 Transport Services

As with the Network service, there are actually two OSI transport services: a *connection-oriented transport service* (COTS); and a *connectionless-mode transport service* (CLTS). Since, at the end of 1988, none of the OSI applications used the CLTS, the discussion will focus primarily on the connection-oriented transport service.

The *transport service* is responsible for moving data *reliably* from one end-system to another. If the underlying network service is also connection-oriented, then the transport protocol supporting the service can be trivial. Otherwise, use of a CLNS requires sophisticated algorithms in the transport protocols that provide the transport service.

OSI provides five (yes, 5) CO-mode transport protocols, termed transport protocols class 0 through class 4 (TP0–TP4). Classes 0–3 work with a CO-mode network service, whilst class 4 works with both CO/CL-mode network services.

The first four classes are increasingly more sophisticated users of a CONS: TP0 does nothing more than transport addressing and segmentation, transparently breaking transport service user-data into smaller units for the network service. In contrast, TP3 performs multiplexing of multiple transport connections to the same destination on a single network connection (for more cost-effective networking) and performs minimal re-routing in the face of network problems.

The final transport class, TP4, is considerably more complex as it is primarily intended for a CLNS. The best description of transport protocols of this type, due to Professor David L. Mills of the University of Delaware, is this:

> *They achieve reliability through retransmission.*

This concisely captures the very essence of a transport protocol making use of a CL-mode network service.

After data is sent, the sending transport entity starts a timer and then goes about performing other tasks. If an acknowledgement is received, then the timer is stopped. Otherwise, if the timer expires, the sending transport entity *retransmits* the data and restarts the timer. Retransmission continues some number of times until eventually the sending transport entity gives up and declares the transport connection to be aborted. Obviously, the important question is how many retransmissions should be attempted and how long the timer should be set for after each retransmission. Recent work reported in [VJaco88,PKarn87] suggests some novel, common sense insights into this problem.

3.3.1   Emulation of OSI End-to-End Services

In Part III, the discussion focuses on the powerful OSI application services. Because of the natural division of the OSI model above the transport service, some have speculated that the upper layers of OSI might be offered on top of end-to-end services from other protocol suites.

soap...

This approach is politically controversial. The self-appointed purists of OSI find the concept of mixed protocol stacks simply abhorrent. Suggesting that OSI application services might be used on top of non-OSI networks is, to them, a heresy that would put Galileo's to shame.

Similarly, for those outside of OSI, the notion of introducing the OSI application services into their networks is also unsavory. Although they claim that the OSI application services are bloated, the author suspects it's really the case that their native application services are simply emaciated.

In response to these diatribes, the author notes that running OSI applications in non-OSI networks may be the only acception solution for the OSI transition problem acceptable to network administrators and users. Reading Part IV permits one better to appreciate this response.

...soap

Ignoring the political concerns for the moment, the technology that makes it possible to offer OSI application services in non-OSI networks is surprisingly simple: emulate the OSI end-to-end services over a non-OSI network. Although the protocols comprising end-to-end services may vary between different protocol stacks, the resulting services are quite similar. Thus, the method is straightforward: start with the end-to-end service offered by the native protocol suite and place on top of this service a small protocol, termed a *transport service convergence protocol*, to provide the OSI transport service. Given that the native end-to-end services already offer a CO-mode transport service, the convergence protocol does nothing more than smooth over the transport service differences between the two protocol suites.

In Section 5.4, this approach is discussed in greater detail. In particular, the RFC1006 method, which provides OSI end-to-end services on top of the Internet suite of protocols (TCP/IP), is presented.

3.3.2 Transport Bridging

Finally, the discussion of transport service closes on the issue of *interworking*. In the OSI sense, interworking refers to two end-systems on different subnetworks being able to communicate.

If a common network service and transport protocol can be negotiated, then this is a non-problem. Otherwise, if no commonality can be found, then in theory interworking cannot occur. Clearly this is unacceptable!

To solve this problem, it is necessary to break purposefully with the OSI model. A fundamental tenet of the Model is that relaying is a function of the network layer. Relaying is not permitted at higher layers for numerous technical reasons; in particular, the reliability of such systems is suspect.

Unfortunately, if problems in interworking are restricted to the network and transport layers, then to achieve interworking, it is necessary to build a relay at the transport layer. Of course, there is no reason why such a solution should be any more "ugly" than need be.

A *transport service bridge*, or TS-bridge, is a "simple" entity that provides transport-layer relaying. A TS-bridge knows nothing of the underlying protocol combinations that comprise the end-to-end services; rather, it is knowledgeable only of the OSI transport service. As such, it "copies" the transport service primitives from one set of end-to-end services to another. When the topic of TS-bridges is presented in detail later, several related topics will also be introduced, such as how their use may be relatively transparent to the end-systems they interwork.

3.3.3 Connectionless-mode Transport Service

Although the CLTS will not be further discussed (owing to a lack of CLTS's maturity in OSI), it is worth noting that experience from other protocol suites has shown a CL-mode transport service to be worthwhile. For example, in the Internet suite of protocols, popular protocols for both remote file access (NFS[2] [SMI86b]) and network management (SNMP [JCase89b]) are based on a CL-mode transport service provided by the User Datagram Protocol[JPost80] (UDP).

As with all connectionless-mode services, there is no explicit relationship established between service users. As such, building application protocols on top of a CL-mode transport service is difficult. Nevertheless, the stateless architecture and support for multicast and broadcast facilities make this task very appealing.

---

[2]NFS is a trademark of Sun Microsystems, Incorporated.

3.4 Roadmap

With the *Introduction to End-to-End Services* drawing to a close, the discussion briefly outlines the remainder of Part II.

As with the introduction, we'll proceed bottom-up, considering the two key layers of the lower-layer infrastructure, network and transport, in greater detail. The physical and data link layers, which comprise the two lowest layers of the infrastructure will not be considered. The technologies that implement them vary too widely and change too quickly to be considered here. Instead, consult [ATane88] for an excellent exploration of these topics.

The discussion of the network and transport layers that follows reflects a bias towards practical rather than theoretical aspects. There are two reasons for this. First, the mechanisms used by OSI are similar to numerous commonplace architectures. As such, anything more than a terse description is unwarranted. Although adequate end-to-end services are required for a functioning network, OSI contributes very little that is new in this area! Second, when OSI does contribute, it emphasizes diversity. Unfortunately, diversity has its price. For OSI end-to-end services, the price is increased complexity of interworking. That is, OSI end-to-end services are applicable to a wide-range of transmission media, but when trying to connect those media together, use of the end-to-end services becomes quite complex. Thus, the discussion focuses on the practical aspects of OSI end-to-end services.

The discussion concludes with a brief comparison of OSI end-to-end services to the end-to-end services from the *de facto* standard for open networking: the Internet suite of protocols, commonly referred to as TCP/IP.

Chapter 4

Network Services

As noted in *Introduction to End-to-End Services*, the network service is responsible for data transfer independent of the underlying media comprising the subnetworks over which the data might traverse.

More formally, the network service is offered to the network user as shown in Figure 4.1. In order to offer this service, two network entities cooperate using a network protocol along with the facilities provided by the underlying data link service. Together, this combination is termed the *network service provider* or NS-provider.

As with all OSI service definitions, the network service is defined in terms of *primitives*. By convention, network primitives are prefixed with "N-". There are two sets of network service primitives: one set for the connection-oriented network service, and the other set for the connectionless-mode network service.

The connection-oriented network service is defined in [ISO87b]. The first addendum to this standard, [ISO87d], defines the connectionless-mode network service.

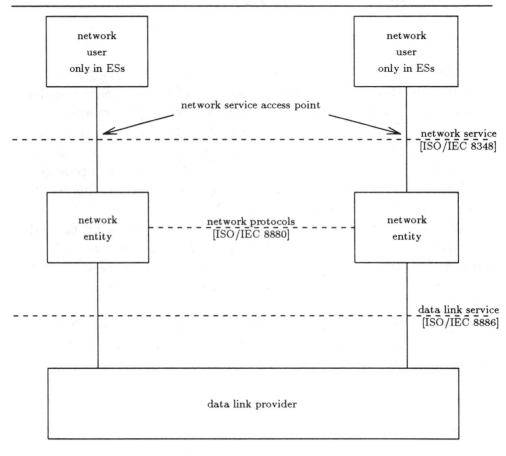

Figure 4.1: The Network Layer

4.1 Concepts

Users of the network service are termed *NS-users*. These are normally transport providers.

The primary goal of the network service is to provide transparency in two forms:

- transparency over the topology of the network; and,

- transparency over the transmission media used in each subnetwork that comprises the network.

Realization of the transparency goal implies three requirements:

addressing: the network service should provide a uniform mechanism for addressing nodes in a network. Because nodes might be physically moved, these addresses should be independent of the network's topology. Further, because network attachment interfaces might be changed on a node, these address must be independent of any media-specific addressing.

In practice, these independencies are not achievable in potentially huge networks. The best that can be achieved with today's technology is to make the dependencies transparent to the network user.

binding: the network service must perform all routing functions during data transfer. Because networks are inherently dynamic, this binding between a connection and the route its data takes must occur on a case-by-case basis. (The distinction between the CONS and CLNS camps is the granularity of this binding — CONS proponents prefer the binding to occur once during connection establishment, whilst CLNS proponents argue for binding to occur for each data packet sent.)

quality of service: different NS-users may very well have different requirements as to the robustness or load carrying of the network connection. This information is communicated during binding. It is then up to the NS-provider to make use of and possibly augment each underlying subnetwork

service with additional mechanisms in order to provide the
desired network QOS. The work required varies considerably — depending on the capabilities of technology implementing the subnetwork in question.

Of course, it should be noted that the NS-provider transfers user-
data transparently. Each *network service data unit* (NSDU) is simply
treated as a string of octets that is uninterpreted by the network
service.

4.1.1   Addressing

The second addendum to the network service, [ISO87c], defines network layer addressing. Because of the transparency goals stated earlier, a network address should make no implications about the physical location of a node; nor should a network address contain explicit
routing information. As such, the primary focus of the OSI network
addressing scheme is to facilitate allocation of network addresses.

The strategy used by OSI is to use hierarchically structured addresses. OSI defines several addressing *domains* and then delegates
administration of these domains to their respective *addressing authorities*. These authorities may create sub-domains and further delegate
authority, and so on.

The responsibility of an addressing authority is to define the structure of an addressing domain and then to allocate values within that
domain. The structure is termed an *abstract syntax*. This means that
the addressing authority is interested only in the conceptual aspects
of the structure and not the actual encoding, the *transfer syntax*, used
by the network protocols that carry those addresses.

At the top-level, an address is divided into two parts:

- an *initial domain part* (IDP); and,

- a *domain specific part* (DSP).

The IDP is further subdivided into two parts:

- the *authority and format identifier* (AFI) that is assigned by the
  ISO/IEC for a particular format to be used by an addressing
  authority; and,

- the *initial domain identifier* (IDI).

Thus, a network address looks like this:

IDP		DSP
AFI	IDI	

The authority and format identifier specifies how the initial domain identifier is interpreted, both in syntax and semantics. The AFI indicates if the IDI is of variable length and whether leading zeros have significance. For example, if the AFI is assigned to the International X.25 community, then the appropriate address format, termed a X.121 address, is used for the IDI.

In addition to defining the semantics of the IDI, the AFI also defines the abstract syntax associated with the domain specific part. In particular, the AFI indicates whether the DSP is formatted using decimal digits or binary information.

The initial domain identifier indicates the entity allowed to assign values to the domain specific part of the address. This is where the first level of delegation from the ISO/IEC occurs. For example, if the IDI refers to an X.121 address, then the entity authorized to use that X.121 address is allowed to assign values to the DSP.

Finally, the DSP has no pre-defined semantics, per se. It is entirely up to the entity indicated by the IDI to allocate DSP values and assign meaning to those values. For example, it will become clear that some routing information may be encoded into the DSP in order to facilitate network binding.

The discussion now considers three examples of network addresses. An X.121 address may be encoded using:

$$\begin{aligned} \text{AFI} &= 36 \\ \text{IDI} &= \text{X.121 address (up to 14 digits)} \end{aligned}$$

as shown here:

36	23421920030013	null DSP

Note that (in theory) this address implies nothing about routing: it identifies a destination that is known to have a particular X.121 address.

An entity recognized by the ISO/IEC may allocate addresses using its international code designator (ICD):

$$\begin{aligned} \text{AFI} &= 47 \\ \text{IDI} &= \text{ICD (4 decimal digits)} \end{aligned}$$

For example, the U.S. National Institute of Standards and Technology (NIST) manages a testing network for OSI, called OSINET. The NIST uses ICD 0004 for this network. As the NIST is the addressing authority for this IDP, it defines the semantics of the corresponding DSP. Note that the AFI value indicates the use of decimal digits in the DSP. An OSINET DSP consists of four parts:

- The first four octets identify a subnetwork of the OSInet. There are actually two sub-identifiers in this field: the first identifies an OSINET member and the second identifies a subnetwork operated by that member. This is an example of further delegation of authority.

- The next several octets identify a *subnetwork point of attachment* (SNPA). SNPAs will be discussed in greater detail when network binding is introduced. For now, think of an SNPA as a media address in a particular subnetwork.

- The next to the last octet identifies a *data link service access point* (DLSAP). Each subnetwork might support several network protocols from different protocol suites (any of which might be non-OSI). In order to distinguish among network protocols, it is necessary to augment the SNPA address by appending a DLSAP.

- The last octet identifies the user of the network service. It is termed a *network selector* (NSEL). Just as different network protocols might use the same transmission media, different transport protocols might use the same network service. The NSEL provides this distinction among users of the network service.

Thus, one particular node in the OSINET might have an address that looks like this:

47	0004	DSP			
		subnet	snpa	dlsap	nsel
		00080001	4152401010	00	00

This identifies OSINET subnetwork number 8.1. The OSI network service resides at DLSAP 0 at the SNPA and the transport protocol using that service resides at NSEL 0.

Finally, OSI provides for a local addressing format that may be used by private enterprises:

$$\text{AFI} \ = \ 49$$
$$\text{IDI} \ = \ \text{null (0 digits)}$$

A common usage is for an organization to divide the DSP into fields similar to the OSINET DSP:

49	DSP			
	subnet	snpa	dlsap	nsel
	0059	080020004053	fe	00

Obviously if two different organizations using the local addressing format connect their collections of subnetworks together, chaos will quickly result — unless they have carefully orchestrated their use of the subnetwork field. The local format is used only in lieu of an established addressing authority for a particular environment.

4.1.2 Binding

Now that nodes in the network have addresses, the next question is, how is data transferred from the originating to the destination end-system? That is, how is routing accomplished? As noted earlier, binding is an issue that both the CO-mode and CL-mode network service must address.

To begin, the network service at the originating end-system must decide the "next hop." If the destination is on the same subnetwork as the originating end-system, then choosing the next hop is simple: it is the destination end-system. Of course, the originating ES needs an algorithm to be able to make this determination.

Otherwise, the next hop must be to an intermediate-system, on the same subnetwork as the originating end-system, which is somehow "closer" to the destination end-system.

Note that the routing responsibilities of ESs and ISs differ considerably: an end-system needs routing information only to make a simple determination as to whether the destination end-system shares a common subnetwork. The intermediate-systems need much more routing information, as they do not originate traffic, they *forward* it. Of course, the extent to which ISs must keep track of routing information varies considerably, depending on whether they support a CO-mode or CL-mode network service. For example, an intermediate-system supporting a CONS needs to know about routing information only when it helps to establish a network connection. In contrast, an intermediate-system supporting a CLNS must know about routing information at all times.

In theory, since network addresses should not contain routing information, they cannot help in determining the next hop. In practice however, the intermediate-systems will have algorithms that somehow map a destination address into a particular subnetwork, and from there a routing table can be used to map the destination subnetwork into the address of a closer intermediate-system.

By the end of 1988, full consensus had not been reached on OSI routing.[1] As such, in accordance with the focus of this book, nothing more will be said in regard to specific OSI routing protocols. At present, only ad hoc methods for routing are in wide-use:

- the semantics of routing based on network addresses (i.e., how to extract a subnetwork address from a network address) are usually hand-coded, and thus are statically defined for intermediate-systems; and,

- routing tables are usually generated from local information, not by routing protocols.

For now, the reader is asked to "take it for granted" that routing actually occurs in OSI networks.

Given this, once the subnetwork attached to the destination end-system is reached, a way is needed of determining the transmission media address of the destination end-system.

---

[1]Indeed, some claim that the issue had hardly been considered.

A node (end-system or intermediate-system) is attached to a subnetwork at a *subnetwork point of attachment* (SNPA), so some mechanisms are needed to map between a network address and its corresponding SNPA. One way of doing this is to run a protocol on the subnetwork that performs this mapping (e.g., ES-IS). This technique provides dynamic mappings, which is consistent with the transparency goals stated earlier. In practice, this is not often the case. A local table might be used. More commonly, the same locally-defined code that knows how to extract the subnetwork identity from a network address will be asked to provide the SNPA from the network address. It is no coincidence that the OSINET addressing format contains fields identifying a particular OSINET subnetwork and an SNPA.

Needless to say, this state of affairs loses a tremendous amount of flexibility. Whilst experience with other protocol suites has shown it to be difficult to avoid identifying the destination subnetwork in a network address, it should be possible, at the very least, to avoid encoding the transmission media address. In short, the lack of widely used *address resolution protocols* in OSI will result in considerable administrative burden.

4.1.3 Quality of Service

Quality of service (QOS) indicates a potential level of service that the NS-users may receive from the network connection. The QOS consists of a collection of parameter/value pairs. As binding is negotiated, the QOS is negotiated, both by the NS-users and the entities providing the network service. As a result, one of the NS-users may decide that the available QOS is insufficient for the application at hand. In this case, the NS-user might choose to abort the network connection rather than continue.

Quality of service exists at the other OSI layers. Most of the layers above the network service simply pass their QOS parameters down directly to the transport service, which, depending on the network service selected, may pass the parameters down to the network service. Table 4.1 shows the network QOS parameters. It should be noted that the values assigned to these parameters need not be scalar values. For example, the throughput parameter consists of several subparameters. For the CONS, the QOS is negotiated during connection establishment, once a network connection is established, no

Phase	Parameter	CONS	CLNS
Connection	Establishment delay	√	
Establishment	Establishment failure probability	√	
Data	Throughput	√	
Transfer	Transit delay	√	√
	Residual error rate	√	√
	Resilience	√	
	Transfer failure probability	√	
Connection	Release delay	√	
Release	Release failure probability	√	
General	Protection from unauthorized access	√	√
	Priority	√	√
	Maximum acceptable cost	√	√

Table 4.1: Network Quality of Service Parameters

further negotiation takes place. For the CLNS, each service primitive carries its own QOS parameter.

4.2   Network Primitives

As noted earlier, there are two sets of network service primitives: one set for the connection-oriented network service, and the other set for the connectionless-mode network service.

4.2.1   Connection-oriented Network Service

The connection-oriented network service goes through three phases: *connection establishment*, *data transfer*, and *connection release*. The service primitives are grouped into these three phases.

Associated with the network primitives are state tables that indicate the order in which various primitives may be invoked. Rather than describe these tables, it is more instructive to view the network service intuitively: the organization of and motivation for the network services are described functionally rather than as a sequence of states.

Whenever an NS-user initiates some action (e.g., sends data), it is termed the *requesting* NS-user; similarly, when the other NS-user is told about this action (e.g., is notified that data has arrived), it is termed the *accepting* NS-user.

NS-users are addressed at a *network service access point* (NSAP). An NSAP address uniquely identifies a user of the network service. As shown in Figure 4.1 on page 52, the NSAP itself makes available the network services to a NS-user.

Connection Establishment Phase

Connection establishment is by far the most complex aspect of the CONS, because of the many options that are negotiated.

The NS-user that initiates the network connection is termed the *calling* NS-user or *initiator*. The NS-user that the initiator is trying to contact is termed the *called* NS-user or *responder*. Note that the concepts of initiator/responder and requestor/acceptor are independent. It is normal for the initiator and the responder either to take turns being requestors of different services, or to request them simultaneously.

A network connection can have only one calling NS-user. If two NS-users simultaneously attempt to establish network connections to each other, then two network connections are established.

Connection Establishment

The connection establishment service, N-CONNECT, sets up the network connection between two NS-users. During the course of execution of this service, various service parameters are negotiated.

N-CONNECT is a confirmed service, therefore the service consists of four primitives:

- N-CONNECT.REQUEST, which is invoked by the calling NS-user;

- N-CONNECT.INDICATION, which is given to the called NS-user;

- N-CONNECT.RESPONSE, which is invoked by the called NS-user; and,

- N-CONNECT.CONFIRMATION, which is given to the calling NS-user;

The relationships among these primitives are straightforward:

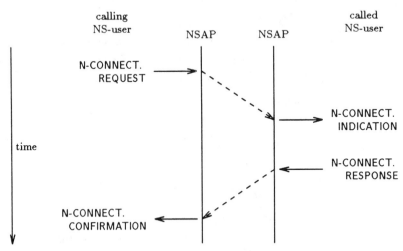

When issuing the N-CONNECT.REQUEST primitive, the calling NS-user uses the following parameters. They are all conveyed to the called NS-user in the corresponding N-CONNECT.INDICATION primitive.

> **calling network address:** the calling NS-user identifies itself via a NSAP address (these were described in Section 4.1.1 on page 54).

calling/called network address: the calling NS-user identifies the intended responder via a NSAP address.

receipt confirmation: one of two values:

> **enabled:** the receipt confirmation service, N-DATA-ACKNOWLEDGE, is to be allowed on this network connection; or,

> **disabled:** the receipt confirmation service is not to be used on this network connection.

> This parameter is examined by the initiating network entity, which may change a value of "enabled" to "disabled." When this parameter is conveyed to the responding network entity, it too is given the opportunity to down-negotiate this value. Finally, the value is conveyed to the called NS-user. This is a classic example of down-negotiation during connection establishment — a practice that is used throughout all the layers of OSI.

expedited data: one of two choices:

> **enabled:** the expedited data transfer service, N-EXPEDI-TED-DATA, is to be allowed on this network connection; or,

> **disabled:** the expedited data transfer service is not to be used on this network connection.

> Again, the value of this parameter is subject to down-negotiation by the network service provider.

quality of service: the calling NS-user indicates its desired QOS. The calling network entity modifies this to reflect its available resources. The resulting information is given to the called network entity, which may perform further modifications.

user-data: from zero up to 128 octets of user-data are sent.

> At present, the author does not know of any OSI transport layer protocols that pass information via this parameter.

Upon receiving the primitive, the local network entity examines the associated parameters and invokes the *network protocol machine* (NPM). As a result, the corresponding N-CONNECT.INDICATION primitive is given to the called NS-user. After some consideration, the called NS-user invokes the N-CONNECT.RESPONSE primitive with these parameters. The parameters are all conveyed to the calling NS-user in the corresponding N-CONNECT.CONFIRMATION primitive.

responding address: this is most often identical to the called network address given in the N-CONNECT.INDICATION primitive, but needn't be. For example, the responder could use this parameter to specify an alternative address to use if the network connection breaks and connection re-establishment is attempted.

receipt confirmation: specifies whether use of the receipt confirmation service is allowed. The value "enabled" may be given only if this value was present in the N-CONNECT.INDICATION.

expedited data: specifies whether use of the expedited data transfer service is allowed. The value "enabled" may be given only if this value was present in the N-CONNECT.INDICATION.

quality of service: the called NS-user indicates its desired QOS, which should be a (logical) subset of the QOS indicated in the N-CONNECT.INDICATION primitive.

user-data: from zero up to 128 octets of user-data are sent.

Of course, it is possible for any number of degenerate error conditions to occur that prevent the primitive from being delivered. For example, the local network entity might be unable to establish a connection to the remote network entity. Alternatively, after a network connection request is received, the remote network entity might be unable to find the called NS-user. In cases such as these, the N-DISCONNECT.INDICATION primitive is returned to the calling NS-user. There are two interesting parameters:

originator: indicates the disconnect was generated by the NS-provider; and,

Class	Reason
Connection rejection	NSAP address unknown — permanent
	NSAP unreachable — transient
	QOS not available — permanent
	QOS not available — transient
	Reason unspecified — permanent
	Reason unspecified — transient
Disconnect	Provider-initiated disconnect — permanent
	Provider-initiated disconnect — transient

Table 4.2: Provider-initiated Disconnect Reasons

reason: indicates why the NS-provider generated the disconnect. Table 4.2 lists the possible reasons for the disconnect. Note that only the reasons with class "connection rejection" may be used; the others are used when releasing an established connection.

Thus, in addition to the exchange described earlier, another valid sequence of primitives occurring during the connection establishment phase is:

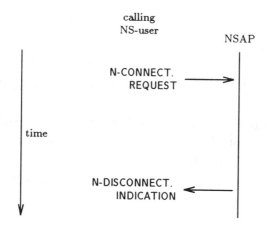

Note that the calling NS-user is unable to distinguish whether it was the local or remote network entity that experienced a problem. This is as expected: from the user's perspective, the network service hides the details of its underlying organization and implementation.

The NS-user knows only that the network service provider ran into a problem.

Of course, the called NS-user might decide to reject the connection. This is accomplished by issuing the N-DISCONNECT.REQUEST primitive (there are other uses for the N-DISCONNECT service, which will be described in due course):

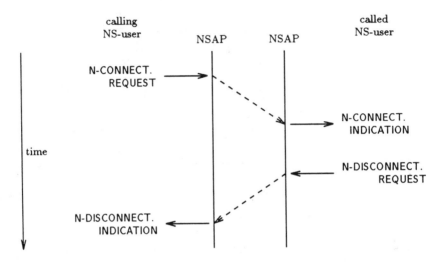

This is termed an NS-user rejection. In this case, the N-DISCON-NECT.INDICATION primitive contains various parameters:

> **originator:** indicates that the disconnect was generated by the NS-user;

> **user-data:** from zero up to 128 octets of user-data are sent.

> **reason:** indicates why the called NS-user generated the disconnect. Table 4.3 lists the possible reason for the disconnect. Note that only the reasons with class "connection rejection" may be used; the others are used for releasing an established connection.

> **responding address:** As with the N-CONNECT.RESPONSE primitive, this is most often identical to the called network address given in the N-CONNECT.INDICATION primitive, but needn't be.

Class	Reason
Connection rejection	user-initiated rejection — permanent
	user-initiated rejection — transient
	QOS not available — permanent
	QOS not available — transient
	Incompatible information in user-data
Disconnect	Normal condition
	Abnormal condition

Table 4.3: User-initiated Disconnect Reasons

Data Transfer Phase

The discussion now turns to the data transfer phase of the network connection. There are only a few services that can be used during this phase.

Data Transfer

The N-DATA service does what most users think the network service should do for them: move data from one place to another. This is an unconfirmed service:

- N-DATA.REQUEST, which is invoked by the requesting NS-user; and,

- N-DATA.INDICATION, which is given to the accepting NS-user.

The relationship between these primitives is straightforward:

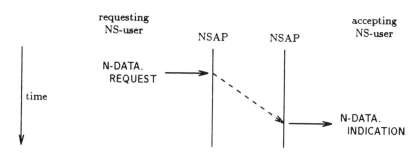

The lack of confirmation has to do with a lack of synchronization, not a lack of reliability. The N-DATA service is unconfirmed but still delivers data reliably between NS-users. If some network failure occurs, the network service will notify the NS-users of this. Of course, the NS-users still have to coordinate between themselves to determine exactly what data was lost.

There are two parameters associated with this service, which are passed uninterpreted from the requesting NS-user to the accepting NS-user:

user-data: a NSDU containing at least one octet.

confirmation request: if the receipt confirmation service was negotiated during connection establishment, then this parameter indicates whether the requesting NS-user desires the accepting NS-user to acknowledge receipt of the user-data.

There is no theoretical limit to the number of octets present in the NSDU. In practice however, many implementations of the network service have severe restrictions as to maximum NSDU size. As such, the NS-user (a transport provider) must often perform explicit segmentation in order to achieve interoperation.

The queuing property of service primitives requires that the NS-provider preserves the ordering of NSDUs by the same user. That is, if two N-DATA.REQUEST primitives are issued, the corresponding N-DATA.INDICATION primitives will occur in the same order.

Receipt Confirmation

If the receipt confirmation service was negotiated during connection establishment, and an N-DATA.INDICATION primitive arrives indicating that the requesting NS-user desires confirmation of the receipt of a NSDU, then the N-DATA-ACKNOWLEDGE service is used to perform this function. Note that this is an advisory, and not mandatory, request for acknowledgement.

It also is an unconfirmed service, but it carries no parameters. Thus, if receipt confirmation is desired when sending a NSDU, the network interaction looks like this:

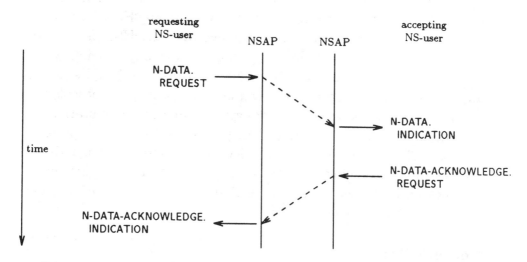

Of course, if a disruptive event occurs that results in either loss of the connection or user-data on the connection, then this sequence of primitives will not complete.

The network service uses the term *confirmation of receipt* (COR) to refer to the logical unit exchanged by the users of the N-DATA-ACKNOWLEDGE service. Thus, in one direction, a NSDU travels through the network provider; and, in the other direction, a COR returns.

Expedited Data Transfer

If use of the expedited transfer service was negotiated during connection establishment, then the N-EXPEDITED-DATA service is available for use by NS-users. This is an unconfirmed primitive with a single parameter: user-data that consists of 1 to 32 octets. User-data sent using the expedited data service are termed *expedited network service data units* or ENSDUs.[2]

When an ENSDU is given to the NS-provider, it is accorded special handling. First, just as the N-DATA service preserves the order of NSDUs, the N-EXPEDITED-DATA service preserves the order of

---

[2]Other layers prefix expedited service data units with "X". The use of the "E" prefix is a historical oddity unique to the transport and network layers.

ENSDUs. However, ENSDUs are sent on a logically different data flow than NSDUs and CORs. This expedited data flow has the property that once an ENSDU is sent, it is *guaranteed* to arrive before any subsequently sent NSDUs or CORs. This is a tricky definition. It means that a NSDU or COR may never overtake any ENSDU that was previously sent, *but* any ENSDU may overtake any NSDUs or CORs that were previously sent, but may not overtake any previously sent ENSDUs. It should be noted that this description of NSDUs, CORs, and ENSDUs is conceptual; the characteristics of the protocols that provide the network service are described, but not the operations.

The upper-layers of OSI, and in particular the session protocol, make use of the expedited data service to facilitate complex activities such as resynchronizing the normal data flow. The transport service provides an expedited data service that maps directly onto the network expedited data service.

Network Reset

The reset service, N-RESET, is used to synchronize (but not to release) a network connection.

Either the NS-user or the NS-provider may initiate this service. If an NS-user initiates this service, then it is a confirmed service:

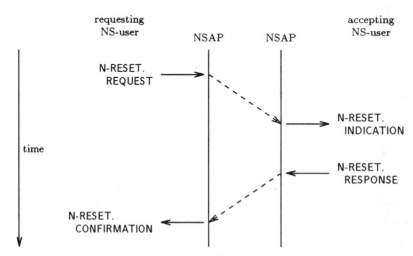

When the N-RESET.REQUEST primitive is issued, it is delivered *after* any previous NSDUs, CORs, or ENSDUs sent by the requesting NS-user. Similarly, when the N-RESET.RESPONSE primitive is issued, it is delivered *after* any previous NSDUs, CORs, or ENSDUs sent by the accepting NS-user. As a result, when the N-RESET service completes, the network connection is in an idle state with no data in transit between the two NS-users.

Otherwise, if the NS-provider initiates this service, then both NS-users receive the N-RESET.INDICATION primitive and any NSDUs, CORs, or ENSDUs in transit are lost. The two NS-users must both issue the N-RESET.RESPONSE primitive. Once both NS-users issue the primitive, the NS-provider returns the network connection to an idle state with no NSDUs, CORs, or ENSDUs in transit:

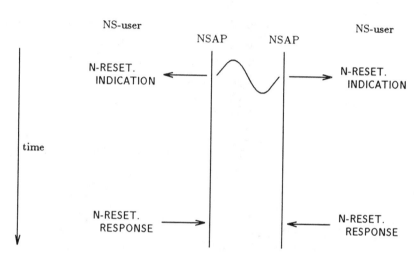

Finally, if both NS-users simultaneously issue the N-RESET.RE-QUEST primitive, then the NS-provider issues the N-RESET.CON-FIRMATION primitive to both NS-users:

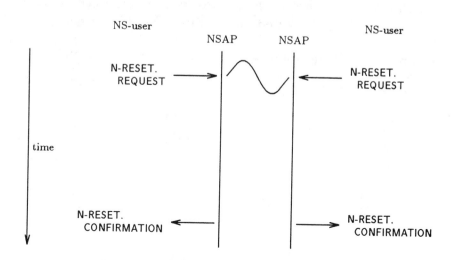

Collisions between a user-initiated reset and a provider-initiated reset are handled in a similar manner. The N-RESET.REQUEST primitive has a single parameter: a reason indicating why the NS-user wishes to reset the network connection. Currently, this always takes the value "user resynchronization." The N-RESET.INDICATION primitive delivered to a NS-user has two parameters:

originator: indicating if the N-RESET service was initiated by an NS-user, the NS-provider, or if the initiator is unknown for some reason; and,

reason: which varies depending on the initiator of this service. If the NS-provider initiated the service, then the value is either "congestion" or "reason unspecified." If the NS-user initiated the service, then (as previously noted) the value is "user resynchronization." Otherwise, the value is "undefined."

By providing a reason of "congestion," it should be clear that proponents of the CONS do not fully believe in the immunity advantage of a CO-mode network service.

Connection Release Phase

There is a single service in the connection release phase.

Connection Release

The N-DISCONNECT service is used to release a network connection. Earlier, the discussion pointed out two uses for this service:

- user-initiated rejection of a network connection; and,

- provider-initiated rejection of a network connection;

Once a connection is established, either the NS-users or the NS-provider may use this service to release the network connection. Once this service is invoked, any NSDUs, CORs, or ENSDUs in transit are lost.

If user-initiated, the N-DISCONNECT service is an unconfirmed service. The N-DISCONNECT.REQUEST primitive contains two parameters:

reason: indicates why the requesting NS-user generated the disconnect. Table 4.3 on page 67 lists the possible reason for the disconnect. Note that only the reasons with class "disconnect" may be used.

user-data: from zero up to 128 octets of user-data is sent.

The corresponding N-DISCONNECT.INDICATION primitive specifies that the disconnection is user-initiated and passes these two parameters unaltered. Note that if both NS-users issue the N-DISCONNECT.REQUEST simultaneously, then the user-data parameter might be lost during the collision.

If the NS-provider initiates the N-DISCONNECT service, then the N-DISCONNECT.INDICATION specifies that the connection release is provider-initiated. A reason code, taken from one of the "disconnect" reasons given in Table 4.2 on page 65, is present.

4.2.2 Connectionless-mode Network Service

There is only one phase associated with the connectionless-mode network service: *data transfer*. As such, there is no concept of a connection: each invocation of a service primitive is considered to be entirely independent of all other invocations. An important consequence of this is that all addressing information must be completely self-contained in the service primitive. Further, there are no ordering considerations: two service primitives addressed to the same entity might arrive in an order different from the one in which they were sent.

Although the CONS views a connection as existing between exactly two NS-users. There is no reason why a CLNS primitive could not involve several recipients. This is usually termed *broadcasting*, or more precisely *multicasting*, since only a well-defined subset of the existing network entities may process the primitive. A special multicast address is used to refer to all of the entities, rather than multiple unicast addresses.

Data Transfer Phase

In the CLNS, there is a single service, N-UNITDATA. This is an unconfirmed service with four parameters:

source/destination address: the requesting NS-user identifies itself and the accepting NS-user.

quality of service: the requesting NS-user indicates its desired QOS. The NS-provider may modify this parameter prior to issuing the N-UNITDATA.INDICATION primitive.

user-data: a NSDU containing between 1 and 64512 octets. The upper limit is chosen to reflect the limitations of the one existing protocol that makes use of the CLNS.

Management

Although not officially part of the International Standard defining the CLNS, there is an Annex, *Facilities for Conveying Service Characteristics*, contained at the back of the International Standard. These facilities include two pseudo-primitives used for logical communication between these two entities on a local system.

OSI does not standardize these primitives because they describe interactions entirely within a single node. Nevertheless, they capture information that is essential for proper implementation of users of the CLNS.

The N-FACILITY service is user-initiated. It allows an NS-user to request information regarding the available network service characteristics in the context of a particular destination address.

The N-REPORT service is provider-initiated and reports on some problem with a previous N-UNITDATA.REQUEST primitive. It contains the "destination address" parameter of the N-UNITDATA.REQUEST primitive along with a reason as to why the report was generated. The reason may be one of the following:

- no reason specified;

- transit delay exceeded;

- NS-provider congestion;

- requested QOS unavailable;

- NSDU lifetime exceeded; or,

- suitable route unavailable.

Note, however, that CLNS does not specify any explicit correlation between the N-REPORT.INDICATION primitive and a *particular* N-UNITDATA.REQUEST primitive.

4.3   Network Protocols

It should be clear that a *single* network protocol cannot offer both
modes of network service over the wide range of current and future
subnetwork technologies. However, there is nothing, outside of implementation costs, to prevent a subnetwork from offering both services
using different protocols.

In OSI, the X.25 packet-level protocol (X.25 PLP) as defined in
[ISO87k], when used over a CO-mode subnetwork service, provides the
CONS. The X.25 PLP as defined by ISO/IEC is technically aligned
with the 1984 CCITT X.25 recommendation.

Similarly, if the CLNS is desired, then the *connectionless-mode
network protocol* (CLNP) [ISO87h] can be used over a CL-mode subnetwork service.

Neither of these protocols is particularly revolutionary. Both are
similar to earlier protocols designed to provide services similar to either CL- or CO-mode.

But this raises an obvious question. Suppose the CONS is desired
but the underlying subnetwork is CL-mode? Or suppose the CLNS
is desired but the underlying subnetwork is CO-mode? Furthermore,
suppose that several subnetworks must be traversed, and the service
they offer is mixed. What protocols can be used to provider either
the CONS or the CLNS?

To provide a framework in which to answer questions like this, OSI
considers the network layer as consisting of three distinct sublayers.
Each sublayer might include a protocol in order to achieve the functions of that layer. This leads us to consider how the network layer is
organized.

4.3.1   Internal Organization of the Network Layer

The document [ISO87a] defines the *internal organization of the network layer* (IONL). The purpose of this document is to provide a
general model of the network layer capable of accommodating the
many possible combinations of subnetwork technologies and network
services.

Viewing the network layer from bottom to top, there are three sublayers:

subnetwork access sublayer: this sublayer is responsible for defining how the network layer interfaces to a particular subnetwork technology, and how it transfers data over that technology. For example, the service offered by a local area network is dramatically different from a point-to-point network. As such, different subnetwork access protocols (SNAcPs) are used.

Potentially a different SNAcP is used for each subnetwork technology, although some subnetwork technologies might use the same SNAcP.

subnetwork dependent sublayer: the sublayer responsible for augmenting the service offered by a subnetwork technology into something close to the desired OSI network service (either CO-mode or CL-mode). Put simply, if both the source and destination end-system reside on the same subnetwork, then the subnetwork-dependent convergence protocol (SNDCP) would be responsible for directly providing the desired network service.

One important function of the sublayer is to map NSAP addresses into SNPA addresses.

Potentially two different SNDCPs exist for each subnetwork technology: one to provide the CONS over the subnetwork, and the other to provide the CLNS over the subnetwork.

If the service offered by the subnetwork access sublayer is close to the desired network service, then the SNDCP might be null. All that would occur at the subnetwork-dependent sublayer is manipulation of the parameters of the subnetwork service. No protocol control information, per se, would be needed for the SNDCP. Otherwise, the PCI for the SNDCP is carried as user-data given to the subnetwork access sublayer.

subnetwork independent sublayer: the sublayer responsible for providing the network service between the two end-systems. The subnetwork-independent convergence protocol (SNICP) is usually null unless the two end-systems reside on different subnetworks. In some cases, the SNDCP and the SNICP might be combined if the service offered by the SNAcP permits. For example, if the subnetwork offers a connectionless-mode transfer service very close to the CLNS, and the desired network service is also the CLNS, then a single protocol might suffice for both the SNDCP and SNICP.

In practice, there are probably only two SNICPs: one supporting the CONS over multiple subnetworks, and the other supporting the CLNS over multiple subnetworks.

It is important to understand that each sublayer builds on the services offered by the sublayer beneath it. Whilst the SNAcP makes it possible to transfer data on a subnetwork, the SNDCP augments this data transfer service to offer the OSI network service on the subnetwork. Next, the SNICP having access to the OSI network service on two connected subnetworks (each realized by their own SNDCP), achieves the relaying necessary to connect the two end-systems.

What makes the IONL so complicated is the vast number of possible combinations. Each subnetwork offers either a connection-oriented or a connectionless-mode service. Thus when trying to interconnect two adjacent subnetworks, say subnet "A" and subnet "B," there are six possible combinations:

Subnetwork service on subnet "A"	Subnetwork service on subnet "B"	Desired OSI Network Service
CO-mode	CO-mode	CONS
CO-mode	CO-mode	CLNS
CO-mode	CL-mode	CONS
CO-mode	CL-mode	CLNS
CL-mode	CL-mode	CONS
CL-mode	CL-mode	CLNS

In achieving these combinations, there are three approaches that might be used:

- if both end-systems reside on the same subnetwork, then they are considered "directly-connected" and may communicate directly;

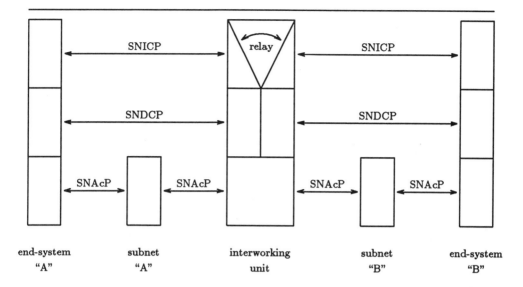

Figure 4.2: Providing the CLNS over CL-based subnetworks

- if the end-systems reside on different subnetworks, then an *interworking unit* (IWU) resides on the intermediate system at the subnetwork boundaries to provide "hop-by-hop" harmonization of the services offered by each subnetwork and desired by the NS-users; or,

- if the end-systems reside on different subnetworks, and the initiating end-system selects an internetworking protocol to be used over the network connection, then an IWU is used at each subnetwork boundary both to harmonize the service used at each hop, and also to propagate the particular interworking protocol.

The IONL document gives examples of all of the possible combinations. For our purposes it is instructive to consider only the two most common cases.

To provide the CLNS over two CL-based subnetworks using an internetworking approach, an organization similar to the one shown in Figure 4.2 is used. In this figure, an identical SNICP is used between the end-systems and the interworking unit. Depending on the service offered by each subnetwork, the SNDCP need not be present.

To provide the CONS over two CO-based subnetworks using hop-by-hop harmonization, an organization similar to the one shown in Figure 4.3 is used. In this figure, one of the subnetworks contains a

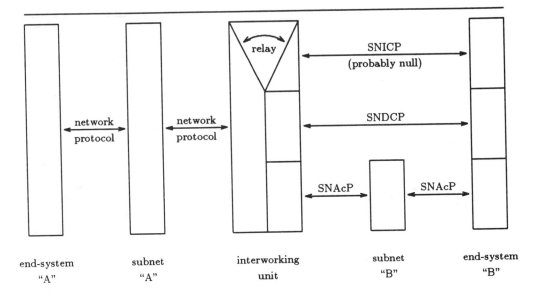

Figure 4.3: Providing the CONS over CO-based subnetworks

network protocol capable of directly offering the CONS. In contrast, the other subnetwork hosts the three network sublayers. This is an example of interworking between a CONS-based wide area network (e.g., one using the 1984 CCITT X.25 recommendation) and a CONS-based local area network (e.g., one using a connection-oriented data link service).

To complete the examination of network services, the discussion closes by looking at some of the protocol combinations used to offer the OSI network service.

The document [ISO87f] defines the general principles used when defining protocol combinations to provide the OSI network service. This is little more than a checklist enumerating the different things that must be defined. The actual work is left to two other standards documents. Each of these defines how one of the OSI network services is realized using several technologies:

- 8802 local area network;

- public switched data network (PSDN);

- point-to-point subnetwork; or,

- circuit switched data network (CSDN).

4.3.2 Providing the CONS

Protocol combinations to provide the connection oriented network service are defined in [ISO87g]. To offer the CONS, this document identifies the protocol(s) used to realize the X.25 packet-level protocol over the subnetwork technology. Using the mechanisms described in [ISO87j], the X.25 PLP provides the OSI CONS.

Providing the CONS over a 8208 subnetwork

For a wide-area network using the 1984 CCITT X.25 recommendation, the OSI CONS is offered directly. The X.25 PLP is used along with the mechanisms defined in [ISO87j] to provide the connection-oriented network service. This architecture corresponds to "subnet A" in Figure 4.3. Thus, in this context, a single network protocol, the X.25 PLP, is used to provide the CONS. It fulfills the roles of all three network sublayers.

Note that for subnets implementing the 1980 CCITT X.25 recommendation, [ISO87j] defines a subnetwork-dependent convergence protocol to augment accordingly the service offered by the subnetwork.

Providing the CONS over a 8802/2 subnetwork

For 8802 local area networks[ISO87l], the following summary proceeds from the bottom up. The connection-oriented subnetwork service (LLC2), a data link protocol defined in [ISO87m], is used to support the protocol defined in [ISO87i]. This protocol implements the X.25 PLP [ISO87k]. The mechanisms defined in [ISO87j] are used to map the service offered by this protocol into the OSI CONS [ISO87h]. This architecture corresponds to "subnet B" in Figure 4.3 on page 80. Thus in this context, the SNAcP is defined by the LLC2 service, and the [ISO87i] protocol is used to provide the roles of the SNDCP and the SNICP.

4.3.3 Providing the CLNS

Protocol combinations to provide the connectionless-mode network service are defined in [ISO87e]. To offer the CLNS, this document identifies the protocol(s) used to realize the OSI connectionless-mode network protocol (CLNP) [ISO87h].[3]

Providing the CLNS over a 8802/2 subnetwork

For 8802 local area networks, the following summary proceeds from the bottom up. The connectionless-mode subnetwork service (LLC1) is used directly to support the CLNP. A section in the CLNP standard defines the minimal SNDCP used for this protocol combination. This architecture corresponds to "subnet A" in Figure 4.2 on page 79. Thus, in this context, and the SNAcP is defined by the LLC1 service, the mechanisms for providing the SNDCP are defined in the CLNP standard, and the CLNP itself fills the role of the SNICP.

Providing the CLNS over a 8208 subnetwork

For a wide area network providing the 1984 CCITT X.25 service, a section in the CLNP standard defines the SNDCP used for that protocol combination. The SNDCP is straightforward: the subnetwork offers a connection-oriented service, hence, before the SNAcP is called to transfer data, the SNDCP uses the SNAcP to establish a connection to the destination node. Once the data is sent, the SNDCP decides if the connection should be released. Owing to the expense (in both time and money) of connection establishment, the connection is most likely maintained until:

- it has been inactive for some reasonable period of time (maintaining a connection is less expensive that establishing one, but is still costly); or,

- a subnetwork connection to a different destination must be established and the 8208 subnetwork service is congested.

In the latter case, the SNDCP will probably use a *least recently used* (LRU) algorithm to select which subnetwork connection should be closed so that a new connection might be formed.

Of course, the SNDCP might be considerably smarter. For example, if it determines that there will be considerable traffic to the

---

[3]An earlier draft of document had an Addendum that defined the SNDCPs used for both 8802/2 and 8208 subnetworks. When the CLNP standard was ratified, the text of this Addendum was folded into the official document [ISO87h].

destination, it might open multiple connections to a single destination. In this case, it would split up traffic addressed to the same destination among the different connections. In OSI, this is termed *splitting* and *recombining*.

4.3.4 A Soapbox on the IONL

It is not a coincidence that many of the professionals familiar with the IONL standard refer to it as the *infernal* organization of the network layer. The reason is simple: the IONL is too complex. This complexity is a direct result of the requirement to supporting two fundamentally different models of the network service, one connection-oriented and the other connectionless.

$\boxed{\text{soap...}}$

In addition to being complex, the IONL doesn't really solve any real world problems! Here's why: when two end-systems establish a transport connection, the initiating end-system selects a network service to support the resulting transport connection. This implies that all subnetworks in between the two end-systems, including the originating and destination subnetworks, must support the network service selected by the initiating end-system. That is, the IONL implicitly assumes that each and every OSI subnetwork is able to support both OSI network services.

If the two end-systems are on the same subnetwork, then it is safe to believe that the network service chosen by the end-system will be acceptable to the subnetwork.

If, however, the two end-systems are on different subnetworks, then, in the real world, it is extremely naive to believe that all subnetworks involved will be able to support the network service selected by the initiating end-system.

- If a subnetwork technology is naturally connection-oriented, then that subnetwork will provide support for the CONS. However, there is then little value in using the CLNS; for a CO-mode subnetwork, using the CLNS and TP4 is more resource intensive, in terms of both end-system computation and network bandwidth, than using the CONS and a less powerful transport protocol.

- If a subnetwork technology is naturally connectionless-mode, then that subnetwork will provide support for the CLNS. However, there is then little value in using the CONS; for a CL-mode

> subnetwork, the CONS is difficult to support and provides no
> additional benefit in (local) communications.

This means that OSI interworking is severely restricted: the real world
simply does not operate the way envisioned by the IONL. As a result,
the IONL is of more theoretical interest than practical significance.

There have been a few solutions proposed to remedy matters. For
example, the so-called "COS 265" proposal defines a method for allowing CO-mode and CL-mode subnetworks to be concatenated.[4] This
means that a subnetwork need only support one network service. Providing that both end-systems run TP4, then interworking is possible.
There are two drawbacks to this approach: first, from the purist viewpoint, it proposes a slight alteration to the OSI model in that a transport connection may be bound to more than one network service;
second, administrators of end-systems attached to CO-mode subnetworks still don't like to run TP4. As such, this solution is politically
unacceptable. As should be clear, with OSI end-to-end services, two
choices is worse than one.

Section 5.6.4 on page 114 presents one possible solution to the OSI

... soap interworking problem.

---

[4]ISO 8473 − 8208 (CLNS minus CONS) is 265.

Chapter 5

Transport Services

As noted in *Introduction to End-to-End Services*, the connection-oriented transport service is responsible for reliable data transfer between end-systems.

More formally, the transport service is offered to the transport user as shown in Figure 5.1. In order to offer this service, two transport entities cooperate using a transport protocol along with the facilities provided by the underlying network service. Together, this combination is termed the *transport provider* or TS-provider.

As with all OSI service definitions, the transport service is defined in terms of *primitives*. By convention, transport primitives are prefixed with "T-". There are two sets of transport service primitives: one set for the connection-oriented transport service, and the other set for the connectionless-mode transport service.

For our purposes, only the connection-oriented transport service is of interest. It is defined in [ISO86c].

For those interested in the connectionless-mode transport service, it is defined in [ISO86b].

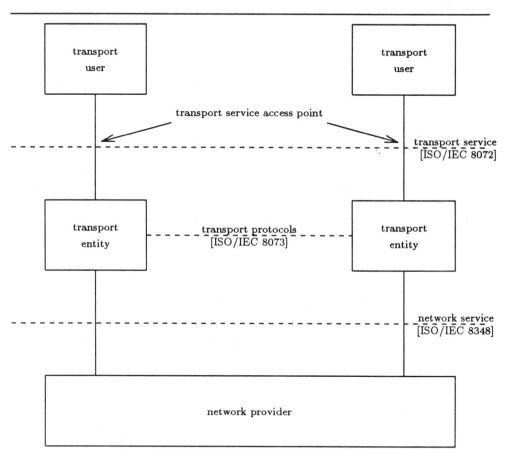

Figure 5.1: The Transport Layer

5.1 Concepts

Users of the transport service are termed *TS-users*. These are normally session providers.

The primary goal of the transport service is to provide transparency over the possibly varying reliability of the network service. The network service is responsible for moving data from one end-system to another, whilst the transport service is responsible for making sure that this happens reliably.

If a connection-oriented network service is used, then the role of the transport service can be vastly simplified. Otherwise, as noted earlier, complex mechanisms are required to ensure a consistent level of service.

As we shall see throughout the discussion, the network and transport layers are tightly bound.

5.2 Transport Primitives

The connection-oriented transport service goes through three phases: *connection establishment, data transfer*, and *connection release*. The service primitives are grouped into these three phases.

Associated with the transport primitives are state tables that indicate the order in which various primitives may be invoked. Rather than describe these tables, it is more instructive to view the transport service intuitively: the organization of and motivation for the transport services are described functionally rather than as a sequence of states.

Whenever a TS-user initiates some action (e.g., sends data), it is termed the *requesting* TS-user; similarly, when the other TS-user is told about this action (e.g., is notified that data has arrived), it is termed the *accepting* TS-user.

TS-users are addressed at a *transport service access point* (TSAP). A transport address consists of two parts: a *transport selector* and one or more *network addresses*. A transport selector is a simple string of zero or more octets that is meaningful only at a particular network address. Earlier, Section 4.1.1 on page 54 discussed the interpretation of network addresses.

A TSAP address uniquely identifies a user of the transport service. As shown in Figure 5.1 on page 86, the TSAP itself makes available the transport services to a TS-user.

5.2.1 Connection Establishment Phase

The TS-user that initiates the transport connection is termed the *calling* TS-user or *initiator*. The TS-user that the initiator is trying to contact is termed the *called* TS-user or *responder*. Note that the concepts of initiator/responder and requestor/acceptor are independent. It is normal for the initiator and the responder to take turns being requestors of different services, or to request them simultaneously.

A transport connection can have only one calling TS-user. If two TS-users simultaneously attempt to establish transport connections to each other, then two transport connections are established.

Connection Establishment

The connection establishment service, T-CONNECT, sets up the session connection between two TS-users. During the course of execution of this service, various service parameters are negotiated.

T-CONNECT is a confirmed service, therefore the service consists of four primitives:

- T-CONNECT.REQUEST, which is invoked by the calling TS-user;

- T-CONNECT.INDICATION, which is given to the called TS-user;

- T-CONNECT.RESPONSE, which is invoked by the called TS-user; and,

- T-CONNECT.CONFIRMATION, which is given to the calling TS-user;

The relationships among these primitives are straightforward:

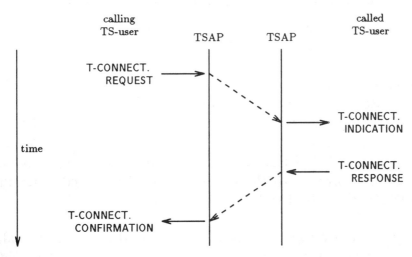

When issuing the T-CONNECT.REQUEST primitive, the calling TS-user uses the following parameters. They are all conveyed to the called TS-user in the corresponding T-CONNECT.INDICATION primitive.

> **calling/called transport address:** the calling TS-user identifies itself and the intended responder via TSAP addresses. (Refer back to the beginning of Section 5.2 for the definition of a TSAP address.)

expedited data: one of two choices:

> **enabled:** the expedited data transfer service T-EXPEDI-TED-DATA, is to be allowed on this transport connection; or,

> **disabled:** the expedited data transfer service is not to be used on this transport connection.

> The value of this parameter is subject to down-negotiation by the transport service provider.

quality of service: the calling TS-user indicates its desired QOS. The initiating transport entity modifies this to reflect its available resources. The resulting information is given to the responding transport entity, which may perform further modifications.

user-data: from zero up to 32 octets of user-data are sent.

> The session protocol does not pass any information using this parameter.

Upon receiving the primitive, the local transport entity examines the associated parameters and invokes the *transport protocol machine* (TPM). As a result, the corresponding T-CONNECT.INDICATION primitive is given to the called TS-user. The called TS-user then invokes the T-CONNECT.RESPONSE primitive with these parameters. They are all conveyed to the calling TS-user in the corresponding T-CONNECT.CONFIRMATION primitive.

responding address: this is most often identical to the called transport address given in the T-CONNECT.INDICATION primitive, but needn't be. For example, the responder could use this parameter to specify an alternative address to use if the transport connection breaks and connection re-establishment is attempted.

expedited data: specifies if use of the expedited data transfer service is allowed. The value "enabled" may be given only if this value was present in the T-CONNECT.INDICATION.

quality of service: the called TS-user indicates its desired QOS, which should be a (logical) subset of the QOS indicated in the T-CONNECT.INDICATION primitive.

user-data: from zero up to 32 octets of user-data are sent.

Of course, it is possible for any number of degenerate errors to occur that prevent the primitive from being delivered. For example, the local transport entity might be unable to establish a connection to the remote transport entity. Alternatively, after a transport connection request is received, the remote transport entity might be unable to find the called TS-user. In cases such as these, the T-DISCONNECT.INDICATION primitive is returned to the calling TS-user. There is only one parameter:

originator: indicates the disconnect was generated by the TS-provider.

The reason for the disconnect is communicated locally (i.e., values are not standardized by the transport service standard), but some possible values are suggested:

- TS-provider congested;

- misbehavior of TS-provider (protocol error);

- available QOS below minimum level;

- called TS-user unknown;

- called TS-user unavailable; and,

- (the ubiquitous) unknown reason.

Thus, in addition to the exchange described earlier, another valid sequence of primitives occurring during the connection establishment phase is:

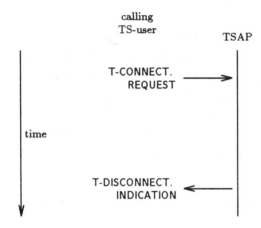

Note that the calling TS-user is unable to distinguish whether it was the local or remote transport entity that experienced a problem. This is as expected; from the user's perspective, the transport service hides the details of its underlying organization and implementation. The TS-user knows only that the transport provider ran into a problem.

Of course, the called TS-user might decide to reject the connection. This is accomplished by issuing the T-DISCONNECT.REQUEST primitive:

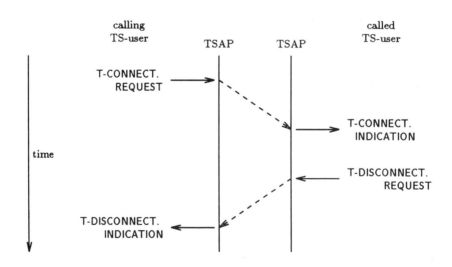

This is termed a TS-user rejection. In this case, the T-DISCON-NECT.INDICATION primitive contains two parameters:

originator: indicates the disconnect was generated by the TS-user;

user-data: from zero up to 64 octets of user-data are sent.

This primitive indicates that it is user-initiated. Any user-specific reason for the disconnect is contained in the user-data parameter.

5.2.2 Data Transfer Phase

The discussion now turns to the data transfer phase of the transport connection. There are only two services that can be used during this phase.

Data Transfer

The T-DATA service does what most users think the transport service should do for them: move data from one end of a connection to the other. This is an unconfirmed service, using two primitives:

- T-DATA.REQUEST, which is invoked by the requesting TS-user; and,

- T-DATA.INDICATION, which is given to the accepting TS-user.

The relationship between these primitives is straightforward:

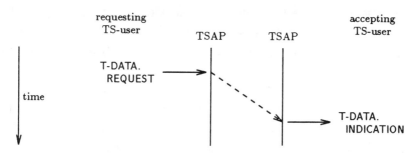

The lack of confirmation has to do with a lack of synchronization, not a lack of reliability. The T-DATA service is unconfirmed, but still delivers data reliably between TS-users. If some transport failure occurs, the transport service will notify the TS-users of this.

There is one parameter associated with this service, a TSDU containing at least one octet. There is no theoretical upper bound on the size of a TSDU. As with all the normal data transfer services of OSI, ordering among TSDUs is preserved by the service.

Expedited Data Transfer

If use of the expedited transfer service was negotiated during connection establishment, then the T-EXPEDITED-DATA service is available for use by TS-users. This is an unconfirmed primitive with a single parameter, user-data consisting of 1 to 16 octets, termed an *expedited transport service data unit* or ETSDU.

As might be expected, the transport service handles expedited data in a fashion identical to the network service: ETSDUs may overtake previously sent TSDUs.

5.2.3   Connection Release Phase

There is a single service in the connection release phase.

Connection Release

The T-DISCONNECT service is used to release a transport connection. Earlier, the discussion pointed out two uses for this service:

- user-initiated rejection of a transport connection; and,

- provider-initiated rejection of a transport connection.

Once a connection is established, either the TS-users or the TS-provider may use this service to release the transport connection. Once this service is invoked, any TSDUs or ETSDUs in transit are lost.

If user-initiated, the T-DISCONNECT service is an unconfirmed service. The T-DISCONNECT.REQUEST primitive contains one parameter, user-data, consisting of zero to 64 octets. The corresponding T-DISCONNECT.INDICATION primitive specifies that the disconnection is user-initiated and passes the user-data parameter unaltered. Note that if both TS-users issue the T-DISCONNECT.REQUEST simultaneously, then, as with the network service, the user-data parameter might be lost during the collision.

If the TS-provider initiates the T-DISCONNECT service, then the T-DISCONNECT.INDICATION specifies that the connection release is provider-initiated.

5.3   Transport Protocols

Based on the available network service, there are five different connection-oriented OSI transport protocols from which to choose. These
are termed transport protocol classes 0 through 4, or more briefly TP0
through TP4. The first four classes work only with the CONS, whilst
the last class, TP4, works with either the CONS or the CLNS.

During connection establishment the transport entities negotiate
which transport protocol is used. This allows implementations of the
more sophisticated transport protocols to provide a superior service
to their users whilst retaining interoperation with simpler implementations.

To distinguish among the five classes of transport protocols, OSI
introduces the notion of "acceptable loss" in a network. In brief,
from the perspective of the transport service, there are three classes
of networks:

> **class A:** networks that detect, as an error, any loss of data.
> These networks *never* duplicate, re-order, or corrupt data.
> Furthermore, a class A network has a relatively small prob-
> ability of actually losing data. Such a network provides the
> CONS.

> **class B:** like class A networks, class B networks detect, as an
> error, any loss of data. However, such losses are more com-
> mon than the transport service would prefer. Class B net-
> works aren't necessarily unreliable, it's just that they are
> *less* reliable than class A networks. The distinction between
> the two classes is decided locally (by each implementation).
> As with the class A networks, a class B network provides
> the CONS.

> **class C:** networks that do not detect errors if data is lost, dupli-
> cated, re-ordered or corrupted. Such networks provide the
> CLNS.

This methodology splits CONS-capable networks into two kinds: those
with error rates acceptable to the transport provider, and those with
unacceptable error rates.

With this in mind, the discussion now considers the five OSI transport protocols.

All five protocols share a few general functions. Each transport entity keeps track of the NSAP that is used to transfer *transport protocol data units* (TPDUs) for the transport connection. The transport entities offers the transport service by exchanging TPDUs. As a consequence, a transport entity must act accordingly if a protocol error occurs.

5.3.1   Simple Class

The simplest of the transport protocols, TP0, does nothing more than *segmentation and reassembly.*

The underlying network service may not be able to accept NSDUs of arbitrary size. By some local mechanism, the local network entity informs the local transport entity as to the largest NSDU that it can manage. The transport entity subtracts from this size the number of octets required for the transport protocol control information. The remaining value is often termed the *atomic TSDU size* for the connection.

When the T-DATA.REQUEST is generated, a TSDU is present. If the TSDU is larger than the atomic TSDU size, then the TSDU is sent as several segments, each in a TPDU. Each TPDU starts with the transport protocol control information. This information contains a flag indicating whether this TPDU contains the end of the TSDU. Following the PCI is the next segment of the TSDU. Upon receiving a TPDU, the remote transport entity checks this flag so that it can pass the T-DATA.INDICATION primitive to the accepting TS-user.

Segmentation and reassembly are transparent to the TS-users. Of course, depending on how the T-DATA.INDICATION primitive is implemented, the accepting TS-user may receive only a part of a TSDU at a time. However, this is a local interface issue. From the OSI perspective, the segmentation is transparent; for the implementor's perspective, it need not be.

TP0 is appropriate for class A networks. As such, if a provider-initiated N-DISCONNECT.INDICATION primitive or a N-RESET.INDICATION primitive is received, indicating a loss of data in the network, TP0 releases the network connection and performs a provider-initiated disconnect.

As a simplifying matter, the TP0 does not offer the expedited data service.

5.3.2   Basic Error Recovery Class

If the transport provider feels that the network does not offer a high
enough level of reliability (i.e., network disconnects occur too fre-
quently), then it might select TP1 instead. As such, TP1 is appropriate for both class A and class B networks.

TP1 handles network disconnects in a different fashion. When
TPDUs are sent, each TPDU is numbered and then retained until an
acknowledgement is received from the remote transport entity. The
acknowledgment takes the form of a special TPDU (that itself is never
acknowledged). However, if negotiated during network connection
establishment, the N-ACKNOWLEDGE-DATA service is used instead
of sending an acknowledgement TPDU.

Thus, when a network disconnect occurs, the transport provider
may decide to establish a new network connection and then resume the
transport connection by re-sending those TPDUs that haven't been
acknowledged. TP1 also has a similar method for recovering when
the N-RESET service is invoked; a transport entity might initiate this
service if it encounters a problem. This is termed "reassignment after
failure." Alternatively, the network provider might initiate the N-
RESET service if a loss of data occurs.

It should be understood that re-establishing a network connection
may involve the network service choosing a route through the subnetworks between the two end-systems. Proponents of the connection-
oriented network service argue that this is adequate recovery for network failures. Of course, network connection re-establishment is expensive in terms of time. As such, if the transport service must recover
often from network failures, performance will suffer tremendously.

Of course, this is politically controversial: proponents of the CO-
mode network service claim that it is extraordinarily reliable. Thus,
they argue that the need for network connection re-establishment is
rare. Naturally, proponents of the CL-mode network service remain
unconvinced. Regardless, ignoring the additional mechanisms necessary for recovery from loss of a network connection, TP1 is essentially
TP0.

5.3.3 Multiplexing Class

Historically, networks offering a connection-oriented service primarily have been public data networks. Although the tariff structures vary among carriers, there are usually two costs associated with such a service: a charge for each connection established, and a charge for each NSDU sent over a network connection. Typically, the cost of connection establishment is the dominant charge for a network connection.

With this in mind, if two or more transport connections need to exist between the same two end-systems, it would be more cost-effective to carry the traffic for all of the transport connections over a single network connection. In OSI, this is termed *multiplexing* and *demultiplexing*.

TP2 contains this functionality. When a transport connection is to be established, TP2 checks whether there is already a network connection to the destination end-system. If so, it uses that existing network connection when sending TPDUs for the new network connection.

In addition, for each transport connection in use, TP2 may optionally perform *flow control*. This means that when the connection is established, the two transport entities negotiate how much data a sender may transmit before additional permission must be granted by the receiver. This allows for independent flow control for each transport connection. Thus, one connection becoming blocked will not affect other connections to the same destination.

TP2 is appropriate only for class A networks, as TP2 is simply a more capable user of the network service than TP0; in addition to segmentation, TP2 also performs multiplexing and, optionally, flow control.

5.3.4 Error Recovery and Multiplexing Class

TP3 simply combines the functions of TP1 and TP2. As such, it is appropriate for both class A and class B networks, and does both multiplexing and flow control.

5.3.5 Error Detection and Recovery Class

TP4 is a protocol whose philosophy is entirely unlike the other transport protocols. It assumes a class C network in which data transfer problems are not detected. In short, TP4 is designed for a connectionless mode network service. Of course, TP4 can be used over a CONS, but many of the mechanisms it employs become redundant at best, and wasteful at worse.

Here's why: as noted in *Introduction to End-to-End Services*, protocols like TP4 achieve reliability through retransmission. The trick is knowing *when* to retransmit. If data is lost in the network and the sending transport entity retransmits too slowly, then throughput suffers. If data is lost due to congestion in the network and the transport entity retransmits too quickly then it merely adds to the congestion and throughput gets even worse! Hence, sophisticated protocols of this variety employ adaptive algorithms to predict the latency characteristics of the network, which may fluctuate considerably because of other traffic.

Hence, there are at least two problems in using a protocol like the TP4 over a CONS. First, the TP4 mechanisms don't come for free; they require considerable skill to implement, and they require significant computational resources on the end-system. For example, checksumming is one of the most computationally expensive aspects of implementing a network or transport protocol. Since the CONS guarantees data integrity, then it is redundant for TP4 to do checksumming. To avoid this non-optimal behavior, OSI provides a way to negotiate non-use of checksumming.

Second, the TP4 must be very careful not to try to "second guess" the network layer. Otherwise, it may retransmit unnecessarily. This increases the economic cost of the connection.

In short, the TP4 is not ideal for use on a class A or a class B network. This shouldn't be surprising; the TP4 wasn't designed for these classes of networks. Hence, OSI provides five different transport protocols. Some argue that it would be preferable to have a single OSI connection-oriented transport protocol. This would have to be the TP4 as it is the only one capable of using a CLNS. However, for the reasons noted above and those noted in the soapbox on the IONL in Section 4.3.4, it is not commonly agreed that operating the TP4 over a CONS is sensible behavior.

5.4 Emulation of OSI End-to-End Services

The OSI applications are quite attractive in the power they offer to end-users. Further, the OSI application services are also quite attractive to application programmers because of the richness they offer in building distributed systems.

However, as of the end of 1988, the actual number of OSI networks was quite small in comparison to networks using other protocol suites.[1] Further, it is not clear how long it will take OSI to achieve widespread dominance. Indeed, Part IV is dedicated to exploring the problems of making this happen and the solutions to those problems. So, an interesting exercise is to consider whether it is technically feasible to offer the OSI application services (and their correspondent applications) over non-OSI networks.

There are many ways in which this might be done. Since most protocol suites are based on layering, it seems natural to consider whether a common layer can be found between the two protocol suites where they can be joined. If the layers are viewed only by their interfaces, then it also seems natural to join the two protocol suites at the two layers that share the most in common. This use of layering is an example of the flexibility described in [DCohe83].

How can commonality be judged? Since the goal is to use the OSI applications and retain their generality, it makes sense to join the protocol suites somewhere below the OSI application services. This means that the session, presentation, and application layers of OSI should remain intact.

Next, since existing networks already contain capable end-to-end services, it makes sense to join the protocol suites somewhere at the top of the OSI end-to-end services.

This narrows to exactly one choice: the protocol suites should be joined at the boundary between the OSI application services and the end-to-end services of the non-OSI protocol suite. From a practical perspective, this is also attractive. The interface to end-to-end services for most protocol suites usually resides at the kernel-user interface for end-systems running an operating system supporting such

---

[1]At the risk of starting a soapbox, perhaps the term *insignificant* is more appropriate.

a model (e.g., UNIX[2]). As such, the emulation can be implemented as a user-level library requiring no modifications to the operating system. Thus, administrators needn't worry about OSI applications causing undue impact on their operating systems.

Since the OSI application services interface to the OSI transport service, the question becomes:

> *Is it possible to provide an emulation of the OSI transport service using the end-to-end services of another protocol suite?*

For the sake of exposition, we use the term *TS-stack* to refer to a particular combination of lower layer protocols used to realize the transport service for the OSI protocol suite. Thus, in order to build an emulator using the architecture shown in Figure 5.2, we need to determine if the lower-layer protocols found in a particular network can be used to implement a TS-stack.

The method for building a TS-stack can be simple. Here is one approach: start with the connection-oriented transport service offered by the protocol suite in question. Next, define and implement a small protocol, termed a *transport service convergence protocol.* The role of this protocol is to smooth over the differences in the services offered by the OSI transport service and the other transport service. For example, the OSI transport service transfers TSDUs, which are discrete units of octets. Other transport services, rather than being packet-oriented, might be stream-oriented. It is the task of the convergence protocol to provide a packet orientation on top of the octet stream offered by the other transport service.

As of the end of 1988, the author knew of only one such transport service convergence protocol that was defined and implemented. Termed "the RFC1006 method" as shown in Figure 5.3 on page 104, this protocol is used to offer the OSI end-to-end services on top of networks based on the Internet suite of protocols (TCP/IP). It must be stressed that this approach is not limited to TCP/IP-based networks. Any protocol suite that offers a protocol providing the functionality of a connection-oriented transport service is a candidate for this emulation (e.g., SNA LU6.2).

The approach taken by the RFC1006 method [MRose87], is to treat TCP, a connection-oriented, stream-based, transport protocol,

---

[2]UNIX is a trademark of AT&T Bell Laboratories.

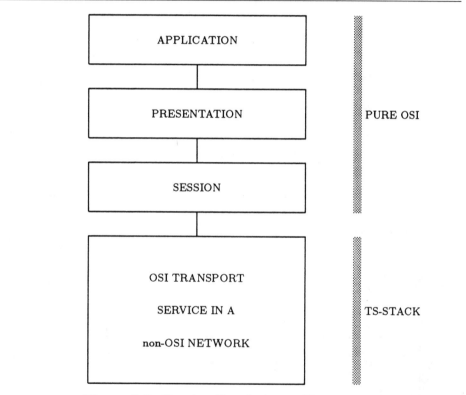

Figure 5.2: Service Emulator at Transport

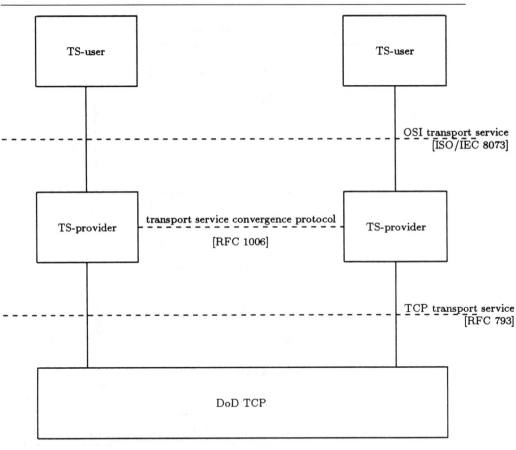

Figure 5.3: OSI Transport Services on top of the TCP

as though it actually offered a connection-oriented network service. The transport service convergence protocol consists of two parts:

- TP0, which naturally uses a CONS; and,

- a packetization protocol, which separates TPDUs when sent over the TCP data stream. In this fashion, the protocol data units exchanged by TP0 are delimited when passing through the TCP service interface. As such, the packetization protocol running over the TCP is able to appear as a CONS to TP0.

If the RFC1006 method is ever modified, this packetization protocol will probably be given one other feature: it will be able to pass full network addresses, so as to be truly indistinguishable from TP0 using the CONS. At present, network addresses aren't fully passed. Whilst this does not impact the workability of the system, it does prevent true hop-by-hop harmonization when connecting adjacent CO-based subnetworks.

5.5 Application Use of End-to-End Services

Before closing this chapter with a discussion on interworking, it is useful to consider how applications use end-to-end services. In particular, it is instructive to follow the process of connection establishment step-by-step.

An application identifies an *application entity* that provides the service desired for communication. For example, an application doing file transfer might identify a "filestore" service provided by a particular application entity. The identity of an application entity is its *distinguished name* in the OSI Directory. This is simply an authoritative description of the application entity; the syntax and semantics of the name are entirely unimportant for the discussion at hand.

5.5.1 Step 1: Map Distinguished Name

The application contacts the OSI directory, presents the distinguished name of the application entity with which it is interested in communicating, and asks for the presentation address attribute associated with that name. A presentation address consists of a presentation selector, a session selector, and a transport address. As noted earlier, the transport address consists of a transport selector and one or more network addresses.

5.5.2 Step 2: Determine Use of Network Addresses

The presentation address is given to the service element in the application layer to establish a connection. This address is passed to the presentation service, which uses the presentation selector. The remainder is given to the session service, which uses the session selector. The ultimate remainder is given to the transport service, and the end-to-end services come into play (at last).

The transport service begins by looking at each network address and deciding which mode of network service (CO-mode or CL-mode) will be used for the address. This decision is a local matter. There is no standard method for making this determination; in practice, there are a few ad hoc rules.

Based on the derived network service and the communications quality of service desired by the application, the transport service selects a transport protocol. Thus, for each network address in the transport address, the transport service selects a TS-stack that might be used to establish a transport connection.

As noted earlier, many environments support only a single mode of network service. This implies that only a portion (or perhaps none) of the network addresses will be usable at the originating end-system. If this is the case, then interworking cannot occur, and a provider-initiated connection rejection is generated.

5.5.3 Step 3: Order Network Addresses

The network addresses are then ordered by preference. The preference is based on both the quality of service desired by the application and the "closeness" of the network addresses. Again, this decision is a local matter: there is no standard method for making this determination.

For example, a transport address might contain two network addresses, each implying use of a CONS. However, one of the network addresses might reside in a private network, whilst the other resides in a public data network. The transport service might prefer the address on the private network for economic or other reasons. This is particularly true if the two networks are not connected, which prevents a single CO-mode network service from being presented to the transport service.

5.5.4 Step 4: Attempt Connections

For each network address, the transport service starts the appropriate transport protocol machine and the underlying network service is invoked. Once a transport connection is established, the remainder of the network addresses is ignored.

5.6   Interworking Revisited

It is now time to reconsider how interworking is accomplished under
OSI. To be sure, the OSI end-to-end services offer a lot of flexibility.
However, is interworking practical?

5.6.1   The Real World of OSI

The so-called "real" world of OSI depends entirely on "where you
live." What this means is that any discussion of interworking must
occur in the context of existing subnetworks.

Earlier, the notion of a TS-stack was introduced. Consider a simplified definition:

>   *A TS-stack offers the OSI end-to-end services.*

Given this, we can introduce a new term, the OSI *community*, which
may be given this definition:

>   *A community is a collection of end-systems connected to-
>   gether and sharing a common TS-stack.*

In other words, a community consists of end-systems that all interwork
with each other.

So, what OSI communities exist today? As of the end of 1988,
there were seven kinds of communities worthy of mention.

Community 1: International X.25

This community uses X.121 network addresses and the 1980 CCITT
X.25 recommendation as a network protocol. This does not provide
a true CONS (being unable to pass full NSAP addresses), and parts
of the network are upgrading to the 1984 X.25. TP0 is the favored
transport protocol in this community.

The TS-stacks used by this community are:

TP0		TP2		TP4
X.25		X.25		X.25

Community 2: Private X.25

Communities of this category are similar to the International X.25 community: they use the 1980 CCITT X.25 recommendation as a network protocol, but are owned by a particular enterprise. For example, the U.K. Academic Community runs a private X.25–based network called JANET, the Joint Academic Network.

The network addresses are X.121–based but are privately allocated. Thus, the OSI X.121 network address format can't be used because of possible collisions in the address space.

The TS-stacks are the same as for the International X.25 community:

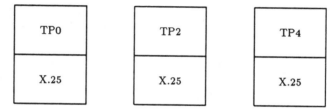

Community 3: Variant U.S. use of X.25

In the United States, where there is a heavy emphasis on use of the CLNS (regardless of the underlying subnetwork technology), 8208-based subnetworks are considered to offer only a CL-mode service, which supports the use of the CLNS.

As such, the TS-stack used by this community is:

Community 4: CONS-based LANs

In Europe, where there is a heavy emphasis on use of the CONS (regardless of the underlying subnetwork technology), 8802/2–based subnetworks are considered to offer a CO-mode service using the protocol defined in ISO 8881.

As such, the TS-stack used by this community is:

```
+-------------+
|             |
|    TP0      |
|             |
+-------------+
|             |
|    8881     |
|             |
+-------------+
|             |
|    8802     |
|             |
+-------------+
```

Community 5: CLNS-based LANs

Of course, there are communities that use 8802/2–based subnets to offer a CL-mode service.

In these communities, the TS-stack is:

```
+-------------+
|             |
|    TP4      |
|             |
+-------------+
|             |
|    CLNP     |
|             |
+-------------+
|             |
|    8802     |
|             |
+-------------+
```

Community 6: The Internet using the RFC1006 method

Given the RFC1006 method, another OSI community is the Internet. This community shares a problem with the Private X.25 community: what kind of OSI network address can be used? A solution to this problem is discussed later on in Section 5.6.3.

The TS-stack used by this community is:

```
+-------------+
|             |
|  RFC1006    |
|             |
+-------------+
|   TCP       |
|   IP        |
```

Community 7: Private TCP/IP-based LANs using the RFC1006 method

Finally, there may be numerous LANs running TCP/IP and using the RFC1006 method. Except for the lack of connectivity, this community is identical to the Internet community.

As such, their TS-stack is:

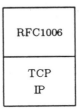

5.6.2 Community Interworking

All of these communities actually exist. So, the question is: can they interwork? For example, is it possible for an end-system in the International X.25 community to interwork with an end-system residing on a CLNS-based LAN?

The answer to this, and many similar questions, is *no*. Under OSI and the way it is implemented, here are the pairs that interwork:

	1	2	3	4	5	6	7
1	I			?			
2		I					
3			I		I		
4	?			I			
5			I		I		
6						I	
7							I

An "I" means that interworking is possible, providing there is an intermediate-system in common between the two communities. A question mark means that interworking is possible, but doesn't happen all that often in practice, as the hop-by-hop harmonization for the CONS is not widely implemented. A blank means that interworking is not possible, even though use of OSI would lead one to believe the contrary.

Here's why: the Private X.25 community and the Internet community need a different address space than any provided by OSI. Thus, communities 2, 6, and 7 are unable to interwork with the other communities.

The remainder of the problems derive from the fact that CONS-based TS-stacks and CLNS-based TS-stacks don't, in practice, interwork. In theory, the TP4 can be selected by the initiating end-system and, if need be, use of the TP4 can be down-negotiated. In practice, the OSI network and transport layers are too closely intertwined. Consider: if the initiating end-system selects TP4, then it must also decide if it wishes to use the CLNP to provide the CLNS. If it does use the CLNP, then it is not possible to down-negotiate the use of TP4, as the other transport protocols do not operate over the CLNP. If the initiating end-systems does not use the CLNP, then it cannot interwork with end-systems residing on subnetworks that offer only a CL-mode service.

The next two sections discuss ways to get around these problems. First, the addressing problem is considered. Next, the mixing of transport protocols on a single transport connection is examined.

5.6.3   Interim use of Network Addresses

It is sensible to accommodate all OSI communities, *regardless* of how they offer OSI services. Let us consider how one can do this in the short-term.[3]

However, as has just been pointed out, the Private X.25 and Internet communities do not follow the OSI network addressing conventions. As such, there must be a way of encoding these addresses as if they *were* OSI network addresses. The solution is to select a new OSI addressing domain and to allocate non-OSI addresses therein. Since it is unlikely that Telex devices will ever be used as OSI end-systems, Stephen E. Kille of University College London (UCL) has proposed that a sub-domain of the Telex AFI be used for this purpose: Under his proposal [SKill89b], which is purposefully an interim solution, non-OSI addresses would be encoded in the OSI addressing sub-domain assigned to UCL by virtue of UCL's Telex address:

$$
\begin{aligned}
\text{AFI} &= 54 \\
\text{IDI} &= 00728722
\end{aligned}
$$

---

[3]At the risk of starting a soapbox, this could also be phrased: let us consider how one can do this until the OSI lower layers are sorted out.

The DSP consists of two parts:

- a two-digit (decimal) subnet number, identifying a particular community using non-OSI addresses; followed by

- an encoding of the non-OSI address for that community.

At present, three subnet numbers are assigned, one for the International X.25(80) community, the JANET (a private X.25 community), and the Internet. Other communities, such as other private X.25 networks, can be easily accommodated using this scheme.

The encoding for X.25–based communities is similar to the OSI X.121 address. So, let's take a look at how an Internet address is encoded using the Interim Approach. An Internet address consists of a 32–bit IP address and a 16-bit TCP port number.

The IP address serves the same purpose as an OSI network address: it identifies a particular node in the network. IP addresses are typically written in dotted-quad notation, e.g., "129.84.2.18". A portion of this address identifies a particular IP-based subnetwork, the remainder identifies a particular end-system on that subnetwork.

Similarly, a TCP port serves the similar purpose to the transport selector: it identifies a particular user of the transport service. TCP ports are typically written as a decimal number.

Interim subnet number 3 is used for the Internet. The IP-address is expressed as four three-digit numbers, one for each quad. Similarly, the port is expressed as a five-digit number; an AFI of 54 indicates a decimal syntax in the DSP. All of these fields are zero-filled to fixed length in order to facilitate parsing:

54	00728722	DSP		
		subnet	ip address	port
		03	129084002018	00102

This example shows two goals of the Interim Approach. First, the OSI community containing the address is easily deducible. By examining the Interim subnet number, the network and correspondent TS-stack are determined. Second, network-specific information (i.e., non-OSI equivalents of the SNPA) are also easily determined.

An interesting exercise for the reader is to consider what conditions have to change in the OSI end-to-end services in order for this Interim Approach to become unnecessary.

5.6.4   Transport Bridging

As should be clear from the discussion on the "real" world of OSI, interworking is presently the exception, not the rule when end-systems on different subnetworks try to communicate. To achieve OSI interworking, one solution is simply to turn a blind eye to a small part of the OSI model. In particular, although the Model states that relaying is a function of the network layer, the interworking problem can be solved, if relaying occurs at the transport layer (level-4).

The Problem with Level-4 Relays

Before diving into this solution, it is important to understand why the OSI model prohibits the use of level-4 relays. The transport layer resides at end-systems. As such, the store-and-forward nature of relaying is bound to cause problems. There are four.

- First, a level-4 relay maintains state for its two existing connections. This means that if the level-4 relay fails, the transport connection between the end-systems will fail, even though both end-systems are operational and an alternative communications path might exist between them. Thus, addition of a level-4 relay to the network potentially introduces an additional single point of failure.

  Of course, a CLNS advocate might argue that TP0 over the CONS has the same problem. In response, a CONS advocate would note that since this is occurring on a class B network, that TP1 and not TP0 should be used, since TP1 will recover from network failure.

- Second, end-to-end integrity is achieved by a checksum at either the transport or network layer in the OSI model. These checksums are re-calculated at the level-4 relay. Thus, there is an inherent impact on performance. In addition, because a new checksum is calculated, it is possible for the level-4 relay to corrupt data as it passes through the relay. Since all users above the transport layer rely on this presumed end-to-end integrity, these layers will now fail.

  A related problem is that a level-4 relay defeats any transport-level encryption mechanisms. The data appears in the clear at the level-4 relay. (Of course, encryption could occur at a higher layer so as to avoid this problem.)

Again, a CLNS advocate might argue that the interworking units used for concatenating multiple CO-mode subnetworks also has the checksumming problem. (Since encryption would occur at the transport layer, the IWU has no effect on this.)

- Third, some end-to-end mechanisms use sophisticated back-pressure techniques to achieve both flow and congestion control. Although introduction of a level-4 relay should not produce instability with respect to the buffering aspects of these techniques, it is possible that round-trip times may vary widely when a level-4 relay is introduced. Hopefully, recent work in sophisticated timer variance algorithms for end-to-end protocols [VJaco88,PKarn87] should compensate for this.

- Fourth, end-to-end addresses may not be carried transparently. When a level-4 relay establishes a connection to the ultimate destination, this destination sees the transport address of the level-4 relay, not the transport address of the actual originator.

With the problems inherent with level-4 relays now on the table, let's see what problems such a relay could solve.

The Transport-Service Bridge

To achieve interworking, we introduce an entity residing above the OSI transport service termed a *TS-bridge*. The TS-bridge knows nothing about transport protocols or the composition of TS-stacks. It does know how to use the relatively simple OSI transport *service*. This service is identically offered by all TS-stacks, regardless of their internal organizations.

Consider the high-level architecture of a TS-bridge as shown in Figure 5.4. The TS-bridge "copies" service primitives from one TS-stack to another. For example, upon receiving a connection indication from one TS-stack, the TS-bridge issues a connection request to the other TS-stack.

Although not shown in Figure 5.4, the TS-bridge is bi-directional: an end-system in either community may initiate a connection to an end-system in a different community.

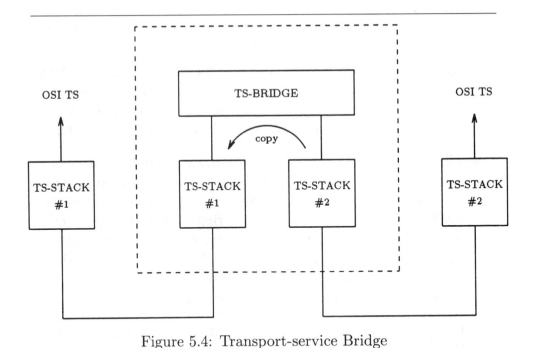

Figure 5.4: Transport-service Bridge

Figure 5.5 shows the high-level architecture of a TS-bridge configuration that solves the most common OSI interworking problem. Of course, the TS-bridge could just as easily have used TP1, TP2, or TP3 over the CONS rather than TP0 over the CONS. In fact, a single TS-bridge can contain more than two TS-stacks, although only two stacks are in use for any given connection.

Conceptually, the TS-bridge simply manipulates transport service primitives by copying them. However, there are two subtle interactions of which the TS-bridge must be aware, owing to slight differences in the OSI transport service depending on the underlying transport protocol. The first is that TP0-based TS-stacks do not support user-data upon connection establishment; connections with such data are refused. The second is that TP0-based TS-stacks do not support the expedited data facility; the TS-bridge must be prepared to down-negotiate use of this facility. Fortunately, the OSI session protocol[ISO87s] doesn't require either facility for correct operation. However, if other users of the transport service are defined, they must take care not to violate these requirements.

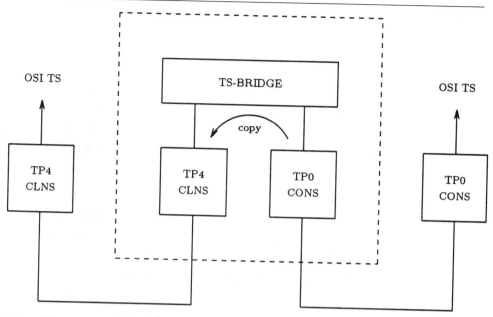

Figure 5.5: TS-bridge between TP4/CLNS and TP0/CONS

The TS-bridge and the OSI Model

Now, the discussion briefly returns to consider see how the TS-bridge copes with the problems inherent to level-4 relays.

In terms of its dual connection-oriented nature, there is no solution. If a TS-bridge fails, then both transport connections are lost, regardless of the availability of alternative paths or other TS-bridges.

In terms of end-to-end integrity, the TS-bridge, per se, does not calculate checksums at all. This functionality occurs beneath the transport service interface: checksums are regenerated by the two TS-stacks that reside beneath the TS-bridge.[4]

From a theoretical perspective, it is possible for the TS-bridge to fail subtly by corrupting data as it passes through the TS-bridge. Further, as with any level-4 relay, this corruption will not be detected by the lower-layer checksums being used in either TS-stack. From the practical perspective however, the TS-bridge performs a simple function, so it can be examined (by hand) for correctness quite thoroughly.

---

[4]In the case where a network service is providing end-to-end integrity, e.g., a connection-oriented network service, then the network provider must regenerate the checksum at the TS-bridge.

This leaves only degenerate failures, such as undetected memory errors, as the only possible causes of such corruption. It is not clear that implementations of network or transport protocols that guarantee integrity would behave correctly under the same circumstances.

In terms of back-pressure, there is currently insufficient experience to determine how buffering in the TS-bridge may affect the two transport connections. Use of a TS-bridge in a heavily-used production environment may be needed to study this phenomenon.

Use of TS-Bridges

Now that we see how a TS-bridge can be used to solve the interworking problem, it is necessary to determine how to modify the application's use of end-to-end services in order to involve a TS-bridge.

The modification to the algorithm presented in Section 5.5 is rather simple; Step 2 is changed. This step determines how the transport service makes use of network addresses contained in the transport address during connection establishment.

Without a TS-bridge, if no usable network addresses are found (i.e., all network addresses refer to end-systems outside of the initiating end-system's communities), then the transport connection service fails.

Alternatively, if at least one TS-bridge is available, then instead, the transport service selects a TS-bridge that services the OSI community for one of the network addresses in the transport address. The transport service takes the network address and transport selector and encodes them as an octet string ([SKill89a] defines such an encoding). This octet string replaces the transport selector given by the initiating TS-user. The network address of the TS-bridge is then given to the network service.

As a result, the transport service establishes a connection to the TS-bridge. Upon receiving the connection indication, the TS-bridge decodes the transport selector to find the transport address of the destination end-system. From this point on, use of the TS-bridge is entirely transparent.

5.7   Comparison to Internet End-to-End Services

Finally, the discussion closes with a comparison of the OSI end-to-end services with the services offered by the Internet suite of protocols (TCP/IP).

All comparisons are partisan by nature. However, since the discussion hasn't entered a soapbox (yet), a balanced perspective will be given.

The Internet suite of protocols is *primarily* based on a connection-oriented transport service provided by the Transmission Control Protocol [JPost81b] (TCP). The TCP is responsible for providing end-to-end reliability. Supporting the TCP is a connectionless-mode network service, provided by the Internet Protocol[JPost81a] (IP). The IP is responsible for providing connectivity over the widest possible range of diverse subnetwork technologies.

5.7.1   Network Service

In terms of network service, the only fair comparison to be made is between the CLNS and the service offered by the IP. By and large, the services are identical.

The interesting question then is to consider the equation when the CONS is added in:

Are two OSI network services one too many?

The answer is yes.

Consider: OSI communities are separated by TS-stacks and connectivity. Connectivity is not a technical issue, but TS-stacks are. So, if there was a single OSI network service, then there could be a single OSI transport protocol.

It should be noted that there is no such thing as a TCP/IP interworking problem (assuming, of course, correct protocol implementations and initial routing information). By using a single network protocol and a dominant transport protocol, the Internet suite of protocols has proven extraordinarily successful.

5.7.2   Transport Service

In terms of transport service, the only fair comparison to be made is between the TP4 and the TCP. The services offered by the two protocols are quite close. There are some differences however:

- the TCP service is stream-oriented, whilst the OSI transport service is packet-oriented;

- the TCP service offers a graceful release, whilst in OSI this is offered by the session service; and,

- the TCP has an urgent data facility, whilst the TP4 has an expedited data service.

Note that these are differences, not necessarily "pros and cons."

For example, the packet-orientation of TSDUs is a mixed blessing. It makes possible better buffer management and possibly can lead to more efficient implementations of the transport provider. On the other hand, a stream-orientation is also advantageous. Here's why: with TP4, TSDUs may be segmented into multiple TPDUs. However, it is not possible for a single TPDU to contain more than one TSDU. If the TSDUs are relatively small, and the transport user is generating them quickly relative to the speed of the network, then it would be desirable to bundle more than one TSDU into a single TPDU. With the TCP, this is easily accomplished by even modestly sophisticated implementations. Furthermore, if the network is suffering from congestion, then when the transport provider goes to retransmit, if the user-data is a stream, then the largest sensible TPDUs can be given to the network. This reduces the number of packets in transmit, and reduces this connection's impact on network congestion. Because of the packet-orientation of TPDUs, the TP4 cannot perform this optimization.

The retransmission algorithms used by the TP4 are woefully simplistic in comparison to those used by the TCP. This is really due more to fervent development and experience in the Internet community than an inherent flaw in the TP4. The OSI community should be encouraged to incorporate as many cutting-edge TCP algorithms (such as those in [VJaco88]) as possible into the TP4, in order to make it more competitive.

Finally, the TP4 uses a modified Fletcher's algorithm [JFlet82] for a checksum to guard against data corruption. The TCP uses a simpler 16–bit one's complement checksum. Although one might think that the TP4 checksum is superior because it is stronger, it is actually *inappropriate* as an end-to-end checksum. Here's why: the purpose of a checksum in a protocol like the TP4 or the TCP is to act as a final sanity check. Modern subnetwork technologies offer very strong checksums at the data link level. As such, the role of a transport-level checksum is to safeguard the data against corruption when it is being handled by software, *not* when it is being transmitted! Experience has shown that the TCP checksum is adequate in these circumstances.

So, what's the harm in using a stronger checksum? Well, the harm is that it's slower. Implementations of the TCP checksum can run at memory speeds (or faster if a vectoring processor is used). This is because the checksum algorithm can be realized using long-word quantities: data fetches and arithmetic and logical operations can be done as efficiently as possible on the end-system. The TP4 checksum is inherently octet-oriented. All operations operate on the octet-level and are slower. ([ANaka88] discusses coding techniques for Fletcher's algorithm that help to make resulting implementations more efficient; even so, all things being equal, a clever coding of the TCP checksum will outperform a clever coding of the TP4 checksum.)

In addition, the TP4 checksum isn't that much stronger. In fact, its additional strength lies in the fact that it can detect certain kinds of octet swapping, whilst the TCP checksum can't. However, this error doesn't happen in production software! Of course, it occasionally happens when developing a transport provider, but the problem is so obvious the first time the system is tested, that it hardly warrants making the checksum algorithm run at one-fourth the speed!

Finally, comparing the OSI transport service to the Internet transport service, it should again be noted that there is no such thing as an TCP/IP interworking problem. The notion of a TS-bridge is unheard of in the Internet protocol suite. The common network protocol and a uniform network addressing format make this completely unnecessary. Interworking simply isn't a problem.

5.8 A Final Soapbox on OSI End-to-End Services

soap...

It should be clear that the concept of ubiquitous OSI is a myth. It simply isn't possible given the poor state of affairs with OSI interworking. As a result, it really doesn't make sense to use OSI end-to-end services internally — there are just too many problems. In their present form, OSI end-to-end services are suitable only for inter-organizational traffic (so-called "Enterprise Networking") when politics takes precedence over technically superior solutions.

This is particularly depressing to the author, because a lack of workable end-to-end services is going to slow severely the ubiquity of the wonderful OSI applications. Considering that users are interested in the applications, and for the most part couldn't care less about the wretched lower layers, OSI has lost significant value — all because the CONS and CLNS camps solved their political problems but couldn't solve the technical problem that resulted.

To add insult to injury, whenever the author attends conferences with some of the committee members who standardized the lower layers, they actually are *proud* of their accomplishment! There is talk of "OSI bearer networks" (an enterprise-wide network based on the OSI end-to-end services), and how the lower layers have finally made this possible. The really amusing part is that many of these professionals think that TCP/IP will never amount to much and "the Internet was an interesting experiment."

It is the author's deepest regret that he is not empowered to sentence these persons to reality, or at the very least, partial sanity.

To summarize the soapbox:

> *The mechanisms implementing the OSI end-to-end services currently lack coherence.*
>
> *Run your powerful OSI applications over TCP/IP.*

...soap

Part III

Application Services

Chapter 6

Introduction to Application Services

Application services are concerned with *information transfer*, unlike end-to-end services, which are concerned with *data transfer*. This important distinction leads to the two sets of services employing entirely different concepts and mechanisms.

application services are
provided by the
upper layer infrastructure

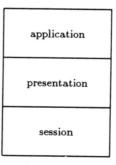

From the perspective of the applications developer, the most outstanding achievement of OSI has been to provide a rich framework for building network applications. To be sure, other protocol suites, such as the Internet suite, also provide an environment for network applications. What distinguishes OSI from its counterparts is the richness and generality of the application services it provides.

The framework used by the application is often termed the *upper-layer infrastructure*. In OSI, the infrastructure is rich, because of the large number of available services that an application can use; the infrastructure is also general, because of the large number of applications that it can support.

There are several reasons why such an infrastructure is desirable, the most notable being:

- It promotes the rapid prototyping of applications. As such, new applications can be designed, implemented, and evaluated more quickly.

- It focuses application design and development on the *application* protocol rather than on issues of underlying support. This ability to focus results in a better implementation of the application itself.

- It minimizes the long-term investment of software-related resources at the expense of the start-up cost. Because applications in a target environment share a common framework, they are likely to share a common software base. This software base needs to be developed in (or ported to) a particular target environment only once. After this initial investment, new applications are much less expensive to field in that target environment. That is, by providing a "toolkit" of facilities, there is less inclination to reinvent tools.

A good argument against this approach is to note that such commonality may be impractical in real applications: there will be some features of the infrastructure that are used by only a few applications and yet all applications will be forced to make use of them. In OSI, the solution to this dilemma is to divide the infrastructure into smaller parts, called *elements*. Each application, as a part of its configuration, declares which elements it requires. These are said to be *active* elements. Other parts of the infrastructure are said to be *inactive* elements. A careful implementation of upper-layer infrastructure will minimize the overhead suffered by an OSI application. For example, this should mean that the executable images, which comprise the application, contain only code and data for those elements that will be active during the lifetime of the execution.

However, an important positive side-effect is that the use of a common framework enforces a discipline on both application designers and developers. It is this rigor that makes possible the advantages described above. Given the rate at which processing, memory, and bandwidth are becoming less expensive, one might argue that the overhead imposed by the upper-layer infrastructure is inconsequential compared to the advantages. This, naturally enough, leads to a soapbox.

The arguments concerning upper-layer infrastructure really fall ┃soap...┃ into two categories. The first is the "best tool" argument. Although the upper-layer infrastructure is rich and general, clearly some applications can make use of specialized services that have been particularly optimized for that application. Such a service comprises the "best tool" for the job. The OSI approach takes the "multi-purpose tool" or the so-called "Swiss army knife" approach. All applications are offered a service that, whilst not particularly optimized for any particular applications, is nevertheless adequate for the job.

The *Cynic of the Internet*, Dr. Paul V. Mockapetris when discussing the OSI Directory service, noted:

> *It is a 200 cubic-feet block of marble sitting in the middle of a highway. Its proponents claim that inside is a beautiful sculpture waiting to be created. Its opponents note that at present it is a huge rock blocking traffic.*

This is most perfectly true of the OSI application service.

The decision as to which approach is more correct depends on perspective. Those interested in performing one task extremely well will favor the best tool approach. In contrast, those taking a more global view may very well favor the multi-purpose tool approach, since it has the potential to provide significant leverage as other applications are developed. As is often true with competing philosophies, correctness is largely defined by perspective. Readers of Part IV, *Transition to OSI*, will find this theme reoccurring time and time again.

However, if one believes that the multi-purpose tool philosophy is superior, this leads to the second category of controversy: the "right tool" argument. Basically, the question is: have we selected the *right* multi-purpose tool for the upper-layer infrastructure? At present, in comparison to our understanding of end-to-end services, our understanding of applications and application protocols is quite immature. Although applications can be viewed as the "product" of networks, the actual number of different applications is (as yet) quite small. As such, it may be presumptuous to claim that the right multi-purpose tools have been selected given our limited understanding.

To illuminate this issue, consider the controversy surrounding applications that are based on either a connection-oriented or a connectionless-mode framework. The upper-layer infrastructure used by OSI is based on a connection-oriented framework. Although modifications have been made in the last two years to introduce an additional connectionless-mode framework, the upper-layer infrastructure is still heavily biased towards the connection-oriented approach. In fact by the end of 1988, there were no OSI applications based on a connectionless-mode framework; all were connection-oriented. However, there is also a class of applications that is best realized using a connectionless-mode framework. For example, the Network File System (NFS) [SMI86b] provides a transparent file service based on connectionless-mode services from the layers beneath it. Many other (non-OSI) protocols are being developed using an upper-layer infrastructure containing a connectionless-mode framework.

Although the NFS is not an OSI service, it is quite popular, performs a very useful (some might say essential) service, and operates quite efficiently. Compare this to OSI file service, as provided by FTAM[ISO88a] in a connection-oriented framework. Although more general, FTAM has a relatively time-expensive set of mechanisms for establishing and releasing the file service. Further, because the NFS uses connectionless-mode facilities, it is more resilient to client and server crashes and is able to recover much more easily than FTAM. These same mechanisms also make it easier for servers to provide simultaneous file service to several clients. Some other differences between FTAM and the NFS, whilst not directly related to connection-oriented issues, are by-products of the frameworks used by the two applications. All other things being equal, today's FTAM implementations are larger, slower, and actually *less* functional than corresponding NFS implementations.

By and large, this is an unfair comparison: the NFS is designed specifically for networks with high throughput, small delay, and a low rate of errors. The NFS is also heavily optimized for UNIX-based systems. FTAM must operate across a more general range of networks and platforms. Nevertheless, today's implementations of FTAM are quite minimal: they simply do not realize enough of FTAM's promise to outshine (or even to compare favorably to) the average NFS implementation.

One might argue that experience with FTAM will one day lead to implementations that not only are much more functional than NFS but also run on a larger range of platforms. Further, at that time, not only will issues such as size and efficiency will be less critical, but the connection-oriented overhead may become reasonable. It is, it would seem, only a matter of time and implementation. Perhaps this is so. But, perhaps it is also true that these problems are fundamental to the upper-layer infrastructure. If this is the case, then no amount of time and experience will be able to make FTAM competitive to the NFS. In fairness, this is an extreme example of an attack on the upper-layer infrastructure. Whilst one certainly cannot dismiss the lessons taught by connectionless-mode protocols such as the NFS, for the majority of applications in use for the next ten years, a connection-oriented framework should prove adequate. Thus, one can convincingly argue that a "right enough" tool has been selected.

```
...soap
```

In order to discuss upper-layer infrastructure, it will be necessary to review first the services provided to the application by the network. Following this, upper-layer services are stepwise introduced, from bottom to top.

When describing upper-layer infrastructure, it is always difficult to decide whether the presentation should be top-down or bottom-up. The top-down approach starts at the goal and then describes the steps taken to reach the destination. It suffers from introducing too much too quickly: the reader is expected to grasp the totality of the environment before understanding the building blocks that comprise the environment. In contrast, the bottom-up approach starts with the foundation and proceeds toward the goal. It suffers from appearing to be contrived: the destination is known to the writer, but not divulged to the reader until the very end. In the discussion which follows, a compromise is taken. That is, although the latter approach is taken for the chapters which follow, the remainder of *this* chapter quickly sketches the upper-layer infrastructure. This provides a brief overview that should be helpful in overcoming the disadvantages inherent to the bottom-up approach.

6.1   Transport Services

As described in Part II, the transport provider offers a simple, but essential set of services:

- connection establishment;

- data transfer; and,

- connection release.

6.1.1   Connection Establishment

For the user, connection establishment consists of three parts: addressing a remote user, negotiating the use of an expedited data facility, and identifying quality of service parameters for the connection.

Complex naming and addressing mechanisms at the application layer have considerable impact on the addresses used by the layers throughout the upper-layer infrastructure. As such, a detailed discussion of addressing will be deferred. For now, note that users of the transport service identify each other through the use of a *transport address*. This address consists of two parts: a *transport selector*, and one or more *network addresses*. A network address identifies a location in the network. A transport selector identifies an entity, a transport service user, at that location. A transport selector is simply a string of octets that is meaningful only at a particular network address.

Finally, the application may have requirements as to the characteristics of the connection. For example, it might have minimal throughput or latency requirements. This is communicated to the transport service by way of the user's *communications quality-of-service* (QOS) parameters. These parameters "customize" the mechanisms used by the transport provider. They affect which network address is selected (if more than one is present in the transport address), which retransmission policy is used, and so on.

6.1.2   Data Transfer

The transport service offers a full-duplex, virtual circuit to its users. Collections of octets, termed *transport service data units* (TSDUs), are exchanged through the transport service. The TSDUs are delivered intact and in order to the remote user of the transport service.

An important ramification of this description is that no restrictions are placed on the order in which data is sent or on which user may send the data. The transport provider offers an "octet pipe" to its users. No restrictions are made as to how that pipe is used.

Some users of the transport service may desire a mechanism for sending "express" data that might overtake previously sent data and be delivered sooner. Usually this expedited data indicates something about the data previously sent. For example, if an action were to invalidate some information recently sent, a "lightning bolt" could be sent to the remote user indicating that an important update would be forthcoming.

6.1.3 Connection Release

Connection release consists simply of marking the connection as terminated, *regardless of the data still in the network*. When a connection is released, the transport service discards any data in transit. Hence, it is the responsibility of the transport users to ensure that their connection is released gracefully. Note that this differs from other transport providers, such as the Transmission Control Protocol (TCP) [JPost81b], which offer both graceful and destructive release mechanisms.

6.2   Session Services

The session provider attempts to add structure to the circuits offered by the transport service. The value added by the session service consists of four areas:

- token management;

- dialogue control;

- activity management; and,

- exception reporting.

Of course, the session service also will provide for the connection establishment, data transfer, and connection release services of transport. Unlike the transport service, the session service provides for a graceful release mechanism, so that applications need not concern themselves with this functionality. (Graceful release is a value-added feature of the session service, although many argue that it should be a function of the transport service.)

6.2.1   Token Management

Although a two-way circuit is necessary for meaningful communications, a surprisingly large number of application exchanges are actually half-duplex, rather than full-duplex, in nature. The session service provides a mechanism for enforcing this kind of behavior. As a result, application protocols are considerably simplified.

In order to provide for half-duplex exchanges over a full-duplex circuit, the session service introduces the notion of a *token*. There are actually four tokens that may be offered by the session service, but for half-duplex exchanges, it is ownership of the *data token* that controls which user may send data.

Obviously, the session service must also provide some mechanism for requesting the token. These requests carry a *priority* that gives the relative importance of the request. When notified that the remote user wants the token, the local session user compares the priority of the request to the priority of the current application exchange. If the remote user's priority is higher, the application may discard or perhaps save the current transaction and then pass the data token to the remote user.

6.2.2 Dialogue Control

Many applications exchange large amounts of data over potentially unreliable networks. Although the transport service attempts to offer a completely reliable circuit service, the network may eventually degrade to the point where it is no longer possible for data to transit the network, even after successive attempts on the part of the transport service. When this happens, the transport service indicates the failure, and the application must decide on what course of action to pursue.

Eventually, the network recovers and a connection is re-established. Ideally, data transfer should continue at the point just before network collapse. To achieve something close to the ideal, the session service introduces the notion of *checkpointing*. A checkpoint is a logical mark placed in the dialogue between users of the session service. Upon receiving a checkpoint, the remote session user may acknowledge the checkpoint. This confirmation is conveyed by the session service back to the originating user and data transfer continues. If, sometime later, the connection is broken and then re-established, the session users agree to resume data exchange at the last confirmed checkpoint.

In addition to exchanging large amounts of data, some applications may wish to interrupt a lengthy data exchange. Consider the case where an interactive file transfer application is sending a file. During the middle of the transfer, the user tells the application to cancel the transfer. Ideally, any part of the file still in the network should be immediately discarded before it is delivered to the remote session user. This saves any resources that the remote application uses locally (e.g., further reads from or writes to disk). To achieve something close to the ideal, the local session provider sends a message using the transport expedited data service, saying to prepare to resynchronize and to discard user data from the network until a special mark is received. The special mark, a resynchronize checkpoint, is sent using the normal transport data service. As the network empties, no further user data is passed up until the two session providers are resynchronized.

6.2.3   Activity Management

Many application exchanges actually consist of several smaller exchanges. A top-level exchange may be considered an *activity*. This distinction provides a coarser granularity to be used when discussing the application protocol. An interesting result from this approach is that it allows a session user powerful mechanisms for manipulating, as a group, the smaller exchanges that comprise an activity.

Consider the case where an electronic mail message is being exchanged. This might be viewed as an activity. More specifically, suppose that a large message sent "4$\underline{\text{th}}$ class" is currently being transferred. Half-way through the transfer, the sending entity finds a high-priority message to deliver. Using the session service, the entity may *interrupt* the current activity, transfer the high-priority message by starting a new activity, and then *resume* the previous activity, picking up where it left off.

Obviously, there must be some kind of relationship between dialogue and activity management. In fact, there are three kinds of checkpoints that are offered by the session service. One of these is used for marking the data in the smaller exchanges; another is used to mark activities; and, the third is the resynchronization mark briefly discussed earlier. So, within a single activity, checkpoints might be used to manage that portion of the dialogue.

In the original work on session services, there was another service, *quarantine*, which allowed the session user to bundle application exchanges and have them delivered, as a unit, to the remote user. The quarantine facility was ultimately dropped from session service since it could be logically provided by activity management.

6.2.4   Exception Reporting

In the course of an exchange, an application may encounter an abnormal situation that requires drastic action. Rather than aborting the session connection, a user of the session service may choose to raise an exception to the remote user. Explicit action is required on the part of the remote user to clear the exception. As a result, the session connection is brought to a known state.

The session provider may also raise exceptions to the users of the session service. As with user-initiated exceptions, some kind of explicit action is required to clear the exception.

It is difficult to determine if an error is important enough to raise an exception but not catastrophic enough to warrant aborting the connection. Unless the designer of an application indicates when exceptions should be generated, the choice is largely a matter of taste. However, consider this example. Earlier, the notion of tokens was discussed. Supposed a session user requests a token and the remote user chooses to ignore the request. After some time, the session user might decide to raise an exception saying: "I want that data token NOW." Lest the reader think this is contrived, it should be pointed out that associated with each exception is a reason. The session service defines the possible reasons that may be conveyed; "demand data token" is one of these.

6.3   Abstract Syntax

Application exchanges involve transmitting data structures. These structures may be quite complex. For example, to a message transfer application, a message may consist of two components: the *envelope* and the *content*. In turn, the envelope may have several components, such as the address of the originator, the addresses of pending recipients, the date of message submission, tracing information, and so on. Further, the addresses themselves might also have structure. In short, the data structures being exchanged may be *arbitrarily* complex.

Although this generality is appealing (it allows powerful services to be built), it raises two questions: first, how can the data structures be defined in an unambiguous fashion; and, second, how can an instance of the data structure (e.g., a message to be transferred) be transmitted in the network so that no information is lost? In response, OSI introduces the notions of *abstract syntax* and *transfer syntax*.

6.3.1   Abstract Syntax Notation

The task of an abstract syntax language is to describe data types in a machine-independent fashion. This means that a level of indirection is placed between the application protocol and how a particular computer architecture (e.g., one using a Motorola 68030 processor) might represent the data exchanged by that protocol. This means that the abstract syntax language is freed from machine-oriented restrictions. For example, many computers use 32 bits to represent an integer quantity, others use 16 bits, whilst still others use 64 bits. Because an abstract syntax language does not target a particular architecture, a protocol specified using an abstract syntax language is immune from considerations such as this.

When a data type is defined using an abstract syntax language, it is often *tagged*. This provides a useful way of distinguishing the data types that might be sent during an application exchange.

By their nature, abstract syntax languages are *formal*. This means that each language has a grammar that defines how data types may be described using this language. As a side-effect, this formality allows the applications writer to build programs that manipulate the abstract syntax. For example, when debugging an application, a very common chore is to "pretty print" the values of the data types being exchanged.

Since the data type is described using an abstract syntax, it is possible for the applications writer to build a pretty-printer that reads each value of a data type occuring in an application exchange and then produces an easy-to-read description of the data. Although crude (no meaningful protocol analysis is taking place), experience shows that the vast majority of interworking problems encountered when first building an application can be isolated using this technique.

A degenerate form of the pretty-printer is a program that simply reads the values of the data types and reports if they are encoded correctly. To be sure, such programs can be built by hand. However, because of the formality introduced by using an abstract syntax language, these tasks can be *completely* automated.

At present, only one abstract syntax language exists in OSI — Abstract Syntax Notation One (ASN.1). Currently, ASN.1 is the only representation used by all OSI applications. However, one might envision several different abstract syntax languages existing in the future.

ASN.1 has a rich syntax for describing data types and provides a powerful macro facility for extending its grammar. This permits an applications designer to define new constructs capturing new semantics. For example, it may be useful to denote a relationship, such as a refinement, between two data types. Using ASN.1, an applications designer might define a REFINES macro to capture these semantics. Although this is a very useful mechanism for conveying meaning to human readers, programmatic tools, such as those sketched above, cannot share in understanding these additional nuances — unless they are given some specialized help. This unfortunate situation will be examined in greater detail.

ASN.1 is destined to become the network programming language of the 90's, just as the *C* programming language is largely seen as having been the systems programming language of the 80's.

6.3.2 Transfer Syntax Notation

The use of abstract syntax separates data types as they appear in the application protocol from how they physically appear in an application. The task of a transfer syntax notation is to represent unambiguously the values of data types as they are transmitted on the network.

Collections of octets, termed *session service data units* (SSDUs), are exchanged through the session service. Thus, the process of applying a transfer syntax consists of taking an internal representation that (somehow) corresponds to the abstract syntax definition of a data type and then *serializing* the information into a contiguous string of octets. To be interoperable across machines of different architecture, the resulting representation must have an unambiguous mapping to its corresponding abstract syntax. Unlike abstract syntax however, the string of octets is a physical quantity; choices concerning word-length, bit-orientation and the like, must all be decided. Because of this, the resulting representation is called a *concrete syntax*.

Thus, applying a transfer syntax consists of mapping between the abstract syntax of a data type and the concrete syntax used to represent an instance of that data type.

Again, one might envision several different transfer syntaxes existing in the future. In fact, there may be several transfer syntax notations that could be applied to a single abstract syntax notation. At present, only one transfer syntax notation exists in OSI — the Basic Encoding Rules (BER) of ASN.1. As experience with applications using the BER grows, new transfer syntax notations, such as those including data compression or encryption, will no doubt be defined.

The Basic Encoding Rules use a "TLV" approach to mapping between the abstract and the concrete: each data type is encoded as a tag, a length, and a value. The tag field corresponds to the tag defined by the data type's abstract syntax. If several different data types can be exchanged, a prudent applications designer will give each data type a unique tag. This allows the receiving end to determine unambiguously what data type it is receiving.

The length field normally indicates how many octets used for the encoding of the value portion of the data type. If instances of several data types are sent in one SSDU, it is helpful to know where one data type ended and the next began! However, sometimes it is inconvenient for the sender to calculate the length of the encoding prior to sending the value of the data type. In this case, a special code is inserted into the length field to indicate an *indefinite length*. Upon finding a encoding that uses an indefinite length, the receiver starts looking for a special *end of contents* sequence. Upon finding this, the receiver knows that the entire value has been read.

Finally, the value portion of the data type is encoded. The BER produces encodings that, whilst concrete, are nevertheless machine-independent. Each quantity, such as an integer, is encoded in the smallest number of octets necessary to preserve precision of the value. Thus, the BER uses a variable-length/minimal-octet encoding scheme.

It is important to understand that this flexibility has its drawbacks: the BER provides an encoding scheme general enough to support all machine architectures; however, the scheme is not particularly efficient to implement on any existing machine architecture. As such, the price of interoperability can be tremendous inefficiency. For example, informal measurements comparing the BER to Sun Microsystems' External Data Representation (XDR) [SMI86a] show that using the BER to encode an integer on a Motorola 68020 processor is anywhere from three to twenty times slower than using the XDR. Further, some claim that even the XDR can be improved upon. This had led to a controversy regarding the cost of using ASN.1 and the BER.

6.4   Presentation Services

The presentation provider does little more than combine the circuit structuring offered by the session service with the data structuring offered by abstract syntax. As such, the value-added of the presentation service consists of two areas:

- context management; and,

- syntax matching.

Of course, the presentation service will also provide for the services offered by the session service (e.g., connection establishment, token management, etc.). In practice, the presentation service provides session layer functionality in a two step process: first, a data type from the application is mapped into a concrete syntax; and, second, that information is presented as an SSDU to the corresponding session service. The inverse operations are performed when the session service provides the presentation provider with data. This operation has led many to note that the presentation service is, by and large, a "pass through" to the session service. That is, some feel that the presentation service does not enhance session services.

6.4.1   Context Management

In the discussion of abstract syntax, it was noted that several transfer syntax notations could be defined for a given abstract syntax notation. Further, for a given presentation connection, several abstract syntaxes might be active. Although ASN.1 might be used to define each abstract syntax, these syntaxes are separate objects. For example, if several entities were cooperating at the application layer — effectively sharing the presentation connection in an orderly fashion — then each entity might use a different abstract syntax for the data structures it exchanges.

The task of context management is to "remember" what combinations of these are in effect on a presentation connection. When connection establishment occurs, a *presentation context identifier* (PCI) is defined that relates a particular abstract syntax to a particular transfer syntax. This relationship is defined via negotiation: the initiator proposes a mapping, by specifying an abstract syntax and one or more transfer syntaxes. The responder then decides if it wants to use that abstract syntax, and if so, which one of the transfer syntaxes shall be used. The collection of these contexts (more than one may be defined) is called the *defined context set* (DCS).

After connection establishment, it is possible to define or remove contexts. This is important for applications such as FTAM that use a separate context for each document type that is exchanged. For example, when a user wishes to transfer a data file, an FTAM implementation might add a context that contains the abstract syntax corresponding to the format of the file along with a transfer syntax appropriate to exchange the file contents. When the transfer is complete, the FTAM implementation would remove the context.

Note however that context alteration is an optional facility. As such, it is perfectly reasonable for another FTAM implementation to negotiate, during connection establishment, all of the presentation contexts that it will need over the lifetime of the connection.

Obviously, if the synchronization mechanisms of session are being used, then the presentation provider will have to pay careful attention if the connection is resynchronized — this action may very well cause the DCS to change implicitly!

6.4.2 Syntax Matching

Once the DCS has been negotiated, then the users of the presentation service may exchange instances of data types. The presentation provider employs *local syntax matching* services to serialize these values. When an application is running on a particular computer, it has its own machine-oriented representation for the data type. This representation, termed the *internal form*, differs based on the machine architecture, programming language, and even language compiler used. The task of the syntax matching services is to map back and forth between the internal form and the concrete representation on the network.

Conceptually, when a data type is to be converted from an internal form to its corresponding concrete syntax, two mappings are performed: first, the internal form of the data type is mapped to the corresponding abstract syntax; and second, the instance of this abstract syntax is mapped to the concrete syntax. The first mapping is strictly a local issue: on some systems, these two steps may be integrated so that it is impossible to distinguish between them. The second mapping consists of consulting the presentation context for the data type and applying the associated transfer syntax.

Once again, the formalism introduced by using an abstract syntax notation permits the use of machine-generated tools to automate this process. One tool might read an abstract syntax definition and produce an equivalent structure in a local programming language, such as *C*. After this, another tool might take both the abstract syntax definition and the programming language structure and produce a program that performs both of the mappings comprising the syntax matching services. The results of applying this technology are quite powerful: applications programmers concern themselves with data structures described using the programming language that they are familiar with. The mappings between those data structures and the network representation can be automatically generated. This capability can greatly speed application prototyping, experimentation, and development.

6.4.3   Lightweight Presentation Services

The power of the notions of abstract syntax and transfer syntax have led some to speculate whether these facilities could be layered directly on top of the end-to-end services. The rationale is as follows: although the session services provide great functionality, there is a class of "no nonsense" protocols that are interested only in very basic services. These protocols have no use for complicated negotiations, exotic services, and the like. Rather, because of resource/performance constraints (in either the target system or in the network), a designer of such a protocol may specifically avoid this kind of complexity. Whilst contrary, in a sense, to the spirit of OSI, such protocols nevertheless form an important class of applications. To meet these requirements, it appears sensible to layer the syntax matching services directly on top of the end-to-end services.

One group suggesting such an architecture is the "Netman" working group of the Internet Engineering Task Force (IETF) of the IAB. This group is tasked with running the OSI network management framework in TCP/IP-based networks. Their architecture is straightforward: a "pure" OSI application environment is run, containing the OSI network management protocol. The subset of presentation (and session) services required by this environment is actually quite small. As a result, a *lightweight presentation protocol* was developed that sits directly on top of the TCP. The protocol provides an emulation of the exact services required by the OSI network management application. This scheme is in many ways similar to the emulation of transport services described in Section 5.4 of Part II. Later, the discussion will consider this architecture, and the lightweight presentation protocol, in much greater detail. At first glance, this may appear to be a rather specialized undertaking; in fact, there is a large class of distributed applications that can be built using OSI that require exactly the same subset of services as OSI network management!

6.5   Application Service Elements

The OSI application layer differs from the layers beneath it by explicitly being divided into *service elements*. Although each of the underlying layers may be decomposed into elements, this decomposition is not fundamental to the organization of the layer. In contrast, the application layer relies heavily on *application service elements* in order to perform its tasks.

Application service elements provide a mechanism for dividing the responsibility of the "total" application protocol. For example, all applications ultimately establish an association with a peer. The Association Control Service Element is responsible for this task. All OSI applications contain the Association Control Service Element in order to perform association establishment and release. In addition to the commonly used service elements, each application contains one or more service elements that are specific to the application protocol. The combination of all service elements that comprise the application, along with the relationship between those service elements (e.g., "who calls whom") forms an *application context*.

There are several application service elements that may be part of an application context. By the end of 1988 however, only three of the commonly used service elements had reached stability:

- association control;

- remote operations; and,

- reliable transfer.

Besides making application protocols more tractable, the use of application service elements promote reuse of application layer facilities. As with the upper-layer infrastructure as a whole, from an implementation viewpoint this effect can provide substantive leverage.

6.5.1   Association Control

The Association Control Service Element (ACSE) is responsible for *association* establishment and release. An association is a binding between two entities, which are referred to as the *initiator* and the *responder*. The primary task of the ACSE is to bind one application process to another. This binding results in an association that is supported by an underlying presentation connection.

The binding process is really two-step: first, the initiator determines which service it requires, and asks to have this service mapped onto the application entities running in the network; and then, second, based on the initiator's communications requirements, an association will be bound to one of those entities that becomes the responder. The first mapping is performed by Directory Services, whilst the second mapping is performed by the initiator's transport provider (as discussed earlier in Section 5.5 on page 106 in Part II).

Although binding implies a client/server model for establishing the association, this needn't have the same relationship for the services provided. It is perfectly reasonable for an initiator to bind to a responder for the purpose of letting the responder request actions to be performed by the initiator. This provider/consumer model is contrary to the client/server model in which the client connects to the server, and then the client proceeds to request actions to be performed by the server.

6.5.2   Naming and Addressing

Directory Services, which will be discussed in much greater detail, is responsible for the management of *names* and associated *attributes*, such as addresses. At the very least, each application needs to use Directory Services in order to ascertain the presentation address of its peer. (Applications may make other uses of the Directory as well.)

The author finds it useful to think of a *Directory Services Element* as responsible for performing the mapping required by the Association Control Service Element in order to perform binding. The element is purely conceptual. There is no OSI standard defining this element; rather the application entity is assumed to somehow contain this functionality. However, these tasks are sufficiently complex, that it is useful to discuss such an entity separately from the ACSE.

Each application entity minimally requires a *nameservice* in order to establish a binding. The Directory Services Element is given the name of a service and returns a presentation address. Cast in terms of the OSI Directory, this is a straightforward "read" in order to obtain the `presentationAddress` attribute of the object in question.

In practice, using the standard Directory mechanisms for reading this information is inefficient in both space and time. When application layer naming and addressing is considered in greater detail, the discussion examines a "higher performance nameservice" that provides specialized, fast, access to the Directory for this particular functionality.

6.5.3   Reliable Transfer

The Reliable Transfer Service Element (RTSE) is responsible for bulk-mode transfers. Although the functionality of the session service provides for explicit checkpointing and connection recovery, many applications, whilst desiring the service (or a portion thereof), may find it daunting to manipulate these services directly. The RTSE is intended to hide the complexity of the session and presentation services to provide a simple transfer facility.

The RTSE itself can be used by other service elements. For example, in message handling systems, the Remote Operations Service Element often uses the RTSE, as the information exchanged may contain large electronic mail messages. Further, the RTSE can use other service elements, such as the ACSE. The idea is that the RTSE provides an additional level of abstraction in which the rich functionality of the underlying services are provided without the additional complexity of knowing how to use them.

6.5.4   Remote Operations

The Remote Operations Service Element (ROSE) is responsible for request/reply *interactions*. An operation is *invoked* by an application process. In response, its peer returns one of three outcomes: a *result*, if the operation succeeded; an *error*, if the operation failed; or, a *rejection*, if the operation was not performed (e.g., due to network failure).

A surprising large number of applications use the ROSE. For example, the ROSE is used by message handling systems, directory services, network management, and remote data base access. The reason for this is that the ROSE can easily support a *remote procedure call* (RPC) facility, which is what many distributed applications are built on. Many feel that the generality of the ROSE and its ability to support a wide range of loosely coupled systems may very well be a key factor in the overall success of OSI.

In addition to support for RPC, the ROSE also supports the notion of *linked operations* (sometimes termed a *callback* or *remote upcall*). The idea is simple: when an invocation is made, one of its arguments contains the name of an operation to be invoked as a part of the original invocation. This is useful if the performer of the original invocation requires additional information from time to time from the invoker. For example, one could imagine an operation called `Traverse` that took two arguments: the name of a directory containing the user's files, and the name of an operation to invoke for each of the files in that directory. To construct the "print directory" command, which prints each of the user's file on a laser printer, one need only invoke `Traverse` with the name of the directory along with the operation `PrintFile`. If instead, the user wanted to list each file to the screen, the second argument would be `ListFile` instead. In both cases, the `Traverse` operation reads the user's directory and for each file found, it simply invokes the second argument with the name of the file.

6.6   OSI Applications

Although the upper-layer infrastructure is appealing to the applications designer, the OSI *applications* are what appeal to users of the network.

Definitions of the term "application" vary greatly: to some, an application refers to a particular program or set of programs running on a computer; to others, an application refers to a collection of application entities that perform some task. These definitions are not really in opposition: they simply employ different levels of granularity. For example, one could view FTAM, the OSI file service, as an application. It provides the capabilities to transfer, access and manage files. Similarly, one could imagine several file transfer programs being built using FTAM.

In an application, OSI considers FTAM to be simply another application service element, just like Association Control (ACSE) or Remote Operations (ROSE). Thus, the *application context* for a file transfer utility not only contains ASEs such as the ACSE, but also the FTAM ASE. Although OSI does not differentiate between ASEs in terms of their importance, it is useful to think of ASEs as being in two classes: *generic* ASEs, which might be present in any OSI application; and, *specific* ASEs, such as FTAM, which are more closely aligned with what persons think of as the raison d'être for an application. Although one might find several generic ASEs present in an application context, each application context usually consists of exactly one specific ASE.

Several specific ASEs are progressing through the standards process. By the end of 1988 however, only three had reached stability and began to see what might be taken for widespread use. These are now examined in turn.

6.6.1   The Directory

The OSI Directory is responsible for the management of *names* and associated *attributes*. Earlier when discussing application naming and addressing, a presentation address was given as a possible attribute that an object might have. Although useful for providing a mapping between names and addresses, the OSI Directory is intended to do much more than "just" that.

One way of looking at the Directory Service is to describe it in terms of *information objects*. The Directory's representation of an information object, typically called an *entry*, contains information about a person, a place, an organization, etc. Each entry consists of one or more attributes.

Each attribute consists of a type, indicating what kind of attribute it is, and one or more values (one of which is termed the *distinguished value*). Attribute values are structured using ASN.1.

Naming

One of the attributes of an entry is particularly special: it is referred to as the *Relative Distinguished Name* (RDN) of the entry. The RDN is formed by taking the name of the attribute and its distinguished value. For example, if the attribute in question was called `countryName` and it had a distinguished value of US, then we might say that the RDN for the entry was `countryName=US`. Of course, this is strictly a "user friendly" notation: the Directory uses a concise binary format for representing an RDN.

In the OSI Directory, information is primarily organized according to a hierarchical tree structure. The top of the tree is termed the *root*, and has no explicit name. To find the name of an object, termed its *Distinguished Name* (DN), one concatenates the RDNs found when traversing the tree by starting at the root and proceeding directly to the object's entry. Thus, the Distinguished Name

```
countryName          =    "United States"
organizationName     =    "Wollongong"
```

refers to an entry with an RDN of `organizationName=Wollongong` whose parent has an RDN of `countryName=US`. In turn, this parent entry is an immediate child of the root.

One attribute of an entry, its `objectClass`, determines what kind of object this entry corresponds to (e.g., a person). The value of this attribute indicates what types of attributes the entry *must* and *may* contain. For example, for an entry corresponding to an organization, one would expect an attribute describing the business category of the organization. On the other hand, if the entry corresponded to a person, then this would be inappropriate. In short, the object class of each entry indicates which attributes "make sense" for the entry to contain.

The Directory itself is distributed, being composed of *Directory System Agents* (DSAs). A group of DSAs under a common administration are responsible for a portion of the tree, termed a *Directory Management Domain* (DMD). When a user wishes to access the Directory, a *Directory User Agent* (DUA) is invoked to form a 1:1 binding between the user and the DUA. On behalf of its user, a DUA will contact a DSA and issue a request. The DSA may have the information locally available. If this is not the case, a decision has to be made: either the DSA can contact another DSA to get the information (this is called *chaining*); or, the DSA can tell the DUA to contact another DSA directly (this is called *referral*).

The operations that the DUA can request of a DSA are fairly general:

- read the attributes of an entry;

- get a list of the entry's children;

- recursively search for entries with certain attribute values;

- compare a given value to the an entry's attribute;

- add new entries, or attributes to an existing entry;

- change the name of an entry or its attributes; and,

- delete entries or its attributes.

In short, the DSAs provide mechanisms for traversing the tree and manipulating the information contained therein. But, do not think of the Directory as a general-purpose database. The design of the Directory is optimized heavily towards a "white pages" service with these characteristics:

- information is updated infrequently in comparison to queries; and,

- the naming architecture is hierarchical and *user-friendly*.

By "user-friendly," it is meant that names are largely deducible by persons, rather than machines. Enough information must be supplied by the user to identify an entry uniquely. This might involve an iterative "guessing" process, which programs aren't very good at.

6.6.2 Message Handling Systems

Electronic mail is by far the most popular of all the existing network-based applications. In general, any mail system offers a third-party delivery service. The user of the service wishes to have some information delivered, termed the *content*. The contents is placed inside an *envelope* that identifies the intended recipients of the information along with other service-related information (e.g., the priority of the message). The originator places the envelope into the delivery system. From this point on, the postal service takes responsibility for delivery of the message until it is successfully delivered or is returned due to some problem.

It is important to understand that this scenario is broadly applicable to both physical delivery facilities (such as the U.S. Post Office) and electronic delivery facilities. Although the actual implementation may be completely different, the concepts, roles, and responsibilities are identical. Just as the Directory contains DSAs and DUAs, a message handling system can be viewed as containing *Message Transfer Agents* (MTAs) that are responsible for relaying messages, and *User Agents* (UAs) that interact with the MTAs on behalf of the user. The *Message Transfer System* (MTS) is the collection of the set of MTAs responsible for delivering messages.

Early electronic mail facilities, and in particular the pioneering work in the original ARPAnet, used a memo-based framework for message contents. This was even reflected in the names used for both the protocols (e.g., *Standard for the Format of ARPA Internet Text Messages* [DCroc82]) and the software (e.g., *Multi-channel Memorandum Distribution Facility* [DCroc79]) that implemented these systems. In a memo-based framework, the content consists of two parts: the *headers* and the *body*. Both parts consist of ASCII text characters. The headers are rigorously structured. Each header consists of a keyword and some value. Depending on the particular keyword, the value may be further structured (e.g., a date, one or more addresses, and so on). In contrast, the body is free-form text and needn't conform to any particular format. Thus, memo-based messages consist of three components: the envelope, which is meaningful to the transport system; the headers, which are meaningful to the user agent; and, the body, which is meaningful to the user.

A tremendous amount of experience has been gained from memo-based systems, and this has led to the development of rather sophisticated programs. These applications are termed *message handlers.* A message handler consists of three parts:

- a user interface, which interprets the user's commands and displays their results;

- a message manager, which contains both messages previously received by the user along with messages in preparation; and,

- a user agent (UA), to interact with the local MTA.

(These terms aren't part of OSI Message Handling, although they do predate MHS.) Existing message handlers vary considerably in their sophistication. For example, the message manager might have complex retrieval facilities that allow a user to examine all messages concerning a certain topic. Other facilities might be available to generate replies automatically (e.g., "the user is on vacation and won't be answering mail for a while"), and so on. These capabilities are made possible by the headers in the messages: by being in a well-defined format, the message manager component can perform meaningful searches and compositions. User interfaces also vary greatly: whilst some might be simple line-at-a-time interfaces, others might have exotic command languages or be window-based. Further, facilities might exist to construct new message handling commands out of a combination of existing ones, to better tailor the message handler to the user's tastes.

In 1979, the International Federation of Information Processing (IFIP) defined a model for *Message Handling Systems* (MHS) to capture the richness of this environment. Rather than focusing on a memo-based framework. They chose a multi-media basis. This means that messages, from the user's viewpoint, now consist of a *heading* and several *body parts*. The heading provides functionality similar to the headers in memo-based messages, although the structure is radically different. The body parts, rather than being limited to ASCII text, might also be facsimile, voice, teletex, or any other well-defined structure. This kind of content is called an *interpersonal message* (IPM).

However, IFIP's vision was more ambitious: rather than provide an electronic version of a letter-carrying service, MHS was to provide a true store-and-forward capability. This meant that the messages needn't be only communications among persons, but could also contain information being sent between arbitrary processes. Thus, the contents actually needn't be an IPM, but could take on some other format. The MTS would faithfully deliver the contents, regardless of what it contained or "what it looked like," to the appropriate recipients. Hence, message handling could be used easily to provide a store-and-forward file transfer service.

Finally, although memo-based message handlers might be quite sophisticated, the service offered by memo-based MTAs is actually quite simple. (This is not surprising considering the name of one of the most commonly used memo-based MTA protocols, *The Simple Mail Transfer Protocol* [JPost82].) MHS has a richer offering by adding new capabilities to the basic store-and-forward service. For example, a *return-receipt* might be associated with a message.

The provision for arbitrary contents, multi-media interpersonal messaging, and a rich service offering has combined to make the MHS very attractive to users.

6.6.3   File Transfer, Access and Management

Files are a major part of any computer system, so it should not be surprising that users of computers might wish to manipulate files over the network. In the simplest case, a user might want to transfer an entire file from one machine to another. A file service can provide more functionality however. For example, a workstation might want to access just a few records from a file server. Alternatively, a diskless workstation might have all of its files residing on another computer. In addition, special applications such as printing and spooling can also be viewed as filesystem activities. Finally, even remote database access can be thought of as being supported by a network file capability. The OSI file service, FTAM, is provided to meet these needs.

Heterogeneity is a part of networking. As a result, the computers in a given network may very well be running several operating systems. Unfortunately, different operating systems usually have different file mechanisms. In some cases the differences are relatively simple, such as naming conventions for files. In other cases, the differences are dramatic. For example, the popular UNIX operating system has a simple view of a file: a stream of bytes (octets) that can be accessed arbitrarily by offset. In contrast, other operating systems support structured files, in which access is key-based.

In order to accommodate such a wide range of philosophies, FTAM adopts a *virtual filestore* model. That is, rather than adopt the file mechanisms from a particular operating system, FTAM defines a conceptual model of a filesystem. How the virtual filestore is mapped onto a local filesystem is an implementation matter. Although achieving the right balance in defining the virtual filestore is difficult, it is also potentially very rewarding.

The virtual filestore (henceforth, just *filestore*) is a collection of files. Each file has a name that uniquely identifies it. Unlike nearly all existing filesystems, there is no directory structure. From FTAM's perspective, filenames are opaque, no explicit relationship between files can be deduced from their names. Each file has a set of *attributes*, such as ownership information, and *contents*, which is the data associated with the file.

There are two classes of attributes: *file attributes*, which exist on a per-file basis. Thus, simultaneous clients of the filestore always see the same information. An example of a file attribute is the file's name. The second class of attributes consists of *activity attributes*, which exist on a per-client basis. As a result, when a client manipulates an activity attribute, this does not affect other clients. For example, when performing some file operation, each client has associated with it a *selected* file. When it changes its own selected file, this (fortunately) does not affect other clients.

In FTAM's virtual filestore, files are structured. One file attribute is the *contents-type* of the file that tells how the file is structured. Typically, the value of the contents-type attribute is a *document type*. A document type fully defines the structure of a file: two files with the same contents-type might contain different data, but both must adhere to the same structuring rules. A document type defines several things about a file's structure both statically and dynamically.

The static characteristics define the file's composition. In FTAM, each file is made up of *File Access Data Units* (FADUs) that are combined to form a hierarchical tree. The document type defines the *constraint set* for a particular file. Thus, an unstructured file might be defined to have exactly one FADU, whilst a record-based file might be defined as having a parent FADU (containing no file data) with one or more children, each child representing a record in the file. In addition to constraining the form of the tree that represents the file, another static characteristic is the data type of the data that might exist in each FADU. For example, each record in the file might be a personnel record. The document type defines the *abstract syntax* for these data units.

The dynamic characteristics define how the file is transmitted and accessed. Since the data contained in a file are defined using abstract syntax, a transfer syntax must be selected when data is actually transferred. Finally, the document type must define what happens when a file is traversed. Just as clients have a currently selected file, they also have a current position within the file. The document type defines, e.g., how the current position changes when data is added to the file.

FTAM's charter is quite broad: to support both whole file transfer between mainframes and diskless workstation access. As noted in a soapbox earlier, there are certainly special-purpose protocols that can perform some of these tasks "better" than FTAM can. Still, FTAM has promise as general-purpose (though not necessarily high-performance) mechanism for file service.

6.7   Roadmap

With the *Introduction to Application Services* drawing to a close, the discussion briefly outlines the remainder of Part III.

As with the introduction, we'll proceed bottom-up, considering each part of the upper-layer infrastructure in much greater detail. As each part is presented, only aspects that have achieved stability and consensus will be discussed. As a result, only connection-oriented services will be examined — connectionless-mode facilities are still in their infancy. Further, network management will not be seriously considered — as of the end of 1988, it had yet to stabilize. However, some issues involved with both connectionless-mode communication and network management will be introduced as a means of exploring other topics.

Throughout the discussion, the infrastructure will be illustrated with discussion of an actual implementation. This is intended to present a balanced perspective: although the theory of the upper-layer infrastructure is important, it is just as important to understand how it is implemented in practice. The implementational framework examined will be that of the *ISO Development Environment* (ISODE). The ISODE was developed primarily as a tool for studying the upper-layers of OSI. As such, it is well suited for the role it will play in the discussion that follows. (Appendix A on page 597 contains ordering information for the package.)

The ISODE is coded in the *C* programming language[BKern78] and runs on several variants of the UNIX operating system. Hence, when reading the sections on implementation, it will be helpful to be familiar with the basics of the UNIX operating system.

Chapter 7

Session Services

As noted in *Introduction to Application Services*, the session service adds structure to the data circuit provided by the transport service. Whilst the transport service provides a reliable full-duplex communication circuit, the session service provides a more applications-oriented stream to its user.

More formally, the session service is offered to the session user as shown in Figure 7.1. In order to offer this service, two session entities cooperate using the session protocol along with the facilities provided by the transport service. Together, this combination is termed the *session provider* or SS-provider.

As with all OSI service definitions, the session service is defined in terms of *primitives*. By convention, session primitives are prefixed with "S-". Unlike the transport service, which has a scant four services consisting of ten primitives, the session service has twenty-two services consisting of over fifty primitives. Further, the rules that determine the order in which session services may be used are quite complex. Thus to the service user, the session service is much more complicated than the transport service.

However, by careful grouping of session facilities, the session service can be made much more tractable. The same is only partially true for the wretched session protocol. (This observation will be considered in greater detail in the soapbox in Section 7.3.4.)

The session service is defined in [ISO87t], for which two addenda have been approved by the ISO/IEC: [ISO87q], which defines the symmetric synchronization service; and, [ISO87p], which defines the use of unlimited user-data at the session service. These addenda will

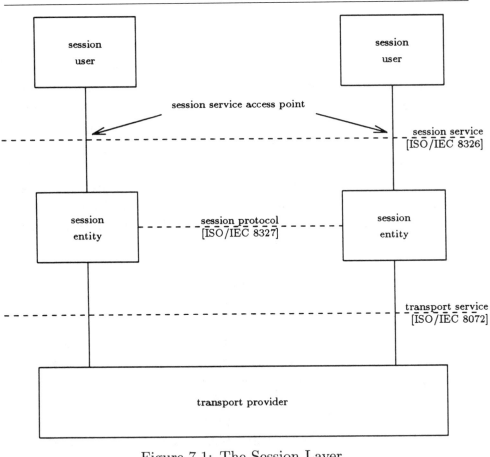

Figure 7.1: The Session Layer

be explained in due course.

The International Standard definition of the session service is technically aligned with the 1984 CCITT recommendation on the session service, [CCITT84e]. The differences between the International Standard definition and the CCITT definition are quite small, and should not affect interoperability between implementations written against either document.

7.1 Concepts

Users of the session service are termed *SS-users*. Although normally this is a presentation provider, this needn't be the case. For example, in the 1984 CCITT recommendations on message handling systems, a presentation layer, per se, did not exist. Therefore the user of the session service was the entity providing reliable transfer (a precursor of the RTSE introduced in Section 6.5.3 on page 146).

The SS-user that initiates the session connection is termed the *calling* SS-user or *initiator*. The SS-user that the initiator is trying to contact is termed the *called* SS-user or *responder*. Whenever either SS-user initiates some action (e.g., asks for ownership of a token), it is termed the *requesting* SS-user; similarly, when the other SS-user is told about this action (e.g., is notified that ownership of a token is being requested), it is termed the *accepting* SS-user. Note that the concepts of initiator/responder and requestor/acceptor are independent. It is perfectly acceptable for the responder to ask the initiator to perform some action.

7.1.1 Session Addresses

SS-users are addressed at a *session service access point* (SSAP). A session address consists of two parts: a *session selector* and a *transport address*. In turn, a transport address consists of a transport selector and one or more network addresses. A network address identifies a location in the network, whilst the selectors identify an entity at that location. Both the transport and session selectors are simple strings of zero or more octets that are meaningful only at a particular network address. Section 4.1.1 in Part II discussed the interpretation of network addresses.

For now, it suffices to note that a SSAP address uniquely identifies a user of the session service. As shown in Figure 7.1 on page 158, the SSAP itself makes available the session services to a SS-user.

7.1.2 Connection Identifier

During connection establishment, the SS-users define a *session connection identifier* to name the session connection uniquely for the application. (This identifier should not be confused with any local mechanism used to bind the session connection between a SS-user and the local session entity such as a connection handle or a file-descriptor).

The connection identifier consists of four parts:

- the *calling SS-user reference*, 64 octets;

- the *called SS-user reference*, 64 octets;

- the *common reference*, 64 octets; and,

- the *additional reference*, 4 octets;

The session service conveys this information transparently. Individual applications, such as Message Handling, decide on the format of the information to be placed in the various parts of the identifier. Although no format is pre-defined, many applications encode a hostname as a string from the alphabet defined in CCITT Recommendation T.61 (Teletex), placing it in the calling SS-user reference portion. Further, the current time, encoded in universal time format, is placed in the common reference portion. The additional reference is empty.[1]

7.1.3 Functional Units

Because the session service is so extensive, it provides a mechanism for only using a subset of its primitives. The *functional units* active for the session connection determine which session primitives are available. In addition to the kernel functional unit, which is always available, there are twelve functional units. These are shown in Table 7.1. Whenever a functional unit makes a token available, then two other services, *give tokens* and *please tokens*, are made available for those tokens.

Functional units are negotiated during connection establishment. The initiator indicates the functional units it is willing to employ, and the responder does the same. The intersection of the two selections determines which functional units are active during the lifetime of the session connection. Regardless of the functional units selected by the initiator and responder, the kernel functional unit is always active. Each service is described in the next section.

---

[1] These are actually ASN.1 encodings using the BER.

Functional Units	Services	Tokens
Kernel	Connection establishment	
	Normal data transfer	
	Orderly release	
	User abort	
	Provider abort	
Negotiated release		Release
Half-duplex		Data
Duplex		
Expedited data	Expedited data transfer	
Typed data	Typed data transfer	
Capability data	Capability data exchange	
Minor synchronize	Minor synchronization point	Minorsync
Symmetric synchronize	Symmetric synchronization	
Major synchronize	Major synchronization point	Majorsync
Resychronize	Resychronize	
Exceptions	User exception reporting	
	Provider exception reporting	
Activity management	Activity start	Activity
	Activity resume	
	Activity interrupt	
	Activity discard	
	Activity end	
	Give control	
	Give tokens	
	Please tokens	

Table 7.1: Session Functional Units

As might be expected, various combinations of functional units have proven popular for various applications. Earlier versions of the session service (up to but not including the 1987 International Standard) defined three subsets of the session service:

- The *Basic Activity Subset* (BAS) is used for applications that make use of activities, such as message handling. This subset contains these functional units:

  - Kernel
  - Half-duplex
  - Typed data
  - Capability data
  - Minor synchronize
  - Exceptions
  - Activity

- The *Basic Combined Subset* (BCS) is used for simpler applications, where the only consideration is whether communications are to be half-duplex or full-duplex. This subset contains these functional units:

  - Kernel
  - Half-duplex
  - Duplex

- The *Basic Synchronization Subset* (BSS) is used for applications that make use of checkpointing, such as file transfer. This subset contains these functional units:

  - Kernel
  - Negotiated release
  - Half-duplex
  - Duplex
  - Typed data
  - Minor synchronize
  - Major synchronize

– Resynchronize

Although these subsets are no longer defined in the session service, they provide a useful grouping of functional units,

Functional units may not be combined in arbitrary ways. For example, the half-duplex and duplex functional units, by definition, are mutually exclusive. The rules are actually pretty simple:

- the Exceptions functional unit may be selected only if the Half-duplex functional unit is also selected;

- the Capability data functional unit may be selected only if the Activity management functional unit is also selected;

- if the initiator proposes both the Half-duplex and Duplex functional units, then the responder must propose only one of them; and,

- if the initiator proposes both the Minor synchronize and Symmetric synchronize functional units, then the responder must propose only one of them.

7.1.4   Tokens

It is important to note that even though a service might be available, a user of the session service might still not be permitted to invoke that service at a given instant. The right to invoke some session services is governed by ownership of a *token*. Table 7.1 indicates which services have tokens associated with them. Although five different tokens are listed, only four of them are distinct. The *majorsync* and the *activity* token are actually the same (for reasons discussed later on).

A token is available only if the corresponding functional unit has been or is being negotiated for use on the session connection. If the token is available, then it is owned by one of the users of the session service.

7.1.5   Serial Numbers

If the appropriate functional units for dialogue control (synchronization services) have been negotiated, then a *serial number* is maintained during the session connection. This serial number takes on a value from 0 to 999998 (decimal). As the dialogue progresses, this serial number is updated as appropriate. For example, if checkpointing is being performed, then the serial number is incremented by one for each synchronization mark. Later on, if the SS-users resynchronize, the serial number might be reset to a previous value.

It is the responsibility of the users of the session service to ensure that the serial number remains within these bounds. The serial number does not wrap. Thus, if a serial number would exceed the upper-limit, one of the SS-users must use the resynchronize service accordingly. During both connection establishment and resynchronization, the SS-user may indicate the serial number for the *next* synchronization point. In this case, the (degenerate) value 999999 may be used.

This is the model used by the International Standard defining the session service. There is a flaw, though, as it assumes that data is being sent in a *two-way alternate* mode or TWA dialogue. That is, since only one serial number is available, this approach will fail if both SS-users are sending data simultaneously (a *two-way simultaneous* mode or TWS dialogue). In response to this problem, the Symmetric Synchronization Addendum to the Session Service[ISO87q] was created. If the Symmetric synchronize functional unit is negotiated, then two serial numbers exist, one for each direction of the session connection.

If the Symmetric synchronize functional unit is active on the session connection, then the session primitives that interact with serial numbers are slightly changed. Normally, these primitives include a serial number as one of their parameters. However, if the Symmetric synchronize functional unit is active, then these primitives include two serial numbers, one for each direction of the data flow. There is one exception: minor synchronization (checkpointing) still takes only one serial number — in the direction of the requesting SS-user's data-flow.

7.1.6   User-Data

After lengthy negotiations and posturing, session users eventually exchange data. This data is termed a SSDU or *session service data unit*. Each SSDU is a collection of one or more octets. These SSDUs pass transparently through the session service.

The session service further distinguishes between the session services used to send data, in order to provide more specific names:

- a NSSDU or *normal data session service data unit* is sent via the normal data transfer service;

- a XSSDU or *expedited session service data unit* is sent via the expedited data transfer service; and,

- a TSSDU or *typed data session service data unit* is sent via the typed data transfer service.

In nearly all cases, it is both simpler and unambiguous to use the term SSDU. Certainly, it is more direct!

The session protocol is based on ECMA-75 (an early session protocol) and also a quaint protocol defined in CCITT recommendation T.62 (Teletex). As a result, certain nuances of the T.62 protocol have come to permeate the session service. The most pervasive of these are the restrictions on user-data. When SSDUs are sent using either the normal or the typed data transfer service, there is no limitation as to the number of octets that may be sent. For the other session services that might contain user-data, e.g., checkpointing, activities, and so on, there is a limit on the size of the SSDU that the service might be given, namely 512 octets.[2] Fortunately, the normal data transfer service is used almost exclusively for the exchange of session user-data. Although other session services might be used for this purpose, usually only a few octets are sent. There is one notable exception however.

When an association is established by an application, this ultimately results in the session connection being established. Connection establishment information is first generated by the application layer and is given to the presentation layer. In turn, the presentation provider generates its own connection establishment information and gives this to the session layer as user-data for the connection establishment service. Now, one might ask:

> *How much data must be sent to establish an association anyway?*

---

[2]There are two exceptions: the expedited data transfer service constrains the size of an XSSDU to 14 octets, whilst the user-initiated abort service constraints the size of its user-data to 9 octets. These constraints are due to limitations in the transport service.

The answer is:

> *Possibly many more than 512 octets!*

The reason for this is that part of the information exchanged in the application layer is *application entity information*. These are most likely to be Distinguished Names from the OSI Directory. In practice, these can be quite large.

In response to this quandary, the Unlimited User-Data Addendum to the Session Service[ISO87p] was created. The effects this had on the already creaky session protocol is discussed in the cathartic soapbox of Section 7.3.4. From the point of view of the session service, the SS-user is somehow supposed to know if the use of this addendum is in effect for a given session connection — the addendum does not define how this information is conveyed to the SS-user.

7.1.7 Quality of Service

Quality of service (QOS) indicates the level of service that the SS-users desire from the session connection. The QOS consists of a collection of parameter/value pairs. As connection establishment is negotiated, the QOS is negotiated — both by the SS-users and the entities providing the session service. As a result, one of the SS-users may decide that the available QOS is insufficient for the application at hand. In this case, the SS-user might choose to abort the session connection rather than continue.

Most QOS parameters are passed directly by the session entities to the transport service, and ultimately map to the network QOS parameters described in Section 4.1.3 on page 59 in Part II. However, a few are specific to the session service:

- *Optimized dialogue transfer* allows a user of the session service to "batch" several primitives together for transmission to the remote host in a single unit. This can result in more efficient use of the network, at the cost of more complicated session entities.

  This is a Boolean parameter.

- *Extended control* directs the session service to bypass the normal flow-control restrictions when attempting a data destructive action. For example, if a SS-user decides to discard an activity, there might be considerable user-data queued in the network. If extended control has been selected, then a "priority" message is sent to the remote session entity, telling it to start discarding user-data from the network as fast as it can until a special mark is encountered.

As a side-effect of the way extended control is implemented by the session protocol, if the session connection has the Expedited data functional unit active, then extended control is always available.

This is a Boolean parameter.

7.2 Session Primitives

The discussion now considers each of the primitives composing the session service. The primitives are grouped according to the services they provide. The session service goes through three phases: *connection establishment*, *data transfer*, and *connection release*. To provide a more structured discussion, the session services are divided into these three categories.

Associated with the session primitives are state tables that indicate the order in which various primitives may be invoked. Rather than describe these tables, it is more instructive to view the session service intuitively: the organization of and motivation for the session services are described functionally rather than as a sequence of states.

7.2.1 Connection Establishment Phase

Connection establishment is by far the most complex aspect of the session service, with its myriad of negotiations and seemingly endless choices. Surprisingly, there is only one service used in this phase.

A session connection can have only one calling SS-user. If two SS-users simultaneously attempt to establish session connections to each other, then two session connections are established.

Connection Establishment

The connection establishment service, S-CONNECT, sets up the session connection between two SS-users. During the course of execution of this service, functional units, tokens, and an initial serial number are negotiated.

S-CONNECT is a confirmed service, therefore the service consists of four primitives:

- S-CONNECT.REQUEST, which is invoked by the calling SS-user;

- S-CONNECT.INDICATION, which is given to the called SS-user;

- S-CONNECT.RESPONSE, which is invoked by the called SS-user; and,

- S-CONNECT.CONFIRMATION, which is given to the calling SS-user;

The relationships among these primitives are straightforward:

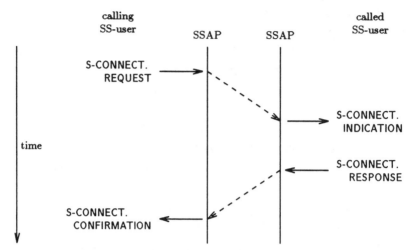

Each primitive has associated with it several parameters, to be described next. When issuing the S-CONNECT.REQUEST primitive, the calling SS-user uses these parameters. They are all conveyed to the called SS-user in the corresponding S-CONNECT.INDICATION primitive.

session connection identifier: (optional) the calling SS-user reference, common reference, and additional reference fields are initialized.

calling/called session address: (mandatory) the calling SS-user identifies itself and the intended responder using SSAP addresses. (Refer back to Section 7.1.1 on page 160 for the definition of a SSAP address.)

quality of service: (mandatory) the calling SS-user indicates its desired QOS. The local session entity modifies this to reflect its available resources. The resulting information is given to the remote session entity that may perform further modifications.

session requirements: (mandatory) the calling SS-user indicates the set of session functional units that it is willing to employ. Both the local and remote session entities might remove functional units from this set, if they are unable to provide the corresponding session services.

initial serial number: (conditional) if the calling SS-user proposes any of the functional units

- Minor synchronize;

- Major synchronize; or,

- Resynchronize

but does not propose the Activity management functional
unit, then an initial synchronization point serial number
must be specified. If the Symmetric synchronization functional unit is proposed for the session connection, then two
serial numbers, one for each direction, are proposed.

If the Activity management functional unit is specified,
then an initial serial number may be specified by the calling
SS-user — the called SS-user does not also propose the Activity management functional unit but does propose one of
the three synchronization function units. Isn't negotiation
wonderful!

initial token assignment: (conditional) for each of the tokens
made available by the proposed functional units, the calling
SS-user indicates who is to be given initial ownership of the
token. The choices are:

- calling SS-user;

- called SS-user; and,

- called SS-user decides.

user-data: (optional) if the Unlimited User-data Addendum to
the Session Service is not in effect, then up to 512 octets
may be given. Otherwise, the size of this parameter is (theoretically) unlimited. In practice, for reasons discussed in
the the soapbox of Section 7.3.4 on page 208, it is wise to
avoid using more than 10240 octets!

The SS-user employs this parameter to pass its initialization information. In the case of the presentation service, a
connect request (CP-PPDU data type) is passed.

Upon receiving the primitive, the local session entity examines
the associated parameters and invokes the *session protocol machine*
(SPM). As a result, the corresponding S-CONNECT.INDICATION primitive is given to the called SS-user. After some consideration, the
called SS-user invokes the S-CONNECT.RESPONSE primitive with the
following parameters. They are all conveyed to the calling SS-user in
the corresponding S-CONNECT.CONFIRMATION primitive.

session connection identifier: (optional) the called SS-user
reference, common reference, and additional reference fields
are initialized.

responding session address: (mandatory) this is most often
identical to the called session address given in the S-
CONNECT.INDICATION primitive, but needn't be. For example, this parameter could specify an alternative address
to use if the session connection breaks and connection re-
establishment is attempted.

result: (mandatory) the called SS-user decides if it wishes to
accept the session connection. If so, it specifies a symbolic
value of *accept*; otherwise, it selects *reject by SS-user* with
one of these associated reasons:

- reason not specified;
- temporary congestion; or,
- rejected (the user-data parameter contains additional
information).

If the called SS-user indicates rejection, then the session
connection is not established.

quality of service: (mandatory) the called SS-user indicates its
desired QOS, which should be a (logical) subset of the QOS
indicated in the S-CONNECT.INDICATION primitive.

session requirements: (mandatory) the called SS-user indicates the set of session functional units that it is willing to
employ. Note that this is independent of the set specified
in the calling SS-user's requirements. As noted earlier, the
actual functional units active over the session connection

will be the kernel functional unit added to the intersection of the two sets.

initial serial number: (conditional) if, owing to the active functional units, a serial number will be used over the session connection, the called SS-user specifies one. The value chosen need have no relationship to the value given in the S-CONNECT.INDICATION primitive. (Actually, if the Symmetric synchronization functional unit is active for the session connection, then two serial numbers, one for each direction, are provided.)

initial token assignment: (conditional) for each of the tokens made available by the actual functional units used on this session connection, the called SS-user indicates who has initial ownership of the token. For each token, the called SS-user is constrained to use the value present in the S-CONNECT.INDICATION primitive, unless the value was "called SS-user decides." In that case, the called SS-user choses either itself or the calling SS-user.

user-data: (optional) the number of octets present depends on whether unlimited user-data is permitted. If not, then no more than 512 octets may be present.

The called SS-user employs this parameter to pass information concerning either the acceptance or rejection of the session connection. In the case of the presentation service, a connect accept (CPA–PPDU data type) is passed if result is *accept*, otherwise a connect refuse (CPR–PPDU data type) is passed.

When the called SS-user accepts the session connection, the primitive received by the calling SS-user is denoted:

S-CONNECT.CONFIRMATION (accept)

Otherwise, the primitive is termed

S-CONNECT.CONFIRMATION (reject)

Of course, it is possible for any number of degenerate errors to occur that prevent the primitive from being delivered. For example, the local session entity might be unable to establish a transport connection to the remote session entity. Alternatively, after a transport connection is received, the remote session entity might be unable to find the called SS-user. In cases such as these, the S-CONNECT.CONFIRMATION primitive is returned to the calling SS-user, with the only interesting parameter being the result, which takes the value *reject by SS-provider*. The reason associated with result takes on one of these values:

- reason not specified;

- SS-provider congestion;

- called session address unknown; or,

- called SS-user not attached to SSAP.

The last two reasons are termed *persistent* errors. This means that it is unhelpful to retry the session connection. Obviously, if rejection by SS-provider is indicated, then the session connection is not established.

Thus, in addition to the exchange described earlier, another valid set of primitives occurring during the connection establishment phase is:

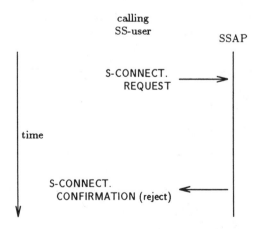

Note that the calling SS-user is unable to distinguish whether it was the local or remote session entity that experienced a problem.

This is as expected: from the user's perspective, the session service hides the details of its underlying organization and implementation. The SS-user knows only that the session provider ran into a problem.

Finally, after issuing the S-CONNECT.REQUEST primitive, the calling SS-user might get impatient and decide to abort the session connection using the user-initiated abort service. The abort service is *destructive*: it can overtake any user-data in transit and cause it to be discarded. Thus, when the calling SS-user aborts the session connection prior to receiving the S-CONNECT.CONFIRMATION primitive, there are any number of possible scenarios: for example, the abort request might reach the remote session entity before the called SS-user responds to the connection request:

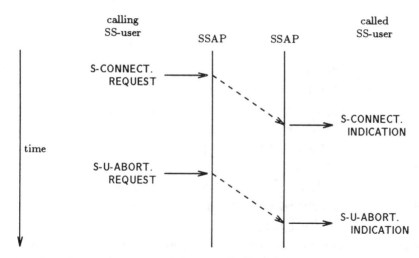

Or, the abort request might reach the remote session entity after it has processed the called SS-user's response. In this case, the called SS-user will consider the session connection as established. It will then receive an indication of the user-initiated abort, indicating that the session connection has gone away. It is even possible for the SS-user's connection response to be received by the the session entity associated with the calling SS-user, after the abort has been sent on the network (the two messages cross in the network).

If this happens, the session entity discards the connection response and does not invoke the S-CONNECT.CONFIRMATION primitive:

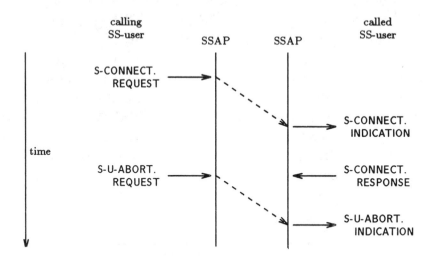

It is even conceivable that the abort request might be made before the local session entity is able even to contact the remote session entity. In this case, the called SS-user is not disturbed at all. Regardless of the scenario, from the perspective of the calling SS-user, as soon as the S-U-ABORT.REQUEST primitive is invoked, the session connection is released.

As can be seen from the discussion, connection establishment is complex primarily due to complex negotiations and numerous rules concerning how options interact with each other. Further, implementations of the session service often must perform extensive error checking (sometimes called *bullet-proofing*) in order to verify that the session service is being invoked in a correct manner. Fortunately, once connection establishment is complete, the majority of these concerns has been dealt with.

The discussion now turns to the data transfer phase of the session connection. There are several sets of services that can be used during this phase. Keep in mind that once a session connection has been established, the service is symmetrical: either the calling or called SS-users may initiate the session services corresponding to the data transfer phase.

7.2.2   Data Transfer Phase: Data Transfer

The data transfer services achieve what most users think the network should do for them: move data from one place to another. However, in the session service, there are four different "flavors" of data transfer, depending on when or how the SS-user wants to send the data. The first three are discussed now; discussion of the fourth kind of data transfer, the capability data exchange service, is postponed until activity management is presented.

Normal Data Transfer

This simplest case is the normal data transfer service, S-DATA, which is an unconfirmed service:

- S-DATA.REQUEST, which is invoked by the requesting SS-user; and,

- S-DATA.INDICATION, which is given to the accepting SS-user.

The relationship between these primitives is straightforward:

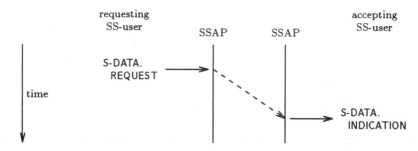

The lack of confirmation has to do with a lack of synchronization, not a lack of reliability. The S-DATA service is unconfirmed but still delivers data reliably between SS-users. If some network failure occurs, the session service will notify the SS-users of this, and if the data was being checkpointed, then the session connection might later be re-established and data transfer would then continue at the last confirmed synchronization point from the previous session connection.

Of course, the lack of confirmation does mean that the accepting SS-user is not given the opportunity to acknowledge that it has safely stored the data it received. The accepting SS-user must initiate another session service interaction to achieve this affect.

A single, mandatory parameter is present on both primitives:

user-data: an NSSDU containing at least one octet.

There is no theoretical limit to the number of octets present in the NSSDU. In implementations of the session services, it may be impractical to pass an arbitrary amount of data in a single procedure call (or by whatever mechanism the SS-user and the local session entity use to communicate). Thus, many implementations provide an additional parameter that indicates if the data being given to the session entity contains the end of the NSSDU. Fortunately, the session protocol is designed to support this implementation scheme rather efficiently.

If the Half-duplex functional unit is active for the session connection, then a SS-user must own the data token before it may invoke the S-DATA.REQUEST primitive. If the SS-user does not own this token, then it might invoke the S-PLEASE-TOKENS.REQUEST primitive and wait for the accepting SS-user to grant ownership of the token at some later time.

Expedited Data Transfer

If the Expedited data functional unit is active for the session connection, then the expedited data transfer service, S-EXPEDITED-DATA, is available for use by the SS-users. Like the S-DATA service, the S-EXPEDITED-DATA service is an unconfirmed service and takes one parameter, user-data. Unlike the normal data transfer service however, only a limited about of user-data may sent using the expedited data transfer service.

This constraint is due to limitations in the underlying expedited data facilities offered by the transport service. Thus, the size of an XSSDU ranges from 1 to 14 octets. Because of this, the expedited service is used only when the data transport is congested (transport flow control has blocked the local user from sending more data), and the user wishes to request its peer to start reading data from the network as quickly as possible until a special mark is encountered. Indeed, if the extended control parameter of QOS is enabled, then the session service uses the expedited data facilities of the transport service for exactly this purpose in order to facility operations such as resynchronization.

Typed Data Transfer

If the Typed data functional unit is active for the session connection, then the typed data transfer service, S-TYPED-DATA, is available for use by the SS-users. From the perspective of the SS-user, the only difference between the normal data and typed data transfer services is that the data token is not required to use the S-TYPED-DATA service.

The typed data transfer service is provided so that SS-users can convey protocol control information outside of the normal stream of data. As a result, user-data for a higher-level protocol (i.e., at the application layer) is not disturbed. For example, the presentation service uses the S-TYPED-DATA service (if available) to perform context management (a topic that was briefly introduced in Section 6.4.1 on page 140).

NOTE: Unless otherwise specified, for the remainder of this section, user-data parameters, if present, contain between 1 and 512 octets of data. However, if the Unlimited User-Data Addendum is in effect, then the size of the SSDU is theoretically unlimited.

7.2.3 Data Transfer Phase: Token Management

There are three services associated with token management. Only two are discussed now; discussion of the third token management service, the give control service, is postponed until activity management is presented.

Give tokens

Table 7.1 on page 162 showed which functional units cause session tokens to be in use. When a SS-user owns one or more tokens, it may decide to transfer ownership to the other SS-user. To do so, the give tokens service, S-TOKEN-GIVE, is invoked. This is an unconfirmed service with only a single, mandatory parameter present on both primitives:

  tokens: the tokens for which the SS-user is relinquishing ownership.

Obviously, in order to include a token in this parameter, the token must both be available on the session connection and owned by the requesting SS-user.

Please tokens

The please tokens service, S-TOKENS-PLEASE, is used to tell the other SS-user that it should relinquish ownership of one or more tokens. As with the give tokens service, the please tokens service is unconfirmed. There are, however, two parameters associated with each primitive:

> **tokens:** (mandatory) the tokens for which the SS-user is requesting ownership and,

> **user-data:** (optional) this is usually an indication of the *priority* associated with the request. As with all user-data, this information is passed transparently by the session service.

Obviously, in order to request a token, the token must be available on the session connection and must not be owned by the requesting SS-user.

Note that the accepting SS-user is under no duress to use the give tokens service in a timely fashion. In fact, as far as the session service is concern, the accepting SS-user can discard the S-TOKENS-PLEASE.INDICATION without even examining it: avoiding anti-social behavior is the responsibility of the SS-users.

7.2.4   Data Transfer Phase: Dialogue Control

Dialogue control entails the use of *synchronization points* in the data stream between two SS-users. There are two types of synchronization points: *major*, which separate *dialogues*, and *minor*, which mark data checkpoints during a dialogue. Associated with each synchronization point is a serial number. When a session connection is established and the dialogue control facilities are to be used, an initial serial number is selected for this purpose — unless, of course, the Symmetric synchronization functional unit has also been selected, in which case two initial serial numbers, one for each direction of transfer, are selected.

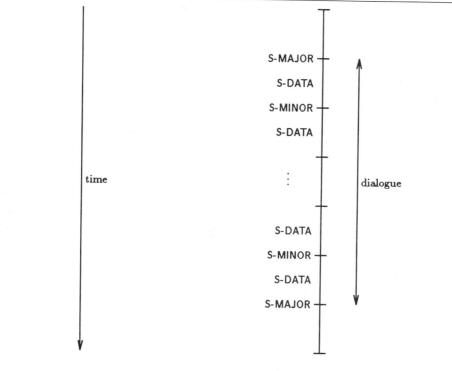

Figure 7.2: A Session Dialogue

Major Synchronization Point

As shown in Figure 7.2, a dialogue is started by an SS-user issuing
a major synchronization point. Dialogues are logically separate from
each other: when a new dialogue is started, the information to be
exchanged pertains to a new application-specific unit. For example, a
file exchange facility might transfer each file in a separate dialogue —
as such, the contents of two different files would not be intermixed in
the same dialogue.

If the Major synchronize functional unit is active for the session
connection, then the major synchronization point service, S-SYNC-
MAJOR, is available for use by the SS-users. This is a confirmed service. Two parameters are present for the S-SYNC-MAJOR.REQUEST
and S-SYNC-MAJOR.INDICATION primitives:

> **serial number:** (mandatory) the next serial number for the ses-
> sion connection. If the symmetric synchronization func-
> tional unit is active, then two serial numbers are provided,

one for each SS-user's data-flow.

user-data: (optional)

This service may be invoked only by the owner of the majorsync token. Further, if the data token and minorsync tokens are available (i.e., the Half-duplex and Minor synchronize functional units, respectively, are active), then these tokens must also be owned by the requesting SS-user.

After issuing the S-SYNC-MAJOR.REQUEST primitive, the requesting SS-user is limited to the session primitives that may be invoked until a confirmation is received. The few primitives that may be used include: giving tokens (usually upon completion of a dialogue), interrupting or discarding an activity (if one is in progress — the relationship between dialogues and activities is discussed later on), resynchronizing the session connection (if some local error is determined while waiting for a confirmation), or aborting the session connection.

When the accepting SS-user receives an indication of a major synchronization point, it is prohibited from taking actions that would affect the state of the dialogue (e.g., issue another synchronization point). Rather, it should confirm the outstanding major synchronization point. Both the S-SYNC-MAJOR.RESPONSE and S-SYNC-MAJOR.CONFIRMATION primitives take a single, optional parameter, user-data. Upon confirmation, the session service increments the serial number by one.

So, major synchronization points denote the boundaries of a dialogue. But, how is the user-data that is sent in a dialogue checkpointed? Minor synchronization provides this facility.

Minor Synchronization Point

After using the S-DATA or S-TYPED-DATA services, the sending SS-user might later issue a minor synchronization point. This information is conveyed to the other SS-user. Upon receipt of a minor synchronization point, the accepting SS-user is somehow supposed to "secure" the data just sent. In this fashion, if recovery is necessary later on, the SS-users can "back up" correctly. For example, during a lengthy file transfer with FTAM, if minor synchronization is use, then a network failure and recovery should result in the file transfer being recovered at the last checkpoint that was both confirmed by accepting SS-user and had the confirmation received by the initiating SS-user.

If the Minor synchronize or Symmetric synchronize functional unit is active for the session connection, then the minor synchronization point service, S-SYNC-MINOR, is available for use by the SS-users. At the option of the requesting SS-user, this is a confirmed service; otherwise, it is an unconfirmed service. Three parameters are present for the S-SYNC-MINOR.REQUEST and S-SYNC-MINOR.INDICATION primitives:

> **type:** (mandatory) indicates if the requesting SS-user would like the minor synchronization point to be confirmed explicitly (the accepting SS-user need not issue a confirmation however, see below).
>
> **serial number:** (mandatory) the next serial number for the session connection. If the symmetric synchronization functional unit is active, then this serial number is for the requesting SS-user's data-flow.
>
> **user-data:** (optional)

This service may be invoked only by the owner of the minorsync token. Further, if the data token is available, then the token must be owned by the requesting SS-user. Upon receiving the S-SYNC-MINOR.REQUEST primitive, the session service increments the serial number by one for use with the next synchronization point.

When the accepting SS-user receives an indication of a minor synchronization point, it may choose to confirm explicitly the minor synchronization point. (It is up to the application protocol to define this behavior.) Both the S-SYNC-MINOR.RESPONSE and S-SYNC-MINOR.CONFIRMATION primitives take two parameters:

> **serial number:** (mandatory) the *highest* serial number being confirmed.
>
> **user-data:** (optional)

However, the accepting SS-user might decide to confirm implicitly the minor synchronization point later on. There are four ways in which this might be done:

- Another minor synchronization point might be indicated. By confirming this minor synchronization point, the accepting SS-user implicitly confirms all previous minor synchronization points.

- A major synchronization point might be indicated (if the appropriate functional unit is active). By confirming this major synchronization point, the accepting SS-user implicitly confirms all previous minor synchronization points.

- The SS-user might gain ownership of the minorsync token and issue its own minor synchronization point. By indicating this minor synchronization point, the SS-user implicitly confirms all previous minor synchronization points.

  Note however, that this approach should only be used if the Symmetric synchronization functional unit was not active — otherwise, the serial numbers used in bi-directional traffic would be unrelated.

- Similarly, the SS-user might gain ownership of both the majorsync and minorsync tokens and then issue its own major synchronization point.

  This will work even if the Symmetric synchronization functional unit is active since a major synchronization point affects the data-flows of both SS-users.

The strategy used by the accepting SS-user is largely application dependent. If each minor synchronization point is confirmed, then this introduces additional network traffic and may reduce pipelining (and hence throughput) in the network. (Because the requesting SS-user waits for a confirmation to arrive, this has the effect of emptying the transport connection being used by the session service.)

At the other extreme, if minor synchronization points are never confirmed, then they do no good whatsoever. Consider: when a session connection breaks and is re-established, the SS-user sending data must back-up to the last confirmed synchronization point — otherwise, it has no way of ensuring that information is not lost in the dialogue.

One strategy that has proven effective is to use the *sliding window*: during connection establishment the SS-users negotiate a window size. This indicates the maximum number of minor synchronization points that are allowed to be outstanding. This approach is used by the RTSE introduced in Section 6.5.3 on page 146. As minor synchronization points are issued, the sending SS-user compares the last minor synchronization point confirmed by the receiving SS-user to the current minor synchronization point. If the difference exceeds some threshold (the window), the sending SS-user waits for a confirmation.

It is important to understand that this scheme ultimately achieves lock-step behavior between the sender and receiver. As such, it is important to negotiate a relatively large sliding window in order to achieve performance. However, a balance is important: if the sliding window is 1, then latency in the network will cause throughput to drop tremendously; if the sliding window is high, then a failure in the network will cause a large amount of data to be retransmitted unnecessarily.

Here's how the lock-step behavior is achieved: one SS-user begins sending data and minor synchronization points quickly. Owing to latency in the network and/or slowness on the part of the other SS-user, the sliding window is exhausted. In some cases, the window is even exhausted before the any minor synchronization points are confirmed. So, the sending SS-user now waits for a confirmation. Upon receiving it, the sliding window, which is closed, opens up by one. so the sending SS-user sends data and then a minor synchronization point. The sliding window is again exhausted and again the sending SS-user blocks. Usually, the dialogue proceeds lock-step until it ends.

In short, if the window is one, the dialogue is lock-step and no more than one unit of data is in the network at any instant. If the window is larger, then more than one unit of data is in transit, and pipelining effect results. As such, the latency in the network is masked.

So, minor synchronization points provide a checkpointing facility for a dialogue. But, if a dialogue is disrupted, how is the dialogue resynchronized? This leads us to consider the final dialogue control mechanism.

Resynchronize

During a dialogue, a degenerate situation may occur that requires resetting the dialogue to a known state. For example, the underlying transport connection may break; or, some local problem might occur that invalidates some of the data previously sent in the dialogue. Two things must be known unambiguously when the dialogue is reset: the next unused serial number and the ownership of any available session tokens.

If the Resynchronize functional unit is active for the session connection, then the resynchronize service, S-RESYNCHRONIZE, is available for use by the SS-users. This is a confirmed service. Four parameters are present for the S-RESYNCHRONIZE.REQUEST and S-RESYNCHRONIZE.INDICATION primitives:

type: (mandatory) indicates what kind of resynchronization is to take place. There are three choices:

- *abandon*, the current dialogue is discarded, and the next unused serial number is assigned to the session connection;

- *restart*, the current dialogue is returned to some point no earlier than the last confirmed major synchronization point; or,

- *set*, the current dialogue is set to an arbitrary synchronization point without affecting unconfirmed synchronization points.

For example, *restart* resynchronization could be used to back-up to the last confirmed minor synchronization point. Of course, the SS-users are responsible for "finding their places" in regards to data previously sent or secured. The relationships among the different types of resynchronization are shown in Figure 7.3.

serial number: (conditional) the next serial number for the session connection. This parameter is not present if this is an *abandon* resynchronization; the session service chooses the serial number. If the symmetric synchronization functional unit is active, then two serial numbers are provided, one for each SS-user's data-flow.

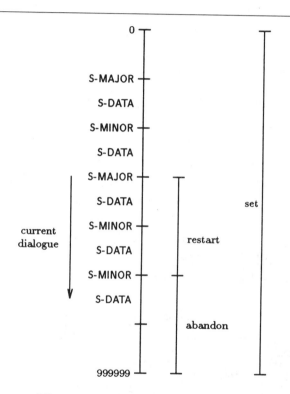

Figure 7.3: Session Resynchronization

token assignment: (conditional) for each of the tokens made available by the actual functional units used on this session connection, the requesting SS-user indicates who is to have ownership of the token.

Just as with the initial token assignment parameter for the S-CONNECT service, there are three choices:

- requesting SS-user;

- accepting SS-user; and,

- accepting SS-user decides.

user-data: (optional)

After issuing the S-RESYNCHRONIZE.REQUEST primitive, the requesting SS-user must wait for a confirmation. The only alternative is to abort the session connection.

When the accepting SS-user receives an indication of a resynchronization, it usually confirms the resynchronization or aborts the session connection. However, there are exceptions, therefore it is now time to discuss session service *collisions*. Given the inherently asynchronous nature of the session service, it is possible for both SS-users to request the S-RESYNCHRONIZE service simultaneously. In this case, which request for resynchronization should be honored? To answer questions like this, the session service has a set of rules for collision resolution. Collision resolution occurs only for those session services that are destructive; non-destructive session services may be safely handled by the session entities. A list of collision winners, from highest to lowest precedence are:

- user-initiated aborts;

- activity discards, then interrupts;

- resynchronization:

    - to abandon the current dialogue; then

    - to set the current dialogue to a specific synchronization point; then

    - to restart the current dialogue;

and,

- user-initiated exception reports.

If the both SS-users invoke resynchronization requests of the same type, then additional rules are used to select a winner.[3] What all of this means for the SS-user is that it must be prepared to "lose." By losing a collision, the SS-user, while waiting a confirnation to a request, may be given a higher-priority request from the other SS-user. In this case, the original request lost the collision and has been discarded by the session service.

Thus, when the accepting SS-user receives an indication of a resynchronization, instead of confirming it or aborting the session connection, it may opt to cause a collision instead — providing that it can invoke a destructive service with a higher priority.

When the accepting SS-user confirms the resynchronization, three parameters are present in the S-RESYNCHRONIZE.RESPONSE and S-RESYNCHRONIZATION.CONFIRMATION primitives:

serial number: (conditional) the next serial number for the session connection. This parameter is not present if this is an *abandon* resynchronization. If the symmetric synchronization functional unit is active, then two serial numbers are provided, one for each SS-user's data-flow.

token assignment: (conditional) for each of the tokens made available by the actual functional units used on this session connection, the accepting SS-user indicates who is to have ownership of the token.

Just as with the initial token assignment parameter for the S-CONNECT service, the accepting SS-user decides this only if the requesting SS-user had given permission to do so ("accepting SS-user decides").

user-data: (optional)

---

[3]The actual rules are tedious and unimportant to the discussion at hand.

A few last words on Dialogue Control

By now, it should be clear that major synchronization, minor synchronization, and resynchronization perform distinct yet complimentary tasks. As such, the session service provides three different functional units that make these services available.

A good question to ask at this point is:

> *Does it make sense to use dialogue control without all three? After all, without either major or minor synchronization facilities, what good is resynchronization?*

In response (but not defense), it should be noted that some combinations might make sense: for example the use of major synchronization services logically separates application actions. If the network connection is highly reliable, then minor synchronization really isn't needed. Of course, one might question the value of this logical facility given that network failure is always a possibility. In most cases, the three dialogue control facilities are used together. Reasons such as this provide motivation for the definition of subsets of functional units. For example, the Basic Synchronization Subset contains those functional units needed to perform dialogue control.

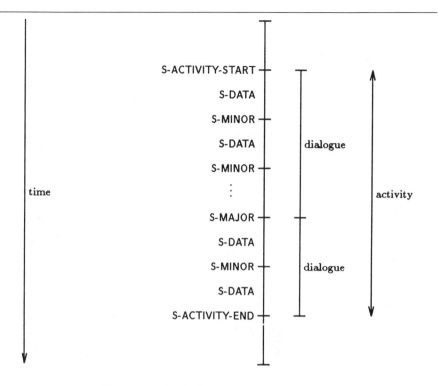

Figure 7.4: A Session Activity

7.2.5 Data Transfer Phase: Activity Management

Activity management concerns itself will managing high-level application exchanges. As shown in Figure 7.4, an activity consists of one or more dialogues. Just as dialogues contain logically separate information, activities represent logically different tasks. Each dialogue within an activity can be thought as containing some independent unit with the task.

All activity management services require that the Activity management functional unit be active for the session connection. Further, in order to use the capability data exchange service discussed in Section 7.2.5 below, the Capability data functional unit must also be active.

Activity Start

The activity start service, S-ACTIVITY-START, is used to start a new activity. This is an unconfirmed service that may be invoked by an SS-

user only if no activity is already in progress. Further, the requesting
SS-user must own the activity token and, if they are available, the
data and minorsync tokens as well. There are two parameters to this
service:

activity identifier: (mandatory) a string of up to 6 octets that
identifies this activity. This value is meaningful only to the
SS-users.

user-data: (optional)

When an activity is started, an implicit major synchronization point
is issued and the next serial number for the session connection is set
to 1.

Activity End

When the activity is completed, the sending SS-user invokes the activity end service, S-ACTIVITY-END. This is a confirmed service with
two parameters:

serial number: (mandatory) the next serial number to use on
the session connection.

user-data: (optional)

As with the activity-start service, the activity end service may be
invoked only by the owner of the activity token (who must also own the
data and minorsync tokens, if available). Thus, in addition to ending
the activity, this service issues a major synchronization point as well.
In fact, there are many similarities between the ending an activity and
issuing a major synchronization point, as Figure 7.4 implies. As such,
the activity and majorsync tokens are actually one and the same.

After issuing the S-ACTIVITY-END.REQUEST primitive, the requesting SS-user is limited to the session primitives that may be invoked until a confirmation is received. The few primitives that may
be used include: giving tokens, interrupting or discarding the activity,
or aborting the session connection.

When the accepting SS-user receives an indication of an activity
end, it is prohibited from taking actions that would affect the state of
the activity (e.g., issue a synchronization point or attempt to interrupt

the activity). Rather, it should confirm the activity's end. Both the S-ACTIVITY-END.RESPONSE and S-ACTIVITY-END.CONFIRMATION primitives take a single, optional parameter, user-data.

So, the activity end service successfully terminates an activity. But, how might an activity be interrupted if something more important happens? This leads us to consider the activity interrupt service.

Activity Interrupt

If the sending SS-user decides to interrupt the activity, possibly wishing to resume it later on, the activity interrupt service, S-ACTIVITY-INTERRUPT, is used. This is a confirmed service that requires that the requesting SS-user own the activity token. There is one mandatory parameter: the reason as to why the activity is being interrupted. Only one of a fixed number of symbolically defined reasons may be given:

- receiving ability jeopardized (the receiving SS-user may be unable to secure further data);

- local SS-user error;

- sequence error;

- demand data token;

- unrecoverable procedural error; or,

- non-specific error (reason not specified).

These reasons are also used by two other services, the activity discard service and the user-initiated exception reporting service.

The activity interrupt service is disruptive. As such, the requesting SS-user may invoke only one session primitive while waiting for confirmation — it may abort the session connection. Similarly, upon receiving the indication that the activity is to be interrupted, the accepting SS-user must either confirm the interruption or abort the session connection. If the activity interrupt is confirmed, then ownership of all available tokens is transferred to the SS-user that requested the activity interrupt.

Activity Resume

At some future point, a SS-user might decide to continue with the old activity by invoking the activity resume service, S-ACTIVITY-RESUME. As with the activity start service, this is an unconfirmed service that may be invoked by a SS-user only if no activity is already in progress and it owns the activity token (as well as the data and minorsync tokens, if available). The activity resume service has several parameters:

activity identifier: (mandatory) a string of up to 6 octets used to identify this activity if it is to be later suspended and then resumed.

previous identifier: (mandatory) what the activity was known as when it was previously started or resumed.

serial number: (mandatory) the next serial number for the session connection indicating where the activity should be resumed at. If the symmetric synchronization functional unit is active, then two serial numbers are provided, one for each SS-user's data-flow.

session connection identifier: (optional) the session connection identifier parameter used to establish the session connection that originally started this activity.

user-data: (optional)

When an activity is resumed, an implicit major synchronization point is issued to the indicated serial number.

Upon receiving an indication that an activity is to be resumed, the accepting SS-user must retrieve from stable storage the information associated with the previously interrupted activity. It uses the previous activity identifier and possibly the session connection identifier in order to find the correct activity. How the information is retrieved from stable storage after it was earlier secured is a local matter. As such, implementations of SS-users may be either simple or quite complex in this regard. For example, some implementations will support activity resumption *only* if it occurs on the same session connection that interrupted the activity. Other implementations have no such

restrictions. Still, an implementation need not support activity resumption at all, by immediately raising an exception (described later
on) when activity resumption is indicated. Note that implementors
of all three systems are really asked one question:

> How long will an interrupted activity be kept in stable stor-
> age?

The answer can range anywhere from "no time at all" to "as long
as you want" (i.e., from zero to infinity). Of course, there may very
well be practical concerns, such as utilization of disk resources, which
focus the implementation choices.

So, the activity interrupt and resume services can be used to save
and restore an activity. But, how might an activity be discarded
if something catastrophic happens? This leads us to consider the
activity discard service.

Activity Discard

If the sending SS-user decides to discard the activity, the activity
discard service, S-ACTIVITY-DISCARD, is used. This is a confirmed
service that requires that the requesting SS-user own the activity token. There is one, mandatory parameter, the reason as to why the
activity is being interrupted. Only one of a fixed number of symbolically defined reasons may be given: these are the same as the reasons
that were listed earlier for interrupting an activity. As with the activity interrupt service, the activity discard service is disruptive. As
such, the requesting may invoke only one session primitive while waiting for confirmation — it may abort the session connection. Similarly,
upon receiving the indication that the activity is to be discarded, the
accepting SS-user must either confirm the action or abort the session
connection. If the activity discard is confirmed, then ownership of
all available tokens is transferred to the SS-user that requested the
activity discard.

Give Control

If it no longer has any activities to initiate, then an SS-user with all
the available tokens might want to transfer ownership to the other SS-
user. The give control service, S-GIVE-CONTROL, is used to perform
this task. This service is unconfirmed and has no parameters.

A good question to ask at this point is:

> *Why have a give control service when the give tokens service is perfectly capable of transferring ownership of all available tokens?*

The answer is that the give control service was introduced to maintain compatibility with the protocol defined in CCITT recommendation T.62. This protocol didn't have tokens, per se, but it did have a notion of which user was controlling the session.

Capability Data Exchange

Finally, if both the Capability and Activity management data functional units are active for the session connection, then the capability data exchange service, S-CAPABILITY-DATA, is available for use by the SS-users.

This service may be invoked only by the owner of the activity token. In addition, capability data may be sent only outside of activities. Further, if the data and minorsync tokens are available, then these must also be owned by the requesting SS-user. Finally, unlike the other data transfer services, capability data exchange is a confirmed service. In fact, use of capability data exchange is *lock-step*: once the S-CAPABILITY-DATA.REQUEST primitive is invoked by the SS-user, it may invoke no other session primitive although it may abort the session connection. All four of the primitives for the S-CAPABILITY-DATA service take a single, optional user-data parameter.

The rationale for all these limitations is that capability data exchange fulfills a very specific purpose: when the Activity management functional unit is active, normal data transfer occurs only during activities. Each activity is viewed as some kind of application-specific task. Suppose that control information not related to a particular task, but which nevertheless might affect subsequent tasks, must be conveyed? The S-CAPABILITY-DATA service is used for this purpose. At this point, the numerous restrictions on the use of this service should be clear, except perhaps for why the service is confirmed. The reason is simple: any data exchange occuring using the service must not be able to overlap a newly started activity. Thus, new activities may not be started until after the capability data has been specifically confirmed.

7.2.6   Data Transfer Phase: Exception Reporting

During the lifetime of a session connection, unanticipated errors may be encountered. the exception reporting services allow either SS-user or the session entity to notify all parties concerned and then wait for someone to return the session connection to a known state.

If the Exceptions functional unit is active on the session connection, then two services are made available: user-initiated and provider-initiated exception reporting.

User-initiated Exception Reporting

When an SS-user detects an error, it invokes the user-initiated exception reporting service, S-U-EXCEPTION-REPORT. It may only do this if it does not own the data token. (As noted earlier, the Exceptions functional unit may be selected only if the Half-duplex functional unit is active.) Further, if the Activity management functional unit is active, then an exception may be raised only if an activity is in progress. Hence, a common use for this service is to demand the data token from the other SS-user ("demand data token") after the give tokens service has been invoked several times.

During an activity, an exception may also be raised if some kind of problem arises with securing the data associated with the activity ("receiving ability jeopardized"). For example: discarding or interrupting an activity may be performed only by the SS-user that started or resumed the activity. The other SS-user must use the user-initiated exception reporting mechanism if it wishes to stop the activity.

User-initiated exception reporting is an unconfirmed service with two parameters. The first is a mandatory reason as to why the exception is being raised (the same as the reasons given for activity disruption listed on page 193). The second is an optional user-data parameter.

After raising an exception, the requesting SS-user waits for the accepting SS-user to clear the exception. This is done either by resynchronizing or by aborting the session connection, interrupting or discarding the activity in progress (if any), or yielding ownership of the data token. If the exception is not cleared fast enough for the requesting SS-user, then its only alternative is to abort the session connection.

Clearing an exception by passing the data token is discouraged if other means are possible (the session protocol is not particularly stable under these circumstances).

Because this is a disruptive service, until the exception is cleared, user-data in transit between the SS-users (NSSDUs, TSSDUs, and XSSDUs) will be discarded. Further, any major or minor synchronization points will not be indicated to the requesting SS-user. In addition, there are a host of other anomalies that may occur until the exception is cleared. In short, a drastic action by a higher-level protocol is required before normal procedures can continue on the session connection.

Provider-initiated Exception Reporting

When the session provider detects an error, the provider-initiated exception reporting service, S-P-EXCEPTION-REPORT, might be invoked. (Alternatively, it could simply abort the connection.) As with exceptions raised by a SS-user, if the Activity management functional unit is active, then an exception may be raised only if an activity is in progress. However, if the Capability data functional unit is active, then an exception may also be raised during capability data exchange.

Provider-initiated exception reporting is one of the two provider-initiated session services (the other is the provided-initiated abort service). Thus, this primitive may (theoretically) occur without warning:

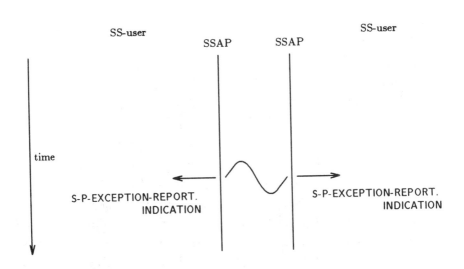

There is only one parameter associated with an exception raised by the SS-provider: a reason. This reason takes one of two values:

- protocol error; or,

- non-specific error (reason not specified).

After an exception is raised by the session provider, either SS-user should try to clear the exception. The same mechanisms (and caveats) for clearing user-initiated exceptions are applicable. As with user-initiated exceptions, until the provider-initiated exception is cleared, all sorts of anomalous behavior may be exhibited.

7.2.7   Connection Release Phase

Finally, the SS-users will eventually wish to release the session connection. There are three services which result in connection release: the orderly release service, which, with the cooperation of the two SS-users, results in all data in transit being safely delivered prior to connection release; the user-initiated abort service, in which an SS-user may unilaterally terminate a session connection; and, the provider-initiated abort service, in which the session provider may inform the two SS-users that the session connection has been lost. The latter two services are destructive: any user-data in transit is lost when they occur.

Orderly Release

The orderly release service, S-RELEASE, is used to terminate a session connection gracefully. Before an SS-user may invoke this service, it must attain ownership of all available tokens. This is a confirmed service. When invoked by the requesting SS-user, there is a single, optional parameter: user-data.

The response contains two parameters, a mandatory result, indicating whether the release is accepted; and, optionally, user-data. If the Negotiated release functional unit is *not* active on the session connection, then the accepting SS-user may not refuse the release. Otherwise, it is free to refuse. The accepting SS-user may choose to do this if, for example, it wishes to start an activity.

User-initiated Abort

When a SS-user detects an error it views as catastrophic, the user-initiated abort service, S-U-ABORT, is invoked. This is an unconfirmed service with a single, optional parameter, user-data. If present, the user-data should indicate to the other SS-user why the session connection was aborted. However, unless the Unlimited User-Data Addendum to the Session Service is in effect, then only 9 octets may be sent. In practice, this is too restrictive to pass any meaningful information.

Provider-initiated Abort

When the session provider detects an error from which it cannot recover, the provider-initiated abort service, S-P-ABORT, is invoked. This is a provider-initiated service with a single, mandatory parameter telling why the session connection was lost. The reason may take one of three values:

- transport disconnect;

- protocol error; or,

- undefined.

After this primitive is delivered to each SS-user, no further primitives may be invoked for the session connection.

7.2.8   The Session Service is Controversial

It is worth noting that although the session service is quite rich, there are many who argue that it is largely superfluous. For example, the *Cynic of the Internet*, Dr. Paul V. Mockapetris of the USC/Information Sciences Institute is credited with the following dialogue:

> *Q: What's the difference between OSI session and a metro bus?*

> *A: Sometimes you miss the bus!*

The point here is that whilst the session services are quite extensive, "real world" applications really don't need them. This is true even of most OSI applications. (Whether OSI applications exist in the real world is not something to be argued here!) For example, OSI applications built using the Remote Operations Service Element introduced in Section 6.5.4 on page 146 usually require only the most basic of underlying services. These are limited to:

- connection establishment;

- data transfer; and,

- (graceful) connection release.

In fact, it was this very observation that led to the development of the *lightweight presentation services* introduced earlier in Section 6.4.3 on page 142.

If the OSI transport service offered a graceful release mechanism, then for these applications, the OSI session layer would be completely superfluous. Given that the end-to-end services in other protocol suites, such as the Internet suite, provide a graceful release mechanism, some have wondered if a graceful release mechanism wasn't purposely left out of the OSI transport service simply to provide an excuse for the session layer.

7.3   Session Protocol

The session protocol is specified in [ISO87s]. There are two addenda, [ISO87o] and [ISO87r], which define the protocol modifications necessary to support the symmetric synchronization service and the use of unlimited user-data (respectively). As with the session service, the International Standard specification of the session protocol is aligned with the 1984 CCITT recommendation on the session protocol, [CCITT84d].

As with many protocols, the session protocol is best described as a *finite state machine*. The session protocol machine (SPM) starts in an initial state. As events occur — the user invokes session service primitives or session protocol data units (SPDUs) are received from the network — activity is triggered on the part of the SPM. During this activity, actions may occur (session service primitives are invoked to the user and/or SPDUs are sent on the network), and possibly a new state is entered. Eventually the session connection is released and the SPM returns to the initial state.

Because of this strong tie to state machines (the session protocol specification includes a state machine description), some implementations of the session layer have been largely generated automatically. Providing that the resulting session entity can be mapped naturally to a session service, automatic generation can provide significant savings to an implementor.

When examining the session protocol, there are three things to be discussed: how the transport service is used; how the SPM behaves (termed the "elements of procedure" for the session protocol); and, how SPDUs are encoded.

7.3.1   Use of the Transport Service

The session entity uses the transport service in a straightforward fashion. The T-CONNECT service is used to establish a transport connection between the two session entities. No initial user-data is exchanged when the transport connection is established.

Only the session entity that initiates a given transport connection is allowed to initiate session connections on that connection. This is because the session entities may choose to reuse the transport connection for multiple session connections. In this case, session connection establishment collisions must be avoided. Further, if the transport connection is to be reused, then when an ABORT SPDU is received, an ABORT ACKNOWLEDGEMENT SPDU is sent.

After a transport connection is established, the T-DATA service is used to carry nearly all SPDUs. However, if the quality of service for the session connection indicates extended control, then the transport expedited service, T-EXPEDITED-DATA, is also used. For these session connections, whenever a major synchronization is confirmed, or resynchronization occurs (either a request or a confirmation), then a PREPARE SPDU is sent on the expedited transport flow indicating the SPDU that is to follow on the normal transport flow. Upon receipt of this SPDU, the SPM knows that it may discard certain SP-DUs that occur until it receives the SPDU associated with the prepare SPDU. In addition, when an abort occurs, its SPDU is also sent on the expedited transport flow. (Recall that aborts are destructive with regards to previously invoked session primitives.)

After a session connection has been released. The session entities may release the transport connection. This determination is made during the negotiations concerning session connection establishment. No disconnect user-data is sent when the transport connection is released.

As a consequence of these rules, note that the SPDUs associated with session connection establishment and release are carried as TS-DUs after the transport connection has been established.

Thus, two possible mappings between session connections and transport connections have been seen: a *one-to-one* mapping, in which a single session connection exists over the lifetime of a transport connection; and, a *many-to-one* mapping, in which a transport connection might support several sequential session connections (simultaneous session connections cannot be multiplexed over a single transport connection).

There is also a third mapping, *one-to-many*, in which several sequential transport connections are used to support a single session connection. This facility may be used when the session entities wish to provide transparent recovery from network failures. As expected, the mechanisms for achieving this are quite complex.

7.3.2 Elements of Procedure

The elements of procedure for the session protocol are largely straight-forward and quite tedious. Suffice it to say that each service primitive invoked by the user results in one or more SPDUs being generated by the local session entity and then sent to the remote session entity as a TSDU. Table 7.2 shows the relationship between session primitives and SPDUs.

However, there are two additional mechanisms used by the session entities that are unknown to the users of the session service. These are to be noted next.

Segmentation is used when the underlying transport service is un-willing to accept TSDUs of arbitrary size. In this case, when large amounts of user-data are sent in a single session primitive, the local session entity divides the user-data into segments, each containing consecutive parts of the user-data. Each segment has session protocol control information (PCI) prepended to it, and is then sent using the T-DATA service. The session PCI attached to the segment indicates the type of data it is (e.g., data associated with the S-TYPED-DATA service) and also contains an *enclosure item*. The enclosure item in-dicates whether this segment is at the beginning of, or the end of, the user-data associated with the corresponding session service. If the user-data fits in an entire segment, then the enclosure item indicates that this segment is both the beginning and the end of the user-data.

The use of segmentation at the session layer is controversial. Many argue that it is the transport service that should be responsible for the transmission of arbitrarily large amounts of user-data. As such, the transport service should always perform segmentation regardless of the underlying protocols that are providing the OSI end-to-end services for the application. However, not all implementations follow this model. As such, the session protocol may use segmentation. (The author suspects that the real reason why session does segmentation may be the same as those described in the soapbox of Section 7.3.4, but has not had the opportunity to talk to the "right persons" to verify this theory.)

Sometimes more than one SPDU is combined to form a single TSDU. This is termed *concatenation*. Note that concatenation occurs when a single service primitive is invoked, which in turn results in sev-eral SPDUs being constructed and then sent as a single TSDU. For

Session Service	.REQUEST **SPDU**	.RESPONSE **SPDU**
S-CONNECT	CONNECT CONNECT DATA OVERFLOW [5]	ACCEPT OVERFLOW ACCEPT [5] REFUSE
S-DATA S-EXPEDITED-DATA S-TYPED-DATA	DATA TRANSFER EXPEDITED DATA TYPED DATA	
S-TOKEN-GIVE S-TOKEN-PLEASE	GIVE TOKENS PLEASE TOKENS	
S-SYNC-MAJOR S-SYNC-MINOR S-RESYNCHRONIZE	MAJOR SYNC POINT MINOR SYNC POINT RESYCHRONIZE [1]	. . . ACK [1] . . . ACK . . . ACK [1]
S-ACTIVITY-START S-ACTIVITY-END S-ACTIVITY-INTERRUPT S-ACTIVITY-RESUME S-ACTIVITY-DISCARD S-GIVE-CONTROL S-CAPABILITY-DATA	ACTIVITY START ACTIVITY END ACTIVITY INTERRUPT [1] ACTIVITY RESUME ACTIVITY DISCARD [1] GIVE TOKENS CONFIRM CAPABILITY DATA	 . . . ACK [1] . . . ACK [1] . . . ACK [1] . . . ACK [2] . . . ACK
S-U-EXCEPTION-REPORT S-P-EXCEPTION-REPORT	EXCEPTION DATA EXCEPTION REPORT [3]	
S-RELEASE	FINISH	DISCONNECT NOT FINISHED
S-U-ABORT S-P-ABORT	ABORT [4] ABORT [3]	. . . ACCEPT [2]

1. If the extended control QOS parameter is enabled, a PREPARE SPDU is sent on the expedited transport flow prior to sending the indicated SPDU on the normal transport flow.

2. This SPDU is generated directly by a session entity in response to an incoming SPDU; there is no corresponding action on the part of a session user that causes this SPDU to be sent.

3. This SPDU is generated directly by a session entity in response to an internal event; there is no corresponding action on the part of a session user that causes this SPDU to be sent.

4. If the extended control QOS parameter is enabled, this SPDU is sent on the expedited transport flow. However, if unlimited user-data is in effect, then a PREPARE SPDU is sent on the expedited transfer flow and the ABORT SPDU is sent on the normal flow.

5. These SPDUs are used if the Unlimited User-Data Addendum is in effect and more than 10240 octets of data were given for the S-CONNECT.REQUEST primitive.

Table 7.2: Session Services and corresponding SPDUs

lack of a better explanation, this is largely because of historical reasons. However, for efficiency reasons, *extended concatenation* might also occur, if the quality of service for the session connection indicates optimized dialogue transfer. This permits the session entity to map certain combinations of session primitives onto several SPDUs, which then are concatenated to form one TSDU. In the best case, three session primitives can be mapped onto a single TSDU. By reducing the interaction between the session entity and the transport entity, greater efficiency may be achieved. The possibility for this efficient behavior is limited, as very few combinations of primitives may be combined for extended concatenation. Further, the protocol mechanisms used to achieve this functionality are relatively complicated.

7.3.3   Encodings

A SPDU is composed of two parts: session protocol control information, or PCI, followed by user-data. The encoding of session PCI is superficially straightforward:

The components are:

SI: The *SPDU identifier* for the SPDU. This indicates what kind of SPDU begins here.

LI: The *length indicator*, which gives the length in octets of the PCI (not the SPDU). If the length of the SPDU is less than 255 octets, then the length is encoded in one octet, taking a value from $2 \ldots 254$. Otherwise, the LI component is encoded in three octets, the first takes the value 255. The other two form an unsigned 16–bit quantity. Thus the maximum length of the PCI is 65535 octets. Hence, for the figure above, if $m < 255$ then LI is encoded in a single octet and takes the value m.

parameters: Parameters associated with the SPDU. This field need not be present (the LI field takes the value 2).

user-data: Any user-data associated with the SPDU. Note that only user-data associated with NSSDUs or TSSDUs is placed here. User-data associated with other session services is considered a parameter to the SPDU.

Unfortunately, the rules for encoding parameters are a bit more complex. In principle, a parameter is encoded as a simple type, length, value tuple. In practice however, the session protocol may combine related parameters into parameter groups. These groups also are type, length, value tuples. However, the value of a group is zero or more parameters (a depth-two recursion). The definition of each SPDU indicates which parameter groups and parameters are valid for use with the SPDU.

Thus, a single parameter to an SPDU or parameter group appears as:

where the PI field is the *parameter identifier*, LI takes the value $p - 2$, and the PV field is the *parameter value*. In turn, a parameter group containing two parameters appears as:

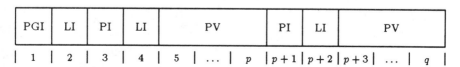

where the PGI field is the *parameter group identifier* and the LI field for the parameter group takes the value q (the other two LI fields take the values $p - 4$ and $q - (p + 2)$, respectively).

In theory a SPDU might contain several parameter groups and parameters. However, in practice the most complicated SPDU contains only three parameter groups and four other parameters.

7.3.4   A Soapbox on the Session Protocol

As the service primitives have been discussed at length, in order to discuss the session protocol, it is now time to examine *session protocol data units* (SPDUs). Unfortunately, the session protocol has been the victim of historical precedent (some would say "hysterical precedent"), and as such it is not a pretty picture.

Consider this interesting quotation:

> *The session protocol is reasonably simple to explain.*

The author of this quotation presumably was referring to the description of the SPM earlier. However, for those who have been unfortunate enough to read the specification of or actually to implement the session protocol, there is an alternative interpretation. This soapbox explores this latter view.

The session service and protocol originated as a blending of two documents, ECMA-75, a 1982 technical report describing a session protocol, and a 1983 revision of CCITT recommendation T.62 (Teletex). For largely hysterical reasons, it was decided to merge these two documents to produce the OSI session definitions. Unfortunately, whilst similar in intent, the two protocols were not that much alike. For example, both protocols had the notion of allowing only one user to perform certain activities. But, only ECMA-75 used the notion of token ownership to accomplish this. In T.62, there was only the notion of passing control. As such, many of the nuances and irregularities of the session service came into existence. Fortunately, the total number of these aberrations is rather small (less than 10), so perhaps it can be explained away.

Sadly, the effects are much more pronounced in the session protocol. For example, the names of the states in the SPM are a mixture of the state names from the two original documents. One side-effect of this is that they aren't numbered consecutively. This is relatively minor, though.

A more substantive problem is that the session protocol mixes the mechanisms from both protocols, largely in an attempt to be compatible with the T.62 protocol. As a result, the rules for encoding SPDUs are obscure and wasteful. The PGI/PI distinction, whilst it looks good on paper, in practice is unnecessary. There are only four parameter groups, and of these, there is only one parameter identifier that conflicts with those used outside of parameter groups. A much simpler encoding scheme would not use parameter groups and would simply assign a unique identifier to each parameter. Further, not all SPDU identifier (SI) codes are unique; the receiving session entity must deduce the actual SPDU by context.

Even worse, the rules for combining SPDUs and user-data to be sent in a single TSDU are complex and largely irregular. For example, when a session primitive is invoked, depending on the particular primitive, this may result in one SPDU being sent in a TSDU, or this may result in several SPDUs being concatenated and sent in a single TSDU. In the absence of extended concatenation, concatenation really doesn't make sense. Why does one session primitive result in multiple SPDUs being sent in a single TSDU when others don't? Why not define SPDUs so that they always map one-to-one onto session primitives? If this were done, then concatenation (and its complicated rules) would be completely unnecessary. It would also remove the artificial separation between the two user-data encodings (for some SPDUs, user-data occurs as a parameter, for other SPDUs, user-data is appended after the session PCI).

Finally, when it became necessary to support potentially unlimited amounts of user-data, SPDU encodings became even more complex. So complex in fact, that profiling organizations (such as the U.S. NIST OSI Implementors Workshop) opted to support only a subset of the protocol additions, because it was simply too difficult to implement in many systems.

As a result, the session protocol is ugliness incarnate. It is *offensive*. It is ... (you get the idea). An important side-effect of this process is that the documents describing session are quite difficult to understand. Indeed, one journal devoted 38 pages to an article that clarified how one interpreted OSI session[FCane86]. Once again, we refer to a dialogue attributed to the *Cynic of the Internet*:

> *Q: What do you get when you cross a gangster with an international standard?*
>
> *A: You get someone who makes you an offer that you can't understand!*

A much simpler, smaller protocol could easily be written that permits the full functionality of the session service. Alas, it was not to
be! Thus,

> *the session protocol is reasonably simple to explain.*

It resulted from a committee process that favored the politics of remaining compatible with an ancient CCITT recommendation, rather
than appreciating the technical merits of a simple protocol with regular procedures and encodings.

...soap

7.4 An Implementation

Finally, the discussion closes with a look at an implementation of the session service. As with the other chapters in Part III, the implementation framework of the ISO Development Environment (ISODE) is examined. The discussion that follows is heavily oriented towards those familiar with the *C* programming language and the UNIX operating system.

In the ISODE, the `ssap` library is responsible for implementing session services. This description of ISODE's session services is only a high-level overview. They are described in considerable detail in *Volume 2: Underlying Services* of the ISODE User's Manual[MRose89]. Although the session protocol is amenable towards automatic generation, it was entirely hand-coded. This is because its implementors decided it would be simpler to write the code once rather than writing the automatic tools and then using them to implement the session entity.

The ISODE implementation of the session services is fairly complete: all functional units are implemented with the exception of Symmetric synchronization. Further, there is only limited support for the use of unlimited user-data at the session service. These restrictions are largely historical: session services were implemented in ISODE prior to publication of these two addenda. As the use of unlimited user-data became necessary, enough of the functionality was implemented to support the needs of the "typical" SS-user.[4]

The `ssap` library is loaded with each UNIX program that needs session services. As such, several processes running on a system may each have their own copies of a session entity. This has the disadvantage of making the programs and processes larger than they need to be. As such, it has been suggested that a single session entity, servicing multiple processes, be placed in the UNIX kernel. There are three reasons why this implementation strategy wasn't used: first, the session service has so many primitives that user/kernel communications would require some kind of message passing facility between the

---

[4]The authors of ISODE felt it was necessary to implement the entire session service to support the widest range of applications. However, when it came time to support unlimited user-data, the authors decided it was such a "hack" on an already hackneyed protocol, that only the essential aspects were supported. Any similarity to laziness on the part of the authors is an unkind coincidence!

session entity and the UNIX processes. Although this can be done, few existing implementations of UNIX are general enough to support this kind of interaction. Second, the ISODE transport switch, which performs tasks such as ordering network addresses during connection establishment, may need access to user files. As such, it is not implemented in the UNIX kernel. Since the session entity ultimately calls on the ISODE transport switch, it would seem strange to place the session entity in the UNIX kernel when the transport switch is not. Finally, kernel code is inherently less portable than user code. Although a session entity could be coded for one variant of UNIX, it would require significant recoding when ported to another UNIX-like system. As a key implementation choice of the ISODE was to promote portability between a wide-range of UNIX platforms, a kernel-based session entity would be contrary to this tenet.

It should be noted that placing the session entity in each user process does not, all other things being equal, decrease the throughput seen by the SS-users; quite the contrary: another implementation of the session service chose to implement a system-wide session entity in a single UNIX process. This process does nothing but offer the session service. Other UNIX processes needing session services use an interprocess communication mechanism (UNIX pipes or fifos) to communicate with this process. Over the IPC mechanism, the two processes exchange messages relating to the session service (just as if the session entity were implemented in the UNIX kernel). This has the advantage of reducing the size of the user processes. The disadvantage is that UNIX IPC is relatively slow. Thus, users of the session service experience considerable delay for each service primitive they invoke.

7.4.1   Session Interface

The ISODE philosophy is that each .REQUEST and .RESPONSE service primitive maps onto a *C* procedure call. Each parameter in a session service maps to a parameter in the corresponding *C* procedure. In addition, there are usually two other parameters. The first is a *session-descriptor*, which is used to indicate which session connection is being manipulated (a UNIX process may use more than one session connection at the same time). The second is an *indication pointer*, which may be updated to reflect the outcome of the call.

Interface Policies

Consider the interface to the S-DATA.REQUEST primitive, which is defined by the procedure SDataRequest:

```
int     SDataRequest (sd, data, cc, si)
int     sd;
char    *data;
int     cc;
struct SSAPindication  *si;
```

which illustrates most of the interface policies defined by the s sap library. The first parameter, sd, is the session-descriptor that indicates which session connection is to be given the data. During a successful connection establishment, the session entity chooses a unique number and communicates this to the caller. This session-descriptor is usually a UNIX file-descriptor, but should not be treated by the user as such. This is the key disadvantage of the ISODE implementation strategy: because the session entity resides in the user process, the semantics of the session service are unknown to the UNIX kernel. As such, using a session-descriptor as a file-descriptor for a UNIX kernel call may very well result in the session entity becoming confused. A kernel-based implementation of the session entity would be able to overcome this limitation. In order to compensate for this, the ISODE contains routines that provide emulations of the UNIX kernel calls that deal with file-descriptors associated with IPC. The most commonly used is xselect, which provides a synchronous event multiplexing facility. By using xselect, a program handling multiple connections can determine which connection is willing to accept data or has data waiting to be read — all without blocking! This is analogous to the select kernel call found in many UNIX variants that provides similar facilities for file-descriptors.

The next two parameters, data and cc, are the data (NSSDU) to be written. The data parameter points to the base of a NSSDU, whilst the cc parameter indicates the length of the NSSDU. Note that this procedure takes an entire NSSDU as an argument. This differs from other implementations that allow a partial NSSDU to be specified along with a flag indicating whether the current argument formed the end of the NSSDU. As a result, users of the ISODE session service must be prepared to transmit entire NSSDUs in a single procedure call. This limitation is not as drastic as it seems: many users of the session service send relatively small (under 8K octets) NSSDUs in order to use checkpointing and other session facilities more effectively.

Consider: although SSDUs of arbitrary size are accepted by the session service, from the implementation viewpoint, it may be more efficient to handle SSDUs that are no larger than a particular threshold. During connection establishment, the user of the ISODE session service is informed as to what this threshold is. The value of this threshold is not chosen arbitrarily. Rather, when a transport connection is established, the local transport entity communicates a threshold to the session entity. The session entity decrements this threshold to account for the worst-case protocol overhead (7 octets), and then passes the result to the session user. The transport entity chooses its threshold based on a negotiation with its peer: the two transport entities decide on the largest amount of user-data that may be placed in a TPDU. By bounding this number, the transport entities may safely implement various buffer-management strategies in order to improve performance. Once such strategy is discussed later on.

The last parameter, si, is a pointer to an SSAPindication structure, which will be updated only if the call fails. This structure is actually a *discriminated union* that is capable of representing any possible .INDICATION that might occur during the data transfer phase of a session connection. A discriminated union is a C structure that contains two top-level elements: a *tag* element followed by a union containing all the possible choices. The tag indicates which choice is present.

If the S-DATA.REQUEST primitive is invoked, then the data has been queued for sending to the peer, and the call to SDataRequest returns the constant OK. Otherwise, the value NOTOK is returned and the SSAPindication parameter si contains the reason for the failure. This is done by simulating a S-P-ABORT.INDICATION primitive and encoding it in the si parameter. With the ISODE session service, the possible reasons associated with the provider-initiated abort are extended considerably. Further, some reasons are termed *non-fatal*, which indicate that the session connection has not been terminated. The list of reasons in shown in Table 7.3.

Confirmed services are implemented using this same paradigm. When the .CONFIRMATION associated with a session service is generated, it is retrieved by the user using a "get next event" procedure. This flexibility is necessary in order to model the complex

Provider-initiated Abort (fatal)	
SC_SSAPID	SSAP identifier unknown
SC_SSUSER	SS-user not attached to SSAP
SC_CONGEST	Congestion at SSAP
SC_VERSION	Proposed protocol versions supported
SC_ADDRESS	Address unknown
SC_REFUSED	Connect request refused on this network connection
SC_TRANSPORT	Transport disconnect
SC_ABORT	Provider-initiated abort
SC_PROTOCOL	Protocol error
User-initiated Abort (fatal)	
SC_NOTSPECIFIED	Reason not specifed
SC_CONGESTION	Temporary congestion
SC_REJECTED	Rejected
Interface Errors (non-fatal)	
SC_PARAMETER	Invalid parameter
SC_OPERATION	Invalid operation
SC_TIMER	Timer expired
SC_WAITING	Indications waiting

Table 7.3: ISODE SSAP Failure Codes

collision resolution mechanisms of the session service. The one exception to this policy is the S-RELEASE service. The procedure that implements the S-RELEASE.REQUEST primitive includes a parameter that, on return, will be updated to reflect the parameters of the S-RELEASE.CONFIRMATION primitive. This exception was made primarily for the convenience of users of the session service.

Reading Events

The procedure SReadRequest is used to return the next event for the session, possibly waiting for something to happen:

```
int     SReadRequest (sd, sx, secs, si)
int     sd;
struct SSAPdata *sx;
int     secs;
struct SSAPindication  *si;
```

The parameters to this procedure are:

sd: the session-descriptor;

sx: a pointer to the SSAPdata structure where the data is to be stored;

secs: the maximum number of seconds to wait for the data (a value of NOTOK indicates that the call should block indefinitely, whereas a value of OK indicates that the call should not block at all, e.g., a polling action); and,

si: a pointer to a SSAPindication structure, which is updated only if data is not read.

This procedure returns one of three values:

- NOTOK, if an abort of some kind occurred;

- OK, if an event associated with data transfer occurred; or,

- DONE, if some event other than data transfer occurred;

Consider how incoming data is handled. If OK is returned, then data has been read into the sx parameter, which is a pointer to a SSAPdata structure:

```
struct SSAPdata {
    int     sx_type;
#define SX_NORMAL       0x00    /* NSSDU */
#define SX_EXPEDITED    0x01    /* XSSDU */
#define SX_TYPED        0x02    /* TSSDU */
#define SX_CAPDIND      0x03    /* cap-data ind */
#define SX_CAPDCNF      0x04    /* cap-data cnf */

    int     sx_cc;
    struct qbuf sx_qbuf;
};
```

The elements of a SSAPdata structure are:

sx_type: indicates how the user-data was received;

sx_cc: the total number of octets that was read; and,

sx_qbuf: the user-data that was read in a buffer-queue form.

```
struct qbuf {
    struct qbuf *qb_forw;
    struct qbuf *qb_back;

    int     qb_len;
    char    *qb_data;

    char    qb_base[1];
};
```

To read the user-data, the user traverses the linked list of qbufs. Each qbuf is a variable-length structure. The initial fixed-part contains pointers to the previous and next buffers, along with the number of octets in this buffer and a pointer to the start of the user-data. Following the fixed part is a character buffer of variable length. The qb_data element points somewhere inside this buffer. A good question might be why such complexity is introduced. Why not just return a pointer to the user-data along with its length. The answer is that it is more time-efficient to use buffer-queues containing variable length buffers and inline pointers.

Here's why:

1. As noted earlier, when the session entity sends an arbitrarily large SSDU, it segments the SSDU prior to sending on the transport service. The receiving session entity must then collect the segments prior to giving the SSDU to the session user.

   This explains why buffer-queues with variable length buffers are used. If the incoming SSDU is split into more than one segment, then several buffers are given to the session user. Since the size of the segments often depend on negotiations occuring on a per-session connection basis, each buffer is of variable length.

2. When the transport entity in the ISODE passes user-data to the session entity, it also uses a buffer-queue to contain the data as some transport implementations also employ segmentation mechanisms. However, user-data for the transport service (TSDUs) contain session protocol control information in addition to session user data (a SPDU).

   This explains why inline pointers are used. The session entity advances the `qb_data` pointer past the session PCI so that it points at the first octet of session user-data.

Thus, by using buffer-queues, the transport and session entities are able to share data efficiently when it is received by the network; the transport entity allocates buffers and fills then with a TSDU; the session entity reads session PCI from each buffer (possibly discarding buffers that contain nothing but session PCI), and advances the inline pointer to where the session user-data begins.

Quality of Service

Finally, the last aspect considered here is how quality of service is represented by the `ssap` library.

```
struct QOStype {
                                        /* transport QOS */
    int    qos_reliability;
#define HIGH_QUALITY   0
#define LOW_QUALITY    1
```

```
                            /* session QOS */
    int     qos_sversion;
    int     qos_extended;
};
```

There are three elements in this structure. The `qos_reliability` element determines the reliability level of the connection. This is used for versions of the ISODE that implement the lightweight presentation protocol introduced in Section 6.4.3. The other two elements are for the session entity. The `qos_sversion` element indicates the version of the session protocol desired (or negotiated). Version 2 of the session protocol incorporates the Unlimited User-Data Addendum. The `qos_extended` element indicates whether extended control is used by the session provider. This quality of service parameter was described in Section 7.1.7.

7.4.2 Session Entity

Next, the discussion considers how the session entity implements a given service.

Every procedure providing a session primitive consists of two parts: an outer *wrapper* and an inner *engine*. The wrapper is responsible for mapping the interface policies of the ISODE session service into a form acceptable for use with the engine. The engine is responsible for actually implementing the session protocol machine.

Figure 7.5 shows the wrapper for the procedure `SDataRequest`. Every procedure providing a session primitive begins by first doing a simple "sanity check" on the parameters it is given. Note that this check is done without knowledge of a particular session connection, so it is primarily a *syntax* check of the parameters. In the ISODE, various macros such as `missingP` are defined that check whether a mandatory parameter has been supplied, and if not, generate a call to the routine `ssaplose`, which sets the correct error code in the `si` parameter. A call to `ssaplose` is equivalent to generating a S-P-ABORT.INDICATION indicating a non-fatal error.

Second, I/O signals are blocked by calling `sigioblock`. Some users of the ISODE enable asynchronous I/O handling. By blocking this signal, internal data structures are safe from undisciplined access. When the procedure is ready to return control, `sigiomask` is called, which restores the signal state to its previous value. At this point,

```
#include "spkt.h"                    /* definitions for SS−provider */

int     SDataRequest (sd, data, cc, si)
int     sd;
char    *data;
int     cc;
struct SSAPindication *si;
{
    int     result;
    SBV     smask;                                                    10
    register struct ssapblk *sb;

    missingP (data);
    if (cc <= 0)
        return ssaplose (si, SC_PARAMETER, NULLCP,
                    "illegal value for SSDU length (%d)", cc);
    missingP (si);

    smask = sigioblock ();
                                                                      20
    ssapPsig (sb, sd);

    if ((sb −> sb_requirements & SR_DAT_EXISTS)
            && !(sb −> sb_owned & ST_DAT_TOKEN))
        result = ssaplose (si, SC_OPERATION, NULLCP,
                    "data token not owned by you");
    else
        result = SDataRequestAux (sb, data, cc, si);

    (void) sigiomask (smask);                                         30

    return result;
}
```

Figure 7.5: Wrapper for a Session Primitive

when the internal structures are again consistent, other actions might be taken by the asynchronous portion of the session provider.

The next step is to map the first parameter, a session-descriptor, into a *session block*, which is a `ssapblk` structure. This block contains all of the information locally known about a session connection. There are several macros that do this; the one used by this routine is called `ssapPsig`. Each of these macros looks for the appropriate session block. If it is not found, then the signal state is restored and `ssaplose` is called to return an error. Otherwise, the state of the connection is checked to see whether this session primitive is permitted to be invoked. Again, if an error occurs, the signal state is restored, `ssaplose` is called, and an error is returned.

After having retrieved the session block, the procedure then verifies that the user is allowed to invoke this primitive with its associated parameters. Unlike, the check made by `ssapPsig`, this is a *semantic* check of the parameters. In this example, the `SDataRequest` procedure checks to see whether the Half-duplex functional unit is active, and if so, that the user has ownership of the data token. If not, `ssaplose` is called: the error code would be `SC_OPERATION` and the associated information would be "data token not owned by you."

After verifying that the user is allowed to invoke the primitive with its associated parameters, the engine is invoked.

Figure 7.6 shows the engine for the primitive. the procedure performs actions appropriate as a session protocol machine. This usually results in one or more SPDUs being sent using the transport service.

Internally, each SPDU is represented by a `ssapkt` structure. This is the *internal form* for SPDUs used by the `ssap` library. For each SPDU to be sent, the procedure calls the routine `newspkt` to allocate a new `ssapkt` structure. Then, based on the parameters and parameter groups that comprise the corresponding SPDU, the procedure fills in the elements comprising this structure.

Next, the routine `spkt2tsdu` is called, which takes a pointer to a `ssapkt` structure and encodes it using the SPDU encoding rules. The encoding is returned in the form of an octet string. After the encoding is returned, the `ssapkt` structure may be freed.

```
static int  SDataRequestAux (sb, data, cc, si)
register struct ssapblk *sb;
char    *data;
int     cc;
struct SSAPindication *si;
{
    int     result;
    register struct ssapkt *s;
    register struct udvec *vv;
    struct udvec vvs[3 + 1];    /* GT + DT + user−data + null */          10
    struct TSAPdisconnect tds;

/* for simplicity of example, this code assumes that no segmentation is necessary... */

    vv = vvs;

    if ((s = newspkt (SPDU_GT)) == NULL)
            return ssaplose (si, SC_CONGEST, NULLCP, "out of memory");
    if (spkt2tsdu (s, &vv −> uv_base, &vv −> uv_len) == NOTOK)
            return ssaplose (si, s −> s_errno, NULLCP, NULLCP);           20
    freespkt (s);
    vv++;

    if ((s = newspkt (SPDU_DT)) == NULL) {
            result = ssaplose (si, SC_CONGEST, NULLCP, "out of memory");
            goto out;
    }
    if ((result = spkt2tsdu (s, &vv −> uv_base, &vv −> uv_len)) == NOTOK)
            (void) ssaplose (si, s −> s_errno, NULLCP, NULLCP);
    freespkt (s);                                                         30
    if (result == NOTOK)
            goto out;
    vv++;

    vv −> uv_base = data, vv −> uv_len = cc;
    vv++;

    vv −> uv_base = NULL;

    if ((result = TWriteRequest (sb −> sb_fd, vvs, &tds)) == NOTOK)       40
            (void) ts2sslose (si, "TWriteRequest", td);

    free (vvs[1].uv_base);

out: ;
    free (vvs[0].uv_base);

    return result;
}
```

Figure 7.6: Engine for a Session Primitive

If multiple SPDUs are to be concatenated, then each SPDU is encoded separately and the resulting octet strings are recorded in a scatter/gather array. Each element of the array contains a `udvec` structure:

```
struct udvec {
    caddr_t uv_base;
    int     uv_len;

    int     uv_inline;
};
```

The `uv_base` element points to the beginning of the encoded SPDU, whilst the `uv_len` element contains the length of the encoding. Then, after all the SPDUs have been concatenated, this procedure invokes the T-DATA service by calling the procedure `TWriteRequest` from the ISODE `tsap` library. This procedure treats a scatter/gather array as a TSDU. Finally, it frees each element of the scatter/gather array (`spkt2tsdu` allocates new memory for each encoding).

There are two important effects of this approach. First, by using an internal form for SPDUs, only one procedure, `spkt2tsdu` need know the arcane rules for encoding SPDUs. Otherwise, each procedure associated with all of the session primitives would need to know how to perform its own specialized encoding. As one might imagine, there is another routine, `tsdu2spkt`, which centralizes knowledge of SPDU decoding rules.

Second, the session entity doesn't have to know the length of the entire TSDU before it encodes the SPDUs. Rather, as each SPDU is encoded, `spkt2tsdu` makes an "educated guess" as to the size of the one encoding and allocates this amount of memory. Then, after all SPDUs have been encoded, a single TSDU is allocated. Hence, each routine is responsible for knowing its own specialized concatenation rules, whilst the `spkt2tsdu` is responsible for knowing how individual SPDUs are encoded.

These two points illustrate an important rule for building complex software: specialized knowledge (such as encoding rules) should be centralized in one procedure or module. If knowledge is shared among different procedure or modules, there is a greater likelihood that unforseen side-effects will cause unexpected behavior (usually termed a *bug*).

Chapter 8

Abstract Syntax

As noted in *Introduction to Application Services*, just as the session service adds *control* mechanisms to data exchange (e.g., dialogues), abstract syntax adds *structure* to the units of data that are exchanged.

Unlike the session service, which resides at a specific layer of the OSI model (level 5), abstract syntax is a concept that permeates the whole of the upper layers: it is used by the presentation layer, the application layer, and, most likely, the user applications as well. As such, we consider abstract syntax as a prerequisite to all of the layers above the session service. A solid grasp of the notation of abstract syntax will facilitate an understanding of the remainder of the OSI stack.

In the early, pioneering days of networking, *virtualization* was a termed used to denote the de-coupling of the virtual data types exchanged by a protocol and the actual data structures that resided in a particular implementation. Then, as now, this separation relied on two notions:

abstract representation: Each *data type* is described without regard to machine-oriented structures and restrictions.

concrete representation: A given instance of a data type might be transmitted on the network using a byte (octet) or bit stream. The representation used must result in an unambiguous understanding between the sender and receiver as to the value of the data type.

In the early days, data types were (by comparison) very simple. As such, abstract representation focused on avoiding the pitfalls of byte and bit ordering of machine-oriented structures. This tended to blur the distinction between the abstract and concrete: data types were defined using diagrams that described the "packet formats" of the protocol.

In the 80's, the data types exchanged by application layer protocols became arbitrarily complex. As such, formal languages are now being used for precise definitions. As we shall see, a key advantage of the use of formal languages is that they may be manipulated by protocol development tools.

In OSI, the *Abstract Syntax Notation One* (ASN.1) language is used to describe data types. This language is distinct from the mechanisms used to produce concrete representations. However, the *Basic Encoding Rules* (BER) were defined for ASN.1 so that data could be unambiguously transmitted. As the discussion of ASN.1 unfolds, the power and flexibility of this language will become clear. It should be noted however, that ASN.1 is only the first of possibly many such descriptive languages. Similarly, whilst the BER was defined for use with ASN.1, other encoding rules might be defined to represent concrete instances of data types defined using ASN.1.

ASN.1 encompasses two distinct specifications: the ASN.1 language and the BER. The term "ASN.1" is somtimes used as an abbrevation for one or the other specifications individually. This is acceptable if the meaning is clear from context.

ASN.1 is defined in [ISO87y], whilst the Basic Encoding Rules of ASN.1 are defined in [ISO87z]. In addition, two addenda have been approved by the ISO/IEC: [ISO87w], which defines several extensions to ASN.1; and, [ISO87x], which defines the corresponding extensions to the Basic Encoding Rules. These addenda will be explained in due course.

Both the specification language and encoding rules of ASN.1 are based on the 1984 CCITT Recommendation X.409[CCITT84a]. The differences between the two works are largely cosmetic: the ISO split X.409 into two documents, one containing the description language and the other containing the encoding rules. Then, as experience was gained with protocols other than the ones defined in the 1984 CCITT Recommendations on Message Handling Systems (X.409 was one of these original documents), the two addenda mentioned above were constructed to reflect this new experience.

8.1 Concepts

Rather than beginning by introducing the formalisms associated with abstract syntax, the discussion pursues a more pragmatic description:

As a part of the operation of a distributed application, instances of data types are exchanged. It is important that this information be *identically* understood by both the sender and receiver. How might this be accomplished?

First, the specification of the protocol used by the distributed application defines each data type using an *abstract representation*. The language used defines the conceptual aspects of a data type, but does not contain rules for how the data type might be realized on a "real" computer.

Second, an implementor defines "concrete" data types equivalent to the abstract data types using a programming language that is "native" to a given machine, (e.g., the *C* programming language). These are *concrete representations* as they are precisely defined by the particular target architecture (e.g., processor), language compiler, and run-time system used on that machine. When it is time to transmit a data type, two mappings must be performed:

- the concrete data structure is mapped to the abstract syntax for the data type; and,

- a transfer syntax is applied to the abstract syntax to obtain the value corresponding to the data type to be transmitted.

When it is time to receive a data type, the inverse mappings, in the reverse order, are applied.

In practice, the first mapping is often conceptual. In the scenario defined by the discussion, there is an explicit mapping between the concrete structures and the conceptual data types. This needn't be the case. For example, when the second mapping is performed, parts of the values could be taken from several unrelated variables.

The second mapping is where the "real work" occurs. The encoding rules take the abstract data type definitions along with a given value and must produce an unambiguous representation. This is called *serializing*, and results in a stream of bits being generated that encodes the value of the data type. Normally, a transfer syntax produces a data stream of octets (the number of bits produced is a multiple of 8). These are termed *octet-aligned* encodings.

8.2   Abstract Syntax Notation

In OSI, ASN.1 is the description language used to define data types. ASN.1 defines a set of primitive data types and provides a facility to construct new elements with their own typing inherent in the structure. This allows new data types to be defined that are uniquely recognizable within an application.

ASN.1 is a formal description language. As such, a grammar exists that defines the rules used for building descriptions using ASN.1.

Although ASN.1 is a formal language, the discussion will not introduce ASN.1 in a formal manner (i.e., the grammar for the ASN.1 language will not be presented). The ASN.1 documents are quite formal. For the most part, they are also quite unreadable (or perhaps they are readable, they're just not comprehensible).[1] Therefore a less formal, more intuitive style of discussion is warranted. The same material will be covered, but hopefully in a fashion that promotes understanding and de-emphasizes pain. Considering the importance that ASN.1 will take in the 90's, competence with ASN.1 is an important

skill to be learned.

8.2.1   Lexical Conventions

Although the discussion presents a top-down view of an ASN.1 module, in order to understand the examples that are given, it is necessary to know how ASN.1 descriptions are put together lexically. An ASN.1 description consists of several tokens or *lexemes*. There are only four kinds of tokens:

1. words, which consist of upper- and lower-case letters, digits, and hyphens (a word must start with a letter);

2. numbers, which consist of digits;

---

[1]In defense of the ASN.1 documents however, they are much more readable than the original 1984 CCITT X.409 Recommendation. It is amusing to note than when the ASN.1 documents were first published, many referred to them as the "English Language" version of the X.409 document — despite the fact that X.409 was also published in English! Opinions vary: those more familiar with the X.409 document think of it as being the "readable" one.

3. strings, which take one of three forms:

   `"character string"`

   `'0123456789ABCDEF'H`

   `'01'B`

   for character strings, hexadecimal strings, or binary strings (respectively); and,

4. punctuation.

Whitespace between tokens (spaces, tabs, and end-of-line) is ignored. In addition, comments may be placed wherever whitespace is valid — in between any two tokens. Commentary text begins with the two-character sequence "--" and continues until another "--" is encountered on that line or the end-of-line character is seen.

Finally, there are several reserved words, or *keywords*, of the language. These appear entirely in upper case. These keywords will be introduced gradually in the discussion.

8.2.2 Modules

A collection of ASN.1 descriptions, relating to a common theme (e.g., a protocol specification), is termed a *module*. The high-level syntax of a module is simple:

```
<<module>> DEFINITIONS ::=
BEGIN

<<linkage>>

<<declarations>>
END
```

The `<<module>>` term names the module. An example might be:

```
MTSAbstractService {
    joint-iso-ccitt mhs-motis(6) mts(3) modules(0)
        mts-abstract-service(3)
}
```

This consists of two parts:

- a module name, such as `MTSAbstractService`, which provides a textual description of the module; and,

- an (optional) *object identifier*, which provides an authoritative name for the module.

The former is useful for humans. The latter unambiguously distinguishes this module from all other ASN.1 modules. How this is accomplished will be discussed further on. For now, think of this identifier as a being a unique handle on the module.

The `<<linkage>>` term relates this module with other modules. An example might be:

```
EXPORTS
    SubmissionPort, DeliveryPort;

IMPORTS
    Name
        FROM InformationFramework {
            joint-iso-ccitt ds(5) modules(1)
                information-framework(1)
        }
    id-pt-delivery
        FROM MTSObjectIdentifiers {
            joint-iso-ccitt mhs-motis(6) mts(3)
                modules(0) object-identifiers(0)
        }
    SIGNED
        FROM AuthenticationFramework {
            joint-iso-ccitt ds(5) modules(1)
                authentication-framework(7)
        };
```

which declares two objects (`SubmissionPort` and `DeliveryPort`) to be available for use by other modules. In addition, several objects from two other modules are **IMPORTed**. (These were **EXPORTed** in their respective modules.) Once an object is **IMPORTed**, it may be used by simply referencing its name.

This format for the `<<module>>` and `<<linkage>>` terms is from the Extensions Addendum. The original ASN.1 (and X.409) did not have a `<<linkage>>` term at all and the `<<module>>` term consisted only of a textual description, as in:

```
MTSAbstractService DEFINITIONS ::=
BEGIN

<<declarations>>

END
```

In those early documents, to reference an object defined in another module, the name of the object was appended to the name of the module that defined it, using a dot as a separator, e.g.,

```
InformationFramework.Name
```

The new syntax provides a clearer description of the objects that cross module boundaries.

Finally, the `<<declarations>>` term contains the actual ASN.1 definitions. Three kinds of objects are defined using ASN.1: *types*, *values*, and, *macros*. Each of these objects is named using an ASN.1 word. However, ASN.1 uses an alphabetic case convention to indicate the kind of object to which the word refers:

- for a *type*, the word starts with an uppercase letter (e.g., Name);

- for a *value* (an instance of a type), the word starts with a lowercase letter (e.g., `id-pt-delivery`); and,

- for a *macro*, the word consists entirely of uppercase letters (e.g., SIGNED).

Note that a side effect of this is that macros appear to be ASN.1 keywords. This is nevertheless consistent, as macros provide a way of changing the ASN.1 grammar. Of course, by this convention, one could define a type whose name consisted entirely of uppercase letters. The author discourages such usage.

8.2.3 Types

An ASN.1 type is defined using a straightforward syntax:

```
NameOfType ::=
    TYPE
```

Similarly, a "variable" (more properly an instance of a data type) corresponding to a pre-defined value of that data type is defined as:

```
nameOfValue NameOfType ::=
    VALUE
```

That is, first the variable is named (`nameOfValue`), then it is typed (`NameOfType`), and then a value is assigned using the ASN.1 value notation. Rather than present the formal rules for defining types and values, ASN.1 is best understood by presenting several succinct examples. The discussion now turns to do so.

Simple Types

The ASN.1 notation defines a collection of simple types that can be viewed as the primitive data elements.

There are several simple types in the ASN.1. For each, a definition is presented along with an example of a type and value declaration.

BOOLEAN

A **BOOLEAN** type is a data type taking one of the two distinguished values **TRUE** or **FALSE**.

```
Multiple-defined-contexts ::=
    BOOLEAN

simple Multiple-defined-contexts ::=
    TRUE    -- or FALSE
```

INTEGER

An **INTEGER** type is a data type taking a cardinal number as its value. Inasmuch as ASN.1 describes conceptual objects, there is no limitat to the precision that may be required to represent the number. That is, ASN.1 deals with integers of unbounded precision. (Later on, a method of restricting the range of values that an integer might take, termed *subtyping*, will be introduced.)

```
ContentLength ::=
    INTEGER


length ContentLength ::=
    100     -- or '64'H
```

An alternative form of this data type is one in which all possible values are enumerated:

```
RegistrationMailType ::=
    INTEGER {
        non-registered-mail (0),
        registered-mail (1),
        registered-mail-to-addressee-in-person (2)
    }


mymail RegistrationMailType ::=
    registered-mail    -- or 1
```

The usefulness of this form led to a new ASN.1 type, **ENUMER-ATED**, being defined in the Extensions Addendum, e.g.,

```
RegistrationMailType ::=
    ENUMERATED {
        non-registered-mail (0),
        registered-mail (1),
        registered-mail-to-addressee-in-person (2)
    }
```

which conceptually is preferrable. Note however that unlike the **INTEGER** type, **ENUMERATED** values do not have significance as *cardinal* numbers. Rather, they represent the complete set of values (the *domain*) that an instance of a data type might take. As such, operations that are valid on integers, such as addition, comparison (other than identity or equality), and so on, cannot be applied to enumerations.

REAL

A **REAL** type is a data type taking a real number as its value. This data type is defined in the Extensions Addendum. As with the **INTEGER** type, from ASN.1's perspective, a real number of arbitrary precision may be specified. This is done by specifying real numbers as a triple of three integers consisting of a *mantissa*, a *base*, and an *exponent*:

$$mantissa * base^{exponent}$$

Whilst the mantissa and exponent can take on the value of any cardinal number, the base is limited to either 2 or 10.

```
TranscendentalNumbers ::=
    REAL

e REAL ::=    -- { mantissa, base, exponent }
              { 27182818, 10,   -7 }
```

BIT STRING

A **BIT STRING** type is a data type taking zero or more bits as its value. This is useful for objects that are not naturally octet-aligned (e.g., encrypted data, facsimile, and so on).

```
RandomNumber ::=
    BIT STRING
```

An alternative form of this data type is one in which individual bits are named (the first bit, by convention, is termed bit 0)

```
Attribute-Groups ::=
    BIT STRING {
        storage(0), security(1), private(2)
    }

groups Attribute-Groups ::=
    { storage, private }    -- or '101'B
```

Note that all bits in an enumerated **BIT STRING** are significant.

OCTET STRING

An **OCTET STRING** type is a data type taking zero or more octets as its value. Each byte in an octet string may take any value from 0 to 255.

```
UserName ::=
    OCTET STRING
```

```
initiator UserName ::=
    "anon"     -- or '616E6F6E'H
```

It is often useful to refine further the **OCTET STRING** notion to reflect a particular character set. ASN.1 defines several character string types.

The three most notable are:

NumericString: a string consisting only of digits (0–9) and spaces;

PrintableString: a string consisting of uppercase and lowercase letters, digits, punctuation marks, and spaces; and,

IA5String: a string containing characters taken from CCITT International Alphabet number 5 (which, for purposes of discussion, is simply the ASCII character set).

Further, it is often useful to define standardized representations for the date and time. There are two ways of doing this. One approach is to define a complex ASN.1 structure containing fields for each element of the date and time. (How such structures are built using ASN.1 constructors is discussed later on.) Another approach is to refine further a character string so that its format provides this structure. This latter method is taken by ASN.1, although nothing prevents a protocol designer to define alternative data types that represent time-oriented structures. ASN.1 defines two data types for time representations:

GeneralizedTime: which contains the date, expressed as a four-digit year, two-digit month, and two-digit day; time, expressed in hours and minutes, optionally with seconds and fractional sections of arbitrary decimal precision; and, an optional indicator of the relation of this time to Coordinated Universal Time (UTC).

```
dateAndTime GeneralizedTime ::=
    "19890304181906.740004Z"
```

UTCTime: which contains the date, expressed as a two-digit year, two-digit month, and two-digit day; time, expressed with a resolution up to one second; and, an optional indicator of the relation of this time to UTC.

```
atTheToneTheTimeIs UTCTime ::=
    "890304101500-0800"
```

To many, these representations might seem overly complex (there are many possible ways to encode a valid date and time), thus reducing the benefits of using a string representation instead of a complex ASN.1 type.

NULL

A **NULL** type is a data type that is simply a place-holder. The only information conveyed is whether the data type is present in some larger structure. For example, suppose a data type normally has a value associated with it, e.g., the time of day. But, under some circumstances, the clock may be known to be wrong (e.g., the battery has failed). In this case, rather than returning the (presumably) incorrect time of day, it may be wiser to return some value that conveys "time of day unknown." Using ASN.1, such a data type would be defined thusly:

```
TimeOfDay ::= CHOICE { UTCTime, NULL }

unixEpoch TimeOfDay ::= { "700101000000Z" }

unknownTime TimeOfDay ::= { NULL }
```

This indicates that the `TimeOfDay` type really takes on values from two domains: the first value domain occurs when the time of day is known; in this case, the time of the day is conveyed. Otherwise, the second value domain is used.

Object Types

There are two ASN.1 types that are simple types, but have such complicated (and important) semantics that they warrant their own section.

OBJECT IDENTIFIER

The first is the **OBJECT IDENTIFIER**, which is a data type denoting an authoritatively named object. **OBJECT IDENTIFIER**s provide a means for identifying some object, regardless of the semantics associated with the object (e.g., a standards document, an ASN.1 module, and so on).

An **OBJECT IDENTIFIER** is a sequence of non-negative integer values that traverse a tree. The tree consists of a *root* connected to a number of labeled *nodes* via edges. Each label consists of a non-negative integer value and possibly a brief textual description. Each node may, in turn, have children nodes of its own, termed *subordinates*, which are also labeled. This process may continue to an arbitrary level of depth. Central to the notion of the **OBJECT IDENTIFIER** is the understanding that administrative control of the meanings assigned to the nodes may be delegated as one traverses the tree.

When describing an **OBJECT IDENTIFIER** there are several formats that may be used. The most concise textual format is to list the integer values found by traversing the tree, starting at the root and proceeding to the object in question. The integer values are separated with a dot. Thus,

```
1.0.8571.5.1
```

identifies the object found by starting at the root, moving to the node with label 1, then moving to the node with label 0, and so on. The node found after traversing this list is the one being identified.

The root node has three subordinates:

- ccitt(0), which is administrated by the International Telegraph and Telephone Consultative Committee (CCITT);

- iso(1), which is administered by the International Organization for Standardization and International Electrotechnical Committee (ISO/IEC); and,

- joint-iso-ccitt(2), which is jointly administered by the ISO/IEC and the CCITT.

Thus, at the first cut, the naming tree looks like this:

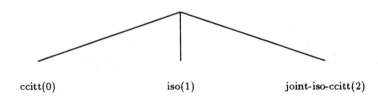

ccitt(0)   iso(1)   joint-iso-ccitt(2)

and, the administrative authority for each node is free to assign further subordinate nodes and optionally to delegate authority to others to name objects under those nodes.

The CCITT has defined four subordinates:

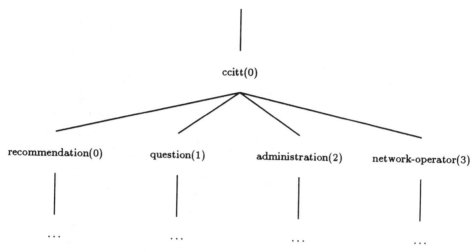

These are:

- `recommendation(0)`, which has 26 subordinate nodes, labeled a through z. Each subordinate corresponds to a series of CCITT recommendations. The committee responsible for a series of CCITT recommendations, such as the "X" series, is delegated responsibility for naming objects. Thus, `0.0.24` is the prefix used by the committee responsible for the "X" series.

- `question(1)`, which is assigned to particular Study Groups in the CCITT. Each CCITT Study Period occurs over four years. During each period, these groups meet to resolve "questions" of interest to the CCITT, such as defining OSI protocols. An **OBJECT IDENTIFIER** has been delegated for the use of each Study Group for each Study Period. The first Study Period in which objects were assigned was in 1984–1988. This is the *epoch* Study Period, taking value 0. The next Study Period is 1988–1992 which takes value 1, and so on. To calculate the **OBJECT IDENTIFIER** used by a particular Study Group at a given time, take the number assigned to the Study Period, multiply it by 32, and then add the number of the Study Group in question. Call this number n. The resulting **OBJECT IDENTIFIER** is `0.1.n`. As a result of this "encoding," it should be clear that there can be no more than 32 Study Groups (numbered 0 to 31) operating during any given Study Period. If this were not the case, then two different organizations would be authorized to assign objects under this prefix!

- `administration(2)`, which is assigned to the PTTs for each country. The value of the label assigned to each node is a *decimal country code* (DCC).

- `network-operator(3)`, which is assigned to the organizations running X.121 networks. The value of the label assigned to each node is a *Data Network Identification Code* (DNIC). In turn, each organization might further delegate their own subordinate nodes to customers.

The ISO/IEC has defined four subordinates:

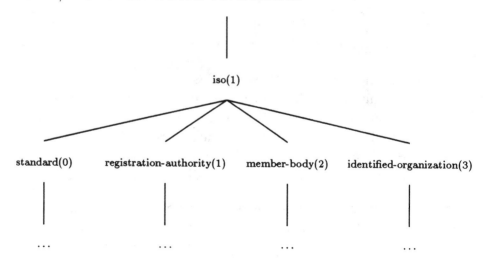

These are:

- `standard(0)`, which has a subordinate assigned to each International Standard. For example, the OSI file service, FTAM, is International Standard 8571. Thus, when FTAM defines objects, these start with the prefix `1.0.8571`. Each standard is then responsible for the naming hierarchy used under its assigned prefix.

- `registration-authority(1)`, which is reserved for use by OSI registration authorities, as they are created.

- `member-body(2)`, which has a subordinate assigned to each member body of the ISO/IEC. The value of the label assigned to each node is a *decimal country code* (DCC). Each member body is then responsible for further organization of its respective naming space.

- `identified-organization(3)`, which has a subordinate assigned to any organization that the ISO/IEC wishes to favor. This permits a way for any organization to name objects (even proprietary objects) without fear of collisions in the naming hierarchy.

Finally, from time to time the ISO/IEC and CCITT form joint committees and delegate naming authority thusly. This is particularly important in the area of initial standards development. In order to coordinate matters, the American National Standards Institute (ANSI) is responsible for delegating authority under the `joint-iso-ccitt(2)` tree.

Returning to ASN.1, the syntax for use with an **OBJECT IDENTIFIER** is straightforward:

```
Document-Type-Name ::=
    OBJECT IDENTIFIER

fTAM-1 Document-Type-Name ::=
    { 1 0 8571 5 1 }
```

In this example, the value declaration shows only the numeric values of the nodes. The textual values may also be used, providing that those strings are unambiguous:

```
fTAM-1 Document-Type-Name ::=
    { iso standard 8571 5 1 }
```

(An unambiguous string is one that uniquely names an immediate sibling of a node.) In order to promote readability, but not risk ambiguity, these two forms can be combined:

```
fTAM-1 Document-Type-Name ::=
    { iso(1) standard(0) 8571 5 1 }
```

An alternative form is to use the **OBJECT IDENTIFIER** keyword explicitly:

```
ftam-documents OBJECT IDENTIFIER ::=
    { iso(1) standard(0) 8571 5 }


fTAM-1 Document-Type-Name ::=
    { ftam-documents 1 }
```

All of these forms are legal ASN.1 value syntax.

OBJECT DESCRIPTOR

A related data type is the **OBJECT DESCRIPTOR**, which denotes a simple textual string that also references an object. Unlike the **OBJECT IDENTIFIER** however, an **OBJECT DESCRIPTOR** is not unique. Although the authors of ASN.1 hope that such conflicts will be uncommon, if ASN.1 is widely used for both OSI and non-OSI enterprises, then collisions will inevitably be quite common.

```
NickName ::=
    ObjectDescriptor


ber NickName ::=
    "Basic Encoding of a single ASN.1 type"
```

Constructor Types

The simple types discussed thus far can be combined to build complex data types. The constructor types are used for this purpose. The process is recursive; constructor types combine both simple and other constructor types, of arbitrarily deep nesting.

SEQUENCE

A **SEQUENCE** type is a data type denoting an ordered list of zero or more *elements*, each of which are ASN.1 types. For example,

```
VarBind ::=
    SEQUENCE {
        ObjectName,
```

```
            ObjectSyntax
    }
```

defines a data type, `VarBind`, which contains two elements. The first is defined by the type `ObjectName`, whilst the second is defined by the type `ObjectSyntax`. Such a definition might be used in a symbol table.

To make these definitions more readable, it is often useful to associate a textual label with the elements in a constructor type. On the surface, this does nothing to change either the syntax nor semantics of the data type, although it may help to disambiguate values in a **CHOICE** (described later on). For example, the textual label may indicate which value in a **CHOICE** type was present:

```
    TimeOfDay ::=
        CHOICE {
            actual-value
                UTCTime,

            not-available
                NULL }

    unixEpoch TimeOfDay ::=
        { actual-value "700101000000Z" }

    unknownTime TimeOfDay ::=
        { not-available NULL }
```

Otherwise, textual labels are provided only for readability purposes. Thus, an equivalent definition might be:

```
    VarBind ::=
        SEQUENCE {
            name
                ObjectName,

            value
                ObjectSyntax
    }
```

allowing one to refer to the **name** element of `VarBind`, or the **value** element. This is particularly helpful when multiple elements are of the same ASN.1 type.

Another interesting capability would be to allow some elements
to be **OPTIONAL**, meaning that the element need not be present
in the data type. In some cases, it may also be useful to assign a
DEFAULT value to be used if the element is not present:

```
Interrupt-Request ::=
    SEQUENCE {
        fatal-error
            BOOLEAN
            DEFAULT TRUE,

        message
            PrintableString
            OPTIONAL
    }
```

Note however, that the data type should be unambiguous in the light
of optional elements. Consider:

```
FuzzyThinking ::=
    SEQUENCE {
        alpha
            INTEGER
            OPTIONAL,

        beta
            INTEGER
            OPTIONAL
    }
```

If an instance of this data type contains two numbers, then the first
corresponds to `alpha` and the second to `beta`. However, suppose that
an instance of this data type contains only one number, does that
number correspond to `alpha` or `beta`? Since these two textual labels
convey no typing information to ASN.1, it is impossible to know, by
looking only at this data type, to what the number corresponds! Later
on, the discussion will describe a way called *tagging* that permits the
use of optional elements without ambiguity.

Finally, it may be useful to define a **SEQUENCE** that includes
all the elements of some other constructor type, but without having
to list them all. This can be done by using a special ASN.1 keyword
as shown here:

```
ORName ::=
    SEQUENCE {
        address
            COMPONENTS OF ORAddress,

        directory-name
            Name
            OPTIONAL
    }


ORAddress ::=
    SEQUENCE {
        ...
    }
```

In this example, we can imagine that the type ORAddress is itself a
SEQUENCE containing many elements. From ASN.1's perspective,
use of the **COMPONENTS OF** keyword defines a simple inclusion
of all of the elements of the given **SEQUENCE**.

Note that this definition differs from:

```
AddressAndName ::=
    SEQUENCE {
        address
            ORAddress,

        directory-name
            Name
            OPTIONAL
    }
```

which contains exactly two components, an ORAddress and a Name.

SEQUENCE OF

A **SEQUENCE OF** type is a data type denoting an ordered list of
zero or more elements of the same ASN.1 type:

```
RoutingTable ::=
    SEQUENCE OF
        RoutingEntry
```

This is analogous to a dynamic array in many programming languages: the number of elements is unbounded (not statically determined), but each element has identical syntax.

SET

A **SET** type is a data type denoting an unordered list of zero or more *members*. Unlike the **SEQUENCE**, which relies on the ordering of its elements in order to avoid ambiguity, ordering in a **SET** is unimportant. Each member is uniquely distinguished by its data type.

```
IMPIdentifier ::=
    SET {
        user
            ORAddress
            OPTIONAL,

        user-relative-identifier
            LocalIPMIdentifier
    }
```

But, what happens if a **SET** includes two **INTEGERs**? Tags, to be described momentarily, permit the use of identical data types as members without ambiguity.

Members of other **SETs** may be including using the **COMPONENTS OF** keyword, as shown here. The syntax is identical to that described earlier; however, the data type referenced by the keyword must be another **SET**. Furthermore, all members of the combined **SET** must be distinguishable by their data type.

SET OF

A **SET OF** type is a data type denoting an unordered list of zero or more members. Each member is the same ASN.1 type:

```
MulticastGroup ::=
    SET OF
        Peer
```

The critical difference between this data type and the **SEQUENCE OF** type is that the latter provides ordering semantics.

Tagged Types

As the discussion above presented constructor types, it was apparent that some means of distinguishing different occurrences of the same ASN.1 type was necessary. In fact, the problem is more general: unique identification of data types also eliminates ambiguity when the data types are transmitted in the network.

To provide for this distinguishing characteristic, ASN.1 associates a *tag* with each data type. This tag is a handle that identifies a particular ASN.1 type. Unfortunately, there may be different requirements on the uniqueness characteristic. In response, there are four different classes of tags in ASN.1 to meet these requirements:

1. The identification must be globally unique. These data types use *universal* tags. Such a tag may be defined only in the ASN.1 document or its addenda. These provide the well-known data types that have been introduced thus far. These data types, and their tags, are shown in Table 8.1.

2. The identification must be unique within a given ASN.1 module. These data types use *application-wide* tags. In any particular ASN.1 module, only one data type may be defined that uses such a tag.

3. The identification must be unique in order to satisfy a constructor type, such as a **SEQUENCE**. In cases such as these, *context-specific* tags are used. These tags have no meaning outside of the ASN.1 type they are defined in.

4. The identification must be unique within an given enterprise, as provided by bilateral agreement. A *private-use* tag is used for these purposes.

All tags consist of a class (one of the four just introduced) and a non-negative integer. Thus, several application-wide tags might be defined in a module, each with a different number. The ASN.1 syntax used to convey the tagging information for cases 1, 2, and 4 is straightforward.

```
IA5String ::=
    [UNIVERSAL 22]
        IMPLICIT OCTET STRING
```

Universal Tag	ASN.1 Type
1	**BOOLEAN**
2	**INTEGER**
3	**BIT STRING**
4	**OCTET STRING**
5	**NULL**
6	**OBJECT IDENTIFIER**
7	**ObjectDescriptor**
8	**EXTERNAL**
9	**REAL**
10	**ENUMERATED**
12–15	Reserved for addenda
16	**SEQUENCE, SEQUENCE OF**
17	**SET, SET OF**
18	**NumericString**
19	**PrintableString**
20	**TeletexString**
21	**VideotexString**
22	**IA5String**
23	**UTCTime**
24	**GeneralizedType**
25	**GraphicsString**
26	**VisibleString**
27	**GeneralString**
28	**CharacterString**
29–...	Reserved for addenda

Table 8.1: ASN.1 Universal Tags

```
Priority ::=
    [APPLICATION 7]
        ENUMERATED {
            normal (0), non-urgent (1), urgent (2)
        }

MagicCookie ::=
    [PRIVATE 0]
        BIT STRING
```

The rule is simple: when defining a data type, after entering the name and the ::= symbol, the tag is entered using the [...] notation.

Context-specific tags are defined differently: rather than occurring at the beginning of a data type definition, they may be used with each element or member of a constructor type.[2] To modify an earlier example:

```
NotSoFuzzyThinking ::=
    SEQUENCE {
        alpha[0]
            INTEGER
            OPTIONAL,

        beta[1]
            INTEGER
            OPTIONAL
    }
```

associates a context-specific tag of 0 with the alpha element and a context-specific tag of 1 with the beta element. Thus, if the alpha element is omitted and the beta element is not, then this is easily determined by looking at the tag of the one data type contained in the **SEQUENCE**.

From a conceptual level, tagging a data type results in "wrapping" the existing data type, tag and all, inside a new data type. Thus,

```
Abstract-Syntax-Name ::=
    [APPLICATION 0]
        OBJECT IDENTIFIER
```

---

[2]Actually, the other three classes of tags may appear anywhere a context-specific tag might appear. It is a convention of ASN.1 that these tags are used only at the beginning of a type definition.

is different from

```
Abstract-Syntax-Name ::=
        OBJECT IDENTIFIER
```

This leads to an important realization: in typed languages such as ASN.1, the tag associated with a data type is an integral part of the structure of the data type.

When a data type is wrapped, additional information must be encoded on the network whenever an instance of that data type is transmitted. Providing that the designer of an ASN.1 module is confident that loss of this information will not prevent interoperation, the **IMPLICIT** keyword may be used when defining a tagged type. Observant readers noticed something peculiar in the earlier definition of **IA5String**:

```
IA5String ::=
    [UNIVERSAL 22]
        IMPLICIT OCTET STRING
```

By using **IMPLICIT**, only the tag associated with `IA5String` (a universal tag with value 22) will be transmitted on the network. The tag associated with the **OCTET STRING** composing the data type (a universal tag with value 4) will not be transmitted.

The **IMPLICIT** keyword is only a "hint" to the transfer syntax, which performs the serialization of the data type. With the ASN.1 Basic Encoding Rules, use of the **IMPLICIT** keyword typically results in an encoding savings of two or three octets for each occurrence of the keyword. Although this seems like a paltry savings, when transmitting large, complex data structures, the increased efficiency is noticeable. In Section 8.3.4 on page 308, the ramifications of the **IMPLICIT** keyword are considered in greater detail.

In the original ASN.1 document, all tags were explicit by default and the **IMPLICIT** keyword was used as desired. In the Extensions Addendum, a new bit of syntax was added to the module definition. This syntax indicates what the "default" case is for the tagged types defined in the module:

```
<<module>> DEFINITIONS <<tags>> ::=
BEGIN
```

```
<<linkage>>

<<declarations>>
END
```

where `<<tags>>`, if present, is one of

```
EXPLICIT TAGS

IMPLICIT TAGS
```

If `<<tags>>` is not present or is EXPLICIT TAGS, then this declares the default behavior of the original ASN.1 document. But, if IMPLICIT TAGS is used, then all tags defined in the module are considered to be **IMPLICITly** tagged.

Meta Types

Finally, there are some ASN.1 types that transcend both the simple and constructor types.

CHOICE

A **CHOICE** type is a data type that is defined as the *union* of one or more data types. Any given instance of this data type takes the value of only one of the member data types of the union. For example, recall an earlier definition:

```
TimeOfDay ::=
    CHOICE {
        actual-value
            UTCTime,

        not-available
            NULL
    }

unixEpoch TimeOfDay ::=
    { actual-value "700101000000Z" }

unknownTime TimeOfDay ::=
    { not-available NULL }
```

As with the **SET**, each of the members of a **CHOICE** must be uniquely distinguishable based on their data types. Note that a **CHOICE** type itself may not be **IMPLICITly** tagged. If it were, then it would not be possible to tell which member of the **CHOICE** was present!

In addition, one or more of the members of a **CHOICE** may be another **CHOICE** data type. Again, as with the **SET**, when all of the members of a **CHOICE** are gathered, they must be distinguishable.

```
PDU ::=
    CHOICE {
        FTAM-Regime-PDU,

        File-PDU,

        Bulk-Data-PDU
    }

FTAM-Regime-PDU ::=
    CHOICE {
        ...
    }


    ...
```

The ellipses (...) aren't part of the ASN.1 syntax; They are used in this example to indicate the presence of additional ASN.1 declarations.

Because of the similarity between **SETs** and **CHOICEs**, the **CHOICE** is often considered a constructor type.

It is important to understand that the interaction between **SETs** and **CHOICEs**, although well-defined, is nevertheless tricky. Consider these two similar definitions:

```
MixedTypes ::=
    SET OF
        CHOICE {
            TypeA,

            TypeB
        }
```

```
EitherType ::=
    CHOICE {
        SET OF
            TypeA,

        SET OF
            TypeB
    }
```

The former definition will produce a type consisting of zero or more TypeA values intermixed with zero or more TypeB values. The latter definition will produce either a type consisting of zero or more TypeA values *or* a type consisting of zero or more TypeB values — the two types will not be intermixed!

ANY

An **ANY** type is a data type that is the union of all possible data types defined using ASN.1. Any given instance of this data type takes any legal ASN.1 value. **ANY** is used whenever the data type being used is not specified by the author of the ASN.1 module. For example, this might occur during development of the protocol specification. Presumably, in order for a sender and receiver to communicate meaningfully, a bilateral agreement has been made as to what data types will actually be transmitted. At a later time, the protocol specification may be further standardized and the **ANY** replaced with a more precise ASN.1 type. For example, the ASN.1 specification for the Association Control Service Element introduced in Section 6.5.1 on page 144 contains the following text:

```
AP-title ::=
        ANY
-- The exact definition and values used
-- for AP-title should be chosen taking
-- into account the ongoing work in the
-- areas of naming, the Directory, and
-- the Registration Authority procedures
-- for AP-titles, AE-titles and
-- AE-qualifiers.
```

Note that an **ANY** type may not be tagged as **IMPLICIT**. If it were, then it would not be possible to tell which ASN.1 type was present! In other words, use of the **IMPLICIT** keyword with **ANY** results in a catastrophic loss of information.

There is also another syntax:

```
AlgorithmIdentifier ::=
    SEQUENCE {
        algorithm
            OBJECT IDENTIFIER,

        parameters
            ANY DEFINED BY algorithm
            OPTIONAL
    }
```

which declares `parameters` to take on any valid ASN.1 type, which is refined by whatever dynamic value is taken by `algorithm`. This is probably the preferred usage of **ANY** in ASN.1.

Finally, from the syntactic perspective, the **ANY** type also makes possible two special abbreviated ASN.1 types. The following two data types are identical:

```
SEQUENCE OF ANY

SEQUENCE
```

So are these:

```
SET OF ANY

SET
```

EXTERNAL

An **EXTERNAL** type is a data type that is defined by some document outside the current module. Unlike the **ANY** type, an **EXTERNAL** type needn't refer to a type defined using ASN.1. Thus, if some data type cannot be modeled using ASN.1, it may be declared as **EXTERNAL** and a more appropriate description language used.

The **EXTERNAL** type is not an ASN.1 intrinsic. Its definition is:

```
EXTERNAL ::=
    [UNIVERSAL 8]
        IMPLICIT SEQUENCE {
            direct-reference
```

```
                OBJECT IDENTIFIER
                OPTIONAL,

         indirect-reference
                INTEGER
                OPTIONAL,

         data-value-descriptor
                ObjectDescriptor
                OPTIONAL,

         encoding
                CHOICE {
                    single-ASN1-type[0]
                        ANY,

                    octet-aligned[1]
                        IMPLICIT OCTET STRING,

                    arbitrary[2]
                        IMPLICIT BIT STRING
                }
         }
```

This definition concisely captures a lot of information: The first goal of the **EXTERNAL** type is to convey information regarding the definition of the data type.

An **OBJECT IDENTIFIER** is used to identify uniquely the document that defines the syntax of the data type. This is carried in the `direct-reference` field. If a number of exchanges involving data types defined in the same document will occur, then it is unwieldy to carry the **OBJECT IDENTIFIER** in each instance of an **EXTERNAL** type. As earlier noted in Section 6.4.1 on page 140, the OSI Presentation layer negotiates which abstract syntaxes are used over the network. After this negotiation, rather than using the **OBJECT IDENTIFIER** directly referencing to a syntax, a small **INTEGER** is used instead. This is carried in the `indirect-reference` field. (During the negotiation, both fields might be necessary; it is for this reason that the two aren't further encapsulated in a **CHOICE** construct.)

Finally, the `data-value-descriptor` field is used to convey textual information about the data type. Use of this field is not recommended as it is inherently ambiguous.

After information regarding the data type's definition has been conveyed, the second goal is to convey the data type's value. The encoding field is used for this purpose.

```
CHOICE {
    single-ASN1-type[0]
        ANY,

    octet-aligned[1]
        IMPLICIT OCTET STRING,

    arbitrary[2]
        IMPLICIT BIT STRING
}
```

The `single-ASN1-type` alternative is used when the data type is defined in terms of ASN.1 and the sender wishes to apply the same transfer syntax on both the data type and the **EXTERNAL** type. As this leads to the simplest case (the usual ASN.1 rules apply), this is usually the preferred implementation choice.

However, the data type might not be defined using ASN.1, or even if it is, some other transfer syntax may be used. For example, if the data type carried by the **EXTERNAL** is amenable to a particular data compression algorithm, then it may be desirable to compress just the value of that one data type (particularly if it is large). The presentation service may not understand about the compression algorithm in use, so it would be desirable to use two different encoding schemes: one for the encoding of the data in the **EXTERNAL** type, and another for the rest of the data. In this scenario, one of the `octet-aligned` or `arbitrary` alternatives is used. If the compression algorithm yields an encoding that is a multiple of 8–bits long, then the `octet-aligned` alternative may be used; otherwise, the `arbitrary` alternative is necessary.

Subtypes

Earlier, it was observed how an **OCTET STRING** may be refined to reflect a particular character set. In the original ASN.1 document, refinements were done by declaring the data type as an **IMPLICIT OCTET STRING** and stating the intent of the data type in the document. Although this is arguably acceptable for an International

Standard defining a few useful data types, it is hardly appropriate in the general case of ASN.1 usage.

In response, the Extensions Addendum introduces the notion of a *subtype*. An ASN.1 subtype is a refinement of some other ASN.1 type, termed its *parent*, although a more apt name may be *prototype*. The parent, in turn, may be a subtype of some other ASN.1 type. The notation for defining a subtype is relatively straightforward. For most data types, a subtype specification, consisting of a parenthesized list, is appended to the type definition, e.g.,

```
SubType ::=
    ParentType (--subtype specification--)
```

Inside the parenthesized list are one or more subtype specifications. If more than one specification is present, they are separated by the "|" character.

However, for the **SET OF** and **SEQUENCE OF** types, such a notation could lead to ambiguity. Consider:

```
AmbiguousSubType ::=
    SET OF
        ParentType (--subtype specification--)
```

Does the subtype specification refer to the **SET OF** or does it refer to ParentType? To resolve this issue, the syntax is slightly different:

```
SetOfSubType ::=
    SET OF (--subtype specification for SET OF--)
        ParentType

ParentSubType ::=
    SET OF
        ParentType (--subtype specification of ParentType--)
```

There are six kinds of subtype specifications. Further, depending on the prototype being refined, not all subtype specifications are valid. Rather than exhaustively listing all of the valid combinations, the discussion presents an example of each of different kinds of subtype specifications.

A *single value* subtype specification is used to indicate a subset of
the explicit values taken on by a prototype:

```
ProtoType ::=
    ENUMERATED {
        first-class (0),
        business-class (1),
        coach-class (2),
        economy-class (3)
    }


SubType ::=
    ProtoType (coach-class | economy-class)
```

In this example, the `ProtoType` may indicate the different air travel
fares available to a passenger, whilst the `SubType` may indicate which
are acceptable to the passenger's employer.

A *contained* subtype is used to combine the values taken on by
different types:

```
OtherType ::=
    ProtoType (INCLUDES Subtype | business-class)
```

In this example, not only may `OtherType` take the same values as
`SubType`, but it may also take the value `business-class` as well.

The *permitted alphabet* subtype is used to refine character strings,

```
TenDigitString ::=
    PrintableString (FROM (  "1" | "2" | "3"
                           | "4" | "5" | "6"
                           | "7" | "8" | "9"
                           | "0"))
```

Note that each string in the permitted alphabet contains a single
logical character. Thus, depending on the repertoire used to define
the character set, each character might be multi-octet-valued. For
example, characters in some national alphabets are represented as
16–bit quantities. Two octets would be needed to represent each
character in such an alphabet.

A *value range* subtype is used to limit the lower- and upper-bounds that the value of a data type may take:

```
ProtoType ::=
    INTEGER

NegativeNumber ::=
    ProtoType (MIN..<0)

NonPositiveNumber ::=
    ProtoType (MIN..0)


PositiveNumber ::=
    ProtoType (0<..MAX)

NonNegativeNumber ::=
    ProtoType (0..MAX)

-- alternatively:
--
--    NonPositiveNumber ::=
--        ProtoType (INCLUDES NegativeNumber | 0)
--
--    NonNegativeNumber ::=
--        ProtoType (INCLUDES PositiveNumber | 0)
--
```

This example exposes the syntax used for *value range* subtypes. If an endpoint of the range is non-inclusive, then the "<" or ">" character is used to indicate this. In addition, the keywords MIN and MAX respectively denote the smallest and largest values that parent may take. In the case of the **INTEGER** prototype, these values are unbounded. But, for refinements of the **INTEGER** prototype, this needn't be the case:

```
OSIlayers ::=
    INTEGER (1 | 2 | 3 | 4 | 5 | 6 | 7)

LowerLayers ::=
    OSIlayers (MIN..4)
```

```
UpperLayers ::=
    OSIlayers (4<..MAX)
```

Of course, only **INTEGER** and **REAL** prototypes may be refined in this fashion.[3] Although one might think that **OCTET STRING** prototypes could be refined based on their collating (alphabetizing) rules, ASN.1 does not permit this.

A *size range* subtype is used to limit the "length" that a value may take. There are two cases:

1. For prototypes that model strings of some kind (either **BIT STRING** or **OCTET STRING**), a size range subtype indicates how many logical units may be present, in effect defining the smallest and largest lengths that the string may take.

   In the case of a **BIT STRING**, a logical unit is simply a bit. But, for character strings, a logical unit needn't be an octet. For example, a repertoire described using a 16–bit character set requires two octets to denote a single logical unit.

2. For prototypes that model arrays (either **SEQUENCE OF** or **SET OF**), a size range subtype indicates how many elements or members may be present, in effect defining the smallest and largest sizes that the array may take.

Consider two examples:

```
-- the North American Numbering Plan:
--      local numbers are 7-digits, others are 10-digits

NANplan ::=
    TenDigitString (SIZE (7..10))

-- all conformant implementations must support up to
-- five bindings in a single transaction

VarBindList ::=
    SEQUENCE (SIZE (1..5)) OF
        VarBind
```

---

[3]Recall that the notation of comparison does not exist for values of the **ENU-MERATED** type.

Finally, the *inner* subtype is used to refine constructor types. The full syntax of this refinement is quite complex. Suffice it to say that inner subtype allows new constructor types to be defined that indicate which portions of other constructor types are:

- present; and (optionally),

- if present, which values they may take on.

The discussion on subtypes closes with a few examples of inner sub-typing:

```
PDU ::=
    SEQUENCE {
        requestID
            RequestID,

        operation
            ENUMERATED {
                get (0),
                put (1)
            },

        error-occuring
            Error-Occuring
            OPTIONAL,

        binding
            Binding
            OPTIONAL
    }

Binding ::=
    SEQUENCE {
        name
            ObjectName,

        value
            ObjectSyntax
            OPTIONAL
    }
```

```
GetRequest ::=
    PDU (WITH COMPONENTS {
        operation (get),
        error-occuring ABSENT,
        binding PRESENT
            (WITH COMPONENTS { value ABSENT })
    })

GetResponse ::=
    PDU (WITH COMPONENTS {
        operation (get),
        binding
            (WITH COMPONENTS { value PRESENT })
    })
```

In this example, PDU defines a **SEQUENCE** in which one element, error-occurring, may be optional. Further, one element, binding, refers to another **SEQUENCE** that also contains an optional element. Next, two subtypes of PDU are defined. Neither make any refinement of the requestID element of PDU; however, both explicitly define the value that must be taken by the operation element. The GetRequest type requires that the error-occuring element not be present, whilst the GetResponse type doesn't make any refinement for this element. Finally, for the binding element, the GetRequest type requires that the value element be absent, whilst the GetResponse type requires that the value element be present.

Conceptually, this meshes with what one might expect a "get request" to contain: a request identifier for the get operation along with the name of a variable to retrieve. In contrast, a "get response" contains the request identifier for the preceding get request. If an error occurred, then an error indication may be present, and possibly the binding may or may not be present as well (depending on the severity of the error). Otherwise, the error indication would be absent and the binding would be present. (The definition of GetResponse makes no requirement as to whether the error-occurring field is present.)

8.2.4 Values

In addition to defining a syntax for data types, ASN.1 also specifies a syntax for describing the values of those data types. Note that this *value notation* should not be confused with the transfer syntax: transfer syntax produces compact encodings for values that may be used on the network. In contrast, the value notation produces human-readable descriptions of those values. The value notation is invaluable (no pun intended) to ASN.1 programmers as they develop new abstract syntaxes and debug the applications that use those syntaxes.

For example, the value notation for an instance of a `GetResponse` PDU might look like:

```
{
    requestID
        17,

    operation
        get,

    binding
        {
            name
                1.3.6.1.2.1.1.1.1.0,

            value
                "unix"
        }
}
```

This simple description relates the fields of the data type to the values present in the instance.

As with the type notation, ASN.1 formally defines the value notation. In *Introduction to Application Services*, it was noted that one of the benefits of such formal mechanisms is that it permits tools to be automatically generated. Rather than detailing the rules for using the ASN.1 value notation, the discussion examines how one might generate a program that prints ASN.1 values corresponding to the data types defined in an ASN.1 module. In detailing the construction of such a program, a high-level natural language description will be given. This approach was taken primarily for brevity, as there are several existing computer programs that perform this task. For example, the *pepy* program described in Section 8.4.4 on page 331 can be invoked to produce a pretty-printer for an ASN.1 module.

Top-Level

Here's how it's done: for each ASN.1 type defined in the module, the program constructs a routine that prints an instance of that data type. The discussion assumes that a primitive routine `vprint` is available. This routine takes at least one argument: a string that indicates how the remaining arguments (if any) are to be formatted when output. (For those familiar with the UNIX *printf*(3s) routine, `vprint` is hardly a new idea.)

Each routine starts by seeing whether a tag and/or label is associated with the data type:

- If a label is associated with the data type, call

    vprint ("%s", LABEL)

  A label occurs inside only constructor types. Thus, at the top-level, this case will never be invoked. However, as will be seen, this algorithm is recursive. Hence, successive calls might take this alternative.

- Otherwise, if the data type is explicitly tagged, call

    vtag (TAG)

The `vtag` routine prints a tag. One of,

    [UNIVERSAL n]

    [APPLICATION n]

    [n]

    [PRIVATE n]

depending on the class of tag (universal, application-wide, context-specific, or private-use, respectively), and the value of the tag, n.

Next, see what kind of data type it is:

- for a **BOOLEAN** type, call either:

    vprint ("TRUE")

  or

```
vprint ("FALSE")
```

depending on the value.

- for an **INTEGER** or **ENUMERATED** type:

    - if the syntax for this data type did not enumerate the list
      of possible values, then call:

    ```
    vprint ("%d", VALUE)
    ```

    - otherwise, scan through the list of possible values, and see
      if there is a label that corresponds to the value present. If
      so,

    ```
    vprint ("%s", LABEL)
    ```

    Otherwise, call:

    ```
    vprint ("%d", VALUE)
    ```

    (ASN.1 does not require each possible value to have a label
    associated with it.)

- for a **REAL** type, call:

  ```
  vprint ("%g", VALUE)
  ```

- for a **BIT STRING** type:

    - if the syntax for this data type did not enumerate the list
      of possible values, then call:

    ```
    vprint ("%s", bit2str (VALUE, {}))
    ```

    - otherwise, construct a list, LIST, which contains the labels
      defined for each bit in the string. Then call:

    ```
    vprint ("%s", bit2str (VALUE, LIST))
    ```

The routine `bit2str` takes a **BIT STRING** value and a list
of labels defined for the bit that defines the label for each bit.
It begins by determining the length of the bit string. Then for
each bit present (those that are "on"), `bit2str` consults the list
of labels to see if a label is defined for that bit. If all bits present
have a label associated with them, then `bit2str` constructs an
ASCII string taking this format:

```
{ labels }
```

where `labels` contains the labels corresponding to all the bits present, separated by commas.

If the list of labels is empty, or a bit is present that doesn't have a label defined, then `bit2str` constructs a different kind of ASCII string:

    'bits'B

where `bits` is a string of 0's and 1's for each bit in the **BIT STRING**.

- for an **OCTET STRING** type, call:

    vstring (VALUE)

The routine `vstring` takes an **OCTET STRING** and determines an accurate representation for its value. It begins by making a pass over each character in the string. If it finds a character that isn't printable ASCII, then it selects a hexadecimal representation:

    'string'H

where each octet in the string is represented by two hexadecimal digits. Otherwise, an alphabetical representation is selected:

    "string"

where each octet in the string is simply copied without interpretation.

- for an **ANY** or an unspecified **SEQUENCE** or **SET** type, call:

    vunknown (VALUE)

- for a **NULL** type, call:

    vprint ("NULL")

- for an **OBJECT IDENTIFIER** type, call:

    vprint ("%s", oid2ode (VALUE))

The routine `oid2ode` takes an **OBJECT IDENTIFIER** and consults a local table that maps **OBJECT IDENTIFIERs** onto brief textual descriptions. If the table contains a mapping for the value in question, then `oid2ode` returns a string containing the description:

```
"description"
```

Otherwise, `oid2ode` constructs a new string containing the components of the value separated by dots — the standard **OBJECT IDENTIFIER** value notation.

- for a **SEQUENCE OF** or **SET OF** type, call:

  ```
  vpush ()
  ```

which simply prints a "{" character.

Next, recursively apply this algorithm to the type contained in the **SEQUENCE** or **SET**. Finally, call:

  ```
  vpop ()
  ```

which simply prints a "}" character.

- for a **SEQUENCE** or **SET** type containing a list of elements or members, call:

  ```
  vpush ()
  ```

Next, for each element or member present, recursively apply this algorithm. Finally, call:

  ```
  vpop ()
  ```

- for a **CHOICE** type, call:

  ```
  vpush ()
  ```

Next, based on the data type that is actually present, recursively apply this algorithm to the that data type. Finally, call:

  ```
  vpop ()
  ```

ANY

The top-level routine knows the complete ASN.1 type information when it generates a printer program for an ASN.1 value. The `vunknown` routine does not have this luxury as it is called to decide how to represent the value of a data type whose abstract syntax is unknown.

The algorithm used by `vunknown` is similar to the top-level algorithm discussed: Look at the tag associated with the value:

- if the tag corresponds to a universal type, then use the top-level algorithm. Note however, that since there is no abstract syntax to use as a template, no labels (e.g., for **INTEGERs** or constructor types) are available.

- otherwise, call:

    vtag (TAG)

    Then, decide if the value came from a constructor type. (The interaction between ASN.1 and its Basic Encoding Rules make this possible. It is not clear if such a determination could be made otherwise.)

    If the value did not come from a constructor type, call:

    vstring (VALUE)

    which is as good a heuristic as any (pun intended).

    Otherwise, call:

    vpush ()

    Then, for each element or member contained in the constructor, call `vunknown` recursively on this value. Finally, call:

    vpop ()

Presentation Policies

The top-level algorithm generates perfectly valid ASN.1 value notation. However, the discussion has not described the particular presentation policy that structures information for the user. This is independent of the ASN.1 value notation.

The primary goal of any presentation policy must be *readability*. soap...

However, readability is in the "eye of the beholder." The author finds
the presentation policy used by the authors of International Standards
documents to be excessively *ugly*. This is true for the ASN.1 type
notation as well as the ASN.1 value notation.

To appreciate the differences a presentation policy makes. Consider the same ASN.1 value, formatted according to different presentation policies. First, the presentation policy used in the ASN.1
document is shown:

```
{              {givenName "John",initial "P",familyName "Smith"    },
 title         "Director"                                          ,
 number        51                                                  ,
 dateOfHire    "19710917"                                          ,
 nameOfSpouse {givenName "Margaret",initial "T",familyName "Smith"},
 children
  {{{givenName "Ralph",initial "T",familyName "Smith"},
    dateOfBirth "19571111"                               },
    {givenName "Susan",initial "B",familyName "Jones"},
    dateOfBirth "19590717"                              }}            }
```

Next, the same ASN.1 value, formatted using the presentation policy preferred by the author is shown:

```
{
   {
      givenName "John",
      initial "P",
      familyName "Smith"
   },
   title "Director",
   number 51,
   dateOfHire "19710917",
   nameOfSpouse {
      givenName "Margaret",
      initial "T",
      familyName "Smith"
   },
   children {
      {
         {
            givenName "Ralph",
            initial "T",
            familyName "Smith"
         },
         dateofBirth "19571111"
      },
      {
         {
            givenName "Susan",
            initial "B",
            familyName "Jones"
         },
         dateofBirth "19590717"
      }
   }
}
```

Although consuming more vertical whitespace than its predecessor, many feel this presentation policy to be more readable. A further bonus is that the pretty-printing can occur incrementally. In order for the preceding presentation policy to get the commas to line up, the entire ASN.1 value had to be examined before generating the first line of output.

8.2.5   Macros

Thus far, the discussion has concentrated on the raw expository power
of ASN.1. As provocative as it might sound, there are some who believe that still more capabilities are required. To meet this challenge,
ASN.1 defines a *macro* notation. The purpose of defining and then
using an ASN.1 macro is to capture some additional semantic information.

The ASN.1 macro facility allows the ASN.1 grammar to be extended to meet the requirements of the abstract syntax designer. Note
that this is in sharp contrast to the macro facilities found in most other
computer languages. The ASN.1 macro notation literally rewrites the
grammar rules of the ASN.1 language. This requires extensive flexibility on the part of an ASN.1 parser. In contrast, the macro facility
for other languages perform textual substitutions on the stream of
input tokens — the language parser remains unchanged. Sadly, this
makes the ASN.1 macro facility a lot more than "syntactic sugar" for
ASN.1 — it is an integral part of the language.

soap... Just as the discussion has purposefully (and hopefully successfully)
avoided spelling out the formalisms involved with the ASN.1 type and
value notations, we now try to explain the ASN.1 macro notation
without using the formal (and largely incomprehensible) description
...soap in the ASN.1 document.

The high-level definition of a macro is straightforward:

```
<<macro>> MACRO ::=
BEGIN

TYPE NOTATION  ::= <<type syntax>>

VALUE NOTATION ::= <<value syntax>>

<<supporting syntax>>
END
```

The `<<macro>>` term names the macro. When the macro is invoked,
by giving a "variable" name and then the macro's name, the `<<type
syntax>>` defines the grammar rules which follow. Each instance of
a macro has a value associated with it, the `<<value syntax>>` term
defines the values that the macro instance may take on. Finally,
the `<<supporting syntax>>` term provides any additional grammar

rules for either the macro's type or value notation. All of this can be somewhat de-mystified with an example. Here's a definition of a macro named OBJECT-TYPE:

```
OBJECT-TYPE MACRO ::=
BEGIN
    TYPE NOTATION ::=
            "SYNTAX" type (TYPE ObjectSyntax)
            "ACCESS" Access
            "STATUS" Status

    VALUE NOTATION ::=
            value (VALUE ObjectName)

    Access ::= "read-only"
                    | "read-write"
                    | "write-only"
                    | "not-accessible"

    Status ::= "mandatory"
                    | "obsolete"
                    | "optional"
END

ObjectSyntax ::=
    CHOICE {
        number
            INTEGER,

        string
            OCTET STRING,

        object
            OBJECT IDENTIFIER,

        empty
            NULL
    }

ObjectName ::=
    OBJECT IDENTIFIER
```

Now here's a use of that macro to define an instance named sysDescr:

```
sysDescr OBJECT-TYPE
         SYNTAX OCTET STRING
         ACCESS read-only
         STATUS mandatory
         ::= { system 1 }
```

The type notation for the macro says that when an instance of the macro is declared:

- the keyword SYNTAX immediately occurs followed by a data type corresponding to the ASN.1 type ObjectSyntax;

- following this, the keyword ACCESS occurs followed by one of four different strings;

- following this, the keyword STATUS occurs followed by one of three different strings; and,

- following this, the symbol ::= occurs followed by a value corresponding to possible values for the ASN.1 type ObjectName.

It should be noted that this is a very simple example of an ASN.1 macro. The macro notation may be used to capture powerful semantics for a wide range of systems. In [JDelg88], for example, the macro facility is used quite extensively to produce succinct yet far-reaching definitions.

A Soapbox on the ASN.1 Macro Facility

soap...

Although the ASN.1 macro facility is attractive in terms of its expressive capabilities. It has two significant drawbacks which, given the current state of ASN.1 compiler technology, make it unusable (or at the very least distasteful).

The first disastrous characteristic is that use of the ASN.1 macro facility rewrites the grammar for the ASN.1 language. To understand why this is problematic, a brief introduction to compiler theory is necessary. Most compilers consist of two parts:

- a *front-end*, which reads the input stream of lexemes and builds
  an internal form that corresponds to the language grammar understood by the compiler; and,

- a *back-end*, which takes the internal form, produces some kind
  of transformation on it, and then writes an output stream of
  lexemes.

For example, a compiler for the C programming language has a front-
end that reads a C file and builds a parse tree corresponding to the
program. The back-end then generates assembly language for the
target architecture. This is an important functional division: modern
compiler technology is based on the notion of having a single front-
end for a programming language, a common internal form, and then
multiple back-ends, one for each kind of supported architecture (i.e.,
processor type and operating system). The internal form provides an
important level of abstraction.

In building the front-end of a compiler, a *compile-time* model is
often used. This means that the grammar rules for the language are
fully specified when the front-end itself is compiled. The good part
about the compile-time model is that other programs can be used
to generate the front-end. On UNIX, for example, the *yacc* and *lex*
programs perform this task: *lex* generates code to read an input file
and produce a stream of lexemes for the compiler, whilst *yacc* generates the code that understands the syntax rules of the language. A
UNIX program augments the *yacc* input file to build the internal form
used by the compiler. Programs such as *lex* and *yacc* can dramatically reduce the time required to build compilers. A further bonus is
that programs like *yacc* generate very sophisticated parsing algorithms
that execute quickly and take up little space. Thus, when building a
front-end to an ASN.1 compiler, there can be many benefits to using
a compile-time model.

Unfortunately, the ASN.1 macro facility permits *any* ASN.1 module to define its own macros. As a result, when writing the ASN.1
compiler, it is not possible to know about all the ASN.1 macros that
might be encountered. Hence, it is not possible to specify fully the
grammar the compiler must know. This means that any ASN.1 front-
end based on a compile-time model will fail when it encounters an
ASN.1 macro.

One solution to this might be to use an interpretive model when building the ASN.1 front-end. This means that the compiler front-end can "learn" new syntax rules when macros are defined. A drawback of the interpretive model is that these front-ends tend to be much slower than their compile-time model counterparts. By the end of 1988, no interpretive model front-ends for the ASN.1 language were well-known. A second solution is to extend the ASN.1 grammar used to cover a small number of select macros. Although this sounds like a "hack," it has the advantage of allowing a compile-time model to be used for the front-end.

The second disastrous characteristic of the macro facility is that it has "buried semantics." The ASN.1 macro notation is fine for relating different ASN.1 constructs. For humans, who are intuitive by nature, such relations can be readily understood (with a little practice). Computer programs, and, in particular, language compilers, aren't nearly so good at seeing things that aren't explicit. Consider the OBJECT-TYPE macro defined earlier. It is part of an ASN.1 module that contains definitions for a particular *network management framework*. The module is preceded by a couple dozen pages of text explaining how the network management framework "works." As a part of this description, the concept of the *managed object* is explained. Finally, the realization of this concept as an ASN.1 macro is defined.

Although a reader of the document in question ([MRose88b]) is now fully primed to understand instances of the OBJECT-TYPE macro, an ASN.1 compiler does not have these benefits. For the moment, assume that an interpretive model is used when building the ASN.1 front-end ("hope springs eternal..."). So, the compiler can understand the syntax of the ASN.1 macros being used. But, what internal form does it build; furthermore, what will the back-end of the compiler do with this form once built? This is where the buried semantics of the ASN.1 macro facility come back to haunt us. The OBJECT-TYPE macro (or any ASN.1 macro, for that matter), contains no information for the compiler when it is encountered. For example,

- how does the compiler know that an object defined using this macro should be entered in the network management symbol table using the object's value as the lookup key?

- how does the compiler know that the ASN.1 type following the SYNTAX keyword describes the syntax of the data type associated with the object?

- how does the compiler know that such an object, if marked "read-only" means that the network management protocol may not alter its value?

- in short, how does the compiler understand the semantics of any of the keywords (SYNTAX, ACCESS, or STATUS) used in the macro?

The answer is:

> *The compiler can't possibly know these things unless it is programmed to know!*

In the case of a front-end based on a compile-time model, this means that in addition to modifying the front-end to know about the syntax of the OBJECT-TYPE macro, the programmer must also modify the back-end of the ASN.1 compiler to use the new internal form. Presumably with a compiler based on a interpretive model, the ASN.1 macro definition would be modified with instructions for the back-end. This would avoid having to hard-wire any additional semantics into the compiler and preserve the interpretive feel. This is an interesting research project.[4]

Until such technology is available, the ASN.1 macro facility introduces tremendous difficulty for automatic tools. To summarize the soapbox:

> *Macros are problematic.*

> `...soap`

8.2.6 An Example

The discussion now turns to an example that unifies much of the preceding text. Rather than stepping through an ASN.1 module, the history surrounding this particular module is explained before the module is introduced. This story doesn't warrant a soapbox, but the discussion isn't exactly unbiased either. Unlike the preceding discussion, the text that follows is narrative rather than expository. (Readers can skip to **An ASN.1 Module** on page 284 if they are uninterested in the historical background.)

---

[4]If someone is interested in pursuing this, contact the author for some ideas.

A Historical Perspective

[VCerf88] defines the technical direction for network management
taken by the Internet community.   This is a large networking community using the TCP/IP protocols described in Part I. In the short-
term, an existing management protocol, the *Simple Gateway Monitoring Protocol*[JDavi87] (SGMP), was modified to reflect the experience gained by its use in operational networks and would be called
the *Simple Network Management Protocol*[JCase89b] (SNMP). In the
long-term, use of the emerging OSI network management protocol, the
Common Management Information Protocol (CMIP) is being investi-
gated. The disadvantage of a two-pronged approach is, of course, that
a transition is needed from the short-term to the long-term solution.
In order to provide for an orderly transition between the technologies, it was essential that a common framework for management of
TCP/IP-based internets be developed.

This strategy, as described in [VCerf88], was issued by the *Internet Activities Board* (IAB), the body that oversees the technical
development of the Internet suite of protocols. As a result of the IAB
recommendations, three working groups of the Internet Engineering
Task Force (IETF) of the IAB were chartered:

- the Management Information Base (MIB) working group was
  formed to develop the common framework for TCP/IP network
  management.

- the SNMP Extensions working group was formed to make minor
  extensions to the SGMP based on operational experience and to
  achieve conformance with the results of the MIB working group.

- the Netman working group was directed to continue exploration
  of the OSI network management framework and develop ·CMIP
  over TCP (CMOT).

The purpose of this discussion is to focus on how the first working
group used ASN.1 to meet its charter.

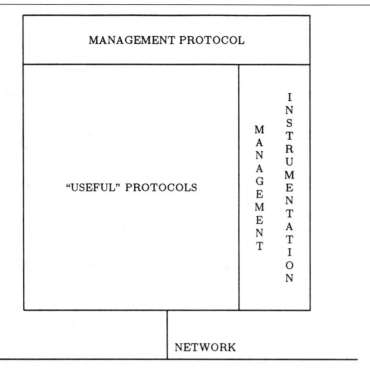

Figure 8.1: A Managed Node

The MIB working group had a difficult task: in addition to enumerating the objects that could be managed, these objects had to be defined in a way that was independent of the actual management protocol in use. This protocol independence is critical if more than one management protocol is ever to be used. To understand why this is so, consider the high-level architecture of a managed node, such as a gateway, as shown in Figure 8.1

A managed node conceptually consists of three parts:

- *"useful" protocols*, which do "real" work;

- a *management protocol*, which permits the monitoring and control of (at least) the "useful" protocols; and,

- *management instrumentation*, which interacts with the local implementation of the "useful" protocols in order to achieve monitoring and control.

In order to do network management, we think of the "useful" protocols as containing *managed objects*, such as routing tables, interface information, virtual terminal connections, and so on. In an implementation, the management instrumentation provides these managed object abstractions to the management protocol. Thus, to the extent that these managed objects are defined in a fashion that is independent of the management protocol, the management instrumentation is also independent of the management protocol. This means that one could conceivably exchange the management protocol used on a node without changing either the "useful" protocols or the management instrumentation.

In any well-designed system, the cost of implementing and maintaining the "useful" protocols should be at least an order of magnitude greater than the associated costs of the instrumentation and management protocols. Thus, if the objects are defined in a management protocol-independent fashion, a significant savings may be realized.

Another benefit of the common framework is obtained in management stations. When the transition from the SNMP to the CMOT occurs, there will undoubtedly be a mixture of managed nodes using either the SNMP or the CMOT. By having a common framework, the network operator can be presented with a common interface for managing the network, independent of what actual protocols are used to manage individual nodes.

To achieve this independence, the working group divided its task into two parts. The first part was to develop a *Structure of Management Information* (SMI) [MRose88b]. The SMI defines the rules for how managed objects are described and how management protocols may access these objects. The second part was to develop a *Management Information Base* (MIB) [KMcCl88]. This is the collection of objects that can be accessed via a network management protocol.

The SMI, a draft standard for the Internet community, is largely an administrative document: it says "how to do things," but not actually "what to do." It is the MIB and the management protocol that are responsible for the "what to do" part, and the SMI is used strictly to provide a well-defined interface between them. The SMI philosophy is to foster:

- *simplicity*, because general understanding of network management is (so far) very limited; by taking a simple approach, future extensions will be less constrained. In addition, there is hope that today's systems will be more workable.

- *extensibility*, because there are many possible approaches that might be followed; by emphasizing extensibility, a larger number of future approaches might be attempted. In addition, since today's systems will be around for a while, it is essential to provide a straightforward way for the new to work with the old.

The *object information model* used in the SMI is simple. Managed objects are defined using ASN.1.

As with much technology, the path taken by the SMI was largely pre-determined. Besides the protocol-independence issue, another important factor was a desire to remain philosophically aligned with the management framework implicitly defined in the SGMP so as to minimize changes to the successor management protocol, the SNMP. However a third factor was the desire to remain technically viable with the management framework used by the CMIP. Finally, a fourth requirement was to be responsive to new experiences with management. As such, the SMI would have to permit rapid, yet controlled, expansion of the MIB as new understandings were gained.

These forces proved too difficult to reconcile completely: when the SNMP was defined in [JCase89b] it proved impossible to remain technically aligned with the SMI and remain compatible with its predecessor the SGMP. As such, when viewing the modifications to the SGMP that resulted in the SNMP, some changes "fixed" things that were "broken," other things were purposefully "broken" and then "fixed" in order to align with the SMI. Obviously, taking something that works and then changing it for "no good reason" is painful.

In early 1988, after the policy statement in [VCerf88] was issued, a colleague of mine at Wollongong, Keith McCloghrie, and I began preparing a proposal for the Internet SMI and MIB. In doing so, we knew that this would have a profound impact on the (as yet) unspecified SNMP. So, we made a pilgrimage to the capital of SGMP, Troy, New York, in the United States. There we met with three of the four authors of the SGMP specification.

Before continuing, it is important to understand the personalities of the characters involved. Keith was born in the United Kingdom and is soft-spoken. Although he is quite capable technically, he does not care to illustrate his points graphically with a lot of shouting and screaming. In contrast, I am the *militant moderate* of networking. Although I prefer simple, elegant technical solutions, I also understand that there is this thing called OSI that is morally equivalent to a moving bulldozer without a driver. As such, I am willing to compromise so as to be able to move out of the way of the bulldozer if it appears to be heading in my direction at an unsafe speed. Sometimes, if the bulldozer is traveling fast enough, "compromise" means using the verbal equivalent of a two-by-four in order to explain things to the parties preventing me from moving out of the way of the very dangerous, yet nevertheless popular, bulldozer.

The authors of the SGMP have a different perspective. They believe in no-frills management protocols. This automatically disqualifies the CMIP and any CMIP-like ideas. A quotation I use from time to time comes from Professor Jeffrey D. Case, one of the originators of the SGMP:

> *I want my dog hunting raccoon, not skinning them!*

What this means is that routers should route, terminal servers should provide terminal service, and printers should print. They should not spend all (or even much) of their time doing activities related to network management. Even though Professor Case was the one SGMP author not present at our meeting, his views were shared (and convincingly argued) by his three co-authors. To appreciate the elegance of their arguments, the article *Network Management and the Design of SNMP* [JCase89a] is highly recommended.

Now, given the success of the SGMP crew (SGMP, and now SNMP, is used internationally to manage TCP/IP-based internets of all sizes), it is important to realize that their perspectives are quite valid. Nevertheless, back in early 1988, Keith and I trekked back to Troy to convince them to be more OSI-like in their thinking.

The key impact of the SMI on a management protocol is how objects are identified (or named) and how they are structured. Fortunately, the SGMP used ASN.1 for both of these purposes, so there was already some commonality in mechanisms.

To identify an object, the SGMP defined **OCTET STRING** values in a hierarchical fashion. In addition, to traverse a tree of managed objects, a lexicographical ordering was imposed on the **OCTET STRINGs**. In OSI, an **OBJECT IDENTIFIER** is used. There are many similarities between the two approaches, so once a lexicographical ordering mechanism was defined for **OBJECT IDENTIFIERs**, there was no real technical difference between the two naming schemes. However, if the SNMP used the **OBJECT IDENTIFIER** for naming purposes, then it would be incompatible with the SGMP. After several hours of heated argument, we tentatively agreed to consider the matter further.

The structuring rules were much more controversial. The SGMP provided two kinds of values for objects: **INTEGERs** and **OCTET STRINGs**. In contrast, the OSI framework permits any valid ASN.1 type to be used to define the structure of an object. Why was the SGMP so restrictive? The answer lies in practicality. Although the OSI approach is general, it also leads to complex systems (violating the "raccoon principle" above). Consider that if one allows any kind of ASN.1 type to be used, then when managed objects are defined in the MIB, one can be assured than virtually every kind of ASN.1 type will be used. This means that both the management protocol and management instrumentation will have to implement these various data types. Implementation does not come for free: in addition to the relatively static cost of coding, the implementation may need to be placed into resource-limited peripherals such as routers or modems. In many cases, this simply isn't practical or cost-effective. Further, even if it were practical to field the code in these environments, there is still the run-time cost of encoding and decoding the objects for transmission on the network. Complex data types have complex encodings that slow down everything. Thus, based on arguments from the SGMP authors, Keith and I adopted an emphasis on simplicity and implementability.

As a result, most ASN.1 constructs, including many seemingly simple ones were not permitted to be used by the SMI. Two simple examples:

- the **ENUMERATED** type may not appear since the **INTEGER** type provides equivalent functionality;

- the **REAL** type may not appear since it is too difficult to encode (the need for additional precision over **INTEGERs** is dubious anyway).

Keith and I nearly got the **BIT STRING** type included, but had to sacrifice this in order to get the **OBJECT IDENTIFIER** type to be used as the naming mechanism.

Although these may seem like small, insignificant points:

> *The road to complex systems is paved with bells and whistles.*

Of course, we provided for an "escape hatch" that permits any arbitrary ASN.1 type to be used, covertly, for the structure of an object. This is used only by bilateral agreement. Naive implementations are expected to ignore such objects.

An ASN.1 Module

With the historical (some say hysterical) digression aside, the discussion next looks at the ASN.1 module that defines the Structure of Management Information for network management of TCP/IP-based internets. The module is shown in Figure 8.2.

To begin, the top-level syntax of the module identifies the name of the module as `RFC1065-SMI`. An object identifier is not present for this module, owing to political reasons not worthy of a soapbox. The module then declares the definitions that it **EXPORTs**. Some of these are ASN.1 types (e.g., `ObjectName`), others are ASN.1 values (e.g., `internet`), whilst one is an ASN.1 macro (i.e., `OBJECT-TYPE`).

The tasks of an SMI are largely administrative. For example, various **OBJECT IDENTIFIER** instances are defined that describe the naming tree. Next, the macro defining a managed object is presented. This is the very same `OBJECT-TYPE` macro discussed in Section 8.2.5 on page 272. As a part of this, the `ObjectName` type is defined. This is explicitly defined for management protocols, such as the SNMP, which need to identify the objects they manage.

Finally, the `ObjectSyntax` type and its supporting types are defined. The `ObjectSyntax` type is a union of two different kinds of data types: simple and application-wide. The `SimpleSyntax` type defines the primitive data types that are used to define the syntax of a managed object. The **INTEGER** and **OCTET STRING** types appear, as these were proven useful by experiences with the SGMP. The **OBJECT IDENTIFIER** type appears since it seems natural to think of managed objects possibly containing references to other objects. Finally, the **NULL** type is permitted for objects that communicate information by their presence in a managed node, rather than by their value.

RFC1065−SMI **DEFINITIONS** ::=

BEGIN

EXPORTS −− *EVERYTHING*
     internet, directory, mgmt, experimental, private, enterprises,
     OBJECT−TYPE, ObjectName, ObjectSyntax, SimpleSyntax,
     ApplicationSyntax, NetworkAddress, IpAddress,
     Counter, Gauge, TimeTicks, Opaque;

                                                                                        10

−− *the path to the root*

internet   **OBJECT IDENTIFIER** ::= { iso identified−organization(3) dod(6) 1 }

directory   **OBJECT IDENTIFIER** ::= { internet 1 }

mgmt   **OBJECT IDENTIFIER** ::= { internet 2 }

experimental **OBJECT IDENTIFIER** ::= { internet 3 }
                                                                                       20

private   **OBJECT IDENTIFIER** ::= { internet 4 }
enterprises **OBJECT IDENTIFIER** ::= { private 1 }

−− *definition of object types*

OBJECT−TYPE MACRO ::=
BEGIN

    TYPE NOTATION ::= "SYNTAX" type (**TYPE** ObjectSyntax)   30
                               "ACCESS" Access
                               "STATUS" Status

    VALUE NOTATION ::= value (**VALUE** ObjectName)

    Access ::= "read-only"
              | "read-write"
              | "write-only"
              | "not-accessible"
    Status ::= "mandatory"   40
              | "optional"
              | "obsolete"

END

Figure 8.2: Structure of Management Information

−− names of objects in the MIB

ObjectName ::=
  OBJECT IDENTIFIER

−− syntax of objects in the MIB

ObjectSyntax ::=
  CHOICE {
      simple   10
          SimpleSyntax,

−− note that simple SEQUENCEs are not directly mentioned here to keep things simple
−− (i.e., prevent mis−use). However, application−wide types that are IMPLICITly
−− encoded simple SEQUENCEs may appear in the following CHOICE

      application−wide
          ApplicationSyntax
  }
                                                                          20
SimpleSyntax ::=
  CHOICE {
      number
          INTEGER,

      string
          OCTET STRING,

      object
          OBJECT IDENTIFIER,   30

      empty
          NULL
  }

ApplicationSyntax ::=
  CHOICE {
      address
          NetworkAddress,
                                                                          40
      counter
          Counter,

      gauge
          Gauge,

      ticks
          TimeTicks,

      arbitrary   50
          Opaque

−− other application−wide types, as they are defined, will be added here
  }

Figure 8.2: Structure of Management Information (cont.)

-- *application−wide types*

NetworkAddress ::=
  CHOICE {
      internet
        IpAddress
  }

IpAddress ::=
  [APPLICATION 0]   -- *in network−octet order*   10
      IMPLICIT OCTET STRING (SIZE (4))

Counter ::=
  [APPLICATION 1]
      IMPLICIT INTEGER (0..4294967295)

Gauge ::=
  [APPLICATION 2]
      IMPLICIT INTEGER (0..4294967295)
                                                                20

TimeTicks ::=
  [APPLICATION 3]
      IMPLICIT INTEGER

Opaque ::=
  [APPLICATION 4]   -- *arbitrary ASN.1 value,*
      IMPLICIT OCTET STRING   --   *"double−wrapped"*

END

Figure 8.2: Structure of Management Information (cont.)

As noted in the ASN.1 comment in the `ObjectSyntax` definition, future extensions to the SMI may include the **SEQUENCE** type. The MIB uses **SEQUENCEs** to define tables in a management protocol-independent fashion (the SNMP and the CMIP use different mechanisms for retrieving and modifying tables).

The `ApplicationSyntax` type defines data types that have been found useful in network management. As experience is gained, this list may be extended.

The `NetworkAddress` type is a choice enumerating the different kind of network addresses that might appear in a managed object. At present, only an address for the Internet Protocol (the IP in TCP/IP) is used.

The `Counter` type is used to represent a non-negative integer that monotonically increases until it reaches a maximum value ($2^{32} - 1$), when it wraps around and starts increasing again from zero. This range was chosen since it can be conveniently represented in a long-word quantity on most machine architectures.

In contrast, the `Gauge` type may increase or decrease, but will latch when it reaches a maximum value (again, $2^{32} - 1$). This type is useful for modeling objects that represent alarm situations.

The `TimeTicks` type is used to represent the time, in hundredths of a second, from some epoch time. The precision of this type was chosen pragmatically: experience shows that this quantum is an effective measurement for network events. It is important to note that the the epoch is not tied to some universal, globally known time. It is impractical, if not impossible, for many managed nodes in the network to synchronize on an agreed upon time. The best that can be hoped for is that two nodes will be able to estimate reliably the network delay between them and then communicate in relative times.

soap... There are some who don't believe this argument and feel that such managed nodes should be "expelled from the network." In response, it should be noted that:

- first, many time synchronization protocols are more complicated than some network management protocols; and,

- second, many of these managed nodes, which don't use a time synchronization protocol, are routers. If these were expelled from the network, I think the network users might have a thing or two to say to the misguided "experts" who hold this position.

It's hard to believe, but there are actually persons (on Standards committees, no less) who think like that!

`...soap`

Finally, the `Opaque` type is used to bypass the type restrictions of the SMI. An arbitrary ASN.1 type may be used to define an object's syntax. Whenever the value associated with the object is to be exchanged on the network, the ASN.1 Basic Encoding Rules are applied to the value. This results in a string of octets. This is then encoded again as an **OCTET STRING**, in effect "double-wrapping" the original ASN.1 value. A managed node conforming to the SMI need only be able to accept and recognize opaquely-encoded data. It does not have to be able to unwrap the data and then interpret its contents. Thus, by bilateral agreement, some nodes might meaningfully communicate more complex objects.

Writing your own ASN.1 Modules

Anyone planning to design an ASN.1 module should read §E.2 in the original ASN.1 document[ISO87y]. This annex to the International Standard contains a large number of useful hints as to how the ASN.1 type notation should be used.

It should be noted that use of ASN.1, per se, is insufficient to define a protocol. In raw form, ASN.1 defines only the data types used by an application. Additional structure is required to defined the interaction between the application entities. However, these interactions may be defined using ASN.1 macros. For example, beginning on page 428 there is a description of the RO-notation, a powerful set of macros that is used to capture the supplier/consumer interactions of many application protocols.

8.3 Transfer Syntax Notation

As well as defining a description language, ASN.1 also defines a set of *Basic Encoding Rules*, the BER. The basic premise of the BER is that instances of ASN.1 types, *values*, are encoded as an stream of octets.

Although an encoding may be quite complex overall, the actual rules used to produce the encodings are actually small in number and quite simple to describe. For example, looking back to Section 8.2.4 on page 263, a recursive algorithm was described that could pretty-print any ASN.1 value. The Basic Encoding Rules can be viewed precisely in this way — the difference being that instead of using human-readable text strings to describe a value, a compact octet encoding is used.

It must be emphasized that the BER is largely a rote topic, as it is a heavily used and well understood technology. Whilst it is important to gain an understanding of the issues that the BER must tackle. The myriad details are usually taken care of by (hopefully well-debugged) programs.

8.3.1 Top-Level

At the top-level, the BER describes how to encode a single ASN.1 type. This may be a simple type such as an **INTEGER**, or an arbitrarily complex type. Conceptually, the key to applying the BER is to understand that the most complex ASN.1 type is nothing more than a number of smaller, less complex ASN.1 types. If this decomposition continues, then ultimately an ASN.1 simple type such as **INTEGER** is encoded.

Using the BER, each ASN.1 type is encoded as three fields:

- a *tag* field, which indicates the ASN.1 type;

- a *length* field, which indicates the size of the ASN.1 value encoding which follows;

- a *value* field, which is the ASN.1 value encoding.

Thus, any ASN.1 type is encoded in three fields:

tag	length	value

It turns out that each of these fields is of variable length. Because ASN.1 may be used to define arbitrarily complex types, the BER must be able to support arbitrarily complex encodings.

Bit Ordering

Before looking at the details, a few words about how the BER views octets are in order. Each octet consists of 8–bits — obviously! But, how are the bits numbered? With the BER, the high-order (most significant) bit is called bit 8, whilst the low-order (least significant) bit is called bit 1. This is important to apply consistently because different machine architectures use different ordering rules (some view the high-order bit as being on the left edge of the octet, others view the high-order bit as being on the octet's right edge). Briefly put:

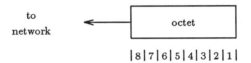

Numeric Representations

Furthermore, a large number of fields encoded by the BER are integer values expressed as binary numbers. There are two ways of representing these numbers, depending on whether negative numbers need to be represented.

To encode an integer that may take on any value (positive, negative, or zero), then a *two's-complement* representation is used. In this scheme, a string of bits comprises the number. Bit 8 of the first octet contains the most significant bit, whilst bit 1 of the last octet contains the least significant bit. Although conceptually it is often easier to think of the representation as being octet-aligned, this needn't be the case; for example, the BER may specify that some fields are only 7 bits long. As long as the most significant previously unused bit in the first octet is used as the most significant bit of the string, and the least significant bit unused in the last octet is used as the least significant bit of the string, then no ambiguity arises.

Rather than explaining how to generate the two's-complement representation, it's much simpler to understand how to interpret an integer value stored in this format. Suppose the length of the string is 32 bits. The least significant bit is assigned the number 0, the next bit is assigned the number 1, and so on, until the most significant bit is assigned the number 31. Now, set a counter, say x, to zero and look at each bit in the string, *except* for the most significant bit. For each bit that is set to one, add 2^n to the counter, where n is the number we assigned to the bit. Next, if the most significant bit is set to one, then subtract 2^n from the counter, again where n is the number we assigned to it (in this case 31). If the most significant bit is set to zero, ignore it. The resulting value in the counter is the integer value represented by the two's-complement representation. Briefly:

$$x = \left(\sum_{i=0}^{n-2} bit(i) * 2^i \right) - bit(n-1) * 2^{n-1}$$

for a string of n bits.

Note that a single contents octet can encode an integer value from $-128 \leq x \leq 127$, whilst two contents octets can encode an integer value from $-65536 \leq x \leq 65535$. (In general, with b bits in the string, numbers from $-2^{b-1} \leq x \leq 2^{b-1} - 1$ may be encoded.) In order to ensure that encodings are as compact as possible, the BER does not permit the first 9 bits to be zero- or one-filled. (The first octet is superfluous in these cases.)

The second representation is used to encode non-negative integer values. This is a simple variation, termed an *unsigned* representation, in which the high-order bit contributes to the counter rather than decrementing from it:

$$x = \left(\sum_{i=0}^{n-1} bit(i) * 2^i \right)$$

for a string of n bits. Because an extra bit is available for representing the magnitude of the integer value, larger numbers may be represented, in the same number of bits, than with a two's-complement encoding; numbers from $0 \leq x \leq 2^b - 1$ may be encoded. With most applications of the unsigned representation, the BER permits the leading octets to be zero-filled. This is done for compatibility with the 1984 CCITT X.409 Recommendation.

8.3.2   Tag Field

The *tag* field is encoded as one or more *identifier octets*. This encoding must somehow capture the definition of the corresponding ASN.1

type. The BER does this by encoding the ASN.1 tag of the type. Recall that a tag is associated with each type defined using ASN.1.

As noted earlier, there are four classes of tags in ASN.1:

- *universal* tags, for the well-known data types (Table 8.1 on page 248 shows these);

- *application-wide* tags, which are defined within a single ASN.1 module;

- *context-specific* tags, which are used to provide distinguishing information in constructor types; and,

- *private-use* tags, which are used by consenting parties.

In addition to belonging to one of these groups, a tag has associated with it a non-negative integer. Thus, the tag field, officially termed the *identifier octets*, generated by the BER must encode not only the tag's class but also the tag's number as well.

In addition, the tag field must encode one other bit of information as well. As noted earlier, an ASN.1 type might be primitive or it might be constructed. Although we think of it as natural that the value of a primitive type should be encoded as a single collection of octets, it may be more efficient for the sending process to break the value up into smaller, more manageable parts. For example, suppose a facsimile image is being encoded. This is represented in ASN.1 using a **BIT STRING**. If the image was large, it would probably be convenient to apply the BER to only a part of the image at a time. This may be done using a constructed encoding: after the BER was applied, the resulting octet-aligned encodings would be sent, the next part of the image fetched and then encoded. This would continue until the image had been entirely consumed. If the sender wishes to use this scheme, then it must indicate to the receiving process that it is doing so. Obviously, if the ASN.1 type is constructed, then it is always sent in constructed form.

So, encoding the tag field as a sequence of octets is rather simple. The tag field consists of one or more octets. The first octet encodes the tag's class along with an indication as to whether the encoding is constructed. Since there are four classes of tags, this can be represented in two of the eight bits in the octet.

Finally, the primitive/constructed indication will require a third bit, which for brevity is termed f:

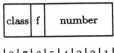

|8|7|6|5|4|3|2|1|

The two high-order bits (bits 8 and 7) are used to encode the tag's class:

Class	Bit 8	Bit 7
Universal	0	0
Application-wide	0	1
Context-specific	1	0
Private	1	1

The next bit (bit 6) indicates whether the encoding is primitive or constructed.

Thus, five bits are left over for encoding the non-negative tag number. These could be used to encode a non-negative integer from 0 to 63. But, this would be rather short-sighted: many more than 64 types are possible! Thus, the BER uses the following rule:

- if the tag's number is less than 31, then it is encoded in the five bits that remain, using the unsigned representation discussed earlier;

- otherwise, bits 5 through 1 are set to all ones, which indicates that the octets that follow contain the tag's number.

So, in many cases (and clearly for all the Universal tags defined thus far), a single octet is sufficient to encode the tag field. In the other cases, one or more octets follow the first octet. The high-order bit (bit 8), if set to zero, indicates whether this particular octet is the last octet of the tag field:

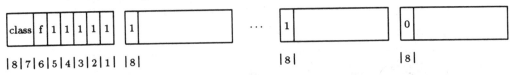

|8|7|6|5|4|3|2|1| |8| |8| |8|

Thus, in the case where the tag's number is greater than or equal to 31, the value is encoded using the unsigned integer representation found by concatenating the 7–bit values that follow the initial identifier octet.

8.3.3 Length Field

The *length* field is encoded as one or more *length octets*. This encoding indicates how many of the octets that follow make up the value of the ASN.1 type being encoded.

Observant readers have probably noticed a contradiction in the BER. Earlier, it was noted that it may be useful to encode a primitive type using a constructed encoding if it was difficult to have the entire primitive type available during encoding. If this is the case, then how can the length field be calculated and sent *before* the value? There are two possible solutions to this dilemma, and the BER permits both of them!

The first solution is to provide for a special value for the length field, termed the *indefinite* form. This means that the length of the encoding is not known ahead of time and that the receiving process should look for a special sequence of octets to indicate the end of the value, termed the *end-of-contents*. Obviously, the BER must ensure that no encoding of an ASN.1 type will be able to generate this sequence as its value.

The second solution is to note that it is possible, although potentially inefficient, to make two passes through the data: the first to calculate the length, and the second to do the actual encoding.

If the length of the encoding is known, then this is termed the *definite* form. In this case, the length field consists of one or more octets encoding the integer-valued length. If the number of octets of the encoding is less than 128, then a single octet can be used to encode the length:

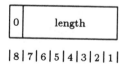

$|\,8\,|\,7\,|\,6\,|\,5\,|\,4\,|\,3\,|\,2\,|\,1\,|$

If the length is longer, then more than one octet is used. The first octet has the high-order bit (bit 8) set to one. The remaining seven bits comprise a number saying how many octets follow in the length field (anywhere from 1 to 126 octets).[5] The length is encoded using the unsigned integer representation found by concatenating the octets that follow the initial length octet. Since all eight bits are used, up to $126 * 8$ or 1008 bits may be used. Since $2^{1008} - 1$ is larger than the

---

[5]The value 127 for bits 7–1 is reserved for possible future extension.

address space on any computer likely to be built for quite some while, this is probably enough bits (a polite understatement). Even so, the BER still provides for future extensibility.

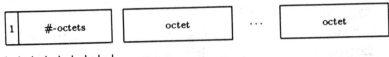

If an indefinite form encoding is used, then the length field consists of a single octet that has the high-order bit set to one and the remaining bits set to zero. After this octet, the value field is encoded, consisting of zero or more ASN.1 encodings. To mark the end of the encoding, the end-of-contents octets are sent.

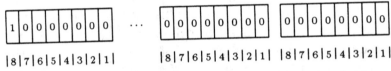

As can be seen, the end-of-contents octets are simply two zero-valued octets. This is equivalent to encoding an ASN.1 type with universal tag value 0 and no length. Since there is no ASN.1 type with this tag, the BER will never produce an ambiguous encoding. Of course, in order to interpret these octets correctly, the BER must know "where to start looking." For this reason, the indefinite length can only be used with constructed encodings. (This will become more clear as the discussion progresses.)

8.3.4   Value Field

We now consider how the ASN.1 types presented in Section 8.2.3 have their values encoded. The value field is encoded as zero or more *contents octets*.

Simple Types

The simple types provide the fundamental encodings that are used by the BER.

BOOLEAN

A **BOOLEAN** value is encoded as a single contents octet, always in primitive form. If the value is **FALSE**, then the contents octet has all bits set to zero. Otherwise, a **TRUE** value is encoded as any non-zero octet.

For example, the value **TRUE** might be encoded as:

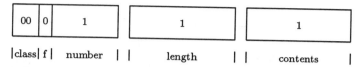

although any non-zero value may be placed in the contents octet.

INTEGER

An **INTEGER** value is encoded as one or more contents octets, always in primitive form. The value is encoded using a two's-complement encoding formed by concatenating the bits in the contents octets.

For example, the value 100 (decimal) is encoded as:

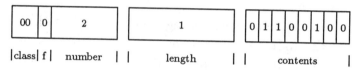

which, ignoring the bits with value zero, is:

$$2^6 + 2^5 + 2^2 = 64 + 32 + 4 = 100$$

REAL

A **REAL** value is encoded as zero or more contents octets, always in primitive form. If the value is zero, then there are no contents octets. This is the "easy" case. Otherwise, the first contents octet identifies the encoding scheme used (there are six or eight, depending on how one counts them).

If the most significant bit of this octet is set to one, then a binary encoding of the **REAL** value is used. If this bit is zero, then the next significant bit of this octet (bit 7) indicates whether a decimal encoding is used (the bit is set to zero) or whether the **REAL** value is a special number. In short:

Encoding	Bit 8	Bit 7
Binary	1	n/a
Decimal	0	0
Special	0	1

There are currently two special **REAL** values: plus- and minus-infinity. Both of these are encoded in the single contents octet:

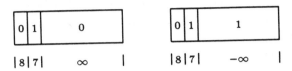

Other values for bits 6–1 are reserved for future addenda to the BER.

If a decimal encoding has been selected, then the remainder of the first contents octet (bits 6–1) defines the format used to represent the **REAL** value in the remaining contents octets. These representations are all taken from International Standard 6093, which defines various character formats for real-valued numbers. The addendum that defines how the BER encodes **REAL** values permits the use of one of three different encodings.

Otherwise, if a binary encoding has been selected, then the remainder of the first contents octet (bits 7–1) defines how the real value is encoded. Recall that any real number may be expressed as

$$mantissa * base^{exponent}$$

for integers *mantissa*, *base*, and *exponent*. In order to simplify the encoding process, the BER express the **REAL** value as:

$$S * N * 2^F * B^E$$

where:

- S is the *sign*, either plus- or minus-one;

- F is the *factor*, a "hack" used to shift the implied decimal point of the mantissa to an octet-boundary;

- N is the *number*, found by dividing the mantissa by $S * 2^F$;

- B is the *base*, limited to one of 2, 8, or 16 (a decimal base requires a decimal encoding); and,

- E is the *exponent*.

Thus, the binary encoding is:

The first contents octet encodes the information for S (if bit 7 is set to one, then the sign is negative) and the base of B:

Base	Bit 6	Bit 5
2	0	0
8	0	1
16	1	0

Other values for bits 6–5 are reserved for future addenda to the BER. Bits 4–3 determine the value for F, which ranges from 0 to 3. Finally, bits 2–1 indicate how many octets are used to encode the exponent:

Size of E	Bit 2	Bit 1
1	0	0
2	0	1
3	1	0

If both bits 2 and 1 are set to one, then the second contents octet indicates how many of the following octets are used to encode the exponent.

Immediately following the first (or second) contents octet is the exponent field, represented using the two's-complement notation. Following this, in however many octets remain in the contents octet, is the value N, also represented using the two's-complement notation.

The encoding for **REAL** values is defined in the Extensions Addendum.

With eight different ways of encoding floating point numbers, it should be obvious that the encoding scheme is designed to accommodate the needs of the sending process — it chooses the one most natural for it. Unfortunately, the receiving process now has to know about eight different decoding schemes. It appears that the authors of the Extensions Addendum seem to have forgot what canonical network representations are all about!

soap...

...soap

BIT STRING

A **BIT STRING** value is encoded as zero or more contents octets, in either primitive or constructed form. A primitive form encoding consists of an initial octet followed by octets encoding the bits in the **BIT STRING**. The initial octet indicates how many bits are unused in the final contents octet (and must take the value 0–7). If no bits are present in the **BIT STRING** value, then a single octet is encoded (the initial octet) with value 0.

First consider a primitive form encoding for the **BIT STRING** value '101'B:

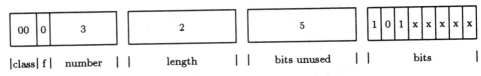

An 'x' in a bit position in a contents octet indicates that the setting is unimportant — that is, the BER does not interpret this information.

A constructed form encoding is simply a collection of smaller **BIT STRINGs**, each with their own tag, length, and value fields.[6] The number of tag field takes the value for **BIT STRING** (which needn't be identical to the number in the parent's tag field), the length field is set appropriately for the substring, and the value field consists of content octets, of which the first octet indicates, for this particular substring, how many bits are unused in the final contents octet.

---

[6]Constructed encodings may be recursive in nature. Thus, substrings may contain substrings, ad infinitum.

Now, consider a constructed form encoding for the same **BIT STRING** value:

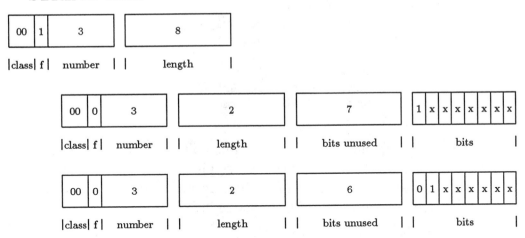

Since this is the first ASN.1 type we've seen that can have a constructed encoding, it should be pointed out that there is no significance as to where the BER divides the **BIT STRING** into substrings. It is merely a convenience for the sending process. Thus, the two encodings shown above have identical semantic meaning.

Observant readers are probably wondering how a **BIT STRING** value can have zero contents octets, given that an initial octet is required to indicate how many bits are unused in the last contents octet. The answer is simple: if a constructed encoding is used for the top-level **BIT STRING**, then there needn't be any contents octets before the end-of-contents octets:

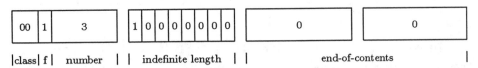

One question that arises when encoding a **BIT STRING** with named bits, such as

```
FunctionalUnits ::=
        BIT STRING {
            eventReportInvoker(0),
            eventReportPerformer(1),
            confirmedEventReportInvoker(2),
            confirmedEventReportPerformer(3),
            linkedReplyInvoker(4),
            linkedReplyPerformer(5),
            confirmedGetInvoker(6),
```

```
                    confirmedGetPerformer(7),
                    setInvoker(8),
                    setPerformer(9),
                    confirmedSetInvoker(10),
                    confirmedSetPerformer(11),
                    actionInvoker(12),
                    actionPerformer(13),
                    confirmedActionInvoker(14),
                    confirmedActionPerformer(15)
            }
```

is: what value should be assigned to named bits that are *not* encoded? One common interpretation is that these bits should be considered to be zero-valued. This can result in slightly more efficient encodings. For example, suppose we wish to encode

```
        eventsOnly FunctionalUnits ::=
            { eventReportInvoker, eventReportPerformer }
```

Only bits 0 and 1 are one-valued. The remainder are zero-valued. In order to encode all of the bits, including the 14 trailing zero-valued bits, three octets are required:

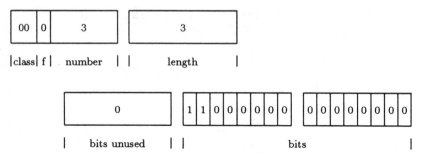

In contrast, if only enough of the **BIT STRING** is encoded to represent all one-valued bits, then one less octet is needed:

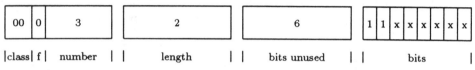

Unfortunately, the BER does not define the interpretation of the unrepresented bits in this encoding — nor does it prohibit such encodings! In the interest of being "conservative in what one generates," implementations should send zero-valued trailing bits; however, in the interest of being "liberal in what one accepts," implementations should also treat any missing bits as zero-valued.

Note that there is no concept of padding for bitstrings. That is, it is not possible to include non-signficant leading zero-valued bits to a value in order to force the significant bits to "line up" on a word boundary.

OCTET STRING

An **OCTET STRING** value is encoded as zero or more contents octets, in either primitive or constructed form. However, all of the contents octets are devoted to the value — unlike a **BIT STRING** encoding, there is no initial octet indicating how many bits are unused in the final octet — by definition, they must all be used!

Here is a primitive form encoding for the **OCTET STRING** value "anon:"

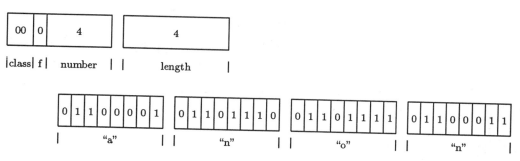

As with **BIT STRING** values, a constructed form of an **OCTET STRING** value is simply a collection of smaller **OCTET STRINGs**. Each substring will have its tag field take the value for **OCTET STRING**. To illustrate this point, here is a correct, but rather non-intuitive, constructor form encoding for IA5String:

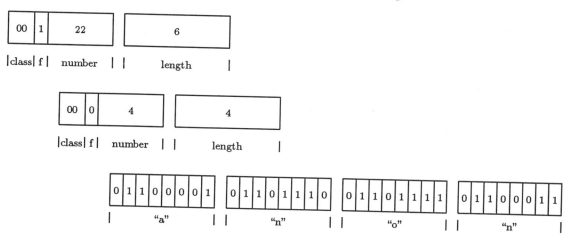

Earlier it was noted that ASN.1 defined several string types, such as **IA5String**, that were refinements of the **OCTET STRING**. How might these be encoded? For the moment, the answer is simple. Given the definition of **IA5String**:

```
IA5String ::=
    [UNIVERSAL 22]
        IMPLICIT OCTET STRING
```

The encoding rules for the **OCTET STRING** are used — except that a different tag is used:

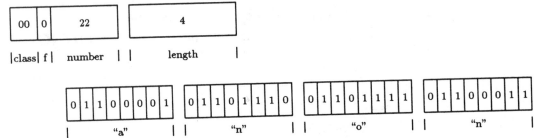

However, this is only true when the **IMPLICIT** clause is present. The actual rules used by the BER are somewhat more complicated. Section 8.3.4 on page 308 discusses how, in general, tagged types are encoded.

NULL

A **NULL** value is encoded as zero contents octets. It is syntatically similar to the end-of-contents octets, but it has a different tag:

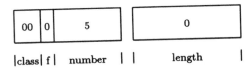

Object Types

The two object types have encodings very similar to the other simple types.

OBJECT IDENTIFIER

An **OBJECT IDENTIFIER** value is encoded as one or more contents octets, always in primitive form.

Recall that an **OBJECT IDENTIFIER** is a sequence of non-negative integer values. The BER mandates certain characteristics of any **OBJECT IDENTIFIER** it encodes: the first element must take the value 0, 1, or 2; and, the second element must take a value less than 40 if the first element is 0 or 1. The reason for these limitations are administrative. Recall that exactly three subordinates to the root note have been defined, coincidentally having values 0, 1, or 2. Since naming authority for these subordinates reside with the ISO and the CCITT, they are responsible for ensuring that any immediate subordinates are not assigned a number greater than 39.

For the purposes of encoding using the BER:

- the first two elements in the sequence form a *sub-identifier* with the value $X * 40 + Y$, where X is the value of the first element, and Y is the value of the second element; and,

- each element following in the sequence also forms a *sub-identifier* with a value equal to that element's value.

For example, the **OBJECT IDENTIFIER**

    { 1 0 8571 5 1 }

consists of four sub-identifiers: 40 ($40 * 1 + 0$), 8571, 5, and 1.

Each sub-identifier is encoded using the unsigned representation in one or more octets. However, the most significant bit of each octet is set to one if another octet follows. Thus, the sub-identifier is represented by concatenating one or more 7–bit values together and treating the resulting string of bits as an unsigned number. In order to ensure a compact encoding, the leading octet may not have bit 8 set to one and all the remaining bits set to zero (i.e., the first seven octets of the encoding must have a non-zero value).

Hence, in order to encode

    { 1 0 8571 5 1 }

four numbers, 40, 8571, 5, and 1 must be encoded. Three of these can be represented in seven or fewer bits, and therefore each can be encoded in a single octet. The other, 8571, requires 14 bits, and hence is encoded using two octets. (If 15 bits had been required to encode the sub-identifier using the unsigned representation, then three octets would be needed for the encoding, as a bit in each octet indicates if another octet is used.)

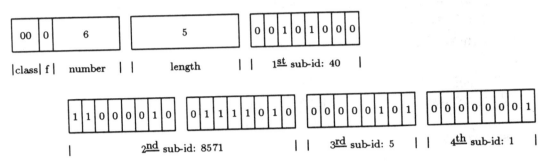

OBJECT DESCRIPTOR

An **OBJECT DESCRIPTOR** value is encoded according to its definition:

```
ObjectDescriptor ::=
     [UNIVERSAL 7]
          IMPLICIT GraphicString
```

which in turn is defined as:

```
GraphicString ::=
     [UNIVERSAL 25]
          IMPLICIT OCTET STRING
```

so the encoding rules for the **OCTET STRING** are used — except that an encoding of an **OBJECT DESCRIPTOR** uses a different tag (universal tag 7 instead of universal tag 4).

Constructor Types

As the ASN.1 language defined complex types in terms of combining simple types with constructors, so the BER encodes complex types by encoding a constructor whose value portion consists of encodings of simpler types.

The complexity in generating an encoding of the constructor types lies in knowing what value to use for the length field. This was one of the key reasons that the notation of an indefinite length was developed — when encoding a constructor type, the sending process generates the tag and length fields (using the indefinite length), generates the encoding for each element of the constructor type, and then generates the end-of-contents octets to "wrap things up." This mechanism allows the sending process to be vastly simplified at the expense of the receiving process, which must now "know how to deal with such things."

SEQUENCE

A **SEQUENCE** value is encoded as zero or more contents octets, always in constructed form. Basically, the tag and length fields are generated. Then, for each element present in the **SEQUENCE**, the BER is recursively applied to those elements.

Note that an element need not be encoded if it is **OPTIONAL**, or if it has the same value as its **DEFAULT**. Regardless, the order of the encodings must match the order that the elements were defined in the ASN.1 module for this type. (Elements of a **SEQUENCE** are distinguished by their positions, not their tags. Of course, in the presence of **OPTIONAL** or **DEFAULT** elements, examination of the tagging information is still necessary to avoid ambiguity.) If none of the elements of a **SEQUENCE** are present, then no contents octets are encoded.

Consider an encoding of:

```
VarBind ::=
    SEQUENCE {
        name
            ObjectName,

        value
            ObjectSyntax
    }
```

Without knowing what types `ObjectName` and `ObjectSyntax` are, the encoding for `VarBind` must look something like this:

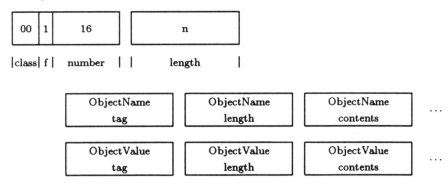

if the definite length is used, or

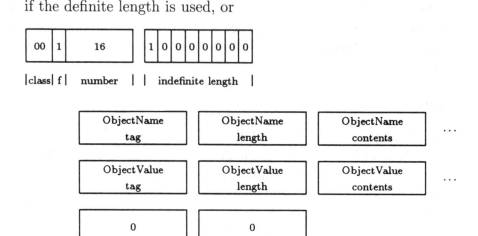

if the indefinite length is used.

SEQUENCE OF

A **SEQUENCE OF** value is encoded identically to a **SEQUENCE** value; even the tags are the same. Note that the tags of the elements are truly redundant here. However, they must be encoded to maintain the TLV format.

SET

A **SET** value is encoded similarly to a **SEQUENCE** value with two exceptions: first, a different tag is used; and, second, since tags, not ordering, distinguishes the members of a **SET**, the members may be encoded in *any* order when the BER is applied.

SET OF

A **SET OF** value is encoded identically to a **SET** value; even the tags are the same.

Tagged Types

Earlier it was noted how ASN.1 definitions of the form:

```
SomeType ::=
    [tag]
        IMPLICIT OtherType
```

were encoded using whatever rules were appropriate for the type OtherType, the difference being that a new value was used in the tag field.

This is straightforward, but leads us to consider how a definition of the form

```
SomeType ::=
    [tag]
        OtherType
```

might be encoded (there is no **IMPLICIT** keyword). The answer is that a tagged definition of this form is treated as a constructor analogous to:

```
SomeType ::=
    [tag]
        IMPLICIT SEQUENCE {
            OtherType
        }
```

The idea is that the tagging information of OtherType is retained intact, being contained within another type that has the new tag. Although the BER does not state the encoding rules for tagged types in this fashion, using this conceptualization tends to make the encoding rules appear much more intuitive.

Thus, an encoding of:

```
SomeType ::=
    [APPLICATION 0]
        OtherType
```

always looks something like this:

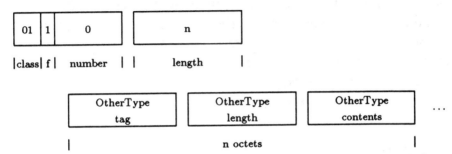

Although the example here does not show use of the indefinite length, this is permitted, as it would be with any type that could be encoded using the constructed form.

Although use of the **IMPLICIT** keyword leads to more compact encodings, there is a price. Tagging information is vital when less knowledgeable (more general) software is used to examine ASN.1 traffic. For example, the OSI Directory, briefly introduced in Section 6.6.1 on page 148, allows users to manipulate attributes for the objects stored therein. The abstract syntax of some of the attributes are pre-defined, such as `presentationAddress`. However, users of the Directory may be permitted to define new attributes using ASN.1. Two related problems might arise from this.

First, another user, perusing the Directory with a *browser* might come upon the new attribute. Since the user's browsing program doesn't know about the ASN.1 definition of the attribute, it must rely on the typing information contained in the tag in order to present this information to the user. For example, a **PrintableString** might be simply printed on the user's terminal without further interpretation. But, when displaying an **OBJECT IDENTIFIER**, a table of "human readable strings" (e.g., the corresponding **OBJECT DESCRIPTOR**) might be consulted first. If an entry was found, then the string, rather than the **OBJECT IDENTIFIER** would be displayed. If the actual typing information is masked by use of the **IMPLICIT** keyword, then the browser cannot perform this function on the data in question.

This is but a simple example of the loss of information. In general, the loss of information is catastrophic: without tagging information it is difficult or impossible to have a program manipulate the information.

Second, since the Directory has built-in knowledge of how to perform certain operations on numerous types, if the **IMPLICIT** keyword is used then the Directory is unable to perform these operations on the new types. For example, the Directory has a comparison operation. It "knows" how to compare to ASN.1 types and how to determine whether they are "equal" in some sense. If the actual typing information is masked by use of the **IMPLICIT** keyword, then the Directory cannot perform this function on the data in question.

Meta Types

Since the meta types transcend the ASN.1 simple and constructor types, it should not be surprising that the BER treats these types specially.

CHOICE

A **CHOICE** value is encoded identically to whichever **CHOICE** is present. Recalling a previous example:

```
TimeOfDay ::=
    CHOICE {
        actual-value
            UTCTime,

        not-available
            NULL
    }

unixEpoch TimeOfDay ::=
    { actual-value "700101000000Z" }

unknownTime TimeOfDay ::=
    { not-available NULL }
```

if the BER is applied to the value denoted by `unixEpoch`, then an encoding for an **OCTET STRING** value is used (since `UTCTime` is an **IMPLICIT OCTET STRING**); otherwise, if the BER is applied to the value denoted by `unknownTime`, then an encoding for a **NULL** value is used.

Note that since the members of a **CHOICE** are required to have unique tags in the ASN.1 language, use of the BER will always result in unambiguous encodings.

ANY

An **ANY** value is encoded identically to whatever ASN.1 type is present. This may seem like a gratuitous statement — but it is strictly accurate.

The sending process must somehow "know" what kind of ASN.1 type it is encoding. It must then apply the appropriate part of the BER to generate the encoding. The receiving process need only apply the BER, and it will correctly decode the corresponding ASN.1 value. As noted earlier, in order for the receiving process to interpret this information correctly, some prior information is necessary.

Interpreting the encoding to generate an ASN.1 value is relatively simple — the difficult part is doing something meaningful with the resulting information.

EXTERNAL

An **EXTERNAL** value is encoded according to its definition as shown on page 255. Basically, a **SEQUENCE** value is encoded that possibly contains an **OBJECT IDENTIFIER** value, an **INTEGER** value, and a **OBJECT DESCRIPTOR** value. Following this, one of three different values is present, distinguished by the given tags.

8.3.5 The Controversy of TLV encodings

Although the BER generates compact encodings, it is not necessarily efficient in terms of processing. In fact, other encoding mechanisms are often 20 times (or more) faster than using the BER. Whilst these mechanisms are not used to encode ASN.1 data types, they nonetheless exist in highly useful, well deployed systems.

The most notable example of such a system is the Network File System (NFS), which provides a transparent file service between machines of different manufacture. The NFS is implemented on a wide-range of platforms and is quite popular as the de facto standard for file-sharing in the 80's, and most likely the 90's as well. To encode messages among different machines, the NFS uses the *External Data Representation* (XDR) [SMI86a]. Unlike the BER, the XDR is optimized for the most common existing machine architectures. As such, although unable to represent *directly* the full range of data types that can be described using ASN.1, the XDR is more than adequate for many of today's existing applications.

The discussion now turns to consider the fundamental basis of TLV encodings to see whether their use is worth the price. (The article [CPart88] presents a more detailed analysis of the BER and the XDR.)

Tags

In a fully general system, tags are useful for discriminating among different data types. However, most real systems usually expect only a single data type at any given instant. Furthermore, when used with remote procedure calls, a common way of constructing distributed systems (described in Section 10.4 on page 420), typing information is usually carried outside of the encoding of the data. As such, in many systems, the tag used by the BER is redundant.

Tags have two disadvantages associated with them: first, even with minimal-length encodings, encoding a tag still takes up space; and, second, whilst space-efficient, the minimal-length encodings used by the BER for tags are computationally expensive. Full support of variable-length encodings require a fair bit of error checking. Thus, *if* tags really aren't needed to disambiguate between data types, *then* smaller, faster encodings can be produced.

In response, it should be noted that more complex data types, such as those involving **CHOICEs** or constructor types with **OPTIONAL** elements, require a method for avoiding ambiguity. In these cases, tags are required. It should be clear that an explicit trade-off is occurring: some encodings (the simple ones) are made slower and longer, so that the full generality of the BER may be applied to produce unambiguous encodings of the more complicated data types.

At this point, opponents of the BER might counter-argue that with a little careful pruning of ASN.1's descriptive capabilities, then tags could be eliminated all around. This pruning would involve techniques such as encoding all members of a **SET** in the order in which they are defined in the ASN.1 description of the data type. In effect, from the encoding perspective, every **SET** becomes a **SEQUENCE**, although from the semantic perspective, the ordering of the elements remains unimportant.

Lengths

Variable-length encodings are inefficient. First, use of the indefinite length form is inherently problematic for the receiving process. For example, the receiving process cannot allocate a fixed-size buffer for incoming data, since it never knows the actual length of the encoding until all of it has been received. Furthermore, it forces the receiving process to use a recursive algorithm that implements the BER. Although both modern computers and programming languages support recursion, this can result in significantly less efficient implementations.

(Again, by providing for extensive generality, efficiency takes a "big hit.")

To understand the gravity of this argument, recall the earlier discussion of the Simple Network Management Protocol. The SNMP uses very simple ASN.1 definitions to describe the messages it exchanges. In fact, rather than designing a highly-optimized data type for each protocol message, a common template is used. If a protocol message doesn't use a field in that template, then the value of that field is ignored by the receiving process. Although clearly a violation of the spirit of ASN.1, this permits highly efficient implementations (in terms of both time and space). For network management, which is commonly used for fire-fighting in the network, there simply isn't time to play games; efficiency is the goal.

Second, variable-length encodings have a profound influence when the value portion is encoded. Here's why: most machine architectures require that common data types, such as integer quantities, obey *alignment* rules. For example, a particular hardware platform might require that all integer quantities begin on even-numbered addresses. (Some platforms don't care, others are more restrictive.)

As a result, when decoding a quantity using the BER, all values must be handled an octet at a time — it is usually not possible to use more efficient word or long-word instructions that are capable of moving two, four, or eight octets at a time. The reason is simple: the variable-length nature of the BER usually results in values being encoded at addresses (e.g., odd-numbered ones) that prevent this more efficient operation. The XDR avoids this complexity and inefficiency by using fixed-length, word-aligned blocks. All quantities are encoded in blocks that are multiples of 4 octets. Whilst this is space-inefficient for Boolean quantities, it ensures that the more efficient hardware instructions may be used. (Of course, since the XDR doesn't use tags, the space inefficiency argument is cancelled!)

At this point, proponents of the BER might counter-argue that fixed-length encodings are short-sighted: 4 octets might be enough to represent the integer quantities used by today's machines, but what about the new architectures that will be introduced? The only defense against this argument is to note that the limitation of 4 octets for integer quantities is a pragmatic one. Consider that many implementations of the BER are simply incapable of handling integer quantities larger than the hardware representation on which they are realized. As such, if a mismatch occurs, then an exception of some sort is raised. Although this defeats the purpose of the BER, it reflects a simple reality — few (if any) implementations are able to deal with arbitrary precision integers. Thus, proponents of fixed-length encodings believe that it is naive to argue that fixed-length encodings are short-sighted. Even when using the BER, everything is going break when machines using 8–octet integers are commonplace!

Values

Finally, the encodings of the commonly used data types, most notably the **INTEGERs**, are amazingly inefficient. Although it is certainly forward-thinking to be able to encode values of arbitrary precision, it is not clear if the real applications found in useful systems will need such generality.

Consider: many computers, even those with different architectures, use surprisingly similar hardware representations for integer quantities. But, no computer existing uses the variable-length representation of the BER **INTEGER** encoding. The resulting inefficiency when using the BER on real machines is, at best, amusing.

When the XDR encodes an integer quantity, it does so using a fixed-length field (noted earlier) and uses a simple two's-complement encoding (which, by some strange coincidence, is identical to the hardware representation used by the vendor that defined the XDR). As such, in many cases, an integer quantity may be encoded using a *single* machine instruction! On other platforms, no more than four machine instructions need be used.

The BER is motivated to provide a consistent format that is naturally recursive. It has excellent generality at the expense of making the individual encodings less than optimal:

the hours are good, but the actual minutes are pretty lousy.

However, because of the great disparity between the encodings used by the BER and the hardware representations in common use, many wonder if the the generalities of ASN.1 and the BER simply cost too much to be deployed in real systems that make efficient use of the network and offer reasonable response time.

8.3.6   An Example

The discussion now turns to an example that shows how the BER may
be applied to the data types defined in the ASN.1 fragment shown in
Figure 8.3.

Consider the ASN.1 value:

```
example Message ::=
    {
        version version-1,
        community "public",
        data {
            get-response {
                request-id 17,
                error-status noError,
                error-index 0,
                variable-bindings {
                    {
                        name 1.3.6.1.2.1.1.1.1.0,
                        value {
                            simple {
                                string "unix"
                            }
                        }
                    }
                }
            }
        }
    }
```

This value was printed by a program that had access to the definition for the Message data type. It is perhaps the most symbolic
representation for this ASN.1 value. For example, whenever possible,
the symbolic labels, rather than the actual values, are used for all of
the primitive types (e.g., for the version field). Furthermore, note
how the nested **CHOICE** for the value field is enumerated. (The
ObjectSyntax type is defined in Figure 8.2 which starts on page 285).

RFC1067−SNMP **DEFINITIONS** ::= **BEGIN**

IMPORTS   ObjectName, ObjectSyntax, NetworkAddress,
                IpAddress, TimeTicks
                    FROM RFC1065−SMI;

−− *top−level message*

Message ::=
        SEQUENCE {
            version   −− *version−1 for this RFC*   10
                INTEGER {
                    version−1(0)
                },

            community   −− *community name*
                OCTET STRING,

            data   −− *e.g., PDUs if trivial*
                −−* *ANY* *−−   −− *authentication is being used*   20
                PDUs
        }

−− *protocol data units*

PDUs ::=
        CHOICE {
            get−request
                GetRequest−PDU,

                                                                             30
            get−next−request
                GetNextRequest−PDU,

            get−response
                GetResponse−PDU,

            set−request
                SetRequest−PDU,

            trap   40
                Trap−PDU
        }

...

GetResponse−PDU ::=
    [1]
        IMPLICIT PDU

...
                                                                             50

Figure 8.3: ASN.1 Fragment of the SNMP Definition

...

```
PDU ::=
      SEQUENCE {
          request−id
              INTEGER,

          error−status                −− sometimes ignored
                 INTEGER {                                                    10
                    noError(0),
                    tooBig(1),
                    noSuchName(2),
                    badValue(3),
                    readOnly(4)
                 },

          error−index                 −− sometimes ignored
                 INTEGER,

          variable−bindings           −− values are sometimes ignored        20
                 VarBindList
      }

...

−− variable bindings

VarBind ::=
      SEQUENCE {                                                             30
          name
              ObjectName,

          value
              ObjectSyntax
      }

VarBindList ::=
      SEQUENCE OF
          VarBind                                                           40

...

END
```

Figure 8.3: ASN.1 Fragment of the SNMP Definition (cont.)

In generating an encoding using the BER for this value, the first step (conceptually) is to view the value as being composed of ASN.1 simple and constructor types:

```
{
    0,
    "public",
    [1] {
        17,
        0,
        0,
        {
            {
                1.3.6.1.2.1.1.1.1.0,
                "unix"
            }
        }
    }
}
```

This gives a more concrete view of the data values to be encoded.

The next step is actually to construct the encoding. For the purposes of brevity, only the definite form length encoding will be used.

A `Message` consists of three parts. The tag field is easy to generate. By scanning the components of the message, and determining their lengths, it is determined that 43 octets will be needed for the value portion.[7] Thus, the first two octets of the encoding are as follows:

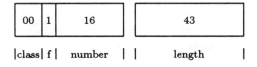

Next, the version number, an **INTEGER**, is encoded:

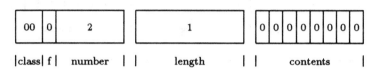

---

[7]A simple recursive algorithm may be used to determine this. Actually, there are many possible implementation strategies that might be used, e.g., generating the value field first and then generating the tag and length fields.

Following this, the community name, an **OCTET STRING**, is encoded:

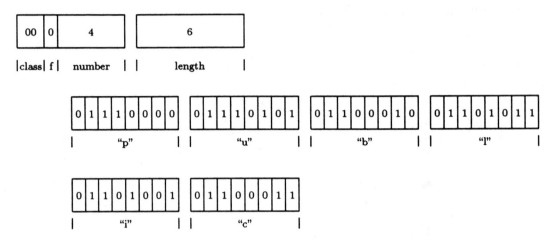

Following this, an instance of the PDUs data type is encoded. Since this is **CHOICE**, whichever data is specified by the value is encoded instead: in this case, an instance of the GetResponse-PDU. This is an **IMPLICITly** tagged type, so in turn, a PDU value is encoded, but with a different tag. A PDU data type is a **SEQUENCE**, so we begin by generating the tag and length fields:

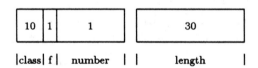

Next, the request identifier, error status, and error index fields are encoded. All three of these are integers:

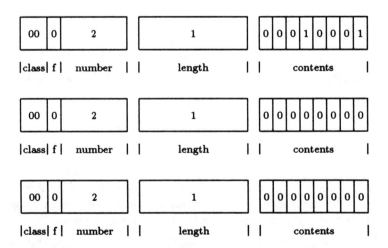

Finally, the variable bindings, a **SEQUENCE OF** value, is encoded. Once again, the tag and length fields are generated:

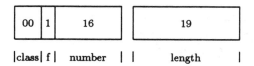

Each element of the **SEQUENCE OF** value is a VarBind value, which is a **SEQUENCE**. Since there is only one element in the **SEQUENCE OF**, only one such value need be encoded. As usual, the tag and length fields are generated:

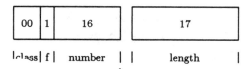

Finally, the components of the VarBind value are generated, starting with an ObjectName value. This is an **OBJECT IDENTIFIER** with value 1.3.6.1.2.1.1.1.1.0, having 9 sub-identifiers:

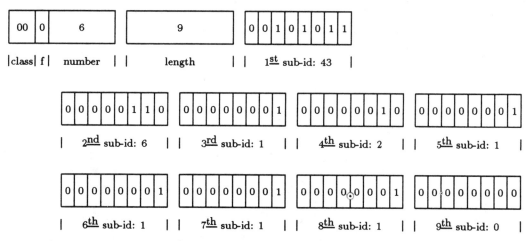

This is followed with an ObjectValue value, which is an **OCTET STRING**:

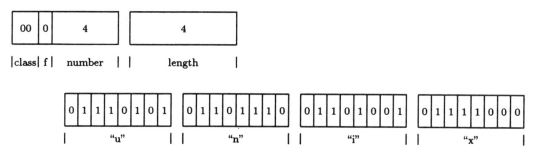

Putting this all together, here are the 45 octets that are generated (in hexadecimal):

```
30 2b
    02 01 00
    04 06 70 75 62 6c 69 63
    a1 1e
        02 01 11
        02 01 00
        02 01 00
        30 13
            30 11
                06 09 2b 06 01 02 01 01 01 01 00
                04 04 75 6e 69 78 00
```

8.4   An Implementation

Finally, the discussion closes with a look at an implementation of ASN.1 and the Basic Encoding Rules. As with the other chapters in Part III, the implementational framework of the ISO Development Environment (ISODE) is examined. As usual, the discussion that follows is heavily oriented towards those familiar with the *C* programming language and the UNIX operating system.

In the ISODE, the `psap` library is responsible for implementing the internal ASN.1 mechanisms and the BER. In addition, several ASN.1 compilers are available. The discussion will focus on two of these. This description of ISODE's ASN.1 service is only a high-level overview. It is described in considerable detail in *Volume 1: Application Services* and *Volume 4: The Applications Cookbook* of the ISODE User's Manual[MRose89].

The ISODE implementation of ASN.1 is fairly complete: the ASN.1 compilers have a few limitations, which are cited below.

8.4.1   Presentation Elements

The fundamental concept behind ISODE's ASN.1 facilities is that of a *presentation element* (PE). A PE is capable of representing any ASN.1 object in a machine-independent form. All of the ASN.1 tools in the ISODE either manipulate presentation elements directly, or they generate programs that perform the manipulation.

From a high-level perspective, a PE is nothing more than a modestly complex *C* structure that represents an ASN.1 value as either a string of octets or bits (primitive types) or as a linked list of other presentation elements (constructor types). Layered on top of this are numerous routines that convert between PEs and the data structures used by a target architecture. These routines are usually accessed by code generated by the two ASN.1 compilers that are described below.

From the programmer's viewpoint, *C* data structures, such as int's are used. At some point, these are converted to PEs just prior to being sent on the network.

Code	Reason
PS_ERR_IO	I/O error
PE_ERR_OVER	Overflow
PE_ERR_NMEM	Out of memory
PE_ERR_BIT	No such bit
PE_ERR_UTCT	Malformed universal timestring
PE_ERR_GENT	Malformed generalized timestring
PE_ERR_MBER	No such member
PE_ERR_PRIM	Not a primitive form
PE_ERR_CONS	Not a constructor form
PE_ERR_TYPE	Class/ID mismatch in constructor
PE_ERR_OID	Malformed object identifier
PE_ERR_BITS	Malformed bitstring

Table 8.2: ISODE Presentation Element Failure Codes

For example, a PE corresponding to an **INTEGER** may be created by calling the routine num2prim:

```
PE      num2prim (i, class, id)
int     i;
PElementClass class;
PElementID   id;
```

This routine dynamically allocates a presentation element and then uses the BER to encode the value taken from the parameter i. The ASN.1 tag is taken from the parameters class and id.

Later on, when encodings are received from the network, they are converted from PEs back to *C* data structures.

For example, an **INTEGER** value may be extracted from a PE by calling the routine prim2num:

```
int     prim2num (pe)
PE      pe;
```

If a conversion routine encounters an error, then it returns a distinguished value, and a field in the presentation element gives the reason for the failure. The list of reasons is shown in Table 8.2.

Obviously, use of presentation elements introduces an inherent inefficiency: at some point two (or perhaps three) copies of data reside in the system. Further, the current implementation of presentation elements is memory-resident. This means that large ASN.1 structures, when converted to and from PEs, must remain entirely in memory. However, the generality is substantial; by using a common internal form, many tools can be built that manipulate them. This encourages reuse and rapid prototyping: by having one set of well-debugged routines that manipulate PEs, developers focus their time on other, higher-level, issues.

8.4.2 Presentation Streams

Hand in glove with the PE is the *presentation stream* (PS). A PS is used to map presentation elements to/from different input-output abstractions such as:

- in-core buffers;

- UNIX files;

- OSI services, such as the session service; and,

- non-OSI services, which permit reading and writing.

A presentation stream is a modestly complex C structure. Layered on top of this are two sets of routines: a uniform interface, termed the *front-end*; and, several sets of domain-specific routines, each knowledgeable about a particular communications domain. These are termed *back ends*. The purpose of the PS abstraction is to allow higher-layer software to read or write presentation elements without regard to the communication mechanisms used to transmit the data.

This flexibility is useful, both for building variant services (such as the lightweight presentation protocol introduced in Section 6.4.3 on page 142), and for debugging purposes, such as maintaining a communications trace.

To read a presentation element from a presentation stream, the routine ps2pe is used:

```
PE      ps2pe (ps)
PS      ps;
```

If an error occurs as the presentation element is being built, a distinguished value, NULLPE, is returned and a field in the presentation stream gives the reason for the failure. The list of reasons is shown in Table 8.3.

PS_ERR_OVERID	Overflow in ID
PS_ERR_OVERLEN	Overflow in length
PS_ERR_NMEM	Out of memory
PS_ERR_EOF	End of file
PS_ERR_EOFID	End of file reading extended ID
PS_ERR_EOFLEN	End of file reading extended length
PS_ERR_LEN	Length mismatch
PS_ERR_TRNC	Truncated
PS_ERR_INDF	Indefinite length in primitive form
PS_ERR_IO	I/O error

Table 8.3: ISODE Presentation Stream Failure Codes

The inverse operation, writing a presentation element to a presentation stream is accomplished by the routine pe2ps:

```
int      pe2ps (ps, pe)
PS       ps;
PE       pe;
```

Although the internal mechanisms of presentation streams are rather mundane, there is one little secret to be told. Earlier it was noted that a PE was little more than a structure containing an octet string or a linked list of other PEs. To simplify the task of presentation streams, it should be noted that PEs actually contain BER encodings. Routines such as int2prim and prim2int are responsible for encoding and decoding (respectively) primitive data types into C structures. Thus, when a BER encoding is generated using a presentation stream, a two-step process is used:

1. First, the PE is examined and the length of the encoding determined:

    (a) if the PE contains an octet string, the length is determined from examination;

    (b) otherwise, the linked list of PEs is examined, and the length recursively calculated.

2. Second, the PE is copied to the back end:

(a) if the PE contains an octet string, the encoding is simply copied;

(b) otherwise, the linked-list of PEs is copied recursively.

The only subtlety to this algorithm is that the tag and length values aren't kept in the octet strings; instead, they are generated dynamically.

8.4.3   An ASN.1 Structure Generator

The ISODE views use of ASN.1 to be a critical activity of the future. Towards this goal, it provides several automatic tools that manipulate ASN.1 definitions. The *posy* program is responsible for reading an ASN.1 module and producing:

- a corresponding set of *C* structures; and,

- an augmented ASN.1 module that relates the *C* structures to their ASN.1 counterparts.

The former is used by human programmers when writing programs that use the ASN.1 definitions in the module. The latter is supplied to another ASN.1 compiler that is tasked with writing a program to generate routines automatically that perform conversion between the two forms.

The name *posy* stands for the P̲epy O̲ptional S̲tructure-generator (Y̲ACC-based), and is probably only of historical interest (*pepy* is the name of the ASN.1 compiler that reads the augmented ASN.1 module, and *yacc*, as noted earlier, is a compiler-compiler).

For purposes of the discussion, our interest is in the *C* structures generated by *posy*. An exhaustive list of the rules and heuristics, is prohibitive. Instead, the discussion considers a few examples.

Simple Types

A commonly used simple type, an **INTEGER**, maps to the *C* int. If additional refinements are present, these are reflected accordingly. Consider the earlier definition found in Figure 8.3:

```
PDU ::=
    SEQUENCE {
```

```
            . . .

                      error-status
                          INTEGER {
                              noError(0),
                              tooBig(1),
                              noSuchName(2),
                              badValue(3),
                              readOnly(4),
                          },
            . . .

                }
```

This might result in the following definition from *posy*:

```
    struct type_SNMP_PDU {

        . . .

          int     error__status;
    #define int_SNMP_error__status_noError 0
    #define int_SNMP_error__status_tooBig 1
    #define int_SNMP_error__status_noSuchName 2
    #define int_SNMP_error__status_badValue 3
    #define int_SNMP_error__status_readOnly 4

        . . .

    };
```

There are several things to be observed from this definition: first, the names of structures are chosen, whenever possible, from the commentary tags in the ASN.1 specification. Second, whilst programmers are good at choosing short, unambiguous names, computer programs aren't. As such, when names are generated, *posy* errs on the side of safety by using an algorithm that produces names that are probably a bit long, but are thought to be unambiguous. To overcome this limitation, *posy* has a method for allowing the programmer choose the names of most of the structures that it generates.

Constructor Types

A constructor type, such as a **SEQUENCE**, maps to a C struct. Again, returning to the ASN.1 fragment found in Figure 8.3:

```
VarBind ::=
        SEQUENCE {
            name
                ObjectName,

            value
                ObjectSyntax
        }
```

This might result in the following definition from *posy*:

```
struct type_SNMP_VarBind {
    struct type_SMI_ObjectName *name;

    struct type_SMI_ObjectSyntax *value;
};
```

which includes pointers to other structures. Note that these structures needn't be defined by *posy*, providing that the definitions follow *posy*'s naming conventions.

Heuristics

There are many possible mappings from ASN.1 onto C. Some of these are straightforward and occur without loss of information. Others are not so clearly understood.

For example, support of the **DEFAULT** and **OPTIONAL** keywords for simple types is straightforward. However, for constructor types, extensive symbol-table management and run-time support is required. The authors of *posy*, Julian P. Onions of the University of Nottingham, and the author of this book, decided that it was too much work to "get right." Thus, *posy* will generate code that handles simple types correctly. For constructor types, a simple heuristic is used. With *posy*, references to all constructors map to a pointer to a C structure. If the pointer takes the value NULL, then this is interpreted to mean that the corresponding ASN.1 value is either the **DEFAULT** value or is not present (**OPTIONAL**).

Limitations

The lack of adequate symbol-table facilities points out one of many deficiencies with *posy*. In general, all of the ASN.1 compilers in the ISODE share the same front-end. As such, they share many of the same limitations.

The most interesting problems are:

Modules: The import/export facilities are rather limited. As a rule, only sketchy information is known about data types defined in other modules. In practice, the choice of a consistent naming and access policy in *posy* has obscured this problem quite well.

VALUEs: Although the full ASN.1 value syntax can be parsed, outside of **BOOLEAN** and **INTEGER** values, there is no effective use of these values in a symbol table. (In other words, the syntax is recognized but otherwise ignored.)

MACROs: Because all of the ISODE's ASN.1 compilers are based on a compile-time model, the macro syntax (both the definition of macros and their use) is not recognized. If someone wants to write an ASN.1 compiler that knows about a particular set of macros, then the front-end for that compiler is duly modified (by hand).

Despite these limitations, *posy* has proven to be a powerful tool in automating a large part of ASN.1 handling.

8.4.4   An ASN.1 Parser

The *pepy* program is responsible for generating and interpreting ASN.1 encodings. It reads an augmented ASN.1 module describing the mappings between *C* structures and their ASN.1 counterparts and produces *C* code fragments that map between the two. In addition, *pepy* can also generate pretty-printers for ASN.1 values that correspond to the data types in the ASN.1 module.

The name *pepy* stands for the Presentation Element Parser (YACC-based), and is probably not of historical interest (the original *pepy* only parsed ASN.1 objects).

Again, an exhaustive list of the rules used by *pepy* is prohibitive. Instead, the discussion considers a few examples.

Simple Types

To generate an encoder, an input to *pepy* might look like this:

```
PDU [[P struct type_SNMP_PDU *]] ::=
    SEQUENCE {

...


        error-status
            INTEGER
            [[i parm -> error__status ]]
            {
                noError(0),
                tooBig(1),
                noSuchName(2),
                badValue(3),
                readOnly(4)
            },

...

    }
```

This tells *pepy* to generate a *C* routine that looks something like the following:

```
int     encode_SNMP_PDU (..., parm)
...
struct type_SNMP_PDU *parm;
{
    PE  pe,
        p;

    /* allocate PE for this data type */

    pe = pe_alloc (PE_CLASS_UNIV, PE_FORM_CONS, PE_CONS_SEQ);

    /* elements are encoded here... */

    return OK;
}
```

Next, when encoding the `error-status` field, the value

```
parm -> error__status
```

should be used. In response, *pepy* will generate something like this:

```
   . . .

        if ((p = int2prim (parm -> error__status)) == NULLPE)
            error (...);

        /* append PE to sequence */

        seq_add (pe, p, -1);

   . . .
```

which does the necessary conversion and then adds the resulting presentation element to the **SEQUENCE** being built.

Decoders are generated in an inverted fashion: first `prim2int` would be called and the resulting value placed in the variable

```
      parm -> error__status
```

Constructor Types

For constructor types, the *pepy* program generates recursive-descent routines: building an encoder or decoder for a constructor type consists mainly of calling other routines. Thus,

```
      VarBind [[P struct type_SNMP_VarBind *]] ::=
          SEQUENCE {
              name
                  SMI.ObjectName
                  [[p parm -> name ]],

              value
                  SMI.ObjectSyntax
                  [[p parm -> value ]]
          }
```

causes *pepy* to produce something like this:

```
      int     encode_SNMP_Varbind (..., parm)
      . . .
      struct type_SNMP_VarBind *parm;
      {
          . . .
```

```
    if (encode_SMI_ObjectName (p, ..., parm -> name) == NOTOK)
        error (...);
    seq_add (pe, p, -1);

    if (encode_SMI_ObjectSyntax (p, ..., parm -> value)
            == NOTOK)
        error (...);
    seq_add (pe, p, -1);

    return OK;
}
```

Limitations

In addition to the front-end limitations discussed earlier, *pepy* does not check to ensure that subtyping constraints are being honored. This responsibility is left to the programmer. Once again, Julian and I decided that the pain was too severe for the possible advantages (although subtyping is a useful notational convenience, we remain unconvinced that it is of practical use). As such, *pepy* will correctly recognize subtype specifications, but will otherwise ignore them.

The primary limitation of *pepy* is that it produces a lot of *C* code, owing to the recursive-descent nature of the routines it generates. In contrast, programs like *yacc* generate table-driven parsers that are much more space-efficient. (The code generated by *pepy*, although not time optimized for execution, is, nevertheless, reasonably fast.)

For example, many implementors of the SNMP use an entirely different technology: they hand-code their ASN.1 support. Whilst optimal in terms of both code size and encoding time, this approach lacks generality (to say the least). Once the programmer time is invested, then the systems perform quite well. Again to quote Jeffrey Case:

> *That dog will hunt!*

As such, these implementors visibly flinch whenever *pepy* is mentioned in polite conversation!

The authors of *pepy*, Julian Onions and myself, are painfully aware of *pepy*'s limitations, and are desperate to retire it. As of the end of 1988, there were no other candidates available — certainly none as capable. This statement is not made lightly: *pepy* has a large number of bells and whistles. It does a lot of useful work. Before it is retired, its successor must be at least as capable.

However, it should be noted that both *pepy* and *posy* started out as rather simple programs with many limitations. Julian has been tireless both in extending the range of ASN.1 semantics supported by these compilers, and in hardening them for the myriad special cases that arise. Julian is clearly the ASN.1 guru for the ISODE.

Chapter 9

Presentation Services

As noted in *Introduction to Application Services*, the presentation service exchanges data structures over the dialogues provided by the session service. Whilst the session service adds *control* mechanisms to the data exchange, the presentation service adds *structure* to the units of data that are exchanged. In brief, the presentation service combines structuring aspects of abstract syntax with the control aspects of the session service.

More formally, the presentation service is offered to the presentation user as shown in Figure 9.1. In order to offer this service, two presentation entities cooperate using the presentation protocol along with the facilities provided by the session service. Together, this combination is termed the *presentation provider* or PS-provider.

As with all OSI service definitions, the presentation service is defined in terms of *primitives*. By convention, presentation primitives are prefixed with "P-". Although on paper, the presentation service appears to be more complex than the session service, it is in fact much simpler: the majority of the complexity in the presentation service is directly related to the underlying session service. As such, the incremental complexity of the presentation service is quite minimal.

The presentation service is defined in [ISO88b]. It uses a newer application model than the landmark 1984 CCITT recommendations, which did not include an explicit presentation layer. However, the application model used by the 1988 CCITT recommendations does include a presentation service. It is defined in [CCITT88e]. The differences between the International Standard definition and the CCITT definition are quite small, and should not affect interoperability be-

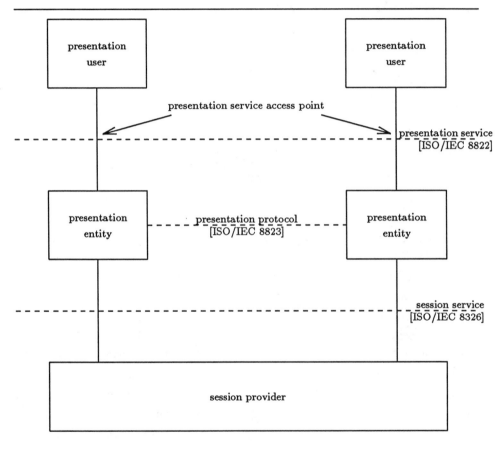

Figure 9.1: The Presentation Layer

tween implementations written against either document.

As such, there are really *two* modes of OSI presentation services. One mode is used for providing backwards compatibility with systems using the 1984 CCITT Recommendations on Message Handling Systems. The other is for the newer presentation service. The remainder of the discussion does not consider the former mode, which provides for the implicit presentation layer used in the application model defined by these early documents.

9.1 Concepts

Users of the presentation service are termed *PS-users*. These are the application service elements described in the next chapter. From the perspective of a local presentation entity, there is a single entity acting as a PS-user: an application entity. From the perspective of an application entity, the various application service elements comprising an application coordinate their actions to appear as a single PS-user.

The PS-user that initiates the presentation connection is termed the *calling* PS-user or *initiator*. The PS-user that the initiator is trying to contact is termed the *called* PS-user or *responder*. Whenever either PS-user initiates some action (e.g., sends data), it is termed the *requesting* PS-user; similarly, when the other PS-user is told about this action (e.g., is notified that data has arrived), it is termed the *accepting* PS-user. Note that the concepts of initiator/responder and requestor/acceptor are independent. It is perfectly acceptable for the responder to ask the initiator to perform some action.

9.1.1 Presentation Addresses

PS-users are addressed at a *presentation service access point* (PSAP). A presentation address consists of two parts: a *presentation selector* and a *session address*. In turn, a session address consists of a session selector and a transport address. In turn, a transport address consists of a transport selector and one or more network addresses. A network address identifies a location in the network, whilst the selectors identify an entity at that location. All three selectors are simple strings of zero or more octets that are meaningful only at a particular network address. Section 4.1.1 in Part II discussed the interpretation of network addresses.

For now, it suffices to note that a PSAP address uniquely identifies a user of the presentation service. As shown in Figure 9.1 on page 338, the PSAP itself makes available the presentation services to a PS-user.

9.1.2 Context Management

The primary purpose of the presentation service is to manage and to apply presentation contexts. A presentation context is a simple pairing between an abstract syntax and a transfer syntax. This pairing is referenced with an integer value, termed the *presentation context identifier* (PCI). [1]

For example, one might imagine a single application entity as being composed of two application service elements. Each service element would define the abstract syntax it uses to communicate with its peer service element residing in the remote application entity. These abstract syntaxes are different for the different application service elements. It would be disastrous if the abstract syntaxes were intermixed. To avoid this problem, during presentation connection establishment, two presentation contexts, one for each application service element would be established. Since all of the user-data passing through the presentation service will be marked with the context to which it belongs, there can be no ambiguity.

From a purist's perspective, the presentation user is aware only of the PCI and the abstract syntax. It is only the presentation service that knows about the transfer syntax associated with the presentation context. From a practical standpoint, it may be necessary for the PS-user to give a hint to the presentation service as to which transfer syntax to use. At present, since the BER is the only defined transfer syntax, this point is moot. In the future, a local mechanism for passing this information may be necessary. The reason for this is simple: if the presentation service selects a transfer syntax, then it is implied that it understands something about the abstract syntax associated with the presentation context. This might be considered a violation of the layering principle.

During connection establishment, a *defined context set* (DCS) is established via negotiation. The initiator indicates the proposed initial contents of the DCS, listing the PCI and abstract syntax for each presentation context. The local presentation entity selects one or more transfer syntaxes that are capable of serializing data types from that abstract syntax. If no transfer syntaxes are available, then this fact is remembered and the presentation context is removed from the DCS.

The information for each of the contexts:

- PCI,

- abstract syntax, and,

---

[1]Do not confuse this term with *protocol control information*, a term defined in Part I. This collision of abbreviations is unfortunate.

- multiple transfer syntaxes

is communicated to the remote presentation entity. The remote presentation entity examines each context and decides if it can support any one of the transfer syntaxes proposed. The remote presentation entity now communicates the contexts to the responder:

- PCI,

- abstract syntax, and,

- an acceptance indicator, taking either symbolic value *acceptance,* or *provider-rejection.* In the latter case, one of these reasons will be indicated:

    - reason not specified;

    - abstract syntax not supported;

    - proposed transfer syntaxes not supported; or,

    - local limit on DCS exceeded;

As its part of the connection establishment process, the responder indicates which presentation contexts it will support.

The responding presentation entity now communicates this information:

- PCI,

- abstract syntax,

- acceptance indicator (taking either the symbolic value *acceptance* or *user-rejection*), and,

- (optionally) a single transfer syntax

to the original presentation entity, which informs the initiator as to the initial contents of the DCS.

If the Context management functional unit is not active, then the contents of the DCS are fixed for the duration of the presentation connection. Otherwise, either presentation user may invoke the P-ALTER-CONTEXT service to add and/or delete presentation contexts from the DCS. A negotiation, analogous to the one just described for connection establishment, is followed.

Functional Units	Services
Kernel	Connection establishment
	Normal data transfer
	Orderly release
	User abort
	Provider abort
Context management	Context addition, deletion
Context restoration	Context restoration

Table 9.1: Presentation Functional Units

When defining a context, the initiator of the presentation connection uses odd-numbered integers when selecting an identifier for a presentation context, whilst the responder uses even-numbered integers. This is necessary to avoid collisions when the P-ALTER-CONTEXT service is used.

9.1.3 Functional Units

The presentation *functional units* active for the presentation connection determine which presentation primitives are available. There are only three functional units, as shown in Table 9.1.

Functional units are negotiated during connection establishment. The initiator indicates the functional units it is willing to employ, and the responder selects which of these it supports. Regardless of the functional units negotiated by the initiator and responder, the kernel functional unit is always active.

Functional units may not be combined in arbitrary ways. Unlike the myriad of regulations for session functional units, there is only one rule for the combination of presentation functional units:

- the Context restoration functional unit may be selected only if the Context management functional unit is also selected.

9.1.4 User Data

After lengthy negotiations and posturing (most of which occurs at the session layer), presentation users eventually exchange data. This data

is termed a PSDU or *presentation service data unit*. Each PSDU is a
collection of one or more *presentation data values*. The presentation
service is purposefully silent as to the format of these data values,
which are said to be in a "local concrete form." (In contrast, the
session service states that an SSDU is a collection of one or more
octets.) Each implementor of a presentation entity is free to choose a
local representation.

Note that although the presentation service is ignorant as to the
content of each presentation data value, it preserves the ordering of
these values in a given PSDU.

Each presentation data value in a PSDU is somehow marked so as
to indicate which presentation context it belongs to. This identifies to
the local presentation entity the abstract syntax and transfer syntax
associated with the data value. The local presentation entity serializes
each data value in the PSDU using the appropriate transfer syntax
and then combines the resulting strings of bits. The resulting string
of octets is then given to the session service as an SSDU.

There is one exception: if the DCS is empty, or if an *expedited
presentation service data unit* (XPSDU) is sent, then the presentation
data values are always bound to a default context that is negotiated
during connection establishment (and may not be changed thereafter).
This limitation for XPSDUs is a side-effect of the transport service
(T-EXPEDITED-DATA) to which XPSDUs are ultimately mapped.

It should be noted that data types from an abstract syntax might
contain data types from other abstract syntaxes. This nesting is permitted, though the transfer syntax for the outermost abstract syntax
will be used for the purposes of serialization.

The presentation service, per se, has no explicit knowledge of either
ASN.1 or the BER. However, as will be seen, the presentation provider
uses both concepts quite heavily internally. Furthermore, as of the end
of 1988, not only did all standardized OSI applications use ASN.1 to
describe their abstract syntaxes, but the BER was the only transfer
syntax available. It is foreseeable that new abstract syntaxes will be
defined using a successor to ASN.1, and that these might be serialized
using a transfer syntax other than the BER.

9.1.5   Session Concepts

Finally, all of the session concepts discussed in Section 7.1 on page 160 are found in the presentation service.

It should be noted that session functional units are considered separately from presentation function units. Both determine which presentation services are available. In general, if an S- service requires a session functional unit to be active, then the corresponding P- service also requires that session functional unit to be active. For example, the S-TYPED-DATA service requires the Typed data functional unit to be active. Hence, the P-TYPED-DATA service also requires this session functional unit to be active.

In contrast, the remainder of the session concepts are simply "pass-through." For example, Quality of Service at the presentation layer is identical to QOS at the session layer.

9.2   Presentation Primitives

The discussion now considers each of the primitives composing the presentation service. The primitives are grouped according to the services they provide. The presentation service, like the session service, goes through three phases: *connection establishment, data transfer,* and *connection release.* In order to provide a more structured discussion, the presentation services are also divided into these three categories.

Associated with the presentation primitives are state tables that indicate the order in which various primitives may be invoked. Rather than describe these tables, it is more instructive to view the presentation service intuitively: the organization of and motivation for the presentation services are described functionally rather than as a sequence of states.

9.2.1   Connection Establishment Phase

Connection establishment is by far the most complex aspect of the presentation service, primarily because session connection establishment is so complicated.

A presentation connection can have only one calling PS-user. If two PS-users simultaneously attempt to establish presentation connections to each other, then two presentation connections are established.

Connection Establishment

The connection establishment service, P-CONNECT, sets up the session connection between two PS-users. During the course of execution of this service, the DCS is negotiated along with the presentation functional units and the various session parameters.

P-CONNECT is a confirmed service, and therefore consists of four primitives:

- P-CONNECT.REQUEST, which is invoked by the calling PS-user;

- P-CONNECT.INDICATION, which is given to the called PS-user;

- P-CONNECT.RESPONSE, which is invoked by the called PS-user; and,

- P-CONNECT.CONFIRMATION, which is given to the calling PS-user;

The relationships among these primitives are straightforward:

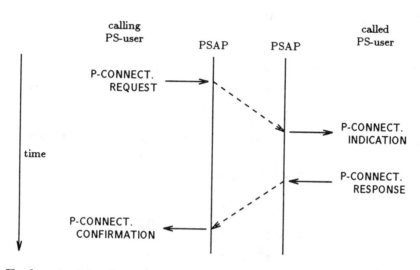

Each primitive has associated with it several parameters that are to be described next. In addition to the normal categories into which a parameter might fall (i.e., mandatory, optional, or conditional), there is a fourth category, *session-dependent.* the user of the presentation service may specify a parameter in this category only if the rules for the session service permit.

When issuing the P-CONNECT.REQUEST primitive, the calling PS-user uses these parameters. They are all conveyed to the called PS-user in the corresponding P-CONNECT.INDICATION primitive.

calling/called presentation address: (mandatory) the calling PS-user identifies itself and the intended responder. (Refer back to Section 9.1.1 on page 340 for the definition of a PSAP address.)

presentation context definition list: (optional) the proposed DCS.

default context name: (optional) the abstract syntax name for the default context.

presentation requirements: (mandatory) the calling PS-user indicates the set of presentation functional units that it is willing to employ. Both the local and remote presentation entities might remove functional units from this set, if they are unable to provide the corresponding presentation services.

mode: (mandatory) one of two choices:

normal: the full presentation service is used; or,

X.410–1984: a mode is used for providing backwards compatibility with systems using the 1984 CCITT Recommendations on Message Handling Systems.

session parameters: (session-dependent) numerous parameters are given that are passed directly as parameters to the S-CONNECT.REQUEST primitive:

- **quality of service**
- **session requirements**
- **initial serial number**
- **initial token assignment**
- **session connection identifier**

See Section 7.2.1 on page 169 for a description of these parameters.

user-data: (optional) one or more presentation data values may be given.

The PS-user employs this parameter to pass its initialization information. In the case of the association control service element, introduced in Section 6.5.1 on page 144, an association request (AARQ-apdu data type) is passed.

Upon receiving the primitive, the local presentation entity examines the associated parameters and invokes the *presentation protocol machine* (PPM). As a result, a P-CONNECT.INDICATION primitive is given to the called PS-user. After some consideration, the called PS-user invokes the P-CONNECT.RESPONSE primitive with these parameters. They are all conveyed to the calling PS-user in the corresponding P-CONNECT.CONFIRMATION primitive.

responding presentation address: (mandatory) this is most often identical to the called presentation address given in the P-CONNECT.INDICATION primitive, but needn't be. For example, this parameter could specify an alternative address to use if the presentation connection breaks and connection re-establishment is attempted.

presentation context definition result list: (conditional) the negotiated DCS.

default context result: (conditional) an indication if the default context was accepted during negotiation:

- accepted;

- user-rejected; or

- provider-rejected;

The provider-rejected indication is used if either presentation entity could not support the transfer syntax required by the context.

presentation requirements: (mandatory) the called PS-user indicates the set of presentation functional units that it is willing to employ. Note that unlike the session requirements, this is a subset of the presentation requirements specified by the calling PS-user. Note that the kernel functional unit is always active.

session parameters: (session-dependent) Numerous parameters are given that are passed directly from the parameters to of the S-CONNECT.CONFIRMATION primitive:

- **quality of service**
- **session requirements**
- **initial serial number**
- **initial token assignment**
- **session connection identifier**

See Section 7.2.1 for a description of these parameters.

user-data: (optional) one or more presentation data values may
be present.

result: (mandatory) the called PS-user decides if it wishes to
accept the session connection. If so, it specifies a symbolic
value of *accept*; otherwise, it selects *user-rejection*. If the
called PS-user indicates rejection, then the session connection is not established.

When the called PS-user accepts the presentation connection, the
primitive received by the calling PS-user is denoted

   P-CONNECT.CONFIRMATION (accept)

Otherwise, the primitive is termed

   P-CONNECT.CONFIRMATION (reject)

Of course, it is possible for any number of degenerate errors to
occur that prevent the primitive from being delivered. For example,
the local presentation entity might be unable to establish a session
connection to the remote presentation entity. Alternatively, after a
session connection is received, the remote presentation entity might
be unable to find the called PS-user. In cases such as these, the P-
CONNECT.CONFIRMATION primitive is returned to the calling PS-
user, possibly without any P-CONNECT.INDICATION primitive being
given to the called PS-user. The only interesting parameter is the
result, which takes the value *provider-rejection*. The reason associated
with the result takes on one of these values:

- reason not specified;

- temporary congestion;

- local limit exceeded;

- called presentation address unknown;

- protocol version not supported;

- default context not supported;

- user-data not readable; or,

- no PSAP available.

There are numerous degenerate cases that might result in the presentation connection not being established. These are analogous to the cases described in Section 7.2.1, e.g.,

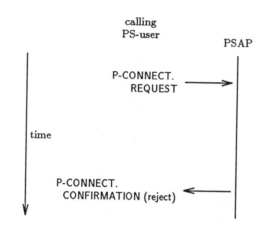

or

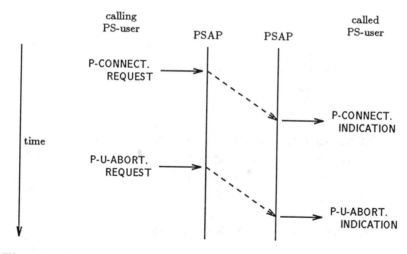

There is, however, one other interesting case. Suppose the initiator includes a presentation data value in the P-CONNECT.REQUEST primitive, which is associated with a presentation context that the remote presentation entity is unable to de-serialize (e.g., the corresponding transfer syntax is unknown). In this case, the presentation service will be unable to pass the user-data to the responder. As a result, the connection will not be established.

The discussion now turns to the data transfer phase of the presentation connection. There are several sets of services that can be used during this phase, which, for the most part, are little more than session services in disguise.

9.2.2   Data Transfer Phase

Almost all of the data transfer services are analogous to the data transfer services offered by the session provider. Basically, a P- service exists for every service described in Section 7.2.2 through Section 7.2.6. The parameters are identical, with two exceptions:

- user-data is serialized when being transformed from a PSDU into an SSDU; and,

- if the Context management functional unit is active, then an additional parameter is available on the P-RESYNCHRONIZE service. This parameter indicates the new DCS.

Context Management

If the Context management functional unit is active, then the P-ALTER-CONTEXT service is available. This service is used to change the DCS after connection establishment. This is a confirmed service.

Three parameters are present for the P-ALTER-CONTEXT.REQUEST primitive:

presentation context addition list: (optional) a list of one more proposed contexts to be added to the DCS. Each context contains a presentation context identifier and an abstract syntax.

presentation context deletion list: (optional) a list of one more proposed contexts to be removed from the DCS. The list contains the presentation context identifier for each context to be removed.

user-data: (optional) one or more presentation data values taken from the existing (not proposed) DCS.

The P-ALTER-CONTEXT.INDICATION primitive contains these parameters and one more:

presentation context addition result list: (mandatory) which indicates, for each of the new presentation contexts proposed, whether the presentation service finds the new context acceptable.

The acceptor now decides which of the contexts acceptable to the presentation service are to be added to the DCS, and which of the contexts proposed to be deleted should be removed. This information is conveyed in the P-ALTER-CONTEXT.RESPONSE primitive:

presentation context addition result list: (mandatory) which, for each of the new presentation contexts proposed, indicates whether the context should be added to the DCS.

presentation context definition result list: (mandatory) which, for each of the presentation contexts marked for deletion, indicates whether the context should be removed from the DCS.

user-data: (optional) one or more presentation data values taken from the new DCS.

The parameters of this primitive are then directly conveyed in the P-ALTER-CONTEXT.CONFIRMATION to the requestor.

After the requestor initiates the P-ALTER-CONTEXT service, it may not invoke any presentation primitive containing a user-data parameter, unless the default context is used.

Context Restoration

If the Context restoration functional unit is active, then an interesting side-effect is introduced for the P-RESYNCHRONIZE service along with the P- services dealing with activity management.

Basically, for resynchronization, the presentation service remembers the DCS previously in effect. As such, when the serial number changes to a previous value, the DCS automatically reverts back to its corresponding value.

Similarly, for activity management, the presentation service remembers the DCS in effect prior to starting an activity. When the activity is terminated, the DCS reverts back to its previous value.

9.2.3 Connection Release Phase

The connection release services are analogous to the connection release services offered by the session provider. Basically, a P- service exists for every service described in Section 7.2.7. The parameters are identical, with two exceptions:

- user-data is serialized when being transformed from a PSDU into an SSDU; and,

- the provider-reason for the P-P-ABORT service is locally defined.

9.3   Presentation Protocol

The presentation protocol is specified in [ISO88c]. As with the presentation service, the International Standard specification of the presentation protocol is aligned with the 1988 CCITT recommendation on the presentation protocol, [CCITT88d].

As with many protocols, the presentation protocol is best described as a finite state machine. The presentation protocol machine (PPM) starts in an initial state. As events occur (the user invokes presentation service primitives or presentation protocol data units (PPDUs) are received from the network), activity is triggered on the part of the PPM. During this activity, actions may occur (presentation service primitives are invoked to the user and/or PPDUs are sent on the network), and possibly a new state is entered. Eventually the presentation connection is released and the PPM returns to the initial state.

It is important to note that the presentation service has a straightforward mapping to the session service. As such, its implementation can be vastly simplified by relying almost entirely on the session state machine. In practical terms, this means that the PPM can be seen as being very simple: the complexities of the state interactions are actually resolved by the underlying SPM.

When examining the presentation protocol, there are three things to be discussed: how the session service is used; how the PPM behaves (termed the "elements of procedure" for the presentation protocol); and, how PPDUs are encoded.

9.3.1   Use of the Session Service

The presentation entity uses the session service in a straightforward fashion. Every P- service maps directly to the corresponding S- service (e.g., the P-CONNECT service maps to the S-CONNECT service). There are two exceptions, to be discussed momentarily. The extra work in the presentation service consists of transforming PSDUs into SSDUs for outgoing session primitives and performing the reverse operation for incoming session primitives.

The P-ALTER-CONTEXT service maps to the S-TYPED-DATA service. This is necessary in order to avoid any session restrictions on sending data. As such, during connection establishment, if the Context management functional unit is selected, then the presentation entity augments the session functional units with the Typed data functional unit. Unless the presentation user also selected the Typed data functional unit, the P-CONNECT service does not indicate negotiation of this session functional unit. (The presentation protocol contains a mechanism for knowing whether the presentation user also wanted the Typed data functional unit.)

9.3.2   Elements of Procedure

The elements of procedure for the presentation protocol is straightforward. Suffice it to say that each service primitive invoked by the user results in a PPDU being generated by the local presentation entity and then the corresponding session service being invoked.

Table 9.2 shows the relationship between presentation primitives and PPDUs. As can be seen, the User-Data PPDU is used for the majority of the presentation services.

9.3.3   Encodings

ASN.1 is used to define each PPDU; further, the Basic encoding rules are used to serialize PPDUs (abstract structures) into/from SSDUs (octet strings). The only interesting PPDU is the User-Data PPDU, which can take several forms as shown in Figure 9.2. All of these different forms are provided to permit more efficient encodings in many common cases.

The `Simply-encoded-data` alternative is used when:

- all the presentation data values in the PSDU are from the default context; or,

- if the DCS contains only one context, and the Context management functional unit is not active (as a result, the DCS cannot change over the lifetime of the presentation connection).

To construct the **OCTET STRING**, the transfer syntax associated with each presentation data value is invoked and the concrete encoding resulting from each presentation data value is concatenated together.

There are three subtleties here (of course). First, this mechanism assumes each encoding is self-delimiting. This means that in a concatenated string of encodings, it is possible to tell where one encoding

Presentation Service	.REQUEST **PPDU**	.RESPONSE **PPDU**
P-CONNECT	CP-type	CPA-type
	CPC-type[1]	CPR-type
P-ALTER-CONTEXT	AC-PPDU	ACA-PPDU
P-DATA	User-Data	
P-EXPEDITED-DATA	User-Data	
P-TYPED-DATA	Typed-data-type	
P-TOKEN-GIVE	User-Data	
P-TOKEN-PLEASE	User-Data	
P-SYNC-MAJOR	User-Data	User-Data
P-SYNC-MINOR	User-Data	User-Data
P-RESYNCHRONIZE	RS-PPDU	RSA-PPDU
P-ACTIVITY-START	User-Data	
P-ACTIVITY-END	User-Data	User-Data
P-ACTIVITY-INTERRUPT	User-Data	User-Data
P-ACTIVITY-RESUME	User-Data	
P-ACTIVITY-DISCARD	User-Data	User-Data
P-GIVE-CONTROL	User-Data	User-Data
P-CAPABILITY-DATA	User-Data	User-Data
P-U-EXCEPTION-REPORT	User-Data	
P-P-EXCEPTION-REPORT		
P-RELEASE	User-Data	User-Data
P-U-ABORT	ARU-PPDU	
P-P-ABORT	ARP-PPDU	

1. If multiple transfer syntaxes are proposed in the CP-type PPDU, then the initiating presentation entity will probably wish to encode each presentation data value using each proposed transfer syntax. This requires the presentation protocol to use a method similar to the session protocol's concatenation procedures.

   The presentation data values are multiply encoded, one encoding for each transfer syntax proposed. Each set of encodings are placed in a CPC-type PPDU (which is simply User-Data). For each transfer syntax, a serialized CPC-type PPDU is then concatenated to the serialized CP-type PPDU.

Table 9.2: Presentation Services and corresponding PPDUs

```
User−data ::=
        CHOICE {
            [APPLICATION 0]
                IMPLICIT Simply−encoded−data,

            [APPLICATION 1]
                IMPLICIT Fully−encoded−data
        }

Simply−encoded−data ::=                                          10
        OCTET STRING

Fully−encoded−data ::=
        SEQUENCE OF
            PDV−list

PDV−list ::=
        SEQUENCE {
                Transfer−syntax−name
                OPTIONAL,                                        20

                Presentation−context−identifier,

            presentation−data−values
                CHOICE {
                    single−ASN1−type[0]
                        ANY,

                    octet−aligned[1]
                        IMPLICIT OCTET STRING,                   30

                    arbitrary[2]
                        IMPLICIT BIT STRING
                }
        }

Presentation−context−Identifier ::=
        INTEGER

Transfer−syntax−name ::=                                         40
        OBJECT IDENTIFIER
```

Figure 9.2: User-data PPDU

ends and the next begins. The BER generates TLV encodings, so this is easy to do. (An advantage over encoding schemes that are not TLV-based.)

Second, transfer syntaxes always produce strings of bits (octet-aligned encodings, such as those generated by the BER, are a special case). Implementors should take note of this when using transfer syntaxes other than the BER.

Finally, in a rather amusing attempt to save a couple of octets, if the User-data maps directly to a session primitive (i.e., it is not enclosed inside of some other ASN.1 type), and if the alternative Simply-encoded-data is used, then the BER tag and length octets of the **OCTET STRING** are not included in the SSDU.[2] Table 9.2 on page 357 lists when the User-data type maps directly to the corresponding session service.

If the Simply-encoded-data alternative is not used, then the Fully-encoded-data alternative is used. Each presentation data value present in the PSDU is considered in order. If adjacent presentation data values belong to the same presentation context, then these are considered as a group. Each group of one or more presentation data-values is encoded in a PDV-list:

- If the group consists of a single presentation data value, and if the transfer syntax for the corresponding context is the BER, then the single-ASN1-type alternative is used.

- If the group consists of more than one presentation data value, and if the transfer syntax for the corresponding context produces octet-aligned encodings, then the octet-aligned alternative is used. Each presentation data value in the group is serialized and the resulting encodings are concatenated to form an **OCTET STRING**.

- Otherwise, the arbitrary alternative is used. Each presentation data value in the group is serialized and the resulting encodings are concatenated to form an **BIT STRING**. As always, if the transfer syntax is not self-delimiting, then ambiguity may result.

---

[2]Presumably, if the constructed form is used to encoded the **OCTET STRING**, then none of the tag or length octets used in any of the encodings appear.

The `Transfer-syntax-name` data type is present only during connection establishment if the initiating presentation entity has proposed more than one transfer syntax. In this case, it is necessary to distinguish which transfer syntax was used to encode the presentation data values in the CP-type PPDU. Note that since the responding presentation entity selects only one transfer syntax, its response (i.e., the CPA-type or CPR-type PPDUs) does not need to include the `Transfer-syntax-name` data type.

9.4   Lightweight Presentation Protocol

Together, the session and presentation services offer a tremendous collection of functionality to networked applications. Unfortunately, their use exacts a heavy price: real implementations of these services tend to be large and slow. This has led some to consider whether a simplied architecture, which captures only the crucial features of both services, might be devised. If so, are there applications that can make use of this "streamlined" approach? The answer is yes.

9.4.1   A Historical Perspective

The initial driving force for developing such an architecture was a desire to use the emerging OSI Network Management Framework in TCP/IP-based internets. The idea is straightforward: the *Common Management Information Service Element* (CMISE) is an application layer element that is used as a part of a network management application. Since CMISE and its corresponding protocol, the *Common Management Information Protocol* (CMIP), are politically acceptable as the unifying technology for network management of different protocol architectures, it makes sense to explore the use of the CMIP in the management of TCP/IP-based internets.

At this point, it would seem logical to use the RFC1006 method, described in Section 5.4 on page 101 in Part II, to host the OSI network management application. The high-level architecture of such a system is shown in Figure 9.3.

However, this approach was not taken by the group charged with exploring OSI network management technology for the Internet, the Netman Working Group of the IAB Internet Engineering Task Force. Their reason is rather interesting: there are some environments in which the richness provided by the OSI application layer is desired, but in which it is nonetheless impractical to implement the underlying OSI infrastructure. That is, implementation of the presentation service, the session service, and even the RFC1006 method, might severely impact the range of platforms on which OSI network management could be fielded.

This philosophy is somewhat contoversial: if only a minimal set of presentation and session services are required, then this subset can be efficiently implemented. As such, the need for a lightweight presenta-

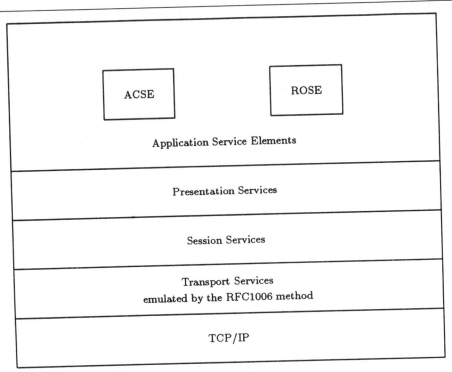

Figure 9.3: Network Management Architecture using RFC1006

tion protocol is suspect. Further, because the OSI protocol stack is
terminated at the presentation interface, mechanisms such as Transport Bridging (described in Section 5.6.4 on page 114) cannot be used.
Thus, the utility of this approach is doubtful. As one industry expert
put it:

Right answer, wrong question.

In many ways, this philosophy is a less extreme position than the
one taken by the SNMP authors described in Section 8.2.6. The difference between the two camps is one of degree, not intent: the SNMP
camp believes that both OSI network management *and* the OSI application services are impractical to use for network management, whilst
the Netman camp believes that the OSI network management framework is a (political) necessity.

9.4.2 An Architecture

Before defining a variant architecture, it is important to understand the bounds of the problem that the architecture must address. In the case of the Netman working group, the criteria are:

- The OSI network management framework must be used. As a result, a "real" OSI application layer containing the application service elements used by the CMIP must be present. These are:

  - the Association Control Service Element (ACSE), which is responsible for establishing and releasing associations between application entities.
  - the Remote Operations Service Element (ROSE), which is responsible for managing request/reply interactions between application entities.

  Both of these service elements are thoroughly examined in Chapter 10.

- The Transmission Control Protocol (TCP) should be used to provide the end-to-end service for network management applications. In addition, use of a less reliable end-to-end service, as provided by the User Datagram Protocol (UDP), should be allowed for experimentation.

A top-down approach is taken to define an architecture that could satisfy these two criteria.

The first step is to determine what kind of presentation services are needed.

- The CMIP uses services from the ACSE and the ROSE; it does not use presentation services directly; and

- The ACSE uses the P-CONNECT, P-U-ABORT, and P-P-ABORT services, whilst the ROSE uses the P-DATA service. Finally, mapping to presentation addresses can be seen as a local matter.

As a result, only four presentation services are needed to host an application entity using the CMISE. In fact this is true of any application entity that uses only remote operations for data transfer. As

such, the approach described here is useful for applications other than
Network Management (e.g., Directory Services).

The next step is to characterize this use of the presentation service.

- The OSI presentation service is being used to exchange ASN.1
  data types over a full-duplex end-to-end service.

- ASN.1 data types, when serialized using the BER, produce self-
  delimiting, octet-aligned encodings.

This is an important realization; for this particular use of the presentation service, the control facilities of the session service, and the
complex mechanisms for negotiation, are *not* needed. This implies
that the session service is superfluous for the application entity we
are considering.

The final step is to observe that because of the self-delimiting
nature of the Basic Encoding Rules, the packet orientation of the
OSI transport service is not needed. All that is needed is a reliable,
full-duplex octet stream. This is *precisely* the service offered by the
TCP!

Figure 9.4 shows the resulting high-level architecture. The "glue"
between the OSI application layer and the TCP-based end-to-end services is termed a *lightweight presentation protocol*. This protocol,
termed the RFC1085 method, is defined in [MRose88a].

9.4.3   An Approach

In defining a lightweight presentation protocol, the RFC1085 method
provides:

- a model for how a lightweight presentation entity might be organized;

- a set of pre-defined values for several of the parameters in the
  P-CONNECT service (this removes the need for negotiation in
  the presentation service); and,

- a finite state machine that defines the protocol.

Only the first two aspects are considered in the discussion.

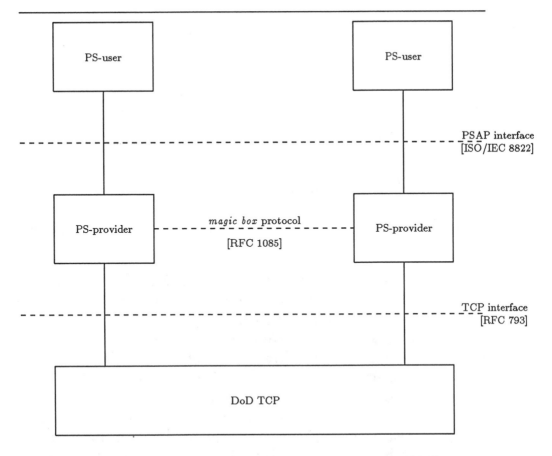

Figure 9.4: Network Management Architecture using RFC1085

Implementation Model

Figure 9.5 shows the high-level architecture of a lightweight presentation entity. Three modules compose the entity:

- a *dispatch* module, which provides the interface to the presentation service (this interface must be indistinguishable from the interface provided by an entity that offers the "real" OSI presentation service);

- a *serialization* module, which applies the Basic Encoding Rules to the ASN.1 data types passing through the presentation service; and,

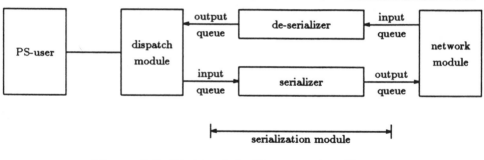

Figure 9.5: Lightweight Presentation Entity

- a *network* module, which manages a TCP-based end-to-end connection.

One may imagine such an entity being implemented in a straightforward fashion: as PSDUs are given to the dispatch module, the serialization module applies the BER and gives the resulting string of octets to the network module. Note that because of the self-delimiting nature of the BER and the stream-orientation of the TCP, elegant software paradigms are possible. In particular, rather than serializing the entire ASN.1 data type before transmitting it on the network, it is possible to serialize in parallel with network transmission. This means that pipelining, a very important technique for reducing latency in the network, can be naturally employed by such a system. In contrast, because of the packet-oriented nature of the session service, an implementation of the presentation protocol must go to great lengths to achieve this characteristic. In some implementations, pipelining can be achieved only by requiring special knowledge and behavior on the part of the application entity as well.

Elimination of Negotiation

A pervasive characteristic of the session service is negotiation. In particular, negotiation during session connection establishment is quite complex. In order to reduce this complexity significantly, the RFC1085 method defines "hard-wired" values that the presentation service will always expect and return. Thus, the appearance of negotiation is maintained, but the actual work is avoided. Note that this strategy is effective only when the requirements of the application entity using the presentation service is well understood. If generality is desired, then the full session negotiation mechanisms are required.

The lightweight presentation service supports exactly two presentation contexts: one for the ACSE, which is used during connection establishment and release; and one for the application service element that uses the ACSE and the ROSE. This second context is used to carry the protocol data units for the ROSE (which in turn carry the data types associated with the other service element). The Basic Encoding Rules are always used as the transfer syntax for the two presentation contexts. Further, no default context is available.

In addition, the lightweight presentation service requires that all data types exchanged be defined using ASN.1. Data types described using other abstract syntaxes are not supported. There is one other requirement: all PSDUs consist of only a single presentation data value.

Finally, in terms of functional units, only the presentation Kernel functional unit, along with the session Kernel and Full-duplex functional units are available.

Although these restrictions might seem constraining, it turns out that these are precisely the requirements of application entities that use only the ACSE and the ROSE. These simplifying assumptions make it possible to construct a presentation entity that is vastly smaller than its full-blown counter-part.

9.4.4 Low-Quality End-to-End Connections

The needs of network management applications differ quite a bit depending on the environment in which they are used. Consider the case of a network management station that is monitoring hundreds or even thousands of managed nodes (e.g., routers) in a large network. Generally, such a station would be interested in being notified when abnormal events, sometimes called *traps*, occur. A trap might indicate, for example, the failure of a link attached to one of the routers.

It would be impractical for the management station to maintain a connection to all of these routers simultaneously. Maintenance of an end-to-end connection usually places significant processing and memory requirements on an end-system. Whilst each individual router could probably shoulder this burden, few, if any, management stations could support such a load. Unfortunately, establishing a connection is an expensive proposition both in terms of time and processing. If a trap occurs, there simply may not be enough time to establish a connection to the management station in order to report the trap. So, there is a dilemma: the management station cannot maintain connections to all of the routers, yet for timely reporting, a connection should already be in place!

Perhaps by examining the traffic between the management station and the routers, some insight might be found. Experience shows that there are two common patterns of traffic between management stations and managed nodes:

1. The station regularly polls the routers for statistical information, such as packets forwarded. This might happen once an hour or so.

2. A particular router sends a trap to the management station when "something bad" happens. Upon receiving this information, the management station might wish to investigate further. If so, it might engage in a brief, but intense, conversation with that router, as the problem is diagnosed.

These patterns suggest that traffic between the station and any individual router is rather sparse. Therefore, it is unnecessary for the management station to maintain a continuous end-to-end connection. Instead, what is needed is a low-quality connection — one that is relatively cheap to establish, and, when not in use, requires virtually no resources on either the management station or the router.

To achieve this, the lightweight presentation service allows a new parameter in the Quality of Service for the connection. This parameter is termed the *transport-mapping*, and takes one of two values:

tcp-based: which indicates that the TCP is used as the transport backing for the end-to-end service (this is the default); or,

udp-based: which indicates that the UDP is used as the transport backing for the end-to-end service.

Use of the TCP-based backing is well understood: the application entity remains ignorant of the composition of the protocol stack beneath it. In contrast, use of the UDP-based backing is experimental: no guarantee of reliability is provided by the presentation service.

If the UDP-based backing is used, then there are two important implications: first, because the UDP is a packet-oriented protocol, the serialization module must serialize the entire ASN.1 data type before passing it to the network module for transmission using the UDP. The second implication is that it is now the responsibility of the application entity to ensure that its reliability characteristics are met. (The lightweight presentation protocol uses a simplistic three-way handshake with retransmission for association establishment and release — for data transfer, no retransmission is attempted.)

As a result, the application entity is free to customize its use of the presentation service to meet whatever reliability characteristics it deems appropriate. For example, certain kind of traps generated by a router might be "informational." In this case, the network management system may not care if they are delivered or not. As such, a UDP-based transport backing would be adequate for this management application.

9.4.5 The Architecture Revisited

The fundamental goal of this variant architecture was minimizing the underlying OSI infrastructure. The disadvantage of selecting this approach over the RFC1006 method is that transport-level bridging between a pure OSI environment and a mixed environment can no longer be performed. As such, in situations where the implementation size of the underlying infrastructure is not as critical, the RFC1006 method is preferable, precisely because it can interoperate, without loss of application layer functionality, with pure OSI environments. Furthermore, two different systems, one using the RFC1006 method, and the other using the RFC1085 method, *cannot* interoperate!

It is important to appreciate that reducing the size and complexity of the system is the primary goal of a system using the RFC1085 method. This means that great care must be taken to avoid featurism in systems built using this method; to fail to do so would invalidate the fundamental reason for using a lightweight presentation protocol.

In comparing the two architectures, applications built using the RFC1085 method were, on the average, twice as fast and half as large as their counterparts built using the RFC1006 method. Clearly, there is a substantial advantage in using lightweight approach! However it should be noted that this portrays the RFC1085 method is the best possible light. The implementation using the RFC1006 method is fully generalized to provide all session and presentation layer functionality, whilst the implementation using the RFC1085 method is not. If a more equal comparison were made, one in which the implementation using the RFC1006 were optimized for precisely the services offered by the RFC1085 method, then the differences between the two methods would be much less pronounced.

It should be noted that systems built using the RFC1085 method are highly portable to a pure OSI environment, or to environments that use the RFC1006 method. Thus, investment in applications programming can be preserved across these differing protocol stacks. This is an important distinction, applications written to use either of the two methods are portable; they just aren't interoperable!

Initial experience with the RFC1085 method has proven successful; at the 3$^{\underline{rd}}$ TCP/IP Interoperability Conference, held in September of 1988, a dozen vendors demonstrated prototype OSI network management systems [GMars89]. These prototypes used the OSI network management framework and the RFC1085 method to manage a local area network running the TCP/IP protocols. The range of platforms participating included minicomputers, workstations, personal computers (PCs), and even terminal servers. This demonstration was important in showing the viability of such a network management architecture.

9.5   An Implementation

Finally, the discussion closes with a look at an implementation of the presentation service. As with the other chapters in Part III, the implementational framework of the ISO Development Environment (ISODE) is examined. The discussion that follows is heavily oriented towards those familiar with the C programming language and the UNIX operating system.

In the ISODE, the `psap2` library is responsible for implementing presentation services. This description of ISODE's presentation services is only a high-level overview. They are described in considerable detail in *Volume 2: Underlying Services* of the ISODE User's Manual[MRose89]. As with the session protocol, the presentation protocol engine was entirely hand-coded. Very little work was involved, as most of the state-checking is done by the underlying session service. Unlike the session implementation, all of the encoding routines were automatically generated by the *posy* and *pepy* programs discussed in Sections 8.4.3 and 8.4.4, respectively.

The ISODE implementation of the presentation services is modest: only the Kernel functional unit is implemented. In practice this is not a severe limitation; the author knows of no other implementations that provide the Context management or Context Restoration functional units. Although any ASN.1 data type can be passed as a presentation data value, the only transfer syntax available is the BER.

9.5.1   Presentation Interface

As with the ISODE interface to session services, each .REQUEST and .RESPONSE service primitive maps onto a C procedure call. Each parameter in a presentation service maps to a parameter in the corresponding C procedure. In addition, there are usually two other parameters. The first is a *presentation-descriptor*, which is used to indicate which presentation connection is being manipulated; the second is an *indication pointer*, which may be updated to reflect what happened as a result of invoking the presentation primitive.

Interface Policies

In brief, the psap2 library follows the same interface policy as the
ssap library that provides session services. The primary difference
between the two interfaces is how user-data is represented:

- the session interface represents an SSDU (a string of octets) as
  two parameters: a pointer to the base of the string, and an
  integer indicating the length of the string;

- the presentation interface represents a PSDU (a list of presentation data values) as two parameters: an array of presentation
  elements, and an integer indicating the size of the array.

Consider the interface to the P-DATA.REQUEST primitive, which is
defined by the procedure PDataRequest:

```
int     PDataRequest (sd, data, ndata, pi)
int     sd;
PE      *data;
int     ndata;
struct PSAPindication  *pi;
```

As with the session interface, only entire SDUs are transferred in a
single call. The ISODE philosophy is that in order to use facilities
such as checkpointing, the user-data sent between checkpoints will be
kept purposely small.

A secondary difference between the two interfaces is that the indication parameter encodes a different set of events. For example,
when an error occurs, the pi parameter is used to encode a P-P-
ABORT.INDICATION primitive. As with the ISODE session service,
the possible errors generated by the provider are extended considerably to indicate non-fatal interface errors, rather than protocol errors.
The list of reasons in shown in Figure 9.3.

Provider-initiated Abort (fatal)	
PC_NOTSPECIFIED	Reason not specified
PC_CONGEST	Temporary congestion
PC_EXCEEDED	Local limit exceeded
PC_ADDRESS	Called presentation address unknown
PC_VERSION	Protocol version not supported
PC_DEFAULT	Default context not supported
PC_READABLE	User-data not readable
PC_AVAILABLE	No PSAP available
PC_UNRECOGNIZED	Unrecognized PPDU
PC_UNEXPECTED	Unexpected PPDU
PC_SSPRIMITIVE	Unexpected session service primitive
PC_PPPARAM1	Unrecognized PPDU parameter
PC_PPPARAM2	Unexpected PPDU parameter
PC_INVALID	Invalid PPDU parameter value
PC_ABSTRACT	Abstract syntax not supported
PC_TRANSFER	Proposed transfer syntaxes not supported
PC_DCSLIMIT	Local limit on DCS exceeded
PC_REFUSED	Connect request refused on this network connection
PC_SESSION	Session disconnect
PC_PROTOCOL	Protocol error
PC_ABORTED	Peer aborted connection
User-initiated Abort (fatal)	
PC_REJECTED	Rejected
Interface Errors (non-fatal)	
PC_PARAMETER	Invalid parameter
PC_OPERATION	Invalid operation
PC_TIMER	Timer expired
PC_WAITING	Indications waiting

Table 9.3: ISODE PSAP2 Failure Codes

Reading Events

The procedure `PReadRequest` is used to return the next event for the session, possibly waiting for something to happen:

```
int     PReadRequest (sd, px, secs, pi)
int     sd;
struct PSAPdata *px;
int     secs;
struct PSAPindication  *pi;
```

The parameters to this procedure are:

sd: the presentation-descriptor;

px: a pointer to the `PSAPdata` structure to be given the data;

secs: the maximum number of seconds to wait for the data (a value of `NOTOK` indicates that the call should block indefinitely, whereas a value of `OK` indicates that the call should not block at all, e.g., it should perform a polling action); and,

pi: a pointer to a `PSAPindication` structure, which is updated only if data is not read.

This procedure returns one of three values:

- `NOTOK`, if an abort of some kind occurred;

- `OK`, if an event associated with data transfer occurred; or,

- `DONE`, if some event other than data transfer occurred.

Consider how incoming data is handled. If `OK` is returned, then data has been read into the `px` parameter, which is a pointer to a `PSAPdata` structure:

```
struct PSAPdata {
    int     px_type;            /* NPSDU, XPSDU, ... */

    int     px_ninfo;
    PE      px_info[NPDATA];
};
```

The elements of a `PSAPdata` structure are:

px_type: indicates how the user-data was received;

px_ninfo: the number of presentation data values in the PSDU; and,

px_info: an array of PEs (presentation data values) that comprises the PSDU.

Note that there is a one to one mapping between the ordering of the presentation data values sent by the requesting PS-user and the presentation data values given to the accepting PS-user. In contrast, the ISODE session service when passing SSDUs to the accepting SS-user, returns a single octet string (the SSDU) in the form of a buffer-queue.

When the presentation entity constructs the array of presentation data values, it uses a special presentation stream abstraction to read from the SSDU, which is supplied as a buffer-queue. This permits the user-data to be extracted efficiently from the encapsulating PPDU with a minimal amount of octet (byte) copying; presentation elements are constructed containing pointers to the original SSDU. In order to avoid "memory leaks," the first presentation element contains a pointer to the base of the original SSDU. When this presentation element is freed, then the SSDU from whence it came is freed as well.

Users of the ISODE presentation service may further extract fields from the presentation element, passing on this inheritance as desired. This method has proven effective in achieving a balance between octet copying and dynamic memory allocation.

9.5.2 Presentation Entity

In the discussion that follows, we examine how the presentation entity implements a given service.

Because the session service is used to enforce the majority of the interface rules for the presentation service, most of the procedures providing a presentation primitive are quite simple: a check on any interface policy specific to the presentation service is done, the user-data is mapped to an SSDU, and then the corresponding session service is invoked. The first step corresponds to the *wrapper* routine used by the ISODE session entity, whilst the other two steps correspond to the *engine* routine.

Figure 9.6 shows the wrapper for the procedure `PPTokenRequest`, which implements the P-PLEASE-TOKEN.REQUEST primitive. The routine begins by checking the presentation-specific parameters, using various macros defined for that purpose. For example, the macro `toomuchP` checks to see whether there are too many presentation data values in the PSDU. If so, it calls `psaplose`, which is equivalent to generating a P-P-ABORT.INDICATION, indicating a non-fatal error.

Second, I/O signals are blocked by calling `sigioblock`. This prevents routines that handle asynchronous I/O activity from tampering with data structures in an uncontrolled fashion. (The ISODE presentation service supports both a synchronous and asynchronous interface.)

Next, the presentation-descriptor is mapped into a *presentation block*, which contains all of the information locally known about a presentation connection. The mapping is done by a macro called `psapPsig`. If it is not found, then the signal state is restored and `psaplose` is called to return an error. No further check of the validity of this primitive is made: the session service will perform that task.

After having retrieved the presentation block, the procedure maps the user-data into an SSDU by calling the routine `info2ssdu`. This examines the presentation data values (if any), constructs an appropriate presentation element, and then invokes a presentation stream to produce an SSDU. If an error occurred during this routine, then one of the two values `NOTOK` or `DONE` will be returned, and a P-P-ABORT.INDICATION will be given to the user. In the former case, the error, although unlikely to occur, is fatal. The latter case indicates an interface error of some kind (e.g., a presentation data value was supplied with an unknown context), and this is reported as a non-fatal problem.

Finally, the routine `SPTokenRequest` is called, which implements the S-PLEASE-TOKEN.REQUEST primitive. If the routine fails, a check is made to see whether the error was fatal, if so, this error will be propagated upwards as a fatal P-P-ABORT.INDICATION. If not, then some kind of interface error occurred (perhaps the user specified tokens that aren't available on this connection), and a non-fatal P-P-ABORT.INDICATION will be returned.

```
#include "ppkt.h"                        /* definitions for PS-provider */

int      PPTokenRequest (sd, tokens, data, ndata, pi)
int      sd;
int      tokens,
         ndata;
PE       *data;
struct PSAPindication *pi;
{
    SBV      smask;
    int      len,                                                          10
             result;
    char     *base;
    register struct psapblk *pb;
    struct SSAPindication   sis;
    register struct SSAPabort  *sa = &sis.si_abort;

    toomuchP (data, ndata, NPDATA, "token");
    missingP (pi);

    smask = sigioblock ();                                                 20

    psapPsig (pb, sd);

    if ((result = info2ssdu (pb, pi, data, ndata, &base, &len,
                        "P-TOKEN-PLEASE user-data", PPDU_NONE)) != OK)
            goto out2;

    if ((result = SPTokenRequest (sd, tokens, base, len, &sis)) == NOTOK)
            if (SC_FATAL (sa -> sa_reason))
                (void) ss2pslose (pb, pi, "SPTokenRequest", sa);           30
            else {
                (void) ss2pslose (NULLPB, pi, "SPTokenRequest", sa);
                goto out1;
            }
out2: ;
    if (result == NOTOK)
            freepblk (pb);
    else
            if (result == DONE)                                            40
                result = NOTOK;
out1: ;
    if (base)
            free (base);

    (void) sigiomask (smask);

    return result;
}
                                                                           50
```

Figure 9.6: Implementation of a Presentation Primitive

Chapter 10

Application Service Elements

[ISO87n] defines the OSI Application Layer Structure. At the coarsest level, *application processes* (APs) execute in the OSI environment. From the OSI perspective, the communication aspects of these processes are represented by *application entities* (AEs).

In the interests of generality, the OSI application layer structure permits an application process to have multiple communication aspects, thereby implying that multiple application entities reside within each application process. Note that the inverse mapping is not permitted: a given application entity must reside entirely within a single application process. In the interests of simplicity, unless otherwise noted, the discussion will consider only application processes containing a single application entity.

An application entity is composed of one or more *application service elements* (ASEs). The way in which these service elements interact with each other, and with the underlying OSI services, defines the *application protocol* used by the application entity. The term *application context name* refers to a particular application protocol. When an application context is defined, it is assigned an object identifier. Figure 10.1 summarizes these relationships.

Note that each of the peer application entities is composed of precisely the same ASEs. Further, each ASE talks only with its peer in the remote application entity. A different presentation context is assigned to each application service element so that the application protocol data units are always delivered to the correct ASE.

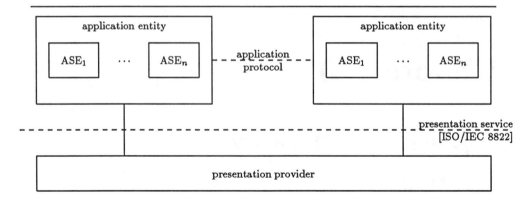

Figure 10.1: The Application Layer

The remainder of this chapter is devoted to presenting three ASEs:

- association control, which manages associations between application entities;

- remote operations, which manage request/reply interactions; and,

- reliable transfer, which manages bulk data transfers.

In addition, there will be a discussion on naming and addressing of application entities following the exposition of association control.

10.1 Association Control

An application association, or *association*, is a presentation connection with additional application layer semantics. Simply put, whilst the connections at each of the underlying layers are general-purpose, each association is specific to a given application task; the combination of application service elements to form an application protocol tends to reinforce this view. Of the ASEs that form an application entity, it is the *Association Control Service Element* (ACSE) that manages associations. As a consequence, note that *all* OSI applications contain an ACSE.

When referring to a connection (at the layers below the application layer), the terms *calling user* and *called user* refer to the entities that request and accept connection establishment (respectively). At the application layer, when referring to an association, the terms *initiating user* and *responding user* refer to the entities that request and accept association establishment (respectively).

At present, beyond the semantics of the underlying presentation connection, an association implies little more than application layer naming. In the future, it is conceivable that authentication, charging, and a whole range of general application layer semantics may be added.

Application layer naming is postponed until Section 10.2.1 on page 399. For now, think of each application entity as having a *title* that identifies the service offered by the application entity. Note that this title is independent of any addressing or routing considerations — it is a name.

10.1.1 ACSE Primitives

The discussion now considers the primitives composing the application control service. By convention, ACSE service primitives are prefixed with "A-". The ACSE service is defined in [ISO88e]. The International Standard definition of the service is technically aligned with the 1988 CCITT recommendation on the ACSE service, [CCITT88b]. The differences between the Interational Standard definition and the CCITT definition are quite small, and should not affect interoperability between implementations written against either document.

Inasmuch as the ACSE is concerned only with the management of associations, there are only two phases: establishment and release.

Association Establishment Phase

Viewed as a whole, association establishment is quite complex. However, the vast majority of all complexity is inherited from the underlying services.

Since an association maps directly onto a presentation connection, an association can have only one initiating application entity. If two application entities simultaneously attempt to establish associations to each other, then two associations are established.

Association Establishment

The association establishment service, A-ASSOCIATE, establishes an association between two AEs. This is a confirmed service, consisting of four primitives:

- A-ASSOCIATE.REQUEST, which is invoked by the initiating application entity;

- A-ASSOCIATE.INDICATION, which is given to the responding application entity;

- A-ASSOCIATE.RESPONSE, which is invoked by the responding application entity; and,

- A-ASSOCIATE.CONFIRMATION, which is given to the initiating application entity.

The relationships among these primitives are straightforward:

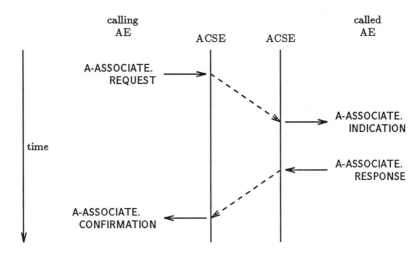

Each primitive has associated with it nearly 20 parameters! This is because of the cascading of connection establishment parameters from the session and presentation services. Easily half of these parameters are simply passed through to the presentation service, which passes a great many of those down to the session service. Rather than list those parameters here, only the ones of particular interest to the application layer will be examined.

When issuing the A-ASSOCIATE.REQUEST primitive, the initiating AE uses the parameters that follow; they are conveyed to the responding AE in the corresponding A-ASSOCIATE.INDICATION primitive.

mode: (optional) one of two choices:

  normal: the full association control service is used (the default); or,

  X.410–1984: a mode is used providing for backwards compatibility with systems using the 1984 CCITT Recommendations on Message Handling Systems.

  The remainder of the discussion does not consider the latter mode. Suffice it to say that it provides for the implicit presentation layer used in the application model defined by these early documents.

application context name: (mandatory) implicitly identifies the ASEs to be used over this association. That is, it doesn't contain a list of the ASEs present, rather it contains a name (**OBJECT IDENTIFIER**) that refers to a collection of ASEs.

calling AE information: (optional) identifies the application process (and application entity within that application process) that is initiating the association.

called AE information: (optional) identifies the intended responding application process (and application entity within that application process).

presentation context definition list: (mandatory) contains an entry for the PCI of each ASE in the application entity, *including* an entry for the ACSE. In addition, if an ASE requires other contexts, these are included here as well.

user-data: (optional) initialization information for other ASEs in this application entity.

Note that the application naming information is entirely optional. This means that an association can be established using only the presentation address of the application entity.

Upon receiving the primitive, the local ACSE examines the associated parameters and invokes the *association control protocol machine* (ACPM). As a result, the corresponding A-ASSOCIATE.INDICATION primitive is given to the responding application entity. After some consideration, the responding application entity invokes the A-ASSOCIATE.RESPONSE primitive with these parameters. They are all conveyed to the initiating application entity in the corresponding A-ASSOCIATE.CONFIRMATION primitive.

application context name: (mandatory) identifies the ASEs to be used over this association. this is most often identical to the name given in the corresponding A-ASSOCIATE.REQUEST primitive, but needn't be. This allows a very simplistic facility for negotiating application layer functional units.

For example, an application making use of remote operations might also wish to use reliable transfer if the data carried in the operations is large. However, use of the RTSE is optional. An initiating application entity that supported use of the RTSE would propose an application context name that included the RTSE. If the responding application entity did not support the use of the RTSE in the application, it would counter with a different application context name — one that did not include the RTSE. If the initiating application entity didn't like this negotiation, it could always abort the association immediately after receiving the A-ASSOCIATE.CONFIRMATION primitive.

Note that this scenario is largely problematic: if an ASE in the initiating application entity provides initialization information, and this ASE is not supported by the responding application entity, then the responder has no way of deciphering this information.

responding AE information: (optional) this is most often identical to the called AE information given in the A-ASSOCIATE.INDICATION primitive, but needn't be. For example, this parameter could specify an alternative application entity to contact if the underlying presentation connection breaks and association re-establishment is attempted.

user-data: (optional) initialization information for other ASEs in this application entity.

result: (mandatory) the responding application entity decides if it wishes to accept the association. If so, it specifies a symbolic value of *accept*; otherwise, it selects either *rejected (permanent),* for serious failures; or, *rejected (transient),* for temporary failures. If the responding application entity indicates rejection, then the association is not established.

diagnostic: (optional) if the association is rejected, there is an associated diagnostic, taking one of these values:

- no reason given;

- application context name not supported;

- calling AE information not recognized; or,

- called AE information not recognized.

result source: (only for A-ASSOCIATE.CONFIRMATION) if the
value of the **result** parameter is *accepted*; or if the responding application entity rejected the association, then this
parameter has the symbolic value *ACSE service-user*; otherwise this parameter has the symbolic value *ACSE service-
provider*.

When the responding application entity accepts the association,
the primitive received by the initiating application entity is denoted

A-ASSOCIATE.CONFIRMATION (accept)

Otherwise, the primitive is termed

A-ASSOCIATE.CONFIRMATION (reject)

Of course, it is possible for any number of degenerate errors to occur that prevent the primitive from being delivered. For example, the
local ACSE might be unable to establish a presentation connection to
the remote ACSE. In cases such as these, the A-ASSOCIATE.CONFIR-
MATION primitive is returned to the initiating application entity, possibly without any A-ASSOCIATE.INDICATION primitive being given
to the responding application entity.

There are three interesting parameters. The first is the result that
takes the value *rejected (permanent)* or *rejected (transient)*. The second is the result source that takes the value *ACSE service-provider* or
presentation service-provider, depending on which entity encountered
the failure. The third parameter is the diagnostic that takes one of
these values:

- null;

- no reason given; or,

- no common acse version.

Because association establishment is so closely tied with both session and presentation connection establishment, the usual degenerate protocol interactions can occur, such as:

- Either the local or remote ACSE encountered a problem; no A-ASSOCIATE.INDICATION primitive was issued, and an A-ASSOCIATE.CONFIRMATION (reject) was returned.

- The initiating application entity, after issuing an A-ASSOCIATE.REQUEST primitive, decides not to wait any longer for a response and issues the A-ABORT.REQUEST primitive. This action might disrupt establishment of the association during any number of possible stages.

Interactions of this sort were described earlier in Section 7.2.1 starting on page 169.

Association Release Phase

There are three services that result in association release: the A-RELEASE service, which, with the cooperation of the two application entities, results in all data in transit being safely delivered prior to association release; the A-ABORT service, in which an application entity may unilaterally terminate an association; and, the A-P-ABORT service, in which the ACSE service provider may inform the two application entities when the association has been lost. The latter two services are destructive; any user-data in transit is lost when they occur.

Orderly Release

The A-RELEASE service is used to terminate an association gracefully. Before an application entity may invoke this service, it must meet the requirements for a release of the underlying session connection (i.e., attain ownership of all available tokens). This is a confirmed service. When invoked by the requesting application entity, there are two parameters, both optional: the first is a reason, taking one of these values:

- normal;

- urgent; or,

- user-defined.

The second parameter is user-data that contains termination information for other ASEs in this application entity.

The response contains three parameters, a mandatory result, indicating if the release is accepted; optionally, a reason for accepting or rejecting the release, and, optionally, user-data. The reason parameter takes on one of these symbolic values:

- normal;

- not finished; or,

- user defined.

whilst the user-data contains termination information for other ASEs in this application entity. Note that the accepting application entity may refuse the release only if release of the underlying session connection could be refused (i.e., the Negotiated release functional unit is active). In this case, the reason *not finished* might appear in order to indicate that the accepting application entity still had additional work to perform prior to release of the association.

User-initiated Abort

When an application entity detects an unrecoverable error, the user-initiated abort service, A-ABORT, is invoked. This is an unconfirmed service:

- A-ABORT.REQUEST, which is invoked by the requesting application entity; and,

- A-ABORT.INDICATION, which is given to the accepting application entity.

The relationship between these primitives is straightforward:

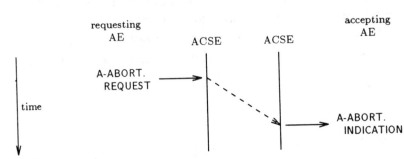

There is a single parameter associated with this service: user-data, which is optional. If present, the user-data should indicate to the other application entity why the association was aborted. Note that unless the session Unlimited User-Data Addendum is in effect, then only 9 octets may be sent as user-data on the session service. In practice, this is too restrictive to pass any information using the ACSE.

This parameter is conveyed in the A-ABORT.INDICATION primitive with a second, mandatory parameter: an abort source, which indicates that the initiating application entity caused the abort.

After this service is initiated or accepted by the application entities, no further primitives may be invoked for the association.

Since the OSI application layer considers all ASEs, including the ACSE, to be a user of the association, if the ACSE service provider encounters an error, it issues an A-ABORT.INDICATION primitive to both application entities. In this case, there is no user-data parameter and the abort source indicates that the ACSE service provider generated the abort. This is why the user-initiated abort service is called A-ABORT rather than A-U-ABORT.

Provider-initiated Abort

When the ACSE service provider detects an error from which it cannot recover, the provider-initiated abort service, A-P-ABORT, is invoked. This is a provider-initiated service with one primitive:

- A-P-ABORT.INDICATION, which is given to both application elements.

As the service is provider-initiated, this primitive may (theoretically) occur without warning:

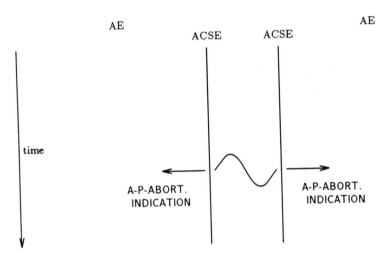

There is only one parameter associated with an abort raised by the ACSE service provider, a reason telling why the association was lost. This reason is identical to the one provided by the P-P-ABORT service:

- unrecognized PPDU;

- unexpected PPDU;

- unexpected session service primitive;

- unrecognized PPDU parameter;

- unexpected PPDU parameter; or,

- invalid PPDU parameter value.

Note that there is a one-to-one mapping between the P-P-ABORT service and the A-P-ABORT service, since the A-ABORT service is used by the ACSE service provider to report its own internal errors.

After this primitive is delivered to each application entity, no further primitives may be invoked for the association.

10.1.2 ACSE Protocol

The ACSE protocol is defined in [ISO88d]. As with the ACSE service, the International Standard specification of the ACSE protocol is technically aligned with the 1988 CCITT recommendation on the ACSE protocol, [CCITT88a].

Once again, the ACSE protocol is best described as a finite state machine. The association control protocol machine (ACPM) starts in an initial state. As events occur (the user invokes presentation service primitives or association control protocol data units (APDUs) are received from the network), activity is triggered on the part of the ACPM. During this activity, actions may occur (association control service primitives are invoked to the user and/or APDUs are sent on the network), and possibly a new state is entered. Eventually the association is released and the ACPM returns to the initial state.

When examining the ACSE protocol, there are three things to be discussed: how the presentation service is used; how the ACPM behaves (termed the "elements of procedure" for the ACSE); and, how APDUs are encoded.

Rather than discuss these separately, as has been done in previous chapters, an integrated view is taken. This is necessary in order to appreciate fully the extremely tight binding the ACSE has with the connection management facilities of the two layers beneath it.

Each ACSE primitive maps one-to-one onto one of the ACSE's APDUs. In turn, each APDU maps onto one of the presentation service connection management primitives. These two mappings are shown in Table 10.1.

In turn, each of these presentation primitives maps onto a PPDU. In turn, each of these PPDUs maps onto one of the session service connection management primitives. These two mappings are shown in Table 10.2.

In turn, each of these session primitives maps onto a SPDU. In turn, each of these SPDUs maps onto one of the transport service data

ACSE Primitive	APDU carried in	Presentation Primitive
A-ASSOCIATE.REQUEST .INDICATION	AARQ	P-CONNECT.REQUEST .INDICATION
A-ASSOCIATE.RESPONSE .CONFIRMATION	AARE	P-CONNECT.RESPONSE .CONFIRMATION
A-RELEASE.REQUEST .INDICATION	RLRQ	P-RELEASE.REQUEST .INDICATION
A-RELEASE.RESPONSE .CONFIRMATION	RLRE	P-RELEASE.RESPONSE .CONFIRMATION
A-ABORT.REQUEST .INDICATION	ABRT	P-U-ABORT.REQUEST .INDICATION
A-P-ABORT.INDICATION		P-P-ABORT.INDICATION

Table 10.1: ACSE mappings onto Presentation Service

Presentation Primitive	PPDU carried in	Session Primitive
P-CONNECT.REQUEST .INDICATION	CP-type	S-CONNECT.REQUEST .INDICATION
P-CONNECT.RESPONSE .CONFIRMATION	CPA-type CPR-type	S-CONNECT.RESPONSE .CONFIRMATION
P-RELEASE.REQUEST .INDICATION	User-data	S-RELEASE.REQUEST .INDICATION
P-RELEASE.RESPONSE .CONFIRMATION	User-data	S-RELEASE.RESPONSE .CONFIRMATION
P-U-ABORT.REQUEST .INDICATION	ARU-PPDU	S-U-ABORT.REQUEST .INDICATION
P-P-ABORT.INDICATION	ARP-PPDU	S-U-ABORT.REQUEST .INDICATION

Table 10.2: Presentation mappings onto Session Service

Session Primitive	SPDU carried in	Transport Primitive
S-CONNECT.REQUEST .INDICATION	CONNECT	T-DATA.REQUEST .INDICATION
S-CONNECT.RESPONSE .CONFIRMATION	ACCEPT REFUSE	T-DATA.REQUEST .INDICATION
S-RELEASE.REQUEST .INDICATION	FINISH	T-DATA.REQUEST .INDICATION
S-RELEASE.REQUEST .INDICATION	DISCONNECT NOT FINISHED	T-DATA.REQUEST .INDICATION
S-U-ABORT.REQUEST .INDICATION	ABORT ABORT ACCEPT	T-EXPEDITED-DATA .REQUEST .INDICATION
S-P-ABORT.INDICATION	ABORT	T-EXPEDITED-DATA .REQUEST .INDICATION

Table 10.3: Session mappings onto Transport Service

transfer primitives. These two mappings are shown in Table 10.3 on page 393. This table makes three simplifying assumptions: first, that the T-EXPEDITED-DATA service is available on the transport connection — if not, then the T-DATA service is used instead. Second, if the T-EXPEDITED-DATA service is available, but the ABORT SPDU is too large to carry on this service, then the PREPARE SPDU sent on the transport expedited flow is not shown. Third, that the amount of user-data exchanged during session connection establishment does not require the use of the additional SPDUs defined in the Unlimited User-Data Addendum for the session protocol[ISO87r].

Now that it is clear how the various services relate to each other, consider Table 10.4, which shows how parameters are passed from the A-ASSOCIATE.REQUEST primitive downward towards the CONNECT SPDU.

10.1.3 An Example

Finally, consider an annotated example that shows these mappings. Suppose that the application entity contains two ASEs: the ACSE and the FTAM ASE (FTAM is the OSI file service, described in Section 11.3 starting on page 475). When an association to the file ser-

A-ASSOCIATE .REQUEST	AARQ APDU	P-CONNECT .REQUEST	CP-type PPDU	S-CONNECT .REQUEST	CONNECT SPDU
mode		√			
application context name	√				
calling AE info	√				
called AE info	√				
user-data	√				
calling P-address		P-address	P-selector	S-address	S-selector
called P-address		P-address	P-selector	S-address	S-selector
presentation context definition list		√	√		
default presentation context name		√	√		
quality of service		√		√	
presentation requirements		√	√		
session requirements		√		√	√
initial serial number		√		√	√
initial token assignment		√		√	√
session connection identifier		√		√	√

Table 10.4: A-ASSOCIATE.REQUEST mappings onto upper-layers

```
{
    service-class {
        management-class, transfer-class,
        transfer-and-management-class
    },
    functional-units {
        read, write, limited-file-management,
        enhanced-file-management, grouping
    },
    attribute-groups { storage },
    ftam-quality-of-service no-recovery,
    contents-type-list {
        1.0.8571.5.3,    -- FTAM-3 document
        1.0.8571.5.1,    -- FTAM-1 document
        1.3.9999.1.5.9   -- NBS-9 document
    },
    initiator-identity "cheetah"
}
```

Figure 10.2: F-INITIALIZE-request FPDU

vice is to be established, the FTAM ASE generates an instance of the F-INITIALIZE-request FPDU and passes this as user-data to the A-ASSOCIATE.REQUEST primitive. This FPDU is defined in the abstract syntax for the FTAM protocol. Thus, the FTAM ASE must request a presentation context for this syntax, along with a presentation context for the ACSE. Furthermore, the FTAM ASE requests a presentation context for each document type that it wishes to exchange over the duration of the association.

In this example, shown in Figure 10.2, there are three document types specified. Presentation context identifier 1 is used for the FTAM PCI, contexts 3, 5, and 7 are used for the abstract syntaxes for the three document types, and context 9 is used for the ACSE PCI.

The local ACSE constructs an AARQ APDU and passes this as user-data to the P-CONNECT.REQUEST primitive, as shown in Figure 10.3. Note that the ACSE pretty-printer, since it does not understand the data types defined in the FTAM abstract syntax, produces a more "concrete" listing than the one shown in Figure 10.2.

The local presentation entity constructs a CP-type PPDU, as shown in Figure 10.4 serializes it, and passes the result, a string of 193 octets, as user-data to the S-CONNECT.PRIMITIVE. Note that

```
{
    application-context-name 1.0.8571.1.1,     -- iso ftam
    user-information {
        {
            indirect-reference 1,                -- indicates FTAM PCI
            encoding {
                single-ASN1-type {
                    [3] '0370'H,
                    [4] '053700'H,
                    [5] '0580'H,
                    [6] '00'H,
                    [7] {
                        [APPLICATION 14] '28c27b0503'H,
                        [APPLICATION 14] '28c27b0501'H,
                        [APPLICATION 14] '2bce0f010509'H
                    },
                    [APPLICATION 22] "cheetah"
                }
            }
        }
    }
}
```

Figure 10.3: AARQ APDU

both abstract syntaxes and transfer syntaxes are defined as object identifiers. The value 2.1.1 denotes the Basic Encoding Rules, which is the only transfer syntax currently defined.

Finally, the local session entity constructs a CONNECT SPDU, establishes a transport connection, and then sends the SPDU using the T-DATA.REQUEST primitive.

```
{
  mode {
    normal-mode
  },
  normal-mode {
    context-list {
      {                    -- ftam pci abstract syntax
        identifier 1,
        abstract-syntax 1.0.8571.2.1,
        transfer-syntax-list { 2.1.1 }
      },
      {                    -- FTAM-3 abstract syntax
        identifier 3,
        abstract-syntax 1.0.8571.2.4,
        transfer-syntax-list { 2.1.1 }
      },
      {                    -- FTAM-1 abstract syntax
        identifier 5,
        abstract-syntax 1.0.8571.2.3,
        transfer-syntax-list { 2.1.1 }
      },
      {                    -- NBS-9 abstract syntax
        identifier 7,
        abstract-syntax 1.3.999.1.2.2,
        transfer-syntax-list { 2.1.1 }
      },
      {                    -- acse pci abstract syntax
        identifier 9,
        abstract-syntax 2.2.1.0.1,
        transfer-syntax-list { 2.1.1 }
      }
    },
    user-data {
      complex {
        {
          identifier 9,            -- indicates ACSE PCI
          presentation-data-values {
            single-ASN1-type {
              [1] { 1.0.8571.1.1 },
              [30] {
                {
                  indirect-reference 1,
                  encoding {
                    single-ASN1-type {
                      [3] '0370'H,
                      [4] '053700'H,
                      [5] '0580'H,
                      [6] '00'H,
                      [7] {
                        [APPLICATION 14] '28c27b0503'H,
                        [APPLICATION 14] '28c27b0501'H,
                        [APPLICATION 14] '2bce0f010509'H
                      },
                      [APPLICATION 22] "cheetah"
} } } } } } } } } } }
```

Figure 10.4: CP-type PPDU

10.2 Naming and Addressing

Many believe that a critical function of the application layer is to provide a uniform mechanism for naming and addressing application entities. Although OSI contains well-defined concepts in this area, as of the end of 1988, it did not have well-defined mechanisms to realize these concepts.

In order to capture this functionality, the author has found it useful to "invent" a new service element, the *Directory Service Element*, which is responsible for implementing these concepts. It should be stressed that the mechanisms contained in this conceptual element are strictly matters of local implementation. Nevertheless, the functionality provided by these mechanisms is sufficiently basic to warrant a separate discussion.

One may view a *binding service* as providing the mechanisms for establishing an association between two application entities. The binding process involves two steps:

1. The initiator determines which service it requires and asks to have this service mapped onto the entities available in the network; and,

2. based on the initiator's communications requirements, an association will be bound to one of those entities, which becomes the responder.

For our purposes, only the first step is of interest. Section 5.5 on page 106 in Part II discusses how the second step is accomplished.

10.2.1 Naming

Recall that it was mentioned that an application process contains one or more application entities. Thus, two components are needed to name an application entity:

- an *application process title*, which identifies a particular application process in the network; and,

- an *application entity qualifier*, which identifies a particular application entity within that application process.

An *application entity title* is the combination of these parts.

The ACSE protocol specification defines the abstract syntax for an AE title as follows:

```
AP-title ::=
    ANY

AE-qualifier ::=
    ANY
```

Thus, the ACSE is capable of carrying any ASN.1 defined data type for these fields. To provide further flexibility, the ACSE protocol permits either of these fields to be optional. It should be noted that this flexibility is due to political indecision rather than technical resolve: the committees responsible for producing the standards on application naming could not agree on the form used for an application layer name.

Fortunately, common agreements exist as to what form should be used. Until its matriculation at the end of 1988, the OSI Directory had little impact on data types used for AE titles. Historically, an object identifier was used for the application process title, with a fixed value, e.g.,

```
nilAPtitle OBJECT IDENTIFIER ::=
    { 1 3 9999 1 7 }
```

Further, since in practice, all APs had a single application entity, the application entity qualifier was absent.

However, with the awesome OSI Directory now poised to make a profound impact on application addressing, the AP title generally takes the form of a *Distinguished Name* (DN).

In order to explain application layer naming, it is necessary now to introduce the concept of a Distinguished Name (DN). A DN is an ASN.1 data type defined by the OSI Directory. Basically it is a **SEQUENCE** of attribute/value pairs, termed attribute value assertions. Because it is a **SEQUENCE**, and not a **SET**, the ordering of the pairs is significant: they imply a superior/subordinate relationship between two adjacent components.

Briefly, each component of a Distinguished Name consists of an attribute type and an attribute value. For example:

```
countryName               =    "United States"
organizationName          =    "The Wollongong Group"
organizationalUnitName    =    "Software Engineering"
commonName                =    "gonzo"
commonName                =    "filestore"
```

contains five components. (Actually, this example is highly conceptualized: the attribute types in a Distinguished Name are object identifiers, and any ASN.1 data type can be used for an attribute value.)

A DN refers to an entry in the OSI Directory. Each entry has an object class that indicates what kind of entry it is, and what kinds of attributes it has. The Directory defines several classes. For purposes of the current discussion, there are two object classes of interest, applicationProcess and applicationEntity, which refer precisely to application processes and application entities.

Thus, when an association is to be established, the initiating application entity constructs the Distinguished Name of the responding application entity. After a brief digression, the discussion will return to how this name is mapped into an application layer address.

Application Entity Information

In Section 10.1 the term *application entity information* was repeatedly used but never defined. When referring to an application entity, there are actually four (not two) components that provide identification. The first two, application process title and application entity qualifier, have already been discussed.

The other two components are *application process invocation-identifier*, and *application entity invocation-identifier*. The reason for their presence is that different instantiations of application processes and entities might exist over time. If an association is re-established (e.g., after network failure), it may be important to identify precisely which application entity was previously involved in the association. For example, this information might be needed to resume a session activity.

Thus, when Section 10.1 mentioned that a parameter to the A-ASSOCIATE service contained AE information, there are actually four parameters given to the service primitive. Although this is quite general, the author suspects that it is likely to be some time before application entity information contains any component other than an application process title.

10.2.2   Addressing

Given that an initiator has constructed an application entity title, before an association to that application entity can be established, the corresponding *presentation address* must be ascertained.

With the help of the OSI Directory, this is straightforward. Since an application entity title contains a Distinguished Name of an entry in the OSI Directory, it is a simple matter of invoking a read operation of the `presentationAddress` attribute of that entry. As with all attributes in the Directory, the value of this attribute is defined using ASN.1:

```
PresentationAddress ::=
        SEQUENCE {
            pSelector[0]
                OCTET STRING
                OPTIONAL,

            sSelector[1]
                OCTET STRING
                OPTIONAL,

            tSelector[2]
                OCTET STRING
                OPTIONAL,

            nAddresses[3]
                SET OF (1..MAX)
                    OCTET STRING
        }
```

Note that this format is used when application entities exchange presentation addresses. If users are ever required to enter a presentation address, then an ASCII encoding of some kind is required. Whilst not an OSI standard, [SKill89a] defines such a format.

10.2.3   The Higher-Performance Nameservice

There are two little problems with the scenario presented thus far. The first is a bootstrapping problem: since the Directory service itself is offered by an application entity, then there must be some means of deducing the presentation address of the local Directory — without using Directory Services! In practice, a local configuration file contains this addressing information.

The second problem is one of efficiency and timeliness. The OSI Directory, like the other OSI applications, offers a rich and varied service. The OSI mechanism for talking to the Directory is quite capable of answering the question:

> *What is the presentationAddress attribute of the object represented by this Distinguished Name?*

In fact, this is hardly a challenge for the Directory.

However, as has been repeatedly discussed, generality is costly. In the case of using the Directory to map names into addresses, there are two costs: first, in order to provide a general-purpose service, the OSI protocol used to talk to the Directory, the *Directory Access Protocol* (DAP), is quite complex. This complexity means that an application must be prepared to handle the numerous nuances of the protocol. The cost here is both the size of code to handle the protocol, and knowledge on the part of the application to use the new code. Experience with nameservices from other protocol suites shows this cost to be largely inappropriate for the task at hand.

The second cost is more devastating however: the DAP is a connection-oriented protocol. This means that an association to the Directory must be established before any "useful work" can be performed. Unfortunately, connection establishment is the single most costly part of OSI, because of both latency in the network and the myriad negotiations that are entailed at each layer. Given that some implementations require 30 seconds or more to establish only a session connection, this cost could be prohibitive. Again, experience with nameservices from other protocol suites shows this cost to be inappropriate for the task at hand.

In experimenting with the landmark QUIPU Directory [SKill88], the need for a higher-performance nameservice became apparent.

Given that name/address mapping would be the primary use of such a service, there are three requirements:

- only a single attribute would be queried in a given transaction;

- only public-readable information would be returned, to avoid the need for access control; and,

- most information would be present in an entity residing locally providing the Directory Service; if not, then that entity and *not* the application would be responsible for using the full Directory protocols to find the information. (This entity is, of course, a Directory System Agent, which was introduced in Section 6.6.1 on page 148.)

The resulting work, whilst not an OSI standard, is nevertheless very useful for nameservice in a local environment. However, it must be stressed that the overriding design criterion was one of simplicity. If some query cannot be performed with this nameservice, then rather than extending the functionality of the nameservice, the DAP should probably be used instead.

The nameservice protocol does not use any of the mechanisms employed by more sophisticated and robust transaction protocols: a query is sent using a connectionless-mode transport service. The requestor waits a fixed amount of time (usually 15 seconds). If no response is returned in this time, another query is sent. This is repeated up to a fixed number of times (usually 3 tries). If no response is returned, the nameservice returns failure. Since the nameservice is limited to a local area environment, this simple-minded approach is a relatively efficient mapping.

Data types defined using ASN.1 are used for the queries and responses of the protocol. The Basic Encoding Rules are used to serialize the data structures.

A query looks like this:

```
Query
    ::=
    [0]
        IMPLICIT SEQUENCE {
            request-id[0]
                IMPLICIT INTEGER,
```

```
            name[1]
                IMPLICIT IA5String,

            attribute[2]
                IMPLICIT IA5String
        }
```

The `request-id` field is used to correlate incoming responses with previous queries. The `name` field contains a concise ASCII string encoding of a Distinguished Name, using a format defined by QUIPU for this purpose. The `attribute` field contains an ASCII string encoding of the attribute to be queried. (It is more efficient to use simple strings, so as to avoid knowing about the Directory's Information Framework abstract syntax.)

Upon receiving a query, the Directory constructs an environment to process the query. This environment is marked for high-priority execution and no access rights. Then a response is prepared using the `request-id` from the query. The string form of the Distinguished Name is mapped into its corresponding ASN.1 syntax. This is placed into the response; the initiator will most likely use this as an application entity title.

Next, a read operation on the Distinguished Name is performed. If the Distinguished Name exists, and if it has the indicated attribute, then the value of that attribute is placed in the response.[1]

The response is then returned:

```
Response
    ::=
    [1]
        IMPLICIT SEQUENCE {
            request-id[0]
                IMPLICIT INTEGER,

            name[1]
                ANY
                OPTIONAL,

            value[2]
```

---

[1]In the case where multiple attribute values are present, one of the values is arbitrarily chosen to be returned.

```
                    ANY
                    OPTIONAL
          }
```

As noted earlier, the `request-id` of the response matches the corresponding field of the query. Note that if the mapping from string-form to DN fails (i.e., an invalid syntax is used), then the `name` field is not present. This is useful information to the initiator. Similarly, if the named object does not exist, or if it doesn't have the named attribute, then the `value` field is not present.

10.2.4   Naming Revisited

The entire discussion thus far has been predicated on one very simple, but nonetheless crucial phrase:

> *Given than an initiator has constructed an application entity title...*

Unfortunately, most application programs aren't given a Distinguished Name by the user — they have to construct one from incomplete information supplied by the user. More precisely, most application programs are supplied a textual string denoting a simple name for an end-system. For example, if a user wished to transfer files to a host called `gonzo`, then an interactive FTAM initiator might be invoked thusly:

```
% ftam gonzo
```

OSI purists argue that this approach is wrong: OSI applications deal with *services*, not *hosts*. As such, a complete service name (i.e., a Distinguished Name) should be given. However, the style of interaction shown in this example is quite common with today's applications.

Although `gonzo` is the name of a computer, it bears no resemblance to a Distinguished Name. It is now the task of the application somehow to translate this into something that is acceptable to the OSI Directory. How this mapping is performed is strictly a local matter. From a practical perspective, there are only crude, ad hoc methods available. Nevertheless, they are proving adequate for the short-term. Here is one approach:

If the information provided by the user is not a Distinguished Name, then build a logical service name consisting of two parts: a *designator*, which specifies some logical point in the network; and, a *qualifier*, which indicates a facility at that point. Each application should know the qualifier associated with the service in which it is interested. For example, generic FTAM applications are interested in the `filestore` qualifier. The designator is derived from information supplied by the user, in this case, gonzo.

Now that we have a logical service name, a local table is used to map this onto a Distinguished Name. This is done by consulting a locally maintained table that maps designators to prefixes of a Distinguished Name. For example, an entry might be:

```
gonzo:    countryName             =    "United States"
          organizationName        =    "The Wollongong Group"
          organizationalUnitName  =    "Software Engineering"
          commonName              =    "gonzo"
```

Next, a new component is added onto the end of the prefix:

```
          commonName              =    qualifier
```

In the FTAM example, `filestore` would be used for the qualifier.

As should be obvious, maintenance of the table is problematic. Further, if one could maintain such a table locally, then there would be no need to use the Directory at all! Finally, not all sites would choose to implement this particular naming scheme for their application entities. Nonetheless, in the absence of other, more workable, alternatives, this scheme is adequate for the short-term. At present, unless the application already knows the Distinguished Name of the application entity with which it wishes to associate, then there is simply no alternative outside of searching the Directory. In this case, the system will still require additional local information in order to limit the scope of the search.

10.3   Reliable Transfer

Independent of its complexity, the user-data exchanged at the application layer might be quite large. For example, an application might treat a multi-page structured document as a single ASN.1 data type. If such an object were exchanged, there is a possibility that the underlying network connection might fail during the transfer. Later on, when the network regains its health and a new connection is established, it would be desirable to continue the application exchange, resuming transfer of the potentially large object.

Earlier, the discussion described how the OSI session service provides this kind of functionality with the notions of checkpointing and activities. Applications require two other facilities:

- the service must deal with ASN.1 data types (APDUs) rather than a string of octets (SSDUs); and,

- the complexity of the underlying session service must be abstracted into a single, easily usable service.

The *Reliable Transfer Service Element* is the application service element that provides this service to other ASEs in the application entity.

The purpose of the RTSE is to provide a service which, whilst not as general as the complete session services, nonetheless captures the essence of reliably moving arbitrarily large objects from one AE to another.

When an application context contains an RTSE, it is the sole user of ACSE services and the presentation service. Skipping ahead, Figure 10.5 on page 427 illustrates this.

The RTSE service is conceptually quite simple: after an association is formed, one or more transfers occur. When a transfer is confirmed, the requesting application entity is assured that the object it sent has been "secured" by the RTSE entity on the accepting side. If a transfer does not complete for some reason (e.g., repeated, catastrophic network failure), then this is signalled to the requesting AE.

10.3.1 RTSE Primitives

The discussion now considers the primitives composing the reliable transfer service. By convention, RTSE service primitives are prefixed with "RT-". The RTSE service is defined in [ISO88h]. The International Standard definition of the service is technically aligned with the 1988 CCITT recommendation on the RTSE service, [CCITT88f]. The differences between the International Standard definition and the CCITT definition are quite small, and should not affect interoperability between implementations written against either document.

The 1984 CCITT recommendations also defined a reliable transfer service, slightly different than the 1988 recommendations. This service, and its corresponding protocol, are defined in [CCITT84b]. They are of historical interest only.

Association Establishment Phase

As noted earlier, the RTSE uses ACSE services in order to establish an association to a responding application entity. Thus, when an RTSE is present, the A-ASSOCIATE service is unavailable to the other ASEs.

Association Establishment

The association establishment service, RT-OPEN, establishes an association between two AEs. This is a confirmed service, consisting of four primitives:

- RT-OPEN.REQUEST, which is invoked by the initiating application entity;

- RT-OPEN.INDICATION, which is given to the responding application entity;

- RT-OPEN.RESPONSE, which is invoked by the responding application entity; and,

- RT-OPEN.CONFIRMATION, which is given to the initiating application entity;

The relationships among these primitives are straightforward:

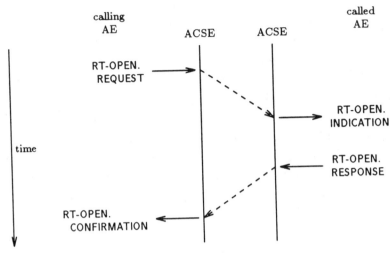

As with the A-ASSOCIATE service, there are over 20 parameters associated with each primitive. Most of these parameters are simply passed through to ACSE, which passes many of these to the presentation service, and so on. Rather than list all the parameters here, only those of particular interest to the users of the RTSE will be examined:

dialogue-mode: (mandatory) one of two choices:

> **monologue:** only the AE that initially has the *turn* is allowed to request transfers; or,

> **two-way alternate:** either AE is allowed to request transfers.

> In order to request a transfer, an application entity must own the turn. Hence, a choice of "monologue" essentially says that ownership of the turn is constant for the association.

initial-turn: (mandatory) one of two choices:

> **initiator:** the initiator owns the turn initially; or,

> **responder:** the responder owns the turn initially.

user-data: (optional) initialization information for other ASEs in this application entity.

mode: (optional) one of two choices:

> **normal:** the full reliable transfer service is used (the default); or,
>
> **X.410–1984:** a mode is used providing for backwards compatibility with systems using the 1984 CCITT Recommendations on Message Handling Systems.
>
> This parameter is passed to the A-ASSOCIATE service.
>
> The remainder of the discussion does not consider the latter mode. It suffices to say that it provides for the implicit presentation layer used in the application model defined by these early documents.

The remaining parameters are passed to the A-ASSOCIATE service.

Data Transfer Phase

There are two aspects of data transfer: reliable transfer and turn management.

Reliable Transfer

There is only one service to transfer user-data, the RT-TRANSFER service. This is a somewhat strange service in that it is confirmed, but has only three primitives:

- RT-TRANSFER.REQUEST, which is invoked by the requesting application entity;

- RT-TRANSFER.INDICATION, which is given to the accepting application entity; and,

- RT-TRANSFER.CONFIRMATION, which is given to to the requesting application entity.

As can be seen, there is no RT-TRANSFER.RESPONSE primitive:

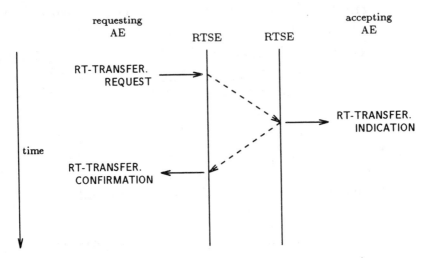

This service attempts to model the notion that the RTSE service provider generates a confirmation directly, rather than having the accepting application entity generate a response that then triggers a confirmation. Hence, the rather strange diagram. Since the reliable transfer service is supposed to issue a confirmation after the user-data is secured by the RTSE entity on the accepting side, this interaction makes sense.

From an implementational standpoint however, great care must be taken to assure that, after confirming the transfer, the RTSE is able to deliver the user-data successfully to the accepting application element. This is most likely a design error in the RTSE. It would probably have been better to have confirmation of the RT-TRANSFER service indicate that the accepting application entity had secured the data, rather than the RTSE associated with the accepting AE. In other words, if there were an RT-TRANSFER.RESPONSE primitive, then this service would be less prone to error.

There are two parameters to the RT-TRANSFER.REQUEST primitive: user-data, a single presentation data value; and, an integer indicating the maximum time permitted for the transfer. The latter parameter is highly conceptualized. For example, one could view the RTSE as providing an application layer queue with the timeout could be measured in days or even weeks.

Turn Management

There are two services associated with turn management: one service requests the turn, the other transfers ownership of the turn. Ownership of the turn is required to request a transfer. In addition, to release the association, the initiating AE must own the turn.

If an application entity desires the turn, it uses the RT-TURN-PLEASE service. This is an unconfirmed service:

- RT-TURN-PLEASE.REQUEST, which is invoked by the requesting application entity; and,

- RT-TURN-PLEASE.INDICATION, which is given to the accepting application entity.

The relationship between these primitives is straightforward:

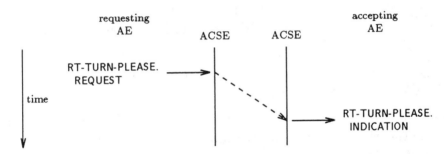

There is a single parameter associated with this service: an integer-valued priority. As with the ROSE, the lower the integer-value, the higher the priority. (It shouldn't be surprising that the "priority" parameter of the ROSE primitives is directly mapped to the parameter of the RT-TURN-PLEASE service).

When an application entity wishes to yield ownership of the turn, it uses the RT-TURN-GIVE service. This is an unconfirmed service with no parameters.

Association Release Phase

There are three services that result in association release: the RT-CLOSE service, which, with the cooperation of the two application entities, results in an orderly release of the association; the RT-U-ABORT service, in which an application entity may unilaterally terminate an association; and, the RT-P-ABORT service, in which the

RTSE service provider may inform the two application entities that the association has been lost. The latter two services are destructive: any user-data in transit is lost when they occur.

Orderly Release

The RT-CLOSE service is used to terminate an association gracefully. Before the initiating application entity may invoke this service, it must own the turn. Further, no transfer may be in progress. This is a confirmed service containing parameters identical to those of the A-RELEASE service, namely, a reason code and user-data.

User-initiated Abort

When an application entity detects an unrecoverable error, the user-initiated abort service, RT-U-ABORT, is invoked. This is an unconfirmed service with one optional parameter, user-data. As expected, this service maps to the A-ABORT service. Hence, after it is invoked, no further primitives may be used on the association.

Provider-initiated Abort

When the RTSE service provider detects an error from which it cannot recover, the provider-initiated abort service, RT-P-ABORT, is invoked. This is a provider-initiated service, with one primitive and no parameters:

- RT-P-ABORT.INDICATION, which is given to both application elements.

As the service is provider-initiated, this primitive may (theoretically) occur without warning:

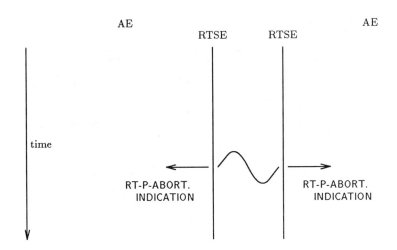

As this primitive is delivered to each application entity, no further primitives may be invoked for the association.

10.3.2 RTSE Protocol

The RTSE protocol is defined in [ISO88i]. As with the ROSE service, the International Standard specification of the RTSE protocol is technically aligned with the 1988 CCITT recommendation on the RTSE protocol, [CCITT88g].

The RTSE services associated with association handling map directly to ACSE services. These mappings are shown in Table 10.5. For the A-ASSOCIATE service, the initiating application entity requests that four session functional units,

- Half-duplex;

- Exceptions;

- Minor synchronize; and,

- Activity

be active. All tokens are assigned to the application entity owning the turn.

RTSE Primitive	APDU carried in	ACSE Primitive
RT-OPEN.REQUEST .INDICATION	RTORQ	A-ASSOCIATE.REQUEST .INDICATION
RT-OPEN.RESPONSE .CONFIRMATION	RTOAC RTORJ	A-ASSOCIATE.RESPONSE .CONFIRMATION
RT-CLOSE.REQUEST .INDICATION		A-RELEASE.REQUEST .INDICATION
RT-CLOSE.RESPONSE .CONFIRMATION		A-RELEASE.RESPONSE .CONFIRMATION
RT-U-ABORT.REQUEST .INDICATION	RTAB	A-ABORT.REQUEST .INDICATION
RT-P-ABORT.INDICATION	RTAB	A-ABORT.REQUEST
RT-P-ABORT.INDICATION		A-P-ABORT.INDICATION

Table 10.5: RTSE mappings onto ACSE Services

For turn management, the RT-TURN-PLEASE service maps directly to the P-TOKEN-PLEASE service. Similarly, the RT-TURN-GIVE service maps directly to the P-CONTROL-GIVE service.

soap...

...soap

Use of the P-CONTROL-GIVE service rather than the P-TOKEN-GIVE service is historical. Consult the soapbox in Section 7.3.4 on page 208 to understand how the creaky old T.62 protocol, to this day, manages to influence things.

For reliable transfer, the protocol is complex, but not unmanageable: Upon receiving the RT-TRANSFER.REQUEST primitive, the P-ACTIVITY-START service is invoked. The data type to be transferred is serialized into a string of octets.

The string is broken into several segments, with the length of each segment being negotiated during association establishment. Each segment is wrapped inside an **OCTET STRING** data type and given to the P-DATA service. The P-MINOR-SYNC service is then used. Based on a window size (also negotiated during association establishment), a small number of checkpoints are allowed to remain outstanding. When this window closes, the local RTSE provider waits until another checkpoint is acknowledged. This allows a small amount of pipelining in the transfer, without having to retransmit too much data if the underlying network connection breaks.

After all of the segments are transferred, the P-ACTIVITY-END service is invoked to acknowledge all outstanding checkpoints. Upon receiving the P-ACTIVITY-END.CONFIRMATION primitive, the local RTSE provider generates the RT-TRANSFER.CONFIRMATION primitive.

Of course, this is the simple, straight-line course through the RTSE protocol. If a problem occurs, the other activity services are invoked to interrupt and later resume, or perhaps discard the activity. Furthermore, if an exception occurs, then the exception reporting services are invoked.

RTSE and the OSI model

Observant readers probably noticed something unusual about the description of the RTSE protocol, namely, that the RTSE serializes a data type and then uses the P-DATA service to send an **OCTET STRING** containing a segment of the serialized information. This seems strange since serialization (the use of a transfer syntax) is supposed to be a function of the presentation layer.

Unfortunately, there is a defect in the interaction between ASN.1, the presentation layer, and the application layer. The RTSE wants to use the P-MINOR-SYNC service in order to insert checkpoints during the transfer of an APDU. But, each APDU is a single presentation data value, and the P-DATA service transfers these as a unit. That is, while several network interactions might occur when a single PDV is sent, to the users of the presentation service, a single interaction occurs.

Thus we have a dilemma: in order to use presentation layer checkpointing, the APDU must be segmented *with* the knowledge of the application layer, but the presentation service hides any segmentation that might occur! The solution taken by the RTSE is to serialize the APDU, break the resulting string of octets into segments, then wrap each segment in an **OCTET STRING** (thus creating a PDV), and then use the P-DATA and P-MINOR-SYNC services.

One solution to this problem would be to create a new presentation service that effectively provides the RT-TRANSFER service. (An interesting exercise is to consider how much RTSE functionality could remain in the application layer.) However, the arbitrary combination of session functions to form a single presentation service is probably a violation of the layering concept.

10.3.3   An Implementation

Finally, the discussion of the RTSE closes with a look at an implementation of the RTSE. As with the other chapters in Part III, the implementational framework of the ISO Development Environment (ISODE) is examined. As usual, the discussion that follows is heavily oriented towards those familiar with the *C* programming language and the UNIX operating system.

In the ISODE, the `rtsap` library is responsible for implementing reliable transfer services. This description of ISODE's RTSE facility is only a high-level overview. It is described in considerable detail in *Volume 1: Application Services* of the ISODE User's Manual[MRose89].

The ISODE implementation of the RTSE is minimal: although it understands the entire protocol, it does not perform connection re-establishment if the network fails. Rather, this is reported back to the user as a RT-P-ABORT.INDICATION primitive.

Of interest for this example is the interface to the RT-TRANSFER service. The routine `RtTransferRequest` is used to request a reliable transfer:

```
int     RtTransferRequest (sd, data, secs, rti)
int     sd;
PE      data;
int     secs;
struct RtSAPindication *rti;
```

The parameters to this procedure are:

> sd: the association-descriptor;

> data: the user-data to be transferred;

> secs: the maximum number of seconds to wait for the data to be transferred (values less than zero indicate no timeout); and,

> rti: a pointer to a `RtSAPindication` structure, which is updated only if the transfer fails.

The routine returns the value OK if the transfer completes (i.e., a RT-TRANSFER.CONFIRMATION event occurs). Otherwise, the value NOTOK is returned, with additional information encoded in the `rti` parameter.

This interface, the original one provided in the ISODE, is rather simple-minded. It assumes that the user-data to be transferred can be kept entirely memory-resident. To provide for applications that deal with objects that are inherently large and queue-based (e.g., message handling), a new interface was added. The routine `RtSetDownTrans` can be called to register a user-data source for the transfer:

```
int     RtSetDownTrans (sd, fnx, rti)
int     sd;
IFP     fnx;
struct RtSAPindication *rti;
```

After the user calls this `RtSetDownTrans`, a subsequent call to the routine `RtTransferRequest` results in `fnx` being repeatedly called to supply the next part of the user-data. For example, `fnx` reads the object from disk in an already serialized form.

A similar, incremental interface is available for receiving transfers. As a result, the P-ACTIVITY-END.RESPONSE (and hence the corresponding RT-TRANSFER.CONFIRMATION) is delayed until after the receiving application entity has secured the user-data. This prevents failures between the RTSE and the rest of the application entity from breaking the RTSE service. In addition, the interface also permits the receiving application entity to cancel the transfer if local problems arise, e.g., no more disk space is available.

10.4 Remote Operations

Remote operations are a popular technique for building distributed applications. OSI provides a powerful notation, the RO-notation, for specifying the external interactions of these systems. This is attractive as the RO-notation specifies the external behavior of systems without placing unnecessary constraints on the internal design of those systems. Many, including the author, feel that this capability is likely to be a key factor in the overall success of OSI standardization.

10.4.1 A Model for Distributed Applications

In many architectures, including OSI, remote operations are viewed as part of a methodology for building distributed applications. In OSI, the landmark document [ECMA85] was the first to describe this methodology as a part of total framework for building distributed applications. Although the latter half of this document has been rendered obsolete by more recent work in the standards bodies, this citation nonetheless provides an excellent insight into the OSI model for distributed applications.

In order to understand this model, it is necessary to re-visit several of the notions introduced in Section 8.1 and relate them to remote operations.

Abstract Data Types

An *abstract data type* is a concept for describing a data structure that is accessed in a well-defined manner. This has several implications:

- Although the data structure may have a *concrete representation* on a given local system (e.g., a *C* struct), its corresponding abstract data type is defined in an implementation-independent fashion, termed its *abstract syntax.*

  In OSI, Abstract Syntax Notation One (ASN.1) provides this function.

- A well-defined set of rules, defined by an *abstract transfer notation,* is used to serialize objects expressed using the abstract syntax so that a data structure corresponding to the abstract data type may be unambiguously transmitted on the network. There are actually two mappings here:

- First, the data structure is mapped to the abstract syntax for the abstract data type.

- Second, the abstract syntax is mapped to the concrete syntax. This is a serializing activity resulting in a string of octets. Do not confuse the concrete representation described above (which deals with programming languages), with the concrete syntax (which deals with transmission properties).

In OSI, the first mapping is a local matter. The second mapping is usually achieved by the Basic Encoding Rules (BER) of ASN.1.

- Access to an abstract data type is defined by a set of unitary actions termed *operations*, which define the complete behavior of an instance of the abstract data type.

In OSI, remote operations serve this purpose.

- *Strong typing* results when operations are the only permitted means of accessing an abstract data type.

An *object model* for programming follows from the use of abstract data types rather than concrete data structures. The use of operations, rather than direct manipulation, provides an important level of indirection; data structures may be accessed without regard to their local implementation.

Operations

Having described the relationships among data structures, abstract data types, and operations, consider the generic structure of an operation. An *operation*, in its most primitive form, is a simple request/reply interaction. The interaction takes the following form:

- The operation is *invoked*. An invocation consists of:

   - an *operation number*, which uniquely identifies the operation to be performed;

The operation number is sometimes termed an *operation value*. Although accurate from the perspective of the RO-notation, this is somewhat confusing, as it could also be interpreted as the result returned by an invocation. The author prefers to use the former term so as to avoid undue confusion.

– an arbitrarily complex *argument*;

– an *invocation identifier*, which is used to distinguish this invocation from other previous invocations; and,

– possibly a *linked invocation identifier*, which is used to indicate that this operation is being invoked as a part of the processing of another invocation.

If an invocation does not contain a linked identifier, then it is termed a *top-level invocation*. Otherwise, it is termed a *child invocation*. Sometimes the term *parent invocation* is also used. This refers to an invocation that results in a child invocation being made. Note that a parent invocation need not be a top-level invocation — it might be the child of some other invocation!

In OSI, it is possible to have several operations being invoked simultaneously: remote operations are inherently asynchronous. It is the responsibility of the application entity, and not the ROSE, to coordinate events.

• If the operation succeeds, then a *result* may be returned. A result consists of:

– an invocation identifier corresponding to the operation that succeeded; and,

– (possibly) an arbitrarily complex *result*.

• If the operation fails, then an *error* is returned. An error consists of:

– an invocation identifier corresponding to the operation that failed;

– an *error number* uniquely identifying the error that occurred; and,

- (possibly) an arbitrarily complex *parameter* that provides clarifying information.

It should be noted that failure, per se, might be a perfectly acceptable outcome for an operation. For example, if one implemented a locking protocol using remote operations, then an error saying "resource already locked" is something that the application should consider a "normal" event.

- If the operation was not performed for some reason (e.g., an unknown operation number, mistyped arguments for the operation, and so on), then a *rejection* is returned. A rejection consists of:

  - an invocation identifier corresponding to the operation that was performed (in degenerate cases, this information may not be available); and,

  - a *reason*, which describes, in general terms, the rejection which occurred.

Although the characteristics of operations will vary between applications, there are two certain guidelines that should be of universal interest.

Reliability Characteristics

When executing an operation in a distributed environment, there is always an element of uncertainity with regard to the occurrence of remote events, particularly when failures occur. One classification of reliability might be as follows: for a given invocation, a guarantee is given that it occurs *exactly once*, *at least once*, or *at most once*.

The first two guarantees require an end-to-end confirmation, with the proviso that the semantics of *exactly once* require a recovery scheme in the event of failures. When an operation has the semantics of *at least once*, it is called *idempotent*. These are operations that produce valid results, regardless of the remote state.

In practice, implementing these semantics is surprisingly straight-forward, given the judicious use of invocation identifiers:

exactly once: The invoker repeatedly requests the operation (using the same invocation identifier) until either a confirmation (result or error) is received or a rejection of "duplicate operation" is received. The performer keeps track of the invocation identifiers of all performed operations requested by an entity from an epoch date. If the performer finds an invocation identifier being repeated, rather than perform the operation, it rejects the operation as a "duplicate operation."

at least once: The invoker repeatedly requests the operation (with any invocation identifier) until a confirmation (result or error) is received. The performer need have no state information regarding previously used invocation identifiers.

at most once: The invoker requests the operation exactly once with any invocation identifier. The performer has no state information regarding previously used invocation identifiers.

The Importance of Totality

It is important to understand the concept of *totality* with respect to operations discussed here: for any given operation, the normal outcome (the result) and all exception outcomes (the errors and rejections) should be well-defined and distinguishable. This is an important feature of any reliable system.

However, it should be noted that use of remote operations does not mandate totality. For example, it is possible to define operations that:

- return only a result;

- return only an exception, if any;

- do not return any outcome.

In these cases, there is an inherent ambiguity since after an operation is started, there is no way of knowing when it has completed. The discussion briefly considers why this is so.

An operation may be thought of as *confirmed* when either a result or error is returned by the performer. However, as just noted, this needn't be the case under the OSI framework for remote operations. This is a subtle point, but one worth emphasizing: defining operations that, on success, do not return a result, leads to ambiguity inasmuch as the invoker cannot determine the "correct" time to terminate the association, since "silence" on the part of the performer could mean that the operation completed successfully or that the operation was still in progress and an error return might be forthcoming. In keeping with the philosophy of total operations, it is important to have an operation return a result, even if no user-data is contained therein. However, it should be noted that some argue that this is an important feature, which should not be denied a sophisticated application protocol.

10.4.2 The Role of the ROSE

The *Remote Operations Service Element* (ROSE) is used to manage these request/reply interactions for an application entity. An application entity that requests an operation is termed the *invoker*; similarly, an application entity that receives the request is termed the *performer*. Note that there needn't be any relationship between the AE that initiates an association and the one that invokes operations. All three combinations are possible:

- initiator invokes operations, responder performs operations;

- responder invokes operations, initiator performs operations; or,

- both initiator and responder invoke and perform operations.

In OSI, these are termed *association classes* 1, 2, and 3 (respectively).

Although one intuitively thinks of only the first combination as likely, this needn't be the case. Returning to the example of network management, an AE running on a management station might initiate an association to an application entity running on an managed node.

This association might be for the sole purpose of having the managed node report unexpected events to the management station — by performing operations using the ROSE.

Each application protocol, by definition, indicates which ASEs are present in an application entity. However, there are certain conventions used when the ROSE is one of those service elements. From the perspective of the ROSE, the application context usually contains three or four service elements:

- the ACSE, to manage associations;

- the ROSE, to manage request/reply interactions;

- (optionally) the RTSE, to provide for bulk-data transfer; and,

- a *user-element*, which is responsible for orchestrating the application entity's actions.

Figure 10.5 shows the architecture of an application context that includes the RTSE. This has two implications:

- the user-element uses RTSE services to manage the association, which, in turn, use ACSE services; and,

- the ROSE uses RTSE services to transfer data which, in turn, use the presentation service.

Figure 10.6 shows the architecture of an application context that does not include the RTSE. In this case:

- the user-element uses ACSE services directly for association management; and,

- the ROSE uses the presentation service for data transfer.

Note that the same configuration must be present in both the application entities using an association. It is not possible for communication to occur if one AE contains an active RTSE and the other does not.

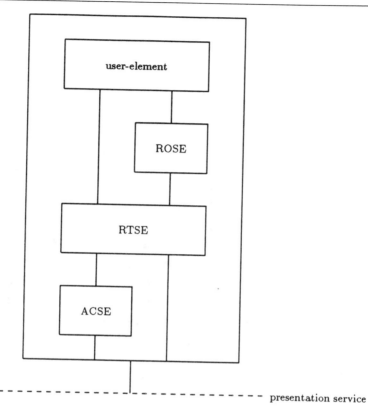

Figure 10.5: Application Context with RTSE

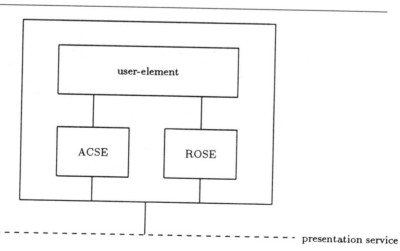

Figure 10.6: Application Context without RTSE

The RO-notation

Given either organization, an application entity containing the ROSE is interested in two activities: binding an association, and invoking operations. In order to facilitate the development of applications using the ROSE, the ASN.1 description of the ROSE provides macros, termed the *RO-notation*, which are used to define:

- application contexts; and,

- the parameters needed for both binding and invocation.

Rather than present the formal grammars associated with the RO-notation, it is more concise to present an intuitive example, as shown in Figure 10.7 starting on page 429. This figure presents a definition of a hypothetical evaluation service, offered by a "compute-engine" in the network. The initiator constructs a program fragment that it provides to the responder. The responder executes the fragment and returns the results of the computation. This example, whilst purposefully simple, is typical of the kinds of uses supported by remote operations.

The service is defined using ASN.1. It begins by defining its name and then importing definitions from three modules. The first two modules form the definition of the RO-notation: the first module defines how application contexts are put together, whilst the second module defines how operations within a single application service element are put together.

At the top-level, an application context, `evalContext`, is defined using the `APPLICATION-CONTEXT` macro and assigned an object identifier. An application entity using this service would supply this object identifier as the application context name for the association.

First, application service elements unrelated to the ROSE are specified. The ACSE is always included. But other ASEs, such as the RTSE, could also be included here as well.

Next, the data types associated with this application context for binding and unbinding are defined. Skipping ahead to the second page of this figure, we see the definition of these data types. They are defined using the `BIND` and `UNBIND` macros of the RO-notation. Basically, each macro is used to define three optional types:

- a data type that is supplied by the initiator when (un)binding;

EvaluationService { iso isode(17) demo(1) eval(8) abstract−syntax(1) }
    −− a fictitious object identifier

DEFINITIONS ::=

BEGIN

IMPORTS
    APPLICATION−CONTEXT, **APPLICATION−SERVICE−ELEMENT**, aCSE,
        aCSE−abstract−syntax
        FROM Remote−Operations−Notation−extension {   10
            joint−iso−ccitt remote−operations(4) notation−extension(2)
        }

    OPERATION, ERROR, BIND, UNBIND
        FROM Remote−Operations−Notation {
            joint−iso−ccitt remote−operations(4) notation(0)
        }

    rOSE
        FROM Remote−Operations−APDUs {   20
            joint−iso−ccitt remote−operations(4) apdus(1)
        };

evalContext **APPLICATION−CONTEXT**
    APPLICATION SERVICE ELEMENTS { aCSE }
    BIND   EvalBind
    UNBIND   EvalUnbind
    REMOTE OPERATIONS   { rOSE }
    INITIATOR CONSUMER OF   { userElement }   30
    ABSTRACT SYNTAXES   { aCSE−abstract−syntax,
                                      eval−abstract−syntax }
        ::= { iso isode(17) demo(1) eval(8) application−context(2) }

−− application service elements

userElement **APPLICATION−SERVICE−ELEMENT**
    CONSUMER INVOKES { evalOperation }   40
        ::= { iso isode(17) demo(1) eval(8) application−service−element(3) }

−− abstract syntaxes

eval−abstract−syntax **OBJECT IDENTIFIER** :: =
    { iso isode(17) demo(1) eval(8) abstract−syntax(1) }

Figure 10.7: Use of the RO-notation

```
-- binding

EvalBind ::=
    BIND
         ARGUMENT  Service-Requirements
         ERROR    Service-Diagnostic

EvalUnbind ::=
    UNBIND
                                                                    10


-- operations

evalOperation OPERATION
    ARGUMENT  EvalObject
    RESULT       EvalObject
    ERRORS      { evalError }
    LINKED      { read, write }
         ::= 0
                                                                    20

read OPERATION
    RESULT       EvalObject
    ERRORS      { endOfInput }
         ::= 1

write OPERATION
    ARGUMENT  EvalObject
         ::= 2

                                                                    30

-- errors

evalError ERROR
    PARAMETER Service-Diagnostic
         ::= 0

endOfInput ERROR
         ::= 1

                                                                    40

-- types

-- for this example, the actual definitions are unimportant...

EvalObject ::=
    ANY

Service-Requirements ::=
    ANY
                                                                    50

Service-Diagnostic ::=
    ANY

END
```

Figure 10.7: Use of the RO-notation (cont.)

- a data type that is returned by the responder if the (un)binding succeeds; and,

- a data type that is returned by the responder if the (un)binding fails.

In this example, the initiator must supply an argument for binding, and the responder returns user-data only if the binding fails. Further, no user-data is exchanged when unbinding occurs. Had binding returned user-data on success, then the data type would have been preceded by a **RESULT** keyword.

Returning to line 30 of the first page of the figure, the application service element providing the remote operations service in the application context is defined. Not surprisingly, this is the ROSE.

Following this, the service elements that use the ROSE are defined. In the RO-notation, three clauses are used for this purpose:

OPERATIONS OF: lists those RO-based ASEs that contain operations that may be invoked by either the initiator or the responder;

INITIATOR CONSUMER OF: lists those RO-based ASEs that contain operations that may be invoked by the initiator of the association; and,

RESPONDER CONSUMER OF: lists those RO-based ASEs that contain operations that may be invoked by the responder of the association.

ASEs listed in the first clause are termed *symmetric*, whilst ASEs listed in the latter two clauses are termed *asymmetric*.

Finally, on lines 32 and 33, the abstract syntaxes used by the application context are defined. An application entity using this service would supply these object identifiers as the presentation context definition list for the A-ASSOCIATE service.

All of the arguments given to the

- **APPLICATION SERVICE ELEMENTS**;

- **REMOTE OPERATIONS**;

- **OPERATIONS OF**;

- **INITIATOR CONSUMER OF**; and,

- **RESPONDER CONSUMER OF**.

clauses of the `APPLICATION-CONTEXT` macro are defined using the `APPLICATION-SERVICE-ELEMENT` macro. The actual definitions for the standard ASEs (e.g., ACSE) are found in other modules.

For each application service element in the application context, the `APPLICATION-SERVICE-ELEMENT` macro lists which operations may be invoked by a *consumer* of the service element, and by a *supplier* the service element.

The critical concept here is that the user-element ASE relates a *collection* of remote operations. Although the ROSE is used to carry these operations, the focus is on the collection of operations that form the user-element ASE, and not the ROSE, per se.

The choice of the terms consumer and supplier is largely artificial. Simply think of them as relating back to the clauses used earlier in the `APPLICATION-CONTEXT` macro, as the term "consumer" in both macros refers to the same application entity. There are three clauses provided by the RO-notation:

OPERATIONS: lists those top-level operations that may be invoked by either the consumer or the supplier;

CONSUMER INVOKES: lists those top-level operations that may be invoked by the consumer; and,

SUPPLIER INVOKES: lists those top-level operations that may be invoked by the supplier.

In our example, the consumer of the ASE is allowed to invoke one operation, `evalOperation`. Note that are several implications of this:

- the supplier of the ASE is allowed to invoke the `read` and `write` operations as these are linked operations of the `evalOperation` invoked by the consumer;

- the supplier of the ASE is allowed to generate the `evalError` error; and,

- the consumer of the ASE is allowed to generate the `endOfInput` error.

Since the `evalContext` defines the initiating AE as the consumer of this ASE, one could accurately replace "supplier" with "responder" and "consumer" with "invoker" (respectively) for these implications.

Note that the value assigned to this user-element is an object identifier. This is strictly for book-keeping purposes. Other application contexts might **IMPORT** this ASE and hence need an unambiguous reference. However, the value chosen has no effect on the parameters given during association establishment.

After defining the user-element, the abstract syntax referenced by the application context is defined on line 46. This brings us to the second page of Figure 10.7.

A single operation, `evalOperation` is defined using the `OPERATION` macro. This lists:

- the argument given to the operation;

- the result to be returned if the operation completes;

- an error that might be returned if the operation does not complete; and,

- the two operations that might be invoked by the performer of this operation during execution.

The value assigned to this operation is an integer. This is unique only within the context of this ASN.1 module. If more than one RO-based ASE is to use this operation, then a globally unique value must be chosen. This is done using an object identifier, rather than an integer value.

After the top-level operation and the two linked child operations, the errors and data types are defined.

To understand how operations are invoked in this service, consider the following interaction: The initiator invokes the `evalOperation` operation.

- If, during the course of execution, more input is required, the responder invokes the `read` operation. The initiator either supplies more input or signals an error (`endOfInput`).

- If, during the course of execution, output is generated, the responder invokes the `write` operation that contains the output (and immediately returns to execution). Asynchronously, the initiator does something with the output provided.

When the execution is complete, the `evalOperation` returns a result.

Although this example may seem tedious, it provides a concise description of the application protocol used by the evaluation service. In a little over 100 lines of ASN.1, the composition of the application entity has been described, along with the rules for the interactions on the association. It is this power that makes ASN.1 and the ROSE so attractive to the application designer. Furthermore, with support from ASN.1 compilers, a great deal of the code that realizes this service may be generated automatically. (For a more even commentary, re-read the soapbox in Section 8.2.5 on page 274.)

10.4.3   ROSE Primitives

The discussion now considers the primitives composing the remote operations service. By convention ROSE service primitives are prefixed with "RO-". The ROSE service is defined in [ISO88j]. The International Standard definition of the service is technically aligned with the 1988 CCITT recommendation on the ROSE service, [CCITT88h]. The differences between the International Standard definition and the CCITT definition are quite small, and should not affect interoperability between implementations written against either document.

The 1984 CCITT recommendations also defined a remote operations service, slightly different than the 1988 recommendations. This service, and its corresponding protocol, are defined in [CCITT84b]. They are of historical interest only.

The 1985 European Computer Manufacturer Association (ECMA) document on remote operations[ECMA85] was inspired by the 1984 CCITT work.

Invocations

To invoke an operation, the RO-INVOKE service is used. This is an unconfirmed service:

- RO-INVOKE.REQUEST, which is called by the invoking application entity; and,

- RO-INVOKE.INDICATION, which is given to the performing application entity.

The relationship between these primitives is straightforward:

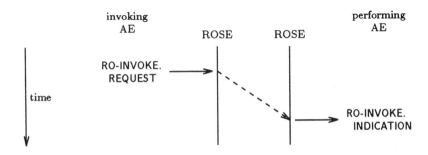

There are several parameters associated with the RO-INVOKE.RE-QUEST primitive. Unless otherwise noted, these are conveyed in the RO-INVOKE.INDICATION primitive given to the performing application entity.

operation value: (mandatory) the operation number, either an integer or an object identifier.

argument: (optional) the argument for the operation.

invocation identifier: (mandatory) the "serial number" for this invocation.

It is the responsibility of the RO-based ASEs to make sure that invocation identifiers are not re-used too soon. Earlier, the discussion on reliability characteristics noted several possibilities.

linked invocation identifier: (optional) the "serial number" of the parent invocation.

operation class: (optional) a hint to the ROSE service provider indicating whether a result or error should be expected. If so, and if the Half-duplex functional unit is active on the session connection supporting this association, then the ROSE service provider may opt to pass the data token immediately after sending the operation.

This parameter is not conveyed to the performing AE.

priority: (optional) a hint to the ROSE service provider indicating how important this invocation is. The value is an integer, with smaller numbers indicating a higher priority. Again, if the Half-duplex functional unit is active on the session connection, and both AEs are generating traffic, this allows the ROSE service provider to determine which application entity should own the data token.

This parameter is not conveyed to the performing AE.

Results

If an operation succeeds, the RO-RESULT service is used. It is an unconfirmed service initiated by the performer.

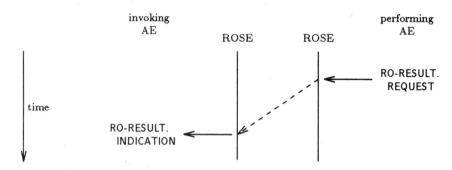

There are four parameters associated with the RO-RESULT.RE-QUEST primitive. Unless otherwise noted, these are conveyed in the RO-RESULT.INDICATION primitive given to the invoking application entity.

invocation identifier: (mandatory) the "serial number" of the invocation that generated this result.

result: (optional) the result generated by the invocation.

operation value: (optional) the operation number of the invocation, supplied if, and only if, a result was generated. This is made available for type-checking purposes. (Although the invocation identifier of the result can also provide this information.)

priority: (optional) a hint to the ROSE service provider to aid in turn management. It is suggested that the priority associated with a result should be at least as high as the priority of the corresponding operation. However, this priority of an operation is not conveyed to the performing application entity.

This parameter is not conveyed to the performing AE.

Errors

If an operation fails, the RO-ERROR service is used. It is an unconfirmed service with four parameters. Unless otherwise noted, these are conveyed in the RO-ERROR.INDICATION primitive given to the invoking application entity.

invocation identifier: (mandatory) the "serial number" of the invocation that generated this error.

error value: (mandatory) the error number that occurred.

parameter: (optional) additional information concerning the error.

priority: (optional) A hint to the ROSE service provider to aid in turn management. Again, it is suggested that the priority associated with an error should be at least as high as the priority of the corresponding operation.

This parameter is not conveyed to the invoking AE.

Rejections

There are two services associated with rejections: RO-REJECT-U, which is used when a user of the ROSE determines a problem with an invocation, result, or error; and, RO-REJECT-P, which is used when the ROSE service provider determines a problem.

Problem with	Reason
Invocation	duplicate invocation
	unrecognized operation
	mistyped argument
	resource limitation
	initiator releasing
	unrecognized linked identifier
	linked response unexpected
	unexpected child operation
Result	unrecognized invocation
	result response unexpected
	mistyped result
Error	unrecognized invocation
	error response unexpected
	unreconized error
	unexpected error
	mistyped parameter

Table 10.6: ROSE User Rejection Reasons

User-Initiated Rejections

If an operation is not performed, the RO-REJECT-U service is used. It is an unconfirmed service with three parameters. Unless otherwise noted, these are conveyed in the RO-REJECT-U.INDICATION primitive given to the peer application entity.

rejection reason: (mandatory) a symbolic value taking on one of the values shown in Table 10.6.

invocation identifier: (mandatory) the "serial number" of the invocation that generated this rejection.

priority: (optional) a hint to the ROSE service provider to aid in turn management. Again, it is suggested that the priority associated with a rejection should be at least as high as the priority of the corresponding operation.

This parameter is not conveyed to the invoking AE.

It should be noted that the the ROSE service provider has no notion as to the syntax or semantics of the invocations it carries. It is

up to the ASE using the ROSE to determine if the argument supplied
to an operation has the correct syntax, the right results are generated,
and so on.

Provider-initiated Rejections

If an operation is not performed due to a failure in the ROSE service provider, the RO-REJECT-P service is used. This is a provider-
initiator service with one primitive:

- RO-REJECT-P.INDICATION, which is given to an application
  entity.

As the service is provider-initiated, this primitive may (theoretically)
occur without warning:

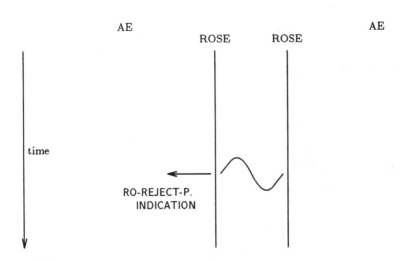

There are three parameters associated with the RO-REJECT-P.IN-
DICATION primitive.

    invocation identifier: (optional) the "serial number" for the
        invocation encountering the problem.

    returned parameters: (optional) if an invocation, result, or
        error could not be sent to the peer application entity, then
        this parameter contains the parameters to the correspond-
        ing RO- service.

    rejection reason: (optional) otherwise, one of three symbolic
        errors is given:

- unrecognized APDU;

- mistyped APDU; or,

- badly structured APDU;

Each of these refers to a ROSE protocol error.

10.4.4   ROSE Protocol

The ROSE protocol is defined in [ISO88k]. As with the ROSE service, the International Standard specification of the ROSE protocol is technically aligned with the 1988 CCITT recommendation on the ROSE protocol, [CCITT88i].

The ROSE protocol is singularly uninteresting. Each user-initiated service maps to a ROSE APDU, which in turn maps to either the RTSE or the presentation services. If the application-context contains the RTSE, then the RT-TRANSFER service, described in Section 10.3.1 is used. Otherwise, the P-DATA service is used.

10.4.5   An Implementation

Finally, the discussion of the ROSE closes with a look at an implementation of the ROSE. As with the other chapters in Part III, the implementational framework of the ISO Development Environment (ISODE) is examined. As usual, the discussion that follows is heavily oriented towards those familiar with the C programming language and the UNIX operating system.

This description of ISODE's ROSE facility is only a high-level overview. It is described in considerable detail in *Volume 4: The Applications Cookbook* of the ISODE User's Manual[MRose89].

The RO-notation is a good way of describing operations, but what can we do to convert this abstract definition into something a little more solid? The answer is to convert the information given in the operation definitions into distinct units. From the given definitions we can (at least) derive:

- a set of remote operation definitions with associated data types;

- a set of error definitions with associated data types; and,

- a set of procedure names that are either invoked or called to provide the functionality of an operation.

The *rosy* program is responsible for reading an ASN.1 module that uses the RO-notation, and for generating these components.

The name *rosy* stands for the Remote Operations Stub-generator (YACC-based).

First, *rosy* simply copies the ASN.1 definitions in the module so that *posy* program, described in Section 8.4.3 on page 328, can do the appropriate annotations.

Next, *rosy* does several things with the operations and errors defined using the RO-notation:

1. A table is built, relating for each operation:

   - its symbolic name and operation value;

   - routines for encoding and decoding its argument (if any); and,

   - a list of the possible errors.

2. A table is built, relating for each error:

   - its symbolic name and error value; and,

   - routines for encoding and decoding its parameter (if any).

3. A stub procedure is defined for each operation. Although it appears to be a *C* procedure, each stub is actually a call to a routine, RyOperation, which uses the ROSE to invoke the operation and wait for a result, error, or rejection. Most importantly, RyOperation takes the *C* structure provided as an argument, and uses a *posy*-generated routine to generate the corresponding ASN.1 value. This is then given to the ROSE service provider. When, for example, the result returns, another *posy*-generated routine is called to transfer the ASN.1 value of the result to the corresponding *C* structure.

   Further, RyOperation enforces all of the rules defined using the RO-notation. Thus, if an error with a mistyped parameter arrives, RyOperation automatically generates a user-initiated rejection on the invoker's behalf.

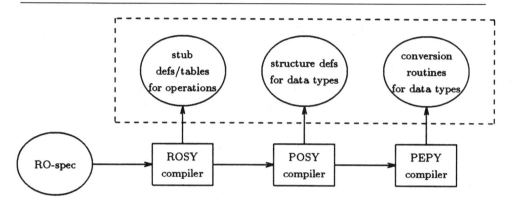

Figure 10.8: Static Facilities of the Applications Cookbook

These tables are also used by the performer, although the interface is slightly more complex. First, the routine RyDispatch is used to register a procedure that is called whenever a particular operation is invoked. When invoked, this procedure will call either:

- RyDsResult, if the operation succeeds;

- RyDsError, if the operation fails; or,

- RyDsUReject, if a user-initiated rejection occurs.

The routine that invokes this procedure does the usual syntax checking, generating user-initiated rejections, if need be.

This is the simplest interface provided to the user. The run-time library used by programs generated by *rosy* contains many other facilities, such as being able to invoke an operation without blocking, with the outcome being reported at a later time.

In this way, *rosy* provides the basic procedure call interface for the operation and provides sufficient information for *posy* and *pepy* to generate routines that perform the the encoding and decoding between ASN.1 and *C* structures. These three programs were not developed entirely independently. Rather, together with a run-time library and a programming methodology, they form *The Applications Cookbook*, a tool set in the ISODE used to build distributed applications that are based on remote operations. Figure 10.8 shows the so-called *static facilities* of *The Applications Cookbook* that these tools provide.

Routines such as RyOperation and RyDispatch are part of the run-time library for programs built using *The Applications Cookbook*.

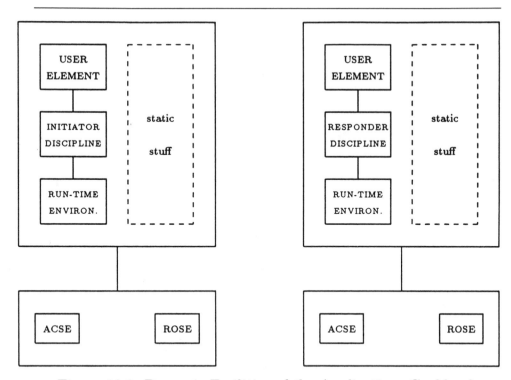

Figure 10.9: Dynamic Facilities of the Applications Cookbook

Together with the libraries implementing the standard application service elements, these form the so-called *dynamic facilities*, as shown in Figure 10.9. The run-time routines are table-driven. They take the tables generated by *rosy* and, with no other information, enforce all of the rules defined using the RO-notation for the application.

Limitations

At present, *rosy* knows only about the OPERATION and ERROR macros. The author would like to extend *rosy* to know about the other macros defined in the RO-notation. (At present *rosy* recognizes and parses the notation, but otherwise ignores the information contained therein.) This would permit association establishment to be automated in addition to operations.

Chapter 11

OSI Applications

The OSI applications offer tremendous power to the user. However, as of the end of 1988, only three applications had reached maturity. In this final chapter of Part III, we consider these applications.

As noted in *Introduction to Application Services*, these are not end-user applications per se, rather, they are collections of application service elements that are used to build applications for the users. Rather than focusing on the ASEs and the protocols they embody, the discussion will focus on the services they offer.

11.1   Directory Services

Directory Services provide a specialized distributed database for OSI applications. The Directory contains information about *objects* and then provides a structured mechanisms for accessing that information.

Directory services are intended to provide this capability for:

- OSI applications to aid in information distribution and retrieval; and

- OSI management processes to aid in network management.

Thus, the Directory is intended not only to be useful to wholly OSI entities, such as applications, but also to interface with the system-specific aspects of the computers that implement OSI.

Directory services are also intended to provide *user-friendly naming*. This permits a user of the Directory (not necessarily a person) to specify an object's name and then to retrieve additional addressing information. There are easily two important uses for this:

- name to presentation address mapping for OSI applications; and,

- name to electronic mail address mapping for use with message handling systems.

The idea of user-friendly naming is simple: both humans and programs are very good at remembering "shorthand" information about things that they're interested in. The goal of the directory is to take that specification and then provide the detailed information actually required for correct operation of the system. Considering the complexity of such things as electronic mail addresses under OSI, the Directory is a truly essential part of a workable OSI mail system.

It is important to understand, however, that the Directory is not intended to be a general purpose database. It particular, it has three simplifying assumptions:

- queries (reads from the Directory) will be much more frequent than updates (writes to the Directory);

- transient conditions, in which the information in the Directory is not entirely consistent, may be commonplace; and,

- a hierarchical, rather than relational, architecture is used for naming.

In other words, Directory Services do not purport to offer a fully distributed, fully reliable, and fully consistent database. Rather, they provide mechanisms for manipulation of information that is distributed. This is an important distinction.

Of course, the Directory must naturally correct transient inconsistencies, so that they are not long-lived. Nevertheless, it cannot guarantee consistency at any given instant.

If we ignore transient conditions momentarily, an important aspect of the Directory is that the answers it returns are independent of either the identity or the location of the application entity that is asking the questions: if the same question is asked by two different entities, the answers returned should be the same.

11.1.1 Models of the Directory

A *directory user* is a person or application process that accesses the Directory. This access is achieved through a *directory user agent* (DUA). The DUA communicates with the Directory on behalf of the user, so that a 1:1 relationship exists between the two. The internal composition of the Directory is completely invisible to the user. As the discussion will detail, very little of the internal composition need be known to the DUA.

The discussion now considers the four models which comprise Directory services.

Informational Model

The *informational model* of Directory Services describes the *Directory Information Base* (DIB). The DIB contains all the information to which the Directory provides access. Note that this model is concerned only with the logical structuring of information. Where that information is physically located is not of concern (yet).

The DIB is composed of information about objects. These are called *entries*. Each entry consists of one or more attributes. In turn, each attribute consists of a *type* and one or more *values*. The attribute's type defines the characteristics of the attribute, e.g., a phone number. In addition, it defines the abstract syntax of the values associated with the attribute, using ASN.1. If there is more than one value associated with an attribute, then one of these is termed the *distinguished value*. This holds no special significance other than it is specifically identified by the Directory:

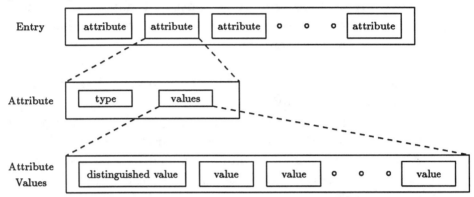

One attribute of an entry, its `objectClass`, determines what kind of object this entry corresponds to (e.g., a person). The value of this attribute indicates what types of attributes the entry *must* and *may* contain. For example, if the value of `objectClass` indicates that the entry corresponds to a person, then it would make sense for that entry to have a `surName` attribute. On the other hand, if the value of `objectClass` indicates that the entry corresponds to an organization, then a `surName` attribute would be inappropriate.

The OSI Directory is flexible in that it defines several common types of objects, and then allows users to define their own objects. Further, object definition is based on the notion of *class inheritance*. This means that an object class can be defined as a "subclass" of a previously defined object class with additional refinements. As a subclass, the newly defined object "inherits" all the semantics of its superclass, in addition to having additional semantics.

The Directory standard defines many object classes and attributes. OSI applications may also define new object classes and attributes. This extensibility will become an important factor as new OSI applications are developed that make use of the Directory.

Entries are related to each other using a hierarchical structure termed the *Directory Information Tree* (DIT). Further, each entry is uniquely identified by its *Distinguished Name* (DN). This name captures the entry's location in the DIT.

To finish the explanation of the informational model, the discussion considers how the structure of the DIT relates to the names of the entries. Each entry has associated with it an attribute called a *relative distinguished name* (RDN) with a single value. [1]

This value is unique with respect to all of the entry's siblings:

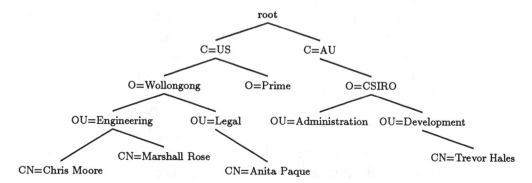

Thus, to determine the distinguished name of an entry, simply traverse the tree starting at the root until the desired entry is reached. The distinguished name is the concatenation of the relative distinguished names of each entry traversed. For example,

```
countryName            =    "United States"
organizationName       =    "Wollongong"
organizationalUnitName =    "Engineering"
commonName             =    "Marshall Rose"
```

might denote the distinguished name of the author in the DIT above.

Finally, some entries in the DIT are called *aliases*. An alias is simply a pointer to another entry. Aliases provide a convenient mechanism to add additional naming policies to the DIT. Thus, a simple DIT with a single alias might be structured as follows:

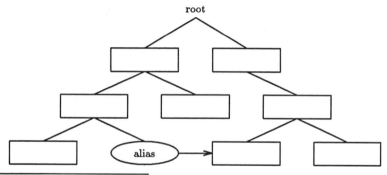

---

[1]More precisely, the entry may have more than one attribute value assertion forming its RDN.

Note that there is no entry present at the root of the DIT.

Earlier it was noted that the naming architecture is based on a hierarchical model rather than a relational model. The choice of architecture is based primarily on the notion of *user-friendliness*. In simplest terms, this means that names should be deducible by humans using incomplete information. In cases where the information available does not uniquely identify an object's entry, then additional information is required to provide uniqueness. For example, if two objects have the same surname, then information in addition to the object's surname must be provided. Further, the Directory should not require that one or both of the objects have their surname modified in order to prevent such ambiguities. Rather, the user is required to provide additional information such as a first name.

In order to make effective use of this architecture, names should be chosen to exploit, rather than hide, the inherent ambiguity of the names used in the real world. The Directory is designed to allow a user to provide incomplete information and then refine the search based on the matches that occur. When searching, different spellings, orderings, and so on should be appropriately matched (commonly known as *imprecise matching*). Finally, aliases may be used to provide further direction. In short, the domain of search and deduction is purposely much larger than the range of entries to which those searches ultimately map.

Functional Model

The *functional model* of Directory Services describes the interactions inside the Directory. The Directory is composed of one or more *Directory System Agents* (DSAs).

To access the Directory, the directory user agent communicates with one or more DSAs.

In the simplest case, the DUA establishes an association to the DSA, asks for information, and the DSA has that information. This is a simple request/reply interaction:

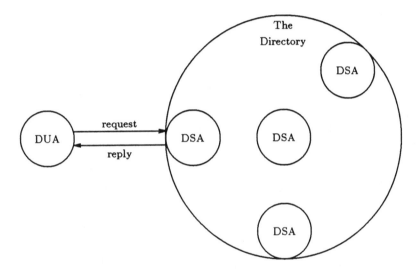

Suppose that the DSA doesn't have that information resident. In this case, it might return a *referral* to the DUA:

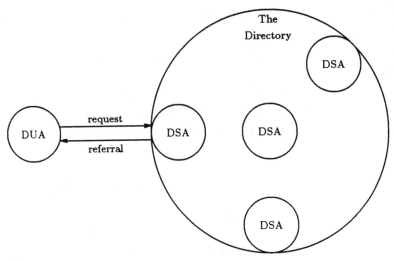

The referral contains the presentation address of another DSA that either has the desired information or is somehow "closer" to the information. The DUA then establishes an association to the second DSA, and the usual request/reply interaction occurs:

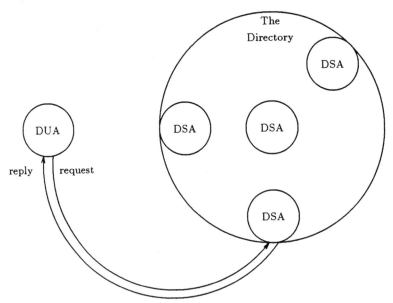

Alternatively, if the original DSA doesn't have the information, it might contact the second DSA directly. This is called *chaining*:

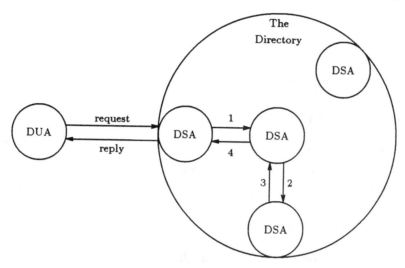

Of course, the original DSA might have to contact several DSAs to find the desired information. This may be done in parallel using a technique known as multicasting. The original DSA establishes an association to multiple DSAs.

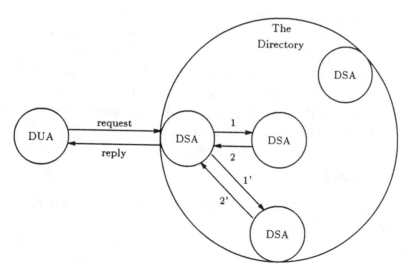

Organizational Model

The *organizational model* of Directory Services describes the service in terms of the policy defining interactions between entities and the information they hold. That is, this model describes how portions of the Directory tree map onto the DSAs. This includes issues of replication and access control. A *Directory Management Domain* (DMD) defines a portion of the Directory Tree and how it is managed.

A DMD consists of:

- one or more DSAs, which collectively hold a portion of the DIT on behalf of that administration;

- zero or more DUAs; and,

- a definition of the external behavior of the DMD, stating how the multiple DSAs in a DMD might be viewed from outside the DMD.

DMDs are further sub-divided into two categories:

- *administrative DMDs* (ADDMDs), which are run by a PTT authority; and,

- *private DMDs* (PRDMDs), which are run by organizations not authorized to assign tariffs.

The architecture of the Directory might lead one to believe that this distinction is necessary. In fact, this division is used solely for political reasons. (The CCITT, a joint-author of Directory Services, by some strange coincidence, is composed of PTTs.) Fortunately, the Directory standards do not really make use of the distinction between ADDMDs and PRDMDs. Thus, one can use the term Directory Management Domain without loss of generality.

Security Model

The *security model* of Directory Services describes the service in terms of authentication and authorization.

An *authentication* policy is used to identify both DSAs and users of the Directory. The purpose of such a policy is to define the mechanisms by which an application entity is identified to the system. In the Directory, there are three kinds of authentication: *none, weak,* and *strong.* Weak authentication is based on password protection. When an entity wishes to be authenticated as acting on behalf of a particular entry in the Directory, it supplies a password. This value is then compared to the userPassword of the appropriate entry. (Obviously, the value of this attribute should not be readable from the Directory!) Strong authentication is based on public key encryption.

An *authorization* policy specifies, enforces, and maintains access rights. In the Directory, a common way of doing this is via an *access control list*. The list defines the actions that a particular application entity may perform on a given object.

The Directory standard does not actually define a security policy. This is considered a local matter. However, the standard does give guidelines on how access rights for the Directory might be specified.

11.1.2 The Directory Service

As noted earlier, the user accesses the Directory Service through a DUA. In turn, the DUA enters into a set of request/reply interactions with the Directory, as represented by one or more DSAs.

Before the interactions occur, a DUA initiates an association (using the ACSE) to a DSA. During the association establishment, authenticating information is exchanged. Each application entity identifies itself using a distinguished name. If authentication is enabled at the DSA, then it consults the entry for the DN to validate the DUA's identity. As noted earlier, authentication may be performed by simple password or by public keys.

After an association is established, the DUA may initiate two kinds of interactions:

- *interrogation* requests, which return information about either the DIT or the DIB;

- *modification* requests, which change either the structure of the DIT or the contents of the DIB; and,

- *interruption* requests, which interrupt a previous request.

The first two kinds of interactions may be qualified:

- by *service controls*, e.g., to limit the depth of a search, or to disallow chaining; and,

- by *security parameters*, e.g., to use digital signatures;

The Directory will always generate a reply to each DUA request. The reply is either a result or an error indication. If a result is returned, then this reply is specific to the particular request issued by the DUA. In contrast, if an error is returned, then this reply is one of several commonly defined exception conditions. One such reply might be a referral telling the DUA to contact a particular DSA and retry the request.

Interrogation Requests

There are four kinds of requests to interrogate the DIT and DIB:

- *read*, which returns some or all of the attributes associated with an object. If a DUA is interested in single or multiple attributes, then it specifies those attributes in the read request. The Directory will return the values of precisely those attributes. Otherwise, if no attributes are specified, all attribute values are returned.

- *compare*, which compares a DUA supplied attribute value to an attribute value for an object. This allows the actual value to remain hidden in the Directory. (Simple authentication makes use of this.)

- *list*, which returns the relative distinguished names of the immediate children of a node.

- *search*, which applies a set of search parameters to the attributes of the subtree starting at a particular node, and returns the names of those nodes satisifying the search criteria. The depth of the search may be limited to:

    - the object at the root of the subtree;
    - the immediate children of the object at the root of the subtree; or,
    - the entire subtree.

The interrogation requests are performed relative to an object in the Directory. In most cases, the request affects only that object. In others (search and list), subordinate objects might also become involved.

Finally, there is a single request that interrupts a previous request:

- *abandon*, which allows the DUA to cancel a previous request. If considerable searching is involved, spanning multiple DSAs (that might span continents), then this can be a useful feature.

Modification Requests

There are four kinds of requests to change the structure of the DIT or modify information in the DIB:

- *add*, which is used to add a new entry to the DIB. Arbitrary insertion into the DIT is not allowed: these entries must be placed beneath entries already containing children that are leaves. This ensures that the DSA responsible for that portion of the DIT is the DSA which performs the addition. Otherwise, confusion would result.

  A second use for the add request is to add arbitrary new attributes to an existing entry in the DIB.

- *remove*, which is used to remove an entry from the DIB. Only leaves in the DIT may be removed.

  A second use for the remove request is to delete attributes from any entry in the DIB.

- *modify*, which is used to change the attributes in an entry.

- *modify RDN*, which is used to change the relative distinguished name of an entry. Note that this is not a general "move" request, since the entry retains its position in the DIT. This ensures that the DSA responsible for that portion of the DIT is the DSA that actually performs the request.

  Of course, leaf entries may be moved by simple deletion and re-insertion. This still does not permit generalized renaming.

The restrictions imposed on the modification requests are quite telling. These are due primarily to the distributed nature of the Directory. The protocol used between DSAs was not designed to provide the functionality necessary to provide general modification of the shape and content of the DIT.

Note that Directory management, per se, is noticeably missing. The Directory standard is conspicuously silent on matters such as:

- management of access control;

- management of replication and caching;

- management of *schema*, which defines the shape and structure of the Directory Tree; and,

- management of *knowledge information*, which defines the semantics of attributes.

11.1.3 Use of Directory Services

Now that the Directory Service has been presented, the discussion now considers how applications might make use of the Directory.

The Directory is designed for large scale and long-lived networks. This means that neither the DIB nor the DIT are static: objects may be added, modified, removed, or moved about.

Because of the large scale that the Directory must address, and the inherent delegation of authority needed for such a vast undertaking, the methods used for identifying objects have been optimized primarily for ease of allocation. This explains why distinguished names, the primary way for identifying an object, are hierarchical rather than relational in nature.

However, to mask this tree-structured name space, two mechanisms are available to make the DIB appear more "friendly":

- aliases, which point to other objects, thereby diverging from a strict tree-structure; and,

- powerful searching mechanisms based on matching attribute values, in order to approximate a *yellow pages* service.

The discussion now considers several applications of the Directory.

Simple Lookup

The DUA supplies the distinguished name of the object it is interested in, and initiates the read interaction. The Directory returns the desired information.

For the general case of interpersonal communications, the Directory defines objects such as:

```
person
organizationalRole
groupOfNames
```

Users of the Directory might ask for various attributes such as

```
surname
telephoneNumber
postalAttributeSet
roleOccupant
description
```

and so on.

OSI requires two directory-related functions:

- mapping an application entity title to a presentation address (this was the entire focus of Section 10.2 on page 399); and,

- mapping a network address to an SNPA address.

The Directory is clearly quite capable of performing either mapping. In the latter case however, it is not anticipated that the Directory will be able to provide timely response as the mapping is needed by the network layer, which must be very fast.

Browsing

A visual interface attached to a DUA selects an object in the tree and displays the values contained therein. The DUA repeatedly initiates the list and search interactions to allow the user to traverse the DIT until the desired object is found.

Yellow Pages

By specifying search parameters, the DUA can find those objects (there may be zero, one, or more than one) that satisfy the user's criteria. For example, the user asks for the phone numbers of all movie theaters in the Palo Alto area. The DUA forms search parameters looking for those entries with:

- an attribute type of `businessCategory` and associated value "Movie Theatre," and,

- an attribute type of `localityName` and associated value "Palo Alto,"

and indicates that it is interested in the `telephoneNumber` attribute of any objects that are matched.

The DUA then initiates the search interaction starting at a particular object in the DIT, termed the *base object*. (Starting at the top of the DIT would result in a very expensive search in terms of both time and economics.) The Directory returns the names of any objects that satisfy the criteria, along with the `telephoneNumber` attribute of each. The DUA then passes this information along to the user.

Group Membership

It is often useful to maintain a list of related objects, e.g., addressees in a mailing list. The Directory defines a group object that has a `member` attribute which takes multiple values. Each of these values is the distinguished name of another object in the Directory!

Thus, the maintainer of the group can use the standard Directory interactions to add and remove members of the group. By simply listing the values of the `member` attribute, the group membership can be listed.

Note that a member of a group can be another group object. For example, the mailing list might be divided into regions. The top-level group would contain a member for each region. Each region would be another group containing the names of the members for that region.

Authentication

The Directory supports two types of attributes to support authentication:

- *simple authentication* is supported by storing passwords for simple comparisons; and,

- *strong authentication* is supported by storing public keys for encryption purposes.

Recall that the Directory is both a user and provider of these services: when DUAs bind to the Directory, they must be authenticated.

11.1.4 Directory Use of Application Services

As should be clear from the repeated use of the term request/reply, both the DSA and the DUA use the remote operations service discussed in Section 10.4 to manage their interactions.

The only interesting requirement of Directory services is the use of the Unlimited User-Data Addendum of the session service. This is necessary owing to the large amount of initialization information exchanged during association establishment.

11.1.5 Directory Standards

The base series of International Standards on the Directory is defined in [ISO88f]. These are technically aligned with the corresponding 1988 CCITT recommendations on the Directory service, [CCITT88j]. The differences between the International Standard definition and the CCITT definition are quite small, and should not affect interoperability between implementations written against either document.

The only substantive difference is that the CCITT mandates that Directory Services be available using a TS-stack consisting of TP0 and X.25.   This is not surprising considering that all the voting members of the CCITT are national carriers that offer X.25 service. In fairness, the CCITT document does allows the Directory Service to be provided by other TS-stacks as well. Of course, the ISO/IEC makes no requirements as to the TS-stack.

In terms of advancing the OSI application services, the Directory standard makes extensive use of the ASN.1 macro facility to define a convention for *abstract service definition*. This allows more concise service protocol definitions using ASN.1 and the remote operations syntax.

There are 8 parts to the Directory Standard:

ISO/IEC 9594	Contents
Part 1	Overview of Concepts, Models, and Service
Part 2	Models
Part 3	Abstract Service Definition
Part 4	Procedures for Distributed Operations
Part 5	Protocol Specifications
Part 6	Selected Attribute Types
Part 7	Selected Object Classes
Part 8	Authentication Framework

11.2   Message Handling Systems

Message Handling Systems (MHS) is the flagship application of OSI. Of all the benefits that OSI may bring, MHS is by far the most visible and the far-reaching. Experience with other protocol suites has shown that electronic mail is the most popular of distributed applications. The technology embodied in the MHS represents major advancements over the services offered by previous users.

MHS is used to exchange structured messages. Primarily for use by humans, MHS defines the *interpersonal message* (IPM) service. But, the IPM service is not the only service that might use MHS.

MHS offers a general-purpose third-party transfer facility. Thus, for long-lived applications that wish to communicate in a store-and-forward environment, MHS is ideal. For example, given proper security considerations, applications for electronic funds transfer (EFT) or electronic data interchange (EDI) could use an MHS backbone for their communications. In fact, in 1989 the CCITT authorized a new work item to define how EDI made use of MHS.

To provide a bit of history, CCITT first published in 1984 set of Recommendations on Message Handling Systems. The remainder of this discussion does not consider the 1984 version. Instead, it focuses on the 1988 definition of MHS, which has been jointly developed by the ISO/IEC and the CCITT. Note that the ISO/IEC defines this series of standards as dealing with *Message Oriented Text Interchange Systems* (MOTIS). As a matter of choice, the discussion will use the term MHS instead.

It should be noted that as a part of defining MHS, numerous additions and improvements were made to OSI. Indeed, many components of the original 1984 CCITT Recommendations on MHS were subsequently incorporated into the OSI application layer for use by all OSI applications. Thus, MHS has been pioneering, not only as the landmark OSI application, but as the driving force behind much of the OSI application services.

11.2.1   Model of Message Handling Systems

The MHS model is based on the original IFIP work in 1979. As shown in Figure 11.1, the model may be layered into three parts. In point of fact, MHS divides the world into two parts; the "user" boxes are

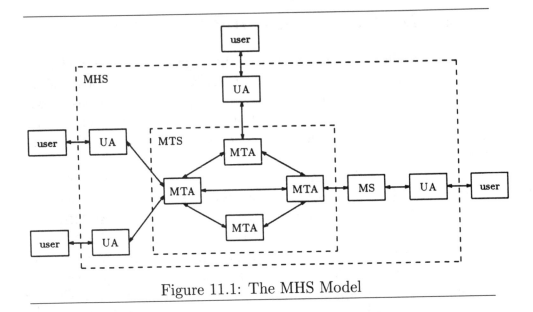

Figure 11.1: The MHS Model

logically part of the User Agents (UA). Nevertheless, the author finds it useful to view a division line between the users, and the agents that act on their behalf.

MHS Environment

The outermost layer is the user's environment. An MHS user is a person or application process that uses a Message Handling System. This access is achieved through a *User Agent* (UA). The UA communicates with the *Message Transfer System* (MTS) on behalf of the user.

The MTS is composed of one or more *Message Transfer Agents* (MTAs). In order to submit or take delivery of a message, a user agent interacts with its local MTA. This is an important division of labor: the MTAs are responsible for cooperatively routing messages through the MTS to their intended destinations. The UAs are responsible for submitting messages to the MTS and for receiving messages. However, there is a potential problem: suppose the UA resides on a computer that is turned off each night when the user goes home. Although we naturally expect the MTS to be continuously available, this is unreasonable to expect of all user agents.

The solution is to introduce a new entity, the *Message Store* (MS). The task of the MS is to act as an intermediary between a UA and its local MTA. When delivering mail, the MTA places it in the message store. Later, when the UA is available (e.g., the user turns on the computer upon arriving at the office), it will *retrieve* the mail from the message store. Further, the UA might even use the message store to submit mail, so that its host computer could perform other tasks. This is termed *indirect submission*. This split of functionality allows user agents to be relatively dumb (performing more of a user interface function), by having the message store be responsible for the interactions with the MTA.

It should be clear that the MHS model is simply an electronic version of the postal mail system. This is particularly attractive since humans understand this model of third-party delivery. As the discussion continues, additional analogies will be found.

There is an organizational model of the MHS that defines *administrative management domains* (ADMDs) and *private management domains* (PRMDs). Management domains provide a means for dividing up the MTS under different authorities. An administrative management domain is run by a PTT authority, whilst a private management domain is run by non-PTTs. ADMDs are required to have a routing capability to all other ADMDs. Outside of this characteristic, the divisions between ADMDs and PRMDs are largely artificial.

Message Structure

A major distinction between MHS and its predecessors, (e.g., the Internet electronic mail protocols [DCroc82,JPost82]), is that MHS defines an unambiguous structure for messages, and in particular, mail messages. In contrast, these earlier systems tended to use a memo-based textual framework. However, MHS is similar to its predecessors in that it divides a message structure into two parts:

- the *envelope*, which contains information used by the MTS; and,

- the *content*, which is the user message carried by the MTS.

Continuing the postal analogy, the envelope contains the return address of the originator, and a list of the recipients. Furthermore, delivery information, analogous to postmarks, is kept as tracing information.

The MTS treats the content in an opaque fashion, just as (one hopes) the postal service does. As such, the content of a message structure could be a message between two humans, or just about anything in digital form that is of interest to the user agents. In the former case, the content will usually be an *interpersonal message* (IPM).

An IPM also consists of two parts:

- a *heading*, which contains memo-like information; and,

- one or more *body parts*, such as text, facsimile, or voice, which may be freely intermixed.

Although more complex from the implementational standpoint, the use of structure gives two important advantages:

- multi-media body parts are easily accommodated; and,

- the content is more amenable to automatic processing.

The addition of multi-media support is an important step forward. For example, 1988 was widely regarded as "the year of fax."[2]   A capable MHS implementation should be integrated in with the user's facsimile resources. This permits information to remain in digital form for the longest time possible, thus making it easier to process.

Experience has shown that automatic processing is an important facility when large amounts of mail must be dealt with on a daily basis. Although several existing text-based mail systems have some automatic support, there are inherent limitations. Historically such systems have proven that whenever structured information is present in a message, automatic aids can be quite successful (e.g., [MRose85]). In contrast, when unstructured text is the only available input, little useful processing can be done.

11.2.2 The Message Handling Service

From the user's perspective MHS offers two services:

- the message transfer (MT) service, which provides third-party delivery of messages; and,

---

[2]Anytime a well-known comedian can get big laughs with a fax joke on national television, you know that "fax has made it."

- the interpersonal message (IPM) service, which provides handling of mail messages.

However, the IPM service is only one of many services that could *potentially* use the MTS.

The Message Transfer Service

The *Message Transfer* service is accessed by a user agent or by a message store on behalf of a user. For the remainder of the discussion, the term *agent* will refer to either a UA or a MS.

The primary MT service is one of *submission* and *delivery*. The agent submits messages to the MTS for other users, and the MTS delivers messages to the agent. For submission, the agent provides a submission envelope containing delivery information along with the content of a message. For delivery, the MTS provides a delivery envelope along with the message content to the agent.

In order to deliver messages, the MTS must contain a *transfer* service. Starting with the MTA local to the agent, the message is forwarded to another MTA until it reaches the MTA associated with the destination. As the message is transferred, it is carried within a transfer envelope that provides delivery and trace information to the MTS:

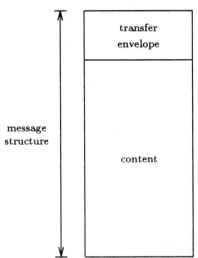

The transfer envelope contains such information as:

- a message identifier, which allows MTS administrators to coordinate messages with problem reports;

- the MHS address of the originator that submitted the message;

- the MHS addresses of the recipients (there may be more than one) and various per-recipient delivery flags;

- the content type, which identifies the class of UA that understands the content (the most common content type specifies an IPM user agent, or simply "P2," the protocol used by IPM UAs);

- the priority of the message, which presumably implies a time/cost trade-off;

- an indication of the types of information carried in the content, which allows the MTS to convert the message content if it cannot be processed on the recipient's UA (e.g., facsimile cannot be displayed on an ASCII terminal); and,

- trace information to record the "postmarks" made as the message traverses the MTS.

Note that with the exception of "type of information" indication, which might require transformation on the content, the MTS treats the content as simple opaque user-data. This can only be done if the content type is an interpersonal message. Since the MTS transfers arbitrary content for any class of UA, conversion is not always possible.

Depending on the agent's specifications when a message is submitted, the MTS will return a *report* to the agent when the message is resolved. That is, if the message was delivered and the agent indicated that it should be notified in this event, then a delivery report will be returned, also via the MTS. Similarly, if the message could not be delivered for some reason, and the agent indicated that it should be notified in this event, then a *non-delivery notification* is also returned.

With prior bilateral agreement, MTAs may define extensions to the transfer envelope. Because of the possibility of intervening MTAs not understanding the nature of the extensions, each extension field in the envelope contains:

- a type, which identifies the extension;

- an associated value; and,

- a flag indicating if knowledge of the extension is critical for submission, transfer, or delivery.

If an MTA receives a message with an extension, doesn't know about the extension, and finds it needs to perform one of the operations listed in the flag (e.g., deliver the message), the MTA rejects the message with the appropriate notification.

The MTS can also be connected to non-MHS services via an *Access Unit* (AU). This allows the MHS to be integrated with physical delivery systems, such as the existing postal system. MHS makes provisions for this capability as a future addition.

MTA use of the Directory

An MTA might use Directory Services to retrieve authentication information, determine addressing information, expand distribution lists, and to determine the capability of UAs (i.e., to discover what body parts are supported by the UA).

The Interpersonal Message Service

The *Interpersonal Message* service provides a basic message facility. This is provided by an IPM user agent directly to a user (human or program).

This service defines a format for the messages exchanged by IPM users. As noted earlier, the message content consists of a heading and one or more body parts. Hence, the relation between an MHS message structure to an IPM is:

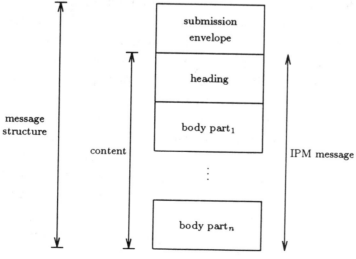

The heading contains such information as:

- a message identifier, which is used by the UA when processing the message;

- the MHS address of the originator;

- a list of primary (To:) recipients;

- a list of copies (cc:) recipients;

- a list of blind copy (Bcc:) recipients, whose addresses do not appear in the heading when it is submitted, but who nevertheless appear as recipients in the submission envelope;

- a textual subject field;

- a list of addresses that should receive any reply; and,

- cross-referencing information, such as the identifier of the message to which this is a reply.

These fields have proven useful with UA software for other message systems. In particular, they permit UAs to automate much of the process of building a reply.

The IPM service defines a number of body parts, such as ASCII text (CCITT international alphabet number 5 — IA5), facsimile, telex, and so on.

In addition, a body part may simply be a forwarded interpersonal message. Prior to the introduction of structured body parts, forwarding messages was problematic. The lack of an unambiguous method for encapsulating messages in text leads to considerable work on the part of the user. With structured body parts, the UA software may easily extract a part of an IPM at the user's request.

In addition, the IPM service allows user-definable body parts. This contains information identifying the body part type and then contains the actual contents. This is essential for providing extensibility in the IPM service, providing the originating and receiving UAs have previously established an agreement as to the syntax and semantics of the body part. For example, users of the powerful TeX processing system might exchange TeX output via MHS using this capability.

UA use of the Directory

A UA might use Directory Services to map "user-friendly names" into MHS names and also to retrieve authentication information.

11.2.3 Use of the Message Handling Systems

The initial use of MHS is fairly obvious. It is intended as the digital analogue (just testing) of the postal system. The potential for further use (e.g., EFT, EDI) has already been mentioned briefly. As such, the discussion now focuses on some aspects of MHS that relate to the basic premises of third-party delivery systems: how recipients are named and addressed, how distribution lists are handled, and how information is kept secure,

Naming and Addressing

The critical function in MHS naming is to determine the address associated with a user.

An MHS name (termed an *O/R name* or originator/recipient name) contains a Directory Distinguished Name, an MHS address (termed an *O/R address*), or both. Thus, when a message is submitted, if a distinguished name is present, and an O/R address is not, MHS will use Directory Services to retrieve the O/R address attribute of the entry identified by the DN.

If the O/R name contains an O/R address, then Directory services is not initially consulted. If, however, during transit, the O/R address is determined to be in error, then the distinguished name associated with the O/R name is used to retrieve a new O/R address.

The critical function in MHS addressing is to determine the route necessary to reach a user. Thus, the O/R address gives hints as to what routing should take place. For example,

```
countryName               =    "United States"
administrative MD          =    "CalBell"
organizationName           =    "Wollongong"
organizationalUnitName =        "Engineering"
commonName                 =    "Marshall Rose"
```

effectively threads a path through a fictitious ADMD called "CalBell," residing in the United States, which is authorized to carry electronic mail for an organization called "Wollongong," which in turn contains an "Engineering" unit with someone named "Marshall Rose."

Distribution Lists

A Distribution List is a means to permit a single O/R name to refer to multiple O/R recipients. As noted earlier, information on distribution lists are intended to be maintained in the Directory. A distribution lists contains:

- a *membership*, identifying users and other distribution lists that receive messages addressed to the distribution list;

- a *submission list*, listing users allowed to submit messages to the distribution list;

- an *owner*, which identifies the user responsible for distribution list maintenance; and,

- an *expansion point*, which identifies the MTA responsible for expanding the addresses when a message is sent to the distribution list.

Because the membership of a list may reference other distribution lists, it is important that looping is prevented. The MTS contains a mechanisms for preventing this form of recursion.

If delivery errors occur after expansion, the MTS refers the non-delivery report back to the MTA that performed the expansion. Based on the distribution list policy, the MTA might forward the notification to the list owner, the message originator, or both.

Security

To fulfill its charter as a third-party delivery service suitable for business applications, MHS must provide a means of protecting the message structure as it traverses the MTS. By using cryptography, various security services may be provided.

These are:

- authentication and non-repudiation of originator;

- data confidentiality and integrity; and,

- security labeling and credential authentication.

Depending on the needs of the application, only a subset of these services need be requested. There is nothing particularly new in these facilities, other than the fact MHS must provide the necessary mechanisms to allow the cryptographic mechanisms to be employed. Readers familiar with security concepts will note that many of these services can be provided only by using public key cryptography. This is one reason of many why the Directory standard defines a public key attribute.

11.2.4 Message Handling Use of Application Services

There are several application entities that reside in the MHS environment. In terms of their use of application services, they may be placed into three categories. Most application entities use reliable transfer. This is appropriate, as electronic mail messages might be quite large. Independent of the use of the RTSE service, some of the application entities use remote operations. This is limited to local interactions, such as indirect submission and retrieval.

As a consequence, MHS application entities never use presentation services directly. Rather, they always use some combination of the RTSE, ROSE, and ACSE services. This is not surprising considering the strategic role that the MHS standards have played in the development of the OSI application services.

Of course, it should also be noted that the application service `soap...` elements provide an important level of abstraction above the session and presentation services. It is not surprising that the RTSE was developed specifically to hide "the sewer of OSI," more commonly known as the session service. `...soap`

11.2.5 Message Handling Standards

The base series of International Standards on Message Handling Systems is defined in [ISO88g]. These are technically aligned with the corresponding 1988 CCITT recommendations on MHS, [CCITT88c]. The differences between the International Standard definition and the CCITT definition are quite small, and should not affect interoperability between implementations written against either document.

As with the Directory standard, MHS makes extensive use of the ASN.1 macro facility to provide more concise service and protocol definitions using ASN.1 and the remote operations syntax.

There are 7 parts to the MHS Standard:

ISO/IEC 10021	Contents
Part 1	System and Service Overview
Part 2	Overall Architecture
Part 3	Abstract Service Definition Conventions
Part 4	Abstract Service Definition and Procedures
Part 5	Message Store Abstract Service Definition
Part 6	Protocol Specifications
Part 7	Interpersonal Messaging System

11.3 File Transfer, Access and Management

FTAM provides the file service for OSI. It is important to understand that FTAM is intended to be more than a file transfer facility: it is the basic building block for moving files with OSI. As such, FTAM is applicable for:

- filestore to filestore transfer;

- diskless workstation file access;

- special applications such as printing and spooling; and,

- remote database access.

This is a particularly ambitious charter.

11.3.1 The Virtual Filestore

The cornerstone of FTAM is the *virtual filestore*. This describes a conceptual model of a file service on a local system. The role of the virtual filestore is to provide an abstraction capable of being emulated on top of the file services offered by a real computer. This is a difficult task, as existing file services are quite different. Nevertheless, it is quite rewarding since it provides a homogeneous view to all applications that interact with files via networking.

It is the role of the FTAM responder to take the services provided by the native filesystem and provide the OSI file service:

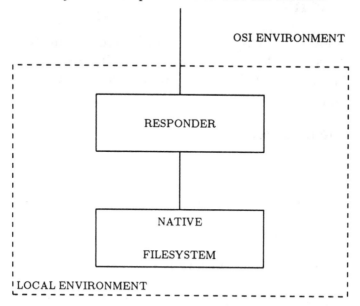

A virtual filestore is a collection of files. (Henceforth, the term *filestore* will be used to refer to a virtual filestore.) Each file has a name that uniquely identifies it. In FTAM, there is currently no explicit relationship among different files in the filestore. That is, the notion of a file directory is not a part of the standard. Experience with file services from other protocol suites have shown file directory representation to be a useful capability. It is anticipated that an Addendum to the FTAM standard covering filestore management and including file directories will be produced soon.

A fundamental notion of FTAM is that a client of the file service interacts with at most one file at a time. This is termed the *selected* file. The discussion now considers how files are viewed in the filestore.

Files have two kinds of components:

- *attributes*, which contain information about the file; and,

- *contents*, which is the data and structuring that comprise the file.

Attributes

Attributes are further separated into two kinds: *file attributes*, which exist on a per-file basis; and, *activity attributes*, which exist on a per-client basis. With file attributes, simultaneous clients of the filestore see the same information, e.g., the name of the file. With activity attributes, interactions by a client are not directly visible to other clients. For example, the method used to traverse the file is something that might differ between clients simultaneously reading a file.

File Attributes

There are four groups of file attributes:

kernel group: The attributes composing this group are necessary for file selection and basic file transfer.

filename: This attribute names the file. It is a sequence of strings. Mapping this name to the native filesystem is a local matter.

In practice, implementors of the filestore require that only one string be present in the sequence. Further, this string is passed, usually uninterpreted, to the native filesystem. As such, although the file service offered by FTAM is homogeneous. The naming conventions in the filestore are not.

permitted actions: This attribute describes the types of data access that can be performed on the file. In addition to indicating how units of data may be accessed (read, write, extend, and so on), this attribute also indicates how the file may be traversed (e.g., random order).

contents type: This attribute describes structuring information for the file. In practice, this is a document type name, which is discussed below.

The remaining three groups are optional. Their use is negotiated during association establishment.

storage group: The attributes composing this group describe the storage characteristics for the file. These are largely used for file management.

storage account: This attribute is a string identifying the filestore user responsible for storage charges.

identity of user/date and time of: These are eight attributes indicating:

- who created the file and when;
- who last modified the file contents and when;
- who last read the file and when; and,
- who last modified the file attributes and when.

file availability: This attribute indicates whether the file may be *immediately* accessed or if access will be *deferred*. The latter value indicates that access to the file may encounter significant delay (e.g., awaiting archival retrieval).

filesize: This attribute gives an estimate (in octets) of the total size of the file's contents.

future filesize: This attribute indicates a soft limit (in octets) on the total size of the file's contents.

security group: The attributes composing this group describe the access control mechanisms for the file.

access control: This attribute is an *access control list.* Each element of the list indicates:

- the file actions permitted;
- concurrency constraints that may be requested (e.g., shared read, exclusive write, etc.);
- (optionally) the filestore user permitted to request the action; and,
- the passwords that must be supplied to validate each action.

legal qualifications: This attribute defines the "legal status" of the file. This is intended as a hook to be used in conjunction with relevant national privacy legislation.

private group: This group provides a mechanism to capture proprietary mechanisms that cannot otherwise be represented by the previous attributes groups. There is a single attribute, termed **private use.** Naturally meaningful use of this attribute requires bilateral agreement. As such, its use is strongly discouraged.

Activity Attributes

The activity attributes are categorized into kernel, storage, and security groups. Because activity attributes potentially differ between clients, it is important to identify precisely when a value is bound to these attributes. For the purpose of immediate discussion, consider three separate events occuring during an FTAM association:

- association established, which occurs when the two application entities successfully complete association establishment;

- file selected, which occurs when the client successfully selects a file in the filestore; and,

- file opened, which occurs anytime when the client has opened the selected file.

Although these are not the precise terms used by the FTAM standard. They serve to given an intuitive explanation of when binding of activity attribute values occur.

kernel group: The activity attributes composing this group are necessary for file selection and basic file transfer.

active contents type: When the file is opened, the value of this attribute is bound to a particular contents type. As with the contents type file attribute, in practice, this value is a document type name.

current access request: When the file is selected, the value of this attribute is bound to the list of actions that the client may request. For file transfer and access, this can be any combination of: read, insert, replace, extend, or erase. If any of these are chosen, then two other actions must also be chosen: open and close. For file management, this can be any combination of read attribute, change attribute, or delete file.

current initiator identity: When the association is established, the value of this attribute is bound to the filestore user supplied for authentication purposes.

current location: As long as the file is opened, the value of this attribute is bound to a particular location inside the file's contents.

current processing mode: When the file is opened, the value of this attribute is bound to the value provided by the initiator.

current calling AET: The value of this attribute is bound to the title of the application entity that initiated the association.

current responding AET: The value of this attribute is bound to the title of the application entity that responded to the association.

storage group: The attributes composing this group describe the storage characteristics for the file.

current account: When the association is established, the default value of this attribute is bound to accounting information given during association establishment. However, when a file is selected, the client may specify a new value to be used until the file is no longer selected.

current concurrency control: When the file is selected (and later if it is opened), the value of this attribute is bound to a vector indicating what concurrency considerations are appropriate. For each of the actions present in the current access request, one of four values may be given as shown here:

Value	Who may perform	
	Client	Others
Not Required	No	Yes
Shared	Yes	Yes
Exclusive	Yes	No
No Access	No	No

current locking style: When the file is opened, the value of this attribute is bound to either enabled or disabled. If enabled, then when data units are transferred, they are locked to prevent other access.

security group: The attributes composing this group describe the access control mechanisms for the file.

current access passwords: the value of this attribute is bound when the file is selected. When the client subsequently requests actions, the access control list is consulted and the appropriate password verified.

active legal qualification: the value of this attribute is bound when the file is opened. The FTAM standard assigns no meaning to this value. Thus, its interpretation is a local matter.

Contents

In FTAM, files are defined in terms of a *document type*. A document type name consists of two parts:

- an object identifier assigned by a registration authority; and,

- a single ASN.1 parameter that defines bounding conditions on the document (e.g., for a document type containing fixed-length records, the parameter might indicate the record length).

The FTAM standard defines five document types:

Name	Document
FTAM-1	Unstructured Text
FTAM-2	Sequential Text
FTAM-3	Unstructured Binary
FTAM-4	Sequential Binary
FTAM-5	Simple Hierarchical File

and various profiling organizations have defined additional document types. FTAM is intended to support a wide-range of document types. As such, it must provide flexible structuring mechanisms.

The *file access structure* defines the composition of the file in terms of *file access data units* (FADUs). This describes how, in general, the file is structured. In contrast, the *identification structure* defines how a particular FADU in the file structure is identified.

File Access Structure

FTAM uses a hierarchical structure to describe the contents of the file. Each node in this structure contains:

- a descriptor, which optionally indicates the name of the node, along with a distance from the parent;

- optionally, a data unit (DU); and,

- optionally, children (other nodes).

The distance from the parent is used to determine the "level" of the child node. The root, by definition, has level 0. Thus, an immediate child of the root having distance 2 is at level 2.

As can be seen, FTAM uses a tree structure to represent a file's contents. As expected, the root node defines the "starting point" for the file.

A tree might be defined using the abstract syntax shown in Figure 11.2. This is a slightly simpler definition than the one that appears in the FTAM standard, in order to emphasize the key aspects.

Given this structure, an FADU refers to a node in tree. This node is the root of a subtree containing structure and data for the FADU. Any FADU can be represented easily using a *preorder* traversal algorithm:

1. Start at the root of the FADU.

2. Create a new sequence for the current node:

   (a) If the node has a name associated with it, set the `node-name` field.

   (b) If the distance to the node's parent is greater than one, set the `arc-length` field.

   (c) If the node contains a DU, insert this in the `data-unit` field.

   (d) If the node has at least one child:

       i. Start a `Children` data type for the `children` field.

       ii. Then, proceeding from the left to the right, recursively apply step 2 and insert the resulting sequence at the end of the `siblings` field.

A hierarchical model is probably general enough to capture the file structuring used by any native filesystem (some have argued for an alternative relational model). However, it is probably *too* general for

```
Subtree ::=
   SEQUENCE {
        node-name[0]
           IMPLICIT GraphicString
           OPTIONAL,

        arc-length[1]
           IMPLICIT INTEGER
           DEFAULT 1,

        data-unit[2]
           ANY
           OPTIONAL,

        children[3]
           SEQUENCE OF
                Children
           OPTIONAL
   }

Children ::=
   SEQUENCE {
        enter-subtree[0]
           IMPLICIT NULL
           OPTIONAL,

        siblings[1]
           IMPLICIT SEQUENCE OF
                Subtree

        exit-subtree[2]
           IMPLICIT NULL
           OPTIONAL
   }
```

10

20

30

Figure 11.2: ASN.1 definition of File Structure

Access Context	Fields Visible
hierarchical all data units (HA)	node-name, arc-length, data-unit, children
hierachical no data units (HN)	node-name, arc-length, children
flat all data units (FA)	node-name, data-unit, siblings
flat one level data units (FL)	for nodes at indicated depth from current node: node-name, data-unit
flat single data unit (FS)	for current node: node-name, data-unit
unstructured all data units (UA)	data-unit, siblings
unstructured single data unit (US)	for current node: data-unit

Table 11.1: FTAM Access Contexts

many native filesystems. The UNIX operating system, for example, imposes no structure on files at all. Each file is simply a stream of octets. Thus, FTAM provides a method for limiting the "structure" of the tree.

An *access context* defines how much of an FADU is referenced by an action. For example, an access context indicates if the node contained in an FADU is retrieved, whether its children will also be retrieved.

The FTAM standard defines seven access contexts as shown in Table 11.1.

This somewhat cryptic table captures the distinctions between the contexts:

- To reference the full structure and data of the FADU having the current node as its root, the HA access context is used. This precisely identifies all structuring information along with the data.

- To reference only the structure and no data, the HN context is used.

- To reference the subtrees (the name and DU) of the current node and all of its children containing data, the FA context is used.

- To reference the subtrees for each of the children of the current node at a given level that contain data, the FL context is used.

- To reference the single subtree at the current node, the FS context is used.

- To reference all the data at or below the current node with no structuring information, the UA context is used.

- Finally, to reference the DU at the current node, the US context is used.

To complete the discussion of access contexts, consider the two extremes. When viewed using the US access context, any FADU appears thusly:

There is no name, nor any children associated with the node. If this node is the root of the entire file, then it should be clear that files can be transferred as a whole or extended. Access to a part is not possible.

In contrast, when viewed using the HA access context, a particular FADU might appear thusly:

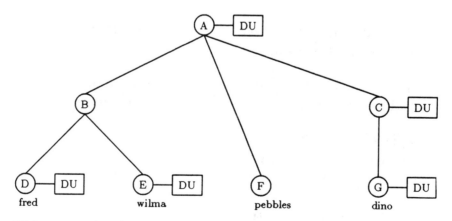

This example also illustrates the difference between a data unit (DU) and a file access data unit (FADU). Figures 11.3 through 11.5 show the level 0, level 1, and level 2 FADUs associated with this

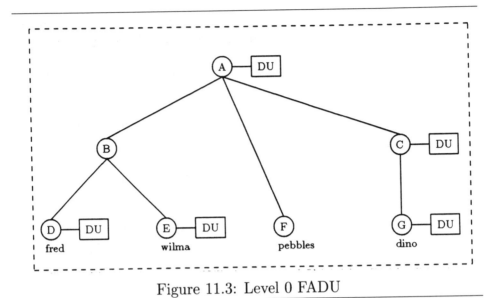

Figure 11.3: Level 0 FADU

FADU. The root of this FADU is the unnamed node marked "A."
The preorder traversal of this FADU would be: A, B, D, E, F, C, G.

Identification Structure

Once the structuring of the FADU has been identified. there need
to be mechanisms for identifying a particular FADU. FTAM provides
several terms and mechanisms to identify an FADU:

- *first* and *last*, identify the first or last (respectively) FADU in
  the preorder traversal;

- *previous*, *current*, and *next*, identify the left adjacent, current,
  or right adjacent (respectively) FADU in the preorder traversal;

- *begin* and *end*, depending upon the document type. However,
  moving to the beginning means that a subsequent next identifies
  the first FADU in the preorder traversal. Similarly, moving to
  the end means that a subsequent previous identifies the last
  FADU in the preorder traversal.

- by node name, which searches for the name at or below the
  current node.

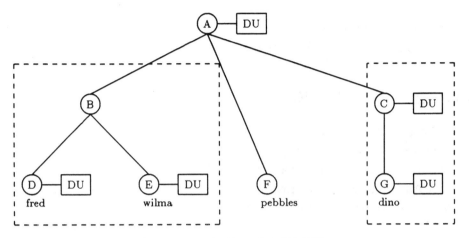

Figure 11.4: Level 1 FADUs

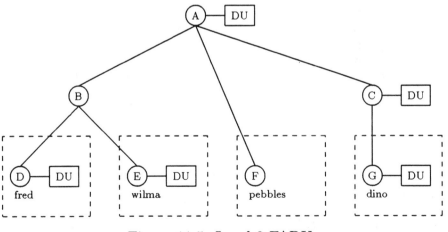

Figure 11.5: Level 2 FADUs

- by sequence of node names, which takes each name as naming an immediate child in the path to the desired node, starting with the FADU's root node. (To stay at the root of the FADU, an empty sequence is given.)

- by node number, which indicates the position of the desired node in the preorder traversal. (The root has number 0).

11.3.2   The File Service

As noted earlier, an application entity accesses the file service by initiating an association to another entity that implements the filestore. When an association is established, this is termed an FTAM association. As the association progresses through various states, different services are offered. This is captured by the notion of the current FTAM *regime*.

There are four regimes in FTAM as shown here:

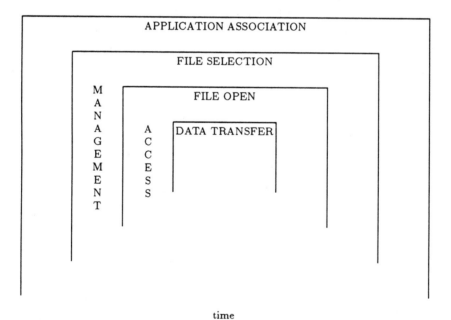

As implied by this diagram, regimes nest. A further relationship is that inner regimes might be repeated before leaving an outer regime. For example, over the lifetime of the application association regime, several file selection regimes might take place.

Application Association Regime

The application association regime is responsible for association establishment and release. During establishment, a few dozen parameters are negotiated between the initiator and responder to define a common subset of the file service. Included in the negotiations are the services available (transfer, access, management, or some combination), the attributes available in the filestore (besides kernel), and so on.

This regime is terminated by the initiator releasing the association, either gracefully or in a disruptive fashion (abort).

File Selection Regime

The file selection regime is responsible for binding a file for subsequent use. This is done by either selecting an existing file, or by creating a new file.

Once a file is selected, file management might be invoked; file attributes may be read and/or changed. After file management, the file may be opened.

This regime is terminated by either deselecting the file (removing the binding) or deleting the file (removing the file from the filestore and then removing the binding).

File Open Regime

The file open regime is responsible for allowing the file to be transferred or accessed. When this regime is entered, the structure of the file is bound (via activity attributes).

Once a file is opened, it may be accessed: FADUs may be located and/or erased. After file access, data transfer occurs.

This regime is terminated by closing the file.

Data Transfer Regime

The data transfer regime is used when data is finally to be transferred. This involves use of the *bulk data transfer* (BDT) mechanism for an FADU. The FADU is read or written.

If either application entity wishes to terminate the transfer prematurely, a cancel facility is involved. Otherwise, the application entity acting as the source of the FADU indicates when the FADU has been entirely transferred. This is necessary as, in order to make effective use of checkpointing, FTAM transfers individual DUs as a sequence of *data elements* (DEs).

The initiator then terminates the regime.

Grouping

Although the file service appears to involve many steps, FTAM provides a convenient mechanism for packaging service requests. This is termed *grouping*.

For example, many file operations have three actions:

- acquire the file for data transfer;

- perform the data transfer; and,

- release the file.

The first and last actions can each be viewed as being indivisible. Grouping permits the FTAM service to bundle these together.

To acquire a file, the typical grouping is:

- begin group;

- select the file;

- open the file; and,

- end group.

The semantics of grouping are such that the initiator can indicate not to proceed if one of these actions fails. Thus, if the file can't be selected for some reason, the open won't be attempted.

To release a file, the typical grouping is:

- begin group;

- close the file;

- deselect the file; and,

- end group.

11.3.3 Use of the File Service

Having presented the file service, the discussion now considers how applications might make use of this.

FTAM is designed for generality. As such it is quite capable, but perhaps not streamlined for time or size critical applications.

File Transfer

To retrieve a complete file from the filestore, the operation is simple:

- enter select and open regimes:

```
begin group
select existing file
open for read
end group
```

- do a read BDT

- return to association regime:

```
begin group
close
deselect
end group
```

Storing a file requires an analogous operation. The only difference (besides doing a write BDT) is that the file is created. The initiator must indicate what actions to take if the file already exists. There are four choices:

- fail;

- select the old file;

- delete the contents of the file and then select it; or,

- delete the file and its contents and then create it.

File Management

To change the name of a file:

```
begin group
select existing file
change filename attribute
deselect
end group
```

Deleting a file is also straightforward:

```
begin group
select existing file
delete
end group
```

To produce a listing of the file attributes:

```
begin group
select existing file
read desired attributes
deselect
end group
```

Remote Paging

In theory, remote paging is nothing more than file transfer done by accessing parts of the file rather than the whole. When a paging partition is to be mounted, the operating system, acting as an FTAM initiator, creates, selects, and opens a file using FTAM. The structure of this file is of a two-level tree:

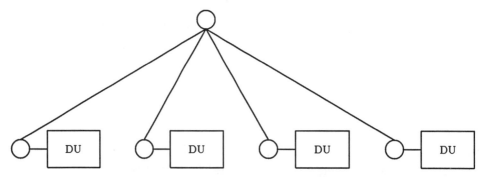

The root node contains no data. Each child contains a DU that corresponds to page of virtual memory.

Whenever a page is to be read or written, the operating system locates the appropriate FADU and then initiates a read or write BDT (respectively).

11.3.4 FTAM Use of Application Services

Although experience has shown that a remote operations paradigm can be used for file service, FTAM does not use remote operations. Rather, it uses the ACSE to manage the association, and then uses presentation services directly for all other activity.

The only interesting aspect of FTAM's use of application services is how presentation contexts are managed. At a minimum, FTAM requires two presentation contexts: one for the ACSE, and one for the FTAM protocol control information. In addition, if file structuring information is to be exchanged by the file service, then a third context is needed. This is termed the FADU PCI.

Finally, FTAM must decide if it is going to make use of the context management facilities of the presentation service. If not, then during association establishment, it must define a presentation context for the abstract syntax of each document type that it intends to transfer.

Section 10.1.3 on page 393 presents an example of how FTAM behaves during association establishment.

11.3.5 FTAM Standards

The base series of International Standards on FTAM is defined in [ISO88a]. There are currently no corresponding CCITT documents. There are 4 parts to the FTAM Standard:

ISO/IEC 8571	Contents
Part 1	General Introduction
Part 2	Virtual Filestore Definition
Part 3	File Service Definition
Part 4	File Protocol Specification

11.3.6 A Soapbox on FTAM

Experience with other protocol suites has shown that two separate | soap... | file services and protocols are desirable.

One protocol provides a general-purpose file transfer service useful over any type of networks, including those with long delays and potentially heavy congestion. Because of the potentially high latency and low reliability, the interface to such a protocol is usually either interactive or through a spooling system.

The other protocol provides file access service over networks known to have no appreciable delays and little congestion. Because of the focused nature of such a protocol, the interface is usually inside the operating system. This is particularly attractive because the combination of local area networks and tight integration makes the file service transparent to the user.

To consider the Internet suite of protocols briefly, the FTP, the file transfer protocol[JPost85], provides the long-haul service, and the NFS, the network file system (NFS), provides the local service. The FTP and NFS are entirely different protocols. Each does a job well for their particular domain.

Many perceive FTAM as failing in both domains because FTAM tries to do both. Consider: for simple file transfer, FTAM is much more complicated and noticeably slower in comparison to the FTP. Further, unless some of the more esoteric features are used, then the services offered by the two protocols are quite similar. (Of course, before the esoteric features can be used, they must be implemented, which isn't as simple as one might hope.)

For transparent file access, FTAM uses a connection-oriented model in which at most a single file may be selected at a given instant. In contrast, the NFS uses a connectionless-mode model in which different transactions may reference different files. As a result, efficiently integrating the NFS into an operating system is more straightforward.

Now consider how FTAM might be integrated into an operating system like UNIX. Ignore, for the moment, FTAM's size or speed, which could be literally two orders of magnitude larger and slower (respectively) than the NFS. Each UNIX process has a file table that is a kernel-resident data structure. Each entry in the table refers to an open file for the process. Since an FTAM association can have at most one selected file, a separate association is needed for each open file. On a diskless workstation, it is not uncommon for 25 or so UNIX processes to be running, each with an average of 8 remote files open. This would require 200 simultaneous FTAM associations! This is fine for a "big" computer. It is not acceptable for a diskless workstation.

(There are even more reasons for why FTAM is incapable of offering an NFS-like service, but these are enough for now.)

In the short-term, probably the only reasonable way of building a transparent file service in an OSI network is to put the NFS over the OSI connectionless-mode transport service.

> ...soap

Part IV

Transition to OSI

Chapter 12

Introduction to Transition

It is interesting to live in a world that is changing. Consider: the Internet suite of protocols (commonly called TCP/IP) is the current solution of choice for achieving interoperability between machines and operating systems of different manufacture, networks of different technology, and communities of different administration. For various technical and political reasons, a new protocol suite, based on the Open Systems Interconnection (OSI) model, will join and eventually displace the Internet protocol suite as the off-the-shelf commodity of choice with which to build open computer networks and user infrastructure in the office, laboratory, and factory floor. The possibilities of OSI are extremely attractive, given the wide range of applications and the far-reaching connectivity and interoperability that it can provide.

It is also irritating to live in a world that must change. Consider: the Internet protocol suite enjoys tremendous success and is becoming even more popular; however the OSI suite eventually will dominate, then eclipse, and finally make the Internet suite "immaterial." The exact point in time when the Internet protocols will be replaced by the OSI protocols is still the center of much debate, but two things are clear: first, the popularity of the Internet suite continues to increase, and second, by the time OSI has replaced the Internet suite as the protocol suite of choice, there will be many thousands more TCP/IP-based systems deployed than there are today! Hence, it is clear that there will be a transition period, perhaps longer than a decade, when both protocol suites will be in widespread use. Unfortunately, although one can achieve connectivity at the lowest layers of protocol suites, interoperability at the highest layers remains an open question. This implies that during the transition period, the fates have conspired to defeat the purpose of having interoperable systems: What's the point of having two kinds of open systems when they don't interoperate, and their user's tools will not work together?

If we believe that both protocol suites will be simultaneously widespread for some period of time, during which one protocol suite (Internet) will lose favor to the other (OSI), then there are two questions that must be given serious attention and consideration, namely:

- how can we protect our investment in the installed base of hosts and networks using the Internet protocol suite, and

- how can we gracefully transition to the new OSI protocol suite?

Hence, we are motivated to explore different strategies for transition and coexistence between the two protocol suites.

Of course, the Internet suite of protocols is not alone in this dilemma: virtually every protocol suite in use today is apt to be competing with OSI in the very near future. However, in order to present technical depth in the discussion that follows, it is necessary to focus on the problem of transition from the Internet suite to the OSI suite. However, it should be stressed that none of techniques and strategies described in Part IV is unique to the Internet-to-OSI transition. Rather, the solutions are quite general, although the actual implementations are specific to the protocol suites in use. The focus on Internet protocols is due to the extraordinary popularity of this "de facto" open interconnection protocol suite and the tremendous problem now faced by those running TCP/IP.

Part IV presents ideas that may be the most controversial in the book. To see why this is so, consider a rather non-intuitive trend. First, sales of technology based on the Internet suite of protocols continues to grow despite OSI having captured the "mind set" of the market. This is particularly true in Europe, which is turning to the use of local area networks (LANs) quite extensively. The failure of the OSI lower-layers to provide effective internetworking capability on local area network media has left little choice but to use the Internet suite, which provides solutions.

For example, on a local area network, transport protocol class four (TP4) is often used over a connectionless-mode network service. But, over wide area networks, a simpler transport protocol (e.g., TP0) is used over a connection-oriented network service. However, these two protocol stacks, each yielding OSI end-to-end services, do not inter-work. Thus, hosts attached to public data networks (PDNs) usually do not interoperate with hosts attached to local area networks even though both hosts involved are "speaking OSI." In contrast, a single protocol stack is used to implement the end-to-end services of the Internet suite (namely the TCP and the IP). These are able to function effectively in both wide and local area networks, and provide internetworking between these two environments.

In other words, if one's idea of networking is simply plugging a host into a public data network operated by a national carrier, then the OSI lower-layers work fine. But, if one's networking requirements involve local area networks *and* long haul networks, with each network potentially under a different administration, then, at present, OSI handles it very poorly.

As a result, the widespread use of local area networks in Europe and the desire to connect them to the various national PDNs have illuminated critical shortcomings of the OSI lower layers. This is particularly ironic considering that Europe has been the most supportive of OSI in the international community, both in terms of technical contributions and political endorsements.

To present an alternative interpretation of events, academic users of networking in Europe have pointed out that:

- the Internet suite is more readily available as it is bundled with most UNIX systems; and,

- implementations of the Internet suite tend to be much more mature than X.25 implementations; in particular, X.25 software in end-systems tends to be unreliable and often results in machine crashes!

To be sure, the second observation may be controversial, as it is only a general perception. Nevertheless, this argument presents things in a somewhat different light, pointing more to a lack of maturity of products rather than inferior technology.

Second, although one might view internetworking as a necessary condition for a successful protocol suite, it is not a sufficient condition. A protocol suite must also be implemented on a wide-range of platforms. By virtue of being deployed at least eight years prior to

OSI, the Internet protocols have already climbed the initial learning curve in terms of product maturity. As a result, many claim that in mainstream computing, it is now more likely than not that a computer being sold has an implementation of the Internet protocols available, if not as a standard feature, then as a third-party package.

Third, this process is self-feeding, largely due to the increased market awareness brought on by the proponents of OSI. Although in 1988, some analysts claimed that sales of technology based on the Internet suite will decrease in the next two years as OSI sales skyrocket, there was no *empirical* evidence to suggest this. There was insufficient experience at this time to do anything more than guess as to what will happen in the market for the next five to ten years.

All of these factors, both technical and market-driven, have combined to entrench the Internet suite of protocols firmly. If it were not for the broad, well-intentioned mandates of national governments, such as the OSI profiles published by both the United States and the United Kingdom[USGOS88,UKGOS88], then OSI might very well find itself "stuck at the starting gate." This leads to a central point to this part of *The Open Book*:

> *Before users will transit from the Internet suite of protocols to the OSI suite, they will have to see added value in OSI applications. Users are interested in services, not protocols.*

soap...   Before starting our technical discussion, let us consider one last marketing issue. If *survival* is the strongest instinct, then it must be said that *fear* is the strongest motivation. Markets are, by and large, based on fear and fear's two co-conspirators, *uncertainty* and *doubt*. The networking market is a high-stakes game for both users and vendors. Users depend on networking products to move and refine information in order to be successful. Vendors depend on their networking products to employ persons, like other kinds of corporations, and to make a profit, like other kinds of corporations. Thus, the large and fast-growing installed base of products using the Internet suite, combined with the looming introduction of the OSI suite, has raised the problems of transition and coexistence to paramount concern.

Unfortunately, few vendors or users actually have any concrete plans as to how they will accomplish transition. There are two common scenarios.

In the first, although Marketing has been "right on top of things" by producing such catchy sayings as:

> ... *protect your investment whilst assuring a path to an OSI future,*

and

> ... *plans for a smooth, painless guaranteed migration to OSI standards as they are approved,*

it appears that Engineering has "dropped the ball" by providing no actual technology behind the words. This is applicable to most vendors who offer some non-OSI suite of protocols (usually proprietary).

In the second scenario, which is appropriate for vendors (usually start-ups) that offer only OSI products, the plans are very simple:

> *Once you've scrapped your existing production networks, come to us for OSI. It will be wonderful!*

These are all actual quotations from various samples of marketing literature seen by the author.

Regrettably, the transition problem isn't that simple. The best one can possibly hope to do is minimize the pain, and the way to do that is to follow a focused, but nevertheless prolonged, period of coexistence.[1] As we examine the various approaches as solutions, this strategy will become more apparent.

`...soap`

To discuss transition and coexistence, a consistent framework must be developed. Initially, the key concepts of transition are presented along with terminology that will be consistently used for the remainder of Part IV. This is followed by a technical perspective of the history of the two protocol suites. In order to compare different approaches, a uniform set of guidelines must be employed. This chapter concludes with the introduction and enumeration of these guidelines.

---

[1] It can be argued that there is no choice about this protracted overlapping of coexistence, since an organization will not be able to cut-over (convert) to OSI all at once. Even if it could, it may need to internetwork with some other organization that has not yet made the transition.

12.1 Concepts

The assumptions fundamental to the discussion are three-fold:

- first, products based on the Internet suite are here today, widely installed, and useful;

- second, OSI will eventually replace the Internet suite as the off-the-shelf technology of choice for building interoperable systems; and,

- third, both will be simultaneously widespread for quite some time (perhaps a decade or more), during which OSI will gain dominance.

For the remainder of this part of the book, these tenets are axiomatic. The discussion that follows will not be meaningful, unless both the author and reader treat these tenets as absolute truth.

The first tenet indicates that there is too much of an installed base to "change overnight." Furthermore, even if the Internet protocols could be replaced overnight, unless the successor protocols had equivalent or superior functionality, then the users of the installed base would be ill-served by such a revolutionary approach.

The second tenet bounds the problem by indicating that the successor to the Internet suite of protocols will be OSI. The reason for this is simple: OSI has received near-unanimous support from industry and users alike. By the end of 1988, every major vendor of computer systems had announced a commitment (of some form) to OSI. In addition, several user organizations (such as the U.S. Government) also had announced the intent to base all computer-communications procurements solely on OSI. For our purposes, it is unimportant as to whether the motivations for OSI are political or technical.

The third tenet defines the overall nature of the problem as being one of transition, moving from one protocol suite to another. There is already a large installed base of computers using the Internet suite of protocols. For both technical and political reasons, there will be resistance towards rapid conversion of these systems to OSI protocols. Thus, a lengthy period of transition will be required.

For purposes of discussion, *transition* means to move from one protocol suite to another. More importantly, however, the third tenet indicates that there will be an extended period of time in which both protocol suites are active. Ideally, this results in *coexistence*, which means to live together without hostility or conflict, despite differences. It also implies a protracted, stable relationship. Of course, a degenerate form of coexistence could be *ignorance*, that is, the two protocol suites simply ignore each other.

Note that the expression *migration* should not enter into the discussion. The reason for this is simple: migration means to move back and forth, as the seasons change. The discussion takes it for granted that once OSI has been achieved, that the market will not move back to the Internet suite of protocols. This is sensible, as users, by and large, are concerned only with getting work done, and not with changing protocol suites at regular intervals! Although this may seem like a fine point, it is probably worth trying to maintain the distinction.

soap...

...soap

12.1.1 Mappings

One abstraction used for describing approaches to transition and co-existence can be described in terms of the mappings they require.

Some mappings are simple. These involve syntactic changes from one protocol suite to another. For example, in electronic mail, dates are represented using a well-defined syntax. Two different mail systems might use different formats to represent dates. One might use a date that is based on Greenwich Mean Time (GMT), whilst another mail system might use a date that is relative to local time followed by an indication of the local time zone. Converting from one form to the other is an example of a straightforward mapping.

In contrast, other mappings are much more complex. These involve semantic changes from one protocol to another. Continuing with electronic mail, two different systems may support different services. For example, one mail system, hypothetically named M, might support a delivery-notification element, which, if present, indicates that the mail system should return a notice to the message's originator when it places the message into the recipient's mailbox. A different mail system, hypothetically named S, might not support such an element, but the two mail systems might be attached through a device termed a *gateway*. What mapping should occur when a message crosses the gateway from M to S? No matter what choice is made by the gateway, that choice will be unacceptable for at least one user of one of the mail systems! The gateway has four choices if the originator desired delivery-notification:

1. ignore the delivery-notification element;

2. return the message, unsent, as the desired service could not be provided;

3. return a delivery-notification message to the originator stating that the message got as far as the gateway, and then forward the message through mail system S; or,

4. make a note in the body of the message that the recipient should send an acknowledgement to the originator.

Clearly, none of the choices is optimal for all situations. The first choice is undesirable if the originator considered that knowing the message was delivered was of the vital importance, but did not know that two different mail systems were involved (i.e., that the two mail systems share a uniform addressing space). The second choice, returning the message, is undesirable if the originator was interested in knowing that the message was delivered, but considered delivery of the message more important than delivery notification. The third choice, returning a message indicating partial success, is undesirable if mail system S is less reliable than mail system M, since the notification message could be misinterpreted by the originator. Further, if notification messages result in a charge for the user, then not only is the message potentially misleading, it might also be expensive! The fourth choice, adding a textual request in the message for the recipient, is unreliable at best. Similar arguments can be made for messages travelling in the reverse direction.

A common rule is that the more complex a mapping, the greater the loss of information or intent. The "acid test" for a mapping is to consider how much information is lost if the mapping, and then its inverse, is applied. Considering that initiating network traffic in one direction will often elicit a new transaction from the opposite direction some time later (e.g., in the case of electronic mail), dual mappings are actually quite common.

A perfect mapping and its inverse will result in no loss of information. However, if information is lost in either direction, then the resulting information has less semantic content than before. In many cases, this loss is not significant. For example, in those cases where a human examines the information directly, it is usually possible to intuit the intended information. In other cases, when the information is subject to further processing, then disastrous misinterpretations may occur as the result of bad mappings. Continuing with our electronic mail example, if the filtered information was given as input to a routing procedure, then routing loops might easily occur. Given the automatic nature of message transfer systems, unless adequate safeguards are installed, a message might spend all of its time going back and forth in the network, consuming resources, without ever being delivered.[2] This is a more important lesson than it might appear: reliability is the responsibility of all protocol layers, having a highly resilient and performant transport layer will only exacerbate the potential misbehavior of upper layer protocols!

12.1.2 Terminology

Since the discussion of transition involves two protocol suites with different terminologies, a choice must be made as to what terminology is to be consistently used. This is necessary to avoid confusion throughout the discussion. As *The Open Book* is focused primarily on OSI, the discussion favors OSI terminology. However, some Internet terminology will be required.

Perhaps the two most widely used and nearly meaningless terms found in the literature are *gateway* and *bridge*. For meaningful discussion, a consistent definition of each is required. A *gateway* is an entity generic to any protocol layer. For this discussion, gateways are responsible for complex mappings, such as translations between the services offered by different peer protocols. As such, they are almost always found at the higher layers of protocol, usually at the application layer.

In contrast, a *bridge* is an entity that also is generic to any protocol layer, but is responsible for simple mappings such as relaying between two implementations of the same protocol. It is convenient to think of bridges as copying information in transit with only mod-

---

[2]One example of such a safeguard would be to keep a "hop count" of the number of times the message had been relayed — once a threshold is exceeded, the message would be returned.

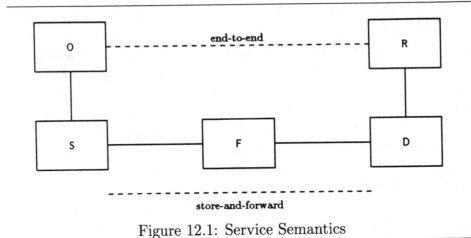

Figure 12.1: Service Semantics

est transformations, whilst gateways munge[3] information, performing great deliberations as to the changes that are made.

These definitions are at best imprecise. An alternative perspective might be to say that a bridge has knowledge of the same layer in two different protocol suites, whilst a gateway has knowledge of more than one layer. This definition reinforces the issues of complexity noted above.

Service Semantics

This distinction introduces the notion of the *service semantics* specifying what mappings are to be performed. Throughout the history of networking, two kinds of service semantics have dominated: *store-and-forward* and *end-to-end*.

Service semantics are termed store-and-forward if they are carried multi-hop via forwarders (i.e., they represent a series of transactions). As shown in Figure 12.1, the service offered by entities S and D involves a hop through entity F. That is, a user of the service, whilst not directly accessing the forwarder, F, nevertheless has some appreciation of F's existence. The classic example of a store-and-forward service is a connectionless-mode network layer in which user information is forwarded from the source end-system (S), through a series of routers (F), to the ultimate destination end-system (D).

---

[3]The term *munge* is technical slang. It is a rather derogatory term meaning that information is imperfectly transformed.

Perhaps the most important characteristic of store-and-forward semantics is that they may involve relatively large delays. However, it is important to emphasize the qualifier *relatively*. In the case of a store-and-forward network service, the delay might be on the order of 30 seconds if several hops are involved; in the case of a store-and-forward mail service, the delay might be in hours or even days. As such, delay may have far-reaching ramifications when performing mappings. Consider that a user running an interactive file transfer application may find the service offered by a transition scheme based on store-and-forward technology to be unacceptably slow — even if the mappings it performs are semantically "better" than a different scheme that isn't store-and-forward, but is faster. Of course, if a spooled file transfer facility was available, then store-and-forward technology might be more appropriate.

The alternative to the store-and-forward scheme is to use end-to-end service semantics. In this case, service semantics exist only between the originator and the recipient. Again referring to Figure 12.1, the service offered by entities O and R involves no third-party. Of course, an end-to-end service may be supported by an underlying store-and-forward service. For example, a connection-oriented transport layer might use a store-and-forward network layer to transmit user information (as described in Part II).

Finally, note that there is no conceptual limitation to the number of times these service semantics might be layered. Electronic mail, for example, is inherently a third-party store-and-forward service. However, each hop the message takes occurs over an end-to-end transport service. Each of these end-to-end transport services might in fact be supported by a store-and-forward network service. In turn, each subnetwork hop might really be over an end-to-end ... and so on.

Protocols and Applications

A *protocol suite* is a collection of services and protocols related in two ways:

- administratively, by an organization; and,

- philosophically, by a reference model.

For the purposes of discussion, there are only two protocol suites of interest. The first is the OSI suite, which is administratively related to the ISO/IEC and is philosophically related to the OSI reference model[OSI84]. The second is the Internet suite, which is administratively related to the IAB (Internet Activities Board) and is philosophically related to the DoD Internet Architecture Model [VCerf83].

Although the discussion considers these two protocol suites exclusively, as noted earlier, many of the concepts presented herein are applicable to other suites. Most are largely based on the same general principles of layering and abstraction that were described in Part I.

Before concluding this introduction on terminology, two terms should be introduced: *application-class* and *application-instance*.

An application-class is a set of applications related to a particular category of activity, regardless of protocol suite. An application-instance is a member of an application class specific to a particular protocol suite. For example, as regards file transfer, a *file-service* is an application-class, whereas FTAM, the OSI File Transfer, Access and Management service, is a particular application-instance. In the discussion, Greek letters, such as α and β, will often be used to refer to different application-instances from the same application-class.

12.2 History

The discussion that follows is intended to be non-partisan. However as pointed out in the Preface, as far as OSI is concerned, technology and politics are painfully intertwined. Thus, whilst the author believes the following to be even-handed, this section may, in fact, generate tremendous controversy!

12.2.1 The Internet Suite of Protocols

The Internet suite of protocols was sponsored by the U.S. DoD and grew out of early research into survivable multi-media packet networking sponsored by the Defense Advanced Research Projects Agency (DARPA). The current generation of protocols is *primarily* based on:

- a connection-oriented transport service, provided by the Transmission Control Protocol[JPost81b] (TCP); and,

- a connectionless-mode network service, provided by the Internet Protocol[JPost81a] (IP).

The major emphasis of the Internet suite is on the connection of diverse network technologies. To this day, excellent research continues on these issues.

There are several applications available for production use in the Internet suite:

- the Simple Mail Transfer Protocol[JPost82] (SMTP), which provides store-and-forward service for textual electronic mail messages, and [DCroc82], which defines the format of those messages;

- the File Transfer Protocol[JPost85] (FTP), which provides file transfer services;

- TELNET[JPost83], which provides virtual terminal services; and,

- the Domain Name System[PMock87] (DNS), which primarily provides mappings from host names to network addresses.

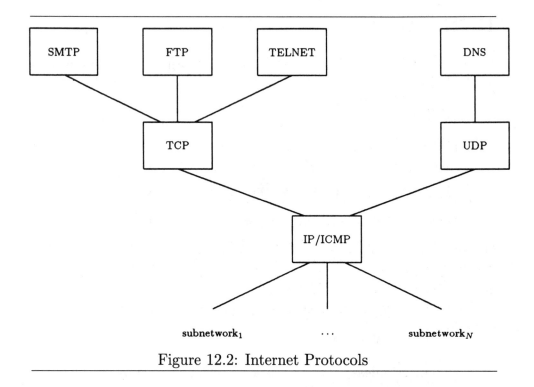

Figure 12.2: Internet Protocols

There are actually many more services, supporting everything from cross-network debugging, to network management, to voice protocols, and so on. [JReyn87] contains a full list, whilst [IAB89] contains a list of protocols that have "official" status.

All of these application protocols are rather "simple." They offer a basic level of service, and they implement this service quite well from the engineering perspective, but the protocols do not exceed this basic level. In retrospect, this is hardly surprising considering that these applications are, with the possible exception of the wonderful DNS, based on 15-year-old models of distributed applications!

The relationship between the application protocols and the end-to-end services is shown in Figure 12.2. This figure, which emphasizes simplicity over detail, also shows a protocol called the UDP. The User Datagram Protocol[JPost80] is a connectionless-mode transport protocol that is little more than a simple pass-through to the IP.

12.2.2   The OSI Suite of Protocols

Definition of the OSI suite of protocols was sponsored by the International community, and in particular the International Organization for Standardization and International Electrotechnical Committee (ISO/IEC). The current generation of protocols are based on:

- a connection-oriented transport service[ISO86c], provided by one of five different transport protocols[ISO86a]; depending on

- the network service available, either connection-oriented or connectionless-mode.

OSI has been the object of such intense effort and public scrutiny that it is truly difficult to identify the "major emphasis" or the single most notable technical accomplishment.[4]

There are several interesting OSI applications, of which the most notable are:

- Directory Services[ISO88f] (DS), which manages names and associated attributes;

- Message Handling Systems[CCITT84c,ISO88g] (MHS), the suite of protocols for multi-media message handling based on the message handling model originally developed by the International Federation of Information Processing (IFIP) in 1979;

- File Transfer, Access and Management[ISO88a] (FTAM), the OSI file service; and,

- Virtual Terminal[ISO87v] (VT), which provides virtual terminal services.

In the last two years, the OSI applications have evolved quite heavily. They are all functionally more capable than the corresponding applications in the Internet suite, at the expense of being much more complex and more difficult to implement with today's technology.

The relationship between the application protocols and the end-to-end services is shown in Figure 12.3. As with the previous figure, simplicity is emphasized over detail. Note that in contrast to the approach taken with the Internet application protocols, OSI-based

---

[4]This is a compliment, not a criticism.

applications protocols use a common set of session, presentation, and application layer facilities. Each of these upper-layers offers several services, and the application chooses the subset of services that it requires. This tends to promote reusability in both application protocol design and the ensuing software implementation. In addition, second-order effects, such as consistency of behavior, also result.

12.2.3 Comparisons

Several studies have been performed comparing the Internet and OSI suites (e.g., [NRC85], which concluded that the TCP and the OSI TP4 were functionally equivalent). From our perspective, we note that concerns differ: network *users* are interested only in application layer functionality — for the most part, they are unconcerned with the actual transport protocols being used; however, *network administrators* are very much concerned with network and transport issues.

Given the vast richness of service described in Part III, it can be seen that in terms of applications, once they are implemented, the OSI suite is superior: a more functional set of application services will be more appealing to the network user. However, the reasons given in Part II of this book suggest that the Internet suite is superior for end-to-end services. This state of affairs will influence the discussion that follows.

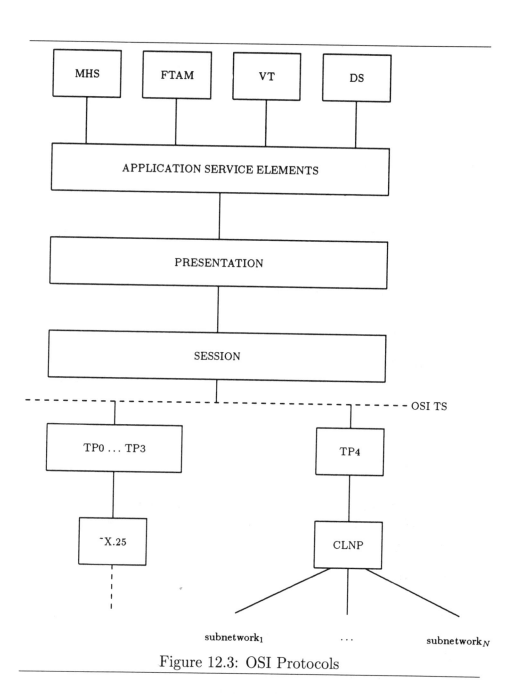

Figure 12.3: OSI Protocols

12.3   Metrics for Comparison

In exploring the strategies for transition and coexistence between the two protocol suites, it is often useful to compare different approaches. In order to be meaningful, these comparisons must be based on a well-defined set of metrics.

Ideally, a rigorous, formal theory of comparison should be developed in order to judge the different approaches. However, there are no metrics agreed upon and no theory in place (to the author's knowledge) that can be used to develop such metrics. Hence, the discussion resorts to less-formal criteria that take the form of a category and then several questions that compose that category:

> **Performance:** How well does the strategy perform in terms of both throughput and latency? How does the strategy impact the performance of other applications running in the network? In short, what throughput does the strategy *deliver* and how is the performance of other applications *impacted*?

> **Flexibility:** What is the range of applicability of the strategy? Is a special-purpose solution (e.g., a dedicated gateway) required for each application, or can one general-purpose solution serve the needs of a wide range of applications?

> **Transparency:** Is it possible for end-users to be unaware that the coexistence/transition strategy is "in the loop?"

> **Amenability:** How manageable is the strategy? Does the strategy impose additional administrative burdens on the network operators?

Note that transparency and amenability are often in conflict: for example, some user communities may opt for a less transparent strategy in order to keep network administrators "out of the loop;" similarly, a strategy that offers seamless integration for the users might pose significant problems for the administrators.

Although these characteristics may be compared objectively given a sufficiently rigorous set of benchmarking definitions, choosing among alternatives is primarily a subjective process. As a result, in answering these questions, evaluations must be made in the context of a target environment. This notion is to be explored towards the end of the discussion.

By its very nature, this part of *The Open Book* is both technical and philosophical. Although the technical issues may be the most interesting, technical solutions to the transition and coexistence problem do not exist in a vacuum — they make sense only in the context of a particular set of requirements that need not be entirely of a technical nature. This leads us to distinguish between a transition strategy and a coexistence strategy. The problem of transition is one where a community consists of networks that currently contain only one protocol suite (e.g., Internet) and that wish ultimately to run only another protocol suite (e.g., OSI). The problem of coexistence is potentially much harder: two communities, each running one protocol suite, wish to interoperate with each other. Of course, as noted earlier, there is a trivial interpretation of coexistence termed *ignorance*. The two protocol suites operate over the same physical media, but otherwise do not interact. Eventually, one of the protocol suites loses favor (i.e., is cancelled via administrative fiat), and the "coexistence period" is over.

Consider: given that many interconnected networks are under different administrative control, transitions to OSI protocols will occur at widely separated times. If the networks are expected to continue to interoperate, then the view must be toward extended (peaceful) coexistence, rather than toward rapid transition.

12.4 Roadmap

With the *Introduction to Transition* drawing to a close, the discussion briefly outlines the approaches to be considered: first, protocol-based approaches are presented. These are the methods traditionally used to interconnect different protocol stacks. Many examples of systems based on these technologies exist today.

Next, service-based approaches are presented. These break away from a vertical- or protocol-oriented perspective, and focus on horizontal- or service-oriented connections. Although much newer, early systems using this technology have begun to appear. For both the protocol-based and service-based approaches, each description will conclude with a "scorecard" outlining how well the approach compares to the metrics defined above.

Finally, the discussion introduces two scenarios for transition. As noted earlier, solutions cannot be evaluated in a vacuum. So, given two real life examples, a determination will be made as to how successfully problems are solved with the various approaches.

Chapter 13

Protocol-based Approaches

Techniques that focus on the interconnection of different protocol suites are labelled "protocol-based." These approaches are documented extensively in the open literature. For example, [PGree86] provides an exploration of the issues involved.

The unifying characteristic of these approaches is that they focus on *vertical integration* between protocol suites. That is, these approaches concern themselves with the protocol interactions that occur between peers from different protocol suites that reside at the same logical layers in their respective protocol hierarchies.

A simple example illustrates this. Consider two protocol entities, E_1 and E_2, performing similar tasks but in different protocol suites:

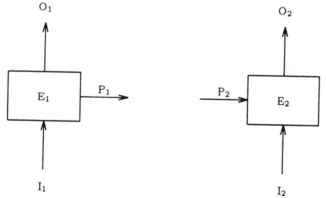

Each entity, E_n, has its own set of definitions for

- the service, I_n, required from the entity below;

- the service, O_n, offered to the entity above; and,

- the protocol, P_n, used with its peers.

The task is to connect the two entities so as to achieve a cross-over between the two protocol stacks. That is, when going from protocol stack 1 to 2, perhaps a mapping function, f, is needed:

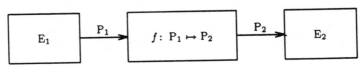

(Of course, communications are often bidirectional, so we can envision an inverse mapping, f^{-1}, which goes from stack 2 to stack 1. Without loss of generality, the discussion considers mappings in one direction.)

Any two protocols will have some functional differences, so that an attempt to map between them will, necessarily, entail some loss of information. In order to determine the loss, the characteristics of the mapping function, f, must be determined. These characteristics depend entirely on the magnitude of the difference between P_1 and P_2, which can be thought of as

$$|P_2 - P_1|$$

This expression has no quantitative value, although it can be compared to other, similarly formed expressions. For now, read the expression as "how hard it is to map between one *protocol* to another.

Note that this mapping focuses on a vertical perspective as it occurs by crossing the two vertical sides of the box containing f. The mapping effects a vertical change on the system: one protocol stack is exchanged for another.

The discussion now turns to three different protocol-based approaches: the dual-stack approach, which is the most straightforward, favoring the "separate but equal" strategy; the application-gateway approach, which highlights much of the discussion thus far on mappings; and, the transport-gateway approach, which is another example of mappings, albeit at the transport layer rather than at the highest layer of the model.

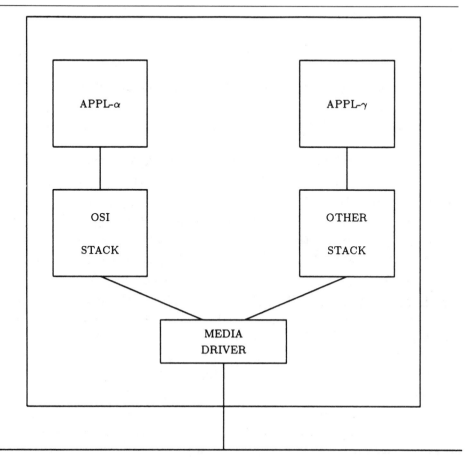

Figure 13.1: The Dual-Stack approach

13.1 Dual-Stack Approach

"Nice work, if you can get it."
– Groucho Marx, Monkey Business, Paramount Pictures
(1931)

The dual-stack approach is simple in concept: As seen from the high-level architecture shown in Figure 13.1, just put both protocol suites in all nodes. For example, if we are interested in the *file service* application-class, then APPL-α might be FTAM, the OSI file service, whilst APPL-γ might be the FTP, the file transfer protocol in the Internet suite.

Although simple in expression, the actual implementation of this

approach is problematic. The dual-stack approach might be unacceptable for either administrative or technical reasons. There are two
general technical reasons that may make this approach impractical:

- lack of infrastructure to support a second set of protocols; or,

- lack of additional hardware capacity.

In the first case, the node might no longer have active software development performed on it, so development resources such as compilers
or programmers may no longer be available.[1] In the second case, there
may just not be enough memory to support a second set of protocols.
To highlight these limitations, suppose that the network capability on
a node is provided by an "intelligent board" or network front-end.

A front-end is usually a single board added to the node. These
boards, each containing its own processor, a modest amount of memory, and some kind of peripheral (e.g., a local area network interface),
run the protocols locally, and then communicate with the node over
the shared bus. When the node enters normal operations, it down-
loads a program to the board containing the protocols to be run.
In some nodes, a network front-end can free significant computing
resources and possibly speed network access. This is not universally
true, however: many nodes have sufficient excess capacity, or are sufficiently faster than the network front-end, that attaching such a board
may actually slow communications! (This issue is quite complex: the
relevant costs of protocol processing and process wake-up differ dramatically among different architectures and operating systems.)

In order to be cost-competitive, these boards are not designed
with much excess capacity. As such, a board designed to support
one protocol suite may simply be too "small" to run a second protocol suite simultaneously. Hence, in order to support a second set of
protocols, a second board, usually with a second network interface,
may be needed. In addition to doubling the cost, there is usually no,
or at best, little, cooperation between the two front-ends. As such,
the node may suffer up to twice the overhead of interacting with the
front-ends.

soap...   One might argue that because the protocols are downloaded from
the node to the front-end, one could simply download software for the

---

[1]In many environments, this is a surprisingly large number of machines.

new protocol suite. (Of course, this wouldn't be done regularly — presumably it would be done only once.) In fact, many vendors of TCP/IP-based network front-ends, claim that this is their "transition strategy." Alone, this is no strategy at all, but a recipe for disaster! Even if it were possible to change all the network front-ends in an internet simultaneously (a dubious proposition), one would still have to change protocols simultaneously on all of the other network nodes as well. This is hardly practical in any internet of reasonable size. Hence, being able to change protocols is not a solution to the transition problem unless one can change everything at once.[2] Furthermore, even if one could change everything at once, then the network administrators would have to have the utmost confidence in the new software; otherwise the network users will have a thing or two to say about the transition...

$\boxed{\text{...soap}}$

13.1.1   Communication with Uni-stack Nodes

It is all too easy to lose sight of a simple fact:

> *Nodes that are incapable of being dual-stack may still offer valuable production services to users.*

For purposes of the discussion, we use the term *uni-stack* system to refer to nodes, that, for one reason or another, do not run both protocol suites.

Of course, since a dual-stack node contains protocols from both suites, it should be able to communicate with these uni-stack nodes. On the surface, it would seem that there is no problem for a uni-stack node to interoperate with a dual-stack node. Referring back to Figure 13.1, the uni-stack node invokes either APPL-α or APPL-γ as appropriate. However, if a uni-stack node wishes to interoperate with another uni-stack node, then both nodes must have the same protocol suite, otherwise communication cannot occur, unless the gateway mechanisms described in Section 13.2 are used.

A more interesting problem occurs when a user on a dual-stack node wishes to interoperate with a uni-stack hosted application: how does the dual-stack node determine which application to use? There

---

[2]This is a situation that Dr. Vinton G. Cerf, co-inventor of TCP/IP, likens to "changing engines in mid-flight."

are two answers. The most common approach is to provide both applications (APPL-α and APPL-γ) to the user, and let the user, based on out-of-band knowledge, decide which application to invoke.

A more sophisticated approach is to provide a new application, APPL-β, as portrayed by the high-level architecture shown in Figure 13.2. This application might use a directory mechanism of some sort to determine which protocol suite to invoke based on the node with which the user wishes to communicate. That is, APPL-β is really a generic file transfer application that presents an interface to the user that is independent of the underlying file transfer protocol. The "switch" used by APPL-β consults its directory and then uses the appropriate protocol machine (either α-PM or γ-PM) to carry out the generic operation requested by the user. The overhead for providing this abstraction occurs only once: when the user directs a connection to be established, a directory is consulted, the appropriate protocol stack is bound, and from that point on, until the connection is released, the switch acts as a simple pass-through.

Note that care must be taken to see that the directory is updated in a timely fashion — otherwise communications may fail even if the two nodes share a common protocol suite! Consider: a host changes protocol stacks, but for one reason or another, its directory entry is not updated. The result is rather predictable: a dual-stack host consults the directory and chooses the incorrect protocol stack; hence communication cannot occur.

13.1.2   Other Considerations

The discussion thus far has centered on finding a common protocol suite between the two nodes. It works quite well when the end-systems are directly attached to the same network. However, when the nodes are attached to different networks, unless all of the intermediate-systems between the two nodes share the same underlying protocols, no end-to-end communication can occur at all! Consider: it only takes one intermediate-system using a different protocol suite to prevent communications. To solve this, tremendous administrative complexity may be introduced. For example, the routing databases for the network would have to take into account that certain links, whilst valid for one kind of traffic, are unusable for other kinds of traffic.

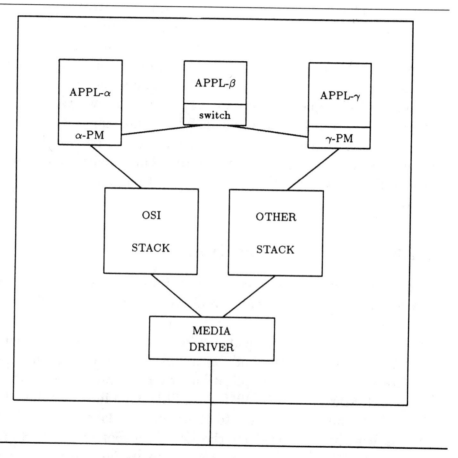

Figure 13.2: Generic Application Instance

It is interesting to note that in some environments there are practical considerations that prevent a dual-stack host from using both stacks simultaneously. For example, in one community, the U.S. Defense Data Network (DDN), hosts are connected via an X.25–based access method, and then use the Internet suite of protocols over this subnetwork. The host/subnet connections are achieved using the *X.25 standard service*, which is defined by the U.S. Department of Defense. This same community, for various administrative and technical reasons, has chosen the *X.25 basic service* (a commercial X.25 definition) to support their OSI-based communications. Unfortunately, the two X.25 services are not compatible, and as such two separate host/network connections are required for dual-stack hosts. Sadly, in the community in question, it can take as long as two years to have a single host/network connection installed, thus throwing doubt on the dual-stack approach as a timely solution for the transition and coexistence problems of this community! One might view this last consideration as a minor point. Try telling that to a network user in this community!

13.1.3   An Implementation

The discussion now turns to consider an implementation of the dual-stack technology. The particular implementation under consideration is a workstation running the AT&T variant of UNIX, UNIX System V release 3. One of the major features found in this version of UNIX is STREAMS[ATT88b], a method for organizing protocol modules in in the UNIX kernel. Network application writers access protocols via the Transport Library Interface[ATT88a] (TLI). One intent of the TLI is to provide a uniform interface to the transport layer. As such, the TLI was heavily influenced by the OSI Transport Service[ISO86c]. However, the TLI is sufficiently general in its interface that it can support other transport providers besides the OSI transport protocol.

An Architecture

In Figure 13.3 the high-level architecture of such a system is shown.

Proceeding from the bottom-up: the end-system has a single network attachment, termed a *network interface* or NI, which supports both the ISO/IEC 8802.3 CSMA/CD local area network standard

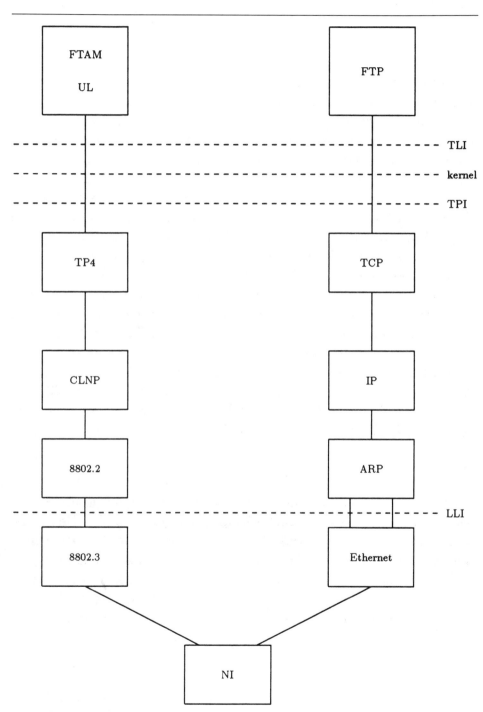

Figure 13.3: An Implementation of the Dual-Stack Approach

and Ethernet (the original but incompatible version of CSMA/CD). The *logical link interface* (LLI) separates the device drivers from the protocols above. As with the TLI, this is an AT&T-defined interface for systems supporting STREAMS. By providing a single, published, interface definition, the hope is that drivers written by one vendor can support the protocols written by another vendor. Above the LLI are various network and transport protocols.[3] To access the drivers, various functions, such as address resolution, are required. These are specific both to the network layer protocol and to the device driver. Hence, the CLNP requires the logical link control mechanisms defined in ISO/IEC 8802.2, whilst the IP uses the Address Resolution Protocol[DPlum82] (ARP). Note that the ARP module actually has two linkages to the Ethernet driver. One is used for IP traffic, whilst the other is used strictly for the Address Resolution Protocol (two links are required since IP and ARP use different packet types on Ethernet). Each transport provider (in Figure 13.3 either the TCP or TP4) is also required to adhere to a *transport provider interface* (TPI) which defines how transport protocols interact with the TLI. The UNIX kernel boundary separates the protocol modules that use the TPI from the user processes that use the TLI. Above the TLI, we have FTAM (and the OSI upper-layers, UL), which use the TLI to access the OSI transport service, and the FTP, which uses the TLI to access the TCP-based transport service.

Programmatic Access

Now the discussion considers some of the programmatic aspects of such a system. In Figure 13.4 on page 529, an example of how one might use the TLI to establish a connection using the OSI transport service is shown. The code fragment, written in the *C* programming language, begins by including a "header file" that defines the various structures employed when using the TLI. Next, the location in the UNIX file system of the OSI transport provider is defined (/dev/osi/tp) along with some variables to be used in the code fragment.

---

[3]Originally, there was a *network layer interface* (NLI), but it proved to difficult too "do right" and it was withdrawn by AT&T. Furthermore, it appears that the LLI itself might be upgraded in the near future — finding the right level of abstraction is difficult!

```
#include <tiuser.h>                    /* TLI user definitions */

#define DEV_TP "/dev/osi/tp"           /* OSI transport provider */

...

int      fd;
struct t_bind *bind;
struct t_call *scall,
          *rcall;                                                        10

...

if ((fd = t_open (DEV_TP, O_RDWR, (struct t_info *) 0)) == NOTOK)
   error ("unable to open transport provider");

if ((bind = (struct t_bind *) t_alloc (fd, T_BIND, T_ALL)) == NULL)
   error ("unable to allocate structure for calling address");

taddr2tp (local, &bind -> addr);                                         20

if (t_bind (fd, bind, (struct t_bind *) 0) == NOTOK)
   error ("unable to bind calling address");

t_free ((char *) bind, T_CALL);

if ((scall = (struct t_call *) t_alloc (fd, T_CALL, T_ALL)) == NULL
      || (rcall = (struct t_call *) t_alloc (fd, T_CALL, T_ALL)) == NULL)
   error ("unable to allocate structures for connection establishment");
                                                                         30
taddr2tp (remote, &scall -> addr);

if (t_connect (fd, scall, rcall) == NOTOK)
   error ("unable to establish connection");

tp2taddr (&rcall -> addr, responding);

t_free ((char *) scall, T_CALL);
t_free ((char *) rcall, T_CALL);
                                                                         40
...
```

Figure 13.4: Use of the TLI to establish a connection

Execution begins by calling t_open. This establishes a relationship between the user process and the indicated transport provider, and returns a *transport endpoint*. This endpoint, which is a UNIX file-descriptor, is used for all further references to the transport provider. If t_open fails (e.g., the indicated transport provider is not running), then the value -1, denoted by the constant NOTOK is returned. In this case, the routine error is called, which presumably prints the given diagnostic string and then terminates the program. (Obviously, we expect production code to be somewhat more robust!) When the TLI routines return an error, they set a variable called t_errno to one of several pre-defined values. The program can then examine the value of this variable and proceed accordingly. We might imagine that the error routine simply prints out a textual description of the error along with the supplied diagnostic.

If t_open succeeds, then t_alloc is called to allocate a structure large enough to accommodate an address for the bound transport provider. Addresses for different transport providers might be of different length. Hence, when t_open was called, the transport provider told the TLI about its maximum address length. the TLI remembers this information and thus t_alloc can act accordingly.

As different transport providers may have different address formats, the user program must have some way of translating whatever address format it uses into the one used by the transport provider. Hence, whilst the interface provided by the TLI is generic enough to support both an OSI and a TCP-based transport service, it is still the user's responsibility to understand the address format specific to a given transport provider. The routine t addr2tp is supplied to perform this mapping for the user. Note that this routine is not a part of the TLI; rather, the vendor that integrates the user program with the transport provider supplies this code. It has been observed that this is perhaps a major shortcoming of the TLI: unless consensus is reached as to address formats for commonly used transport providers, then it is unlikely that a user program supplied by one vendor will actually work when using a transport provider provided by any arbitrarily chosen second vendor. Indeed, even the UNIX file system name of the OSI transport provider varies among vendors.

Once the address is in a format suitable for the transport provider, then the TLI routine t_bind is called. This binds the local address for the transport-endpoint. Following this, t_free is called to release the memory allocated earlier by `t_alloc`.

Next, two other structures are allocated. These are used to contain connect information that is protocol-specific. For example, `taddr2tp` is once again called to provide an address acceptable to the transport provider. In this case, the "called" address, the address to which we wish to connect, must be mapped.

Finally, `t_connect` is called to establish the connection. Upon success, protocol-specific connection information is returned. The routine `tp2taddr`, which performs the inverse function of `taddr2tp`, is called to provide the responding transport address in a format suitable for the user program.

An interesting observation is that by simply replacing the name of the transport provider with, e.g., `/dev/internet/tp`, and by supplying replacements for routines `taddr2tp` and `tp2taddr`, then the code fragment in Figure 13.4 could just as easily show how to use the TLI to establish a connection using the Internet protocol suite (or even some other suite of protocols).

The Myth of Protocol Independence

The success of the TLI in handling the transport service semantics of both the OSI and Internet protocol suites has led some vendors to conclude that dual stack hosts can provide transport service independence to naive processes. For example, one could run the FTP, unmodified, on top of the OSI transport service. Similarly, one should be able to run FTAM (and the OSI upper-layers), unmodified on top of the TCP-based transport service.

The high-level architecture of such a system is shown in Figure 13.5. The problem with this proposal is that although the TLI provides a uniform interface, it does not provide a uniform service. As Figure 13.4 was discussed, several protocol-dependent aspects of the transport provider were mentioned. These aspects, by and large, differ between the OSI transport provider service and the TCP-based transport service.

There are four key sets of differences between the two transport services: first, the TSDU-orientation is different between the two. The OSI transport service passes discrete transport service data units (TSDUs). These units are preserved across the transport service boundary. For example, if two TSDUs are sent, one of length 20 octets, and

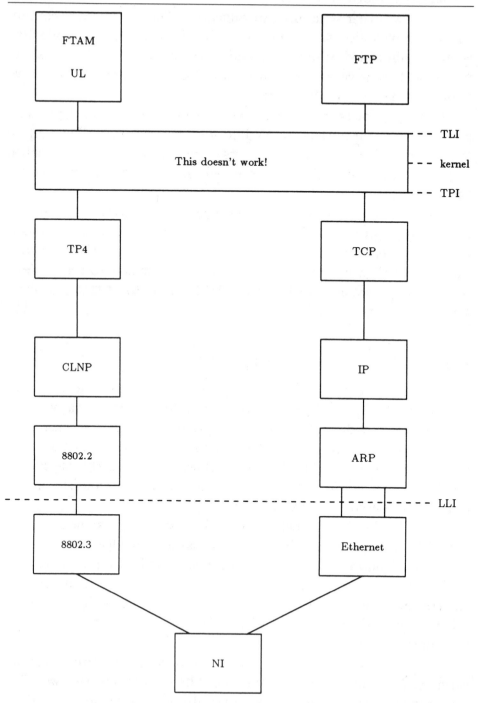

Figure 13.5: The Myth of Transport Service Independence

the other of length 1004 octets, then two TSDUs of the same sizes, respectively, are given to the receiving transport user. In contrast, the TCP provides an octet-stream orientation to its users. As such, if 20 octets are sent followed by another 1004 octets, the receiving TCP entity is free to give its transport user, either:

- 1024 octets, all at once; or,

- 512 octets followed by 512 octets; or,

- 341 octets followed by 341 octets followed by 342 octets; or,

- even 1024 octets, one octet at a time (a very silly TCP implementation).

The OSI session protocol relies on TSDU-boundaries being preserved by the transport service. Hence, using the TCP to provide the OSI transport service, without using some additional mechanisms such as those found in the RFC1006 method, will result in the session provider becoming confused.

The second difference deals with loss of data when a connection is released: *graceful* release mechanisms ensure that all data is delivered before the connection is terminated; in contrast, *destructive* release mechanisms terminate the connection immediately and any user-data in transit is lost. The OSI transport service has only a destructive release mechanism (graceful release mechanisms are provided by the session protocol), whilst the TCP has both a graceful and a destructive release mechanism. Many TCP applications rely on the graceful release mechanism in order to allow data to drain. For example, the FTP uses a second transport connection to transmit files. Briefly put, the two FTP applications establish a second connection that is used to send the file. When all data in the file has been completely passed to the local TCP, the sending FTP requests the connection be terminated using the graceful release mechanism. When all data on the connection has drained, the connection is released. Hence, using TP4 to support the FTP will typically result in the last buffer being lost for each transferred file!

The third difference is in the support of out-of-band signaling. The OSI transport service supports expedited data transfer that allows a small amount of data *potentially* to be delivered before normal data previously sent. In contrast, the TCP supports urgent data notification: when the urgent data information is read from the network by the receiving TCP, the user is told that urgent data is available and how much more information must be read before the urgent has been read. There are good properties of each of these techniques: in the case of expedited data, one could imagine a lengthy transfer being aborted by the user, the session protocol would send an expedited message to the receiver stating that information should be discarded until a resynchronization mark is found. This has the advantage over the urgent data method that no processing need be performed by the user on information that is no longer valid. In the case of urgent data, one could imagine some important event occuring that, whilst not invalidating previously sent data, should be given to the remote user as soon as possible. When the urgent notification is given, the remote user can give priority to the processing of incoming network information. Although both methods of out-of-band signaling are useful, they have different semantics. Hence, replacing TP4 with TCP or vice-versa will only confuse the upper layer protocols.

The fourth and final difference is in addressing. OSI transport addresses have a different format than TCP addresses. Whilst one might argue that routines such as `taddr2tp` and `tp2taddr` hide these differences, there is one counter-example. Earlier, the discussion mentioned how the FTP negotiates use of a second transport connection. In doing this negotiation, the FTP sends (within the data stream) the addressing information for the second connection. Thus, without modifying the FTP, this will fail horribly if the TCP is replaced by the TP4.

All of this emphasizes an important point: a uniform interface to different services is not the same as a uniform service interface. The former is what is provided by the TLI (which does quite an excellent job). The latter is what is required in order to move transport users from one protocol suite to the other.

13.1.4 Scorecard

It is now time to evaluate the dual-stack approach against the metrics developed in Section 12.3 on page 516.

Performance: No degradation of performance occurs.

Flexibility: Good, although it's a lot of work to implement both protocol suites for any reasonable number of platforms.

Transparency: The presence of uni-stack hosts may make inter-operations impossible in some cases. However, from dual-stack hosts, generic applications can provide a seamless user-interface, but only for the common set of functions between the two application protocols in the different protocol suites. The user will see either full or partial functionality, depending on host combinations.

Amenability: Requires most end-systems and all intermediate-systems to be dual-stack capable. In addition, the dual-stack approach in effect produces two logical networks with all of the management problems of both (making the operations at *least* twice as difficult). For example, two routing protocols, one for each protocol suite, will most likely be run over the same physical network. It is difficult to overstate the significance of this problem.

13.2   Application-Gateway Approach

"Sometimes when you try to turn an apple into an
orange you get back a lemon."
    – Michael A. Padlipsky, The Elements of Networking
                                Style, Prentice-hall (1985)

The application-gateway approach is a well-known, but little understood, technology used to achieve interoperability between similar
applications from different protocol suites. The most common use
of this strategy is for store-and-forward applications such as message
handling. For example, gateways between the SMTP-based systems
and other systems using other mail protocols have been in existence
for quite some time (e.g., [JQuar89] contains a tediously exhaustive
list). For end-to-end applications such as the FTP and Telnet, this
strategy usually performs too poorly to be effective. (There are notable exceptions however — the MITRE FTAM/FTP gateway briefly
mentioned in Section 15.1.1 provides an excellent counter-example.)

Consider Figure 13.6, which shows the the high-level architecture
of an application-gateway host. It is important to emphasize that this
strategy joins together two different application protocols and applies
some sort of translation mechanism between the two.

13.2.1   Imperfect Mappings

Although translating between similar protocols may sound simple,
there are both theoretical and practical limits to the effectiveness of
this technique. Let us imagine that we are interested in a particular
application-class, e.g., *mail service*, and that APPL-α is MHS, the
OSI message handling service, whilst APPL-γ is the SMTP, the message transfer protocol in the Internet suite (which carries messages
formatted according to [DCroc82]).

Both are applications performing the store-and-forward functions
of electronic mail, but the services offered by the protocols differ a
great deal. The differences come from divergent views as to what
"electronic mail" means. At the coarsest level of distinction, MHS
offers a multi-media mail facility, whereas the SMTP (together with
the standard describing the format of messages[DCroc82]) permits
the exchange of text-oriented messages. The services offered by MHS

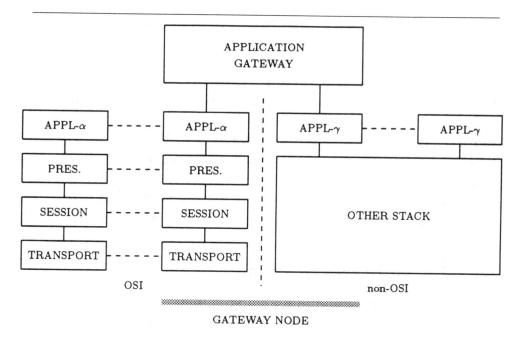

Figure 13.6: The Application-Gateway approach

are wide and varied, whereas the SMTP, the Simple Mail Transfer Protocol, offers a simple, basic, store-and-forward capability, as its name suggests.

Obviously, a mapping function, f, between these two "electronic mail" protocols must result in a loss of information. (To appreciate the full difficulty in building such a mapping function, the reader is encouraged to consult [SKill86].) As a result, passing a message, m, through f and then f^{-1} cannot result in m being returned. This implies that extreme care must be used when constructing a network in which several application-gateways might be concatenated.

In some cases, the resulting loss of information is "only" annoying. For example, mail addresses passing through the gateway, whilst syntactically valid on the receiving end, may look "funny." Even a casual user of electronic mail in a SMTP-based network would consider

```
"/C=UK/ADMD=GOLD 400/PRMD=UK.AC/RFC-822=stef(a)nma.com/"@twg.com
```

to be rather strange. If such addresses become the rule when application-gateways between MHS and SMTP come into heavy use, then user interfaces to the mail system will have to compensate with powerful facilities in order to reduce both user type-in and complexity.

In other cases, the loss of information is catastrophic. For example, [CPart86] begins to argue that unless f and f^{-1} are inverses, then routing loops are quite easily achieved, and the only sure prevention is by regular, manual administration. Another example can be found at the network layer. When connecting networks that employ different routing metrics, a common understanding of the metrics is crucial in order to avoid routing loops (as noted in [DMill87]). Again, this problem occurs from a possible loss of information due to imprecise mapping functions.

Because of these problems, application-gateways are said to provide *connectivity* solutions but are poor for *interoperability* solutions.

13.2.2   An Implementation

There are two kinds of implementations of application-gateways, *staging* and *in-situ*. They differ in the granularity in which translations occur.

From the top-level, gateways built using either kind appear similar. Consider an FTP-FTAM application-gateway. A user establishes an FTP connection to the application gateway. When prompted for authentication information, the user identifies the actual destination host and the authentication information for that destination:

```
% ftp file-gateway
Name (file-gateway:): user@osi-host
Password:
```

In this example, the user invokes the FTP user interface and directs it to establish an FTP connection to the application-gateway residing at host `file-gateway`. The user interface then prompts the user for authentication information — in this example, a username and a password for what it believes is the remote host. For the username, the user supplies a string that designates both the actual destination (`osi-host`) and the username valid there (`user`). The FTP user interface, completely unaware that it is connected to an application-gateway, passes this information on. The gateway parses the username into the actual destination and establishes an FTAM association to the filestore there. For authentication, it uses the remainder of the original username and the password provided by the user.

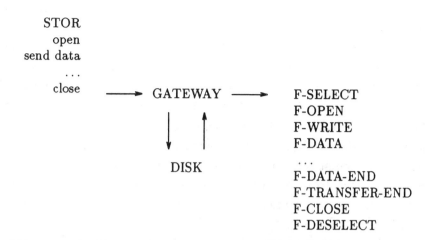

Figure 13.7: Data transit through a Staging Gateway

The two implementation approaches differ not in how they establish associations, but in how they transfer files. The discussion now considers each technique.

Staging Gateways

An application-gateway designed using staging is a true store-and-forward gateway. The data transits through a gateway between the FTP and FTAM are shown in Figure 13.7; top-level protocol transactions are grouped at the gateway. When a file is stored using the FTP,

1. the FTP STOR command is given;

2. a second TCP connection is opened;

3. the data comprising the file is sent; and,

4. the second TCP connection is closed.

At the gateway, the file is captured to disk. Once the entire file is stored, the (roughly) corresponding FTAM protocol sequence is invoked: the file is selected on the remote OSI system and then opened, and so on, until the information is transferred, and the file ultimately deselected.

Because the staging gateway has the entire file available before it transmits to the ultimate destination, it can optimize the mappings it performs in order to minimize loss of information.

However, there are three disadvantages: performance, resource requirements, and timing considerations. In terms of performance, both throughput and latency are affected. Throughput is reduced because no pipelining occurs between the gateway and its two correspondents. Only one network connection is actually transmitting data at any one time. Latency is increased because final top-level protocol acknowledgements must wait until the corresponding acknowledgements have been received from the destination. Consider: after the second TCP connection is closed and the file is on the gateway's disk, the gateway *must not* perform the final acknowledgement for the FTP transfer. Rather, it must wait until the file is successfully sent to the ultimate destination and an acknowledgement is received before it can reply that all is well. Failure to do so would lead to inconsistent results if the gateway should crash or the ultimate destination malfunction before the file is safely stored. Of course, nothing so degenerate need occur in order to delay the final acknowledgement: any number of recoverable, temporary failures, such as access failures, could occur when initially trying to send the file to the ultimate destination.

A second disadvantage is that the gateway may require extensive local resources, such as disk space, which may not be available. If the file being transferred is too large to be stored on the gateway, then the transfer will fail, even if there is sufficient storage on the ultimate destination.

The final disadvantage is a subtle one. Most application protocols employ a high-level timer in addition to relying on the robustness facilities of the end-to-end services. This is primarily a defense against a misbehaving peer at the application layer (i.e., the network is running fine but the remote application is confused). Typically, if an application layer protocol response is not received within a certain amount of time, then the application decides that the remote peer has somehow failed. By introducing a staging gateway, there is the potential to confuse this application layer timer; that is, the timer will expire indicating that there is a problem when in fact the staging gateway is still busy completing the second phase of the transfer. Unfortunately, the use of application layer timers is poorly understood. Hence, use of a staging gateway may very well perturb marginal implementations

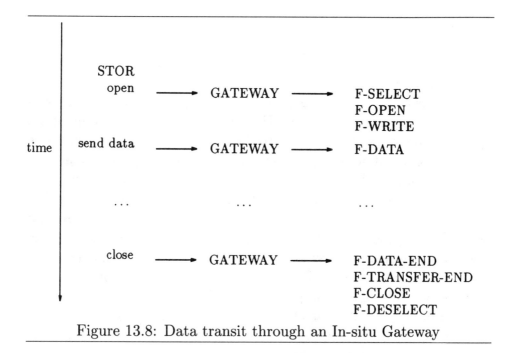

Figure 13.8: Data transit through an In-situ Gateway

into failure. Actually, if the application is interactive, the user might mistake the long delay as a malfunctioning network. This could easily lead to unnecessary user-initiated aborts, even when the transfer was proceeding without problems!

In-situ Gateways

An alternative design is to use a virtual end-to-end or in-situ approach. As shown in Figure 13.8, the data transit here is more granular. When a file is stored using the FTP, the FTP STOR command is given and a second TCP connection is opened. The gateway immediately selects the file on the remote OSI system and continues with the FTAM protocol actions necessary to write to the file. As data is sent via FTP, the gateway sends it immediately via FTAM, performing mappings "on the fly." If properly implemented, not only does the file never touch the gateway's disk, but both network connections can be kept busy, thus increasing throughput and reducing latency. Finally, when the file has been fully transmitted, the second TCP connection is closed, and the gateway initiates the FTAM protocol actions necessary to finish the transaction.

It is important to remember that a gateway built using the in-situ approach is still using a store-and-forward technology. Although in-situ gateways have a higher granularity, they still perform as relays above the network layer.

This leads us to consider whether the increased performance is worth the less precise mappings. Here we come to a great failing of the application-gateway technology: to the author's knowledge, regardless of the time spent at the gateway, the mappings are almost always of equal quality! Thus, the nature of the application, either store-and-forward or end-to-end, determines which approach is appropriate. For example, in the case of file service, staging gateways, by and large, do not produce better mappings than in-situ gateways. Hence, since file service is inherently end-to-end in nature, it makes sense to use an in-situ gateway for file service. In contrast, for electronic mail, almost all application-gateways are of the staging variety. This is natural considering that electronic mail is inherently a store-and-forward service. The quality of the mappings is determined by how difficult it is to map from one message format to another and not by how long the gateway is allowed to massage the message!

13.2.3   A Soapbox on Application-Gateways

soap... Application-gateways are often touted as *the* coexistence solution. This soapbox disputes that claim.

It is true that given time, one can probably build an application-gateway between any two application-instances in a given application-class. Some vendors even suggest that their OSI strategy, particularly in the case of electronic mail, is to offer OSI services only as interfaces to their proprietary systems. For example, to support the OSI message handling service, the vendor might offer an MHS to XYZ application-gateway. Once inside the vendor's system, the XYZ mail system, and not MHS, is used.

As mentioned earlier, the possible semantic loss when information crosses an application-gateway can range from annoying to catastrophic. Thus, although one can attach such a vendor device to an OSI network, the OSI mail service is not offered to the user of such a device. If the MHS and XYZ mail systems are very close, then perhaps such a solution might be adequate. But, if this is not the case, or if the vendor device is going to be used to forward mail from one MHS system to another, the degradation of service may be unacceptable.

Thus, application-gateways, although useful in preserving existing services, are inappropriate as the cornerstone of a coexistence strategy.

`...soap`

13.2.4 Scorecard

Performance: Acceptable for store-and-forward application-classes; usually too poor for other application-classes requiring end-to-end "interactive" response.

> Of course, if there are few application gateways and a lot of traffic, then this leads to a substantive bottleneck.

Flexibility: None, as each application-gateway is a special purpose system. If a new application-class is considered, a new application-gateway must be built.

Transparency: with respect to:

> **service:** Significant functionality often is lost because of inability to perform invertible mappings of services offered.

> **users:** Possible to achieve transparency; however, user is often required to apply out-of-band knowledge, e.g., embed a second host name (somehow) in the connection command.

Amenability: No end-system modifications are required. For a large installed base, this is important. However, management of the application-gateways introduces administrative problems for end-to-end application-classes, e.g., authentication.

13.3   Transport-Gateway Approach

"We could do it, but it would be wrong."
        – Richard M. Nixon, Watergate Tapes (1974)

The transport-gateway approach is similar to the application-gateway approach. Consider the high-level architecture of such a system, as shown in Figure 13.9. The transport-gateway converts TCP segments to TP4 TPDUs (and vice-versa). These terms are discussed in Part II. For now, think of them as the protocol data units exchanged by the respective transport providers.

Earlier in the discussion, four key differences between the transport services offered by the two protocols were described. By careful negotiation and implementation, many of these differences can be blurred. The reason is quite simple: the two protocols (and their respective services) are more alike than they are different. Although the gateway will somewhat degrade the service offered by both protocols, the remaining functionality is quite substantial.

Of course, as the transport-gateway is a level-four relay, it suffers from all of the deficiencies inherent to this kind of technology:

- a single point of failure is added to the connection,

- data integrity is potentially compromised, and this compromise will not be detected; and,

- the two transport protocols may become confused owing to round-trip time perturbations.

These reasons were discussed in greater detail when TS-bridges were presented in Section 5.6.4 on page 114 in Part II.

Note that a transport-gateway is much more complicated than a TS-bridge: the TS-bridge knows only about the OSI transport *service* (SDUs). In contrast, the transport-gateway knows about the internals of *two* different transport protocols (PDUs). Obviously, building a transport-gateway is quite a complex undertaking!

13.3.1   An Implementation

An implementation of a transport-gateway is described in [IGroe86]. The work involved in constructing such a technology is, given the complexity of the protocols, quite detailed.

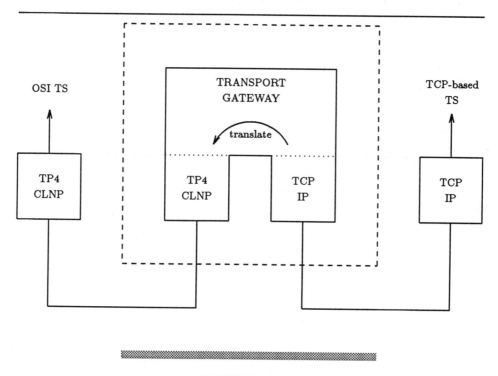

Figure 13.9: The Transport-Gateway approach

13.3.2   What's Wrong Here

One might ask, however: what protocols do we run above the transport service on each host? Because different services are offered at each endpoint, *different* protocols must be run on each end! It is not even a simple matter of making an OSI application such as FTAM run over TCP, because whatever encapsulation scheme is used at the TCP-based end-system will also manifest itself at the OSI-based end-system. Furthermore, this manifestation will be visible above the TP4 interface. Hence, in the OSI-based environment, the OSI session protocol cannot be used above the OSI transport service! Clearly this is unacceptable.

13.4 Summary

With the *Protocol-based Approaches* drawing to a close, the discussion now turns to the characteristics common to the three approaches presented.

Protocol-based approaches focus on *transition*, not coexistence. Although they are limited in several ways, they are nonetheless used quite heavily.

The flaw in these approaches is that they are really caricatures of [soap...] a line from one of Robert Frost's poems:

Good fences make good neighbors.

That is, since they emphasize *protocols* rather than *services*, they naturally tend to reinforce the boundaries between the Internet suite of protocols and the OSI suite. If the lifetime of the Internet suite of protocols were to be short-lived, then this may be an appropriate strategy. However, this underestimates the size of the transition problem many organizations face. This motivates us to search for approaches that tend to blur, rather than highlight, the differences between the two protocol suites: an approach that encourages a lengthy period of coexistence may very well be much more successful in many situations.

[...soap]

Chapter 14

Service-based Approaches

The so-called "service-based" approaches are those that focus on the emulation of services from different protocol suites. They emphasize using a homogeneous service over different protocols, rather than trying to interconnect different protocol suites.

The unifying characteristic of these approaches is that they focus on *horizontal-integration* between protocol suites. That is, these approaches concern themselves with providing the service from one protocol suite at the same logical layer in a different protocol suite.

This is illustrated in a return to the two protocol entities, E_1 and E_2, introduced in the first example of *Protocol-based Approaches*:

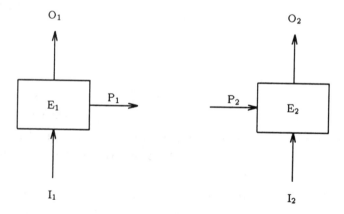

Rather than trying to connect the two entities to achieve a cross-over, the task is to have one entity, E_1, emulate the service O_2, offered by the other:

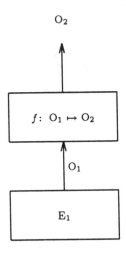

To determine the information loss suffered by such a mapping, the characteristics of the mapping function

$$f\colon O_1 \mapsto O_2$$

must be determined. These characteristics depend entirely on the magnitude of the difference,

$$|O_2 - O_1|$$

between O_1 and O_2 which is read as "how hard it is to map between one *service* to another." As with the expression introduced in *Service-Based Approaches*, this expression has no quantitative value. However, as seen later in the discussion, expressions such as these can be used for *relative* comparisons.

Note that this mapping function focuses on a horizontal perspective as it occurs by crossing the two horizontal edges of the box containing f. The mapping effects a horizontal change on the system: one service is exchanged for another.

This discussion now turns to two different approaches characterized by this kind of mapping: the transport-service bridge approach, which attempts to "paper the world over" with the OSI transport service; and, the network-tunnel approach, which will "complete the circle" of approaches discussed.

14.1 Transport-service Bridges

"Users are interested in services, not protocols."
– Marshall T. Rose, The Open Book (1989), page 551

By way of introduction, consider a hypothesis known as the *D-day conjecture*:

> *At some point in the future, OSI will achieve dominance over the Internet suite of protocols in the marketplace, and the problem of transition and coexistence for existing TCP/IP-based networks will be unavoidable. Let us call this point in time, whenever it might be, the* D-day. *Note that the* D-day *is meaningful in the context of a given community. Different networking communities will probably reach this threshold at different times.*

> *The* D-day *conjecture states that on* D-day *TCP/IP-based networks will already offer a mix of application services; that is, in addition to running the FTP and the SMTP, some, perhaps many, TCP/IP-based networks will be running FTAM and MHS.*

This hypothesis is not far-fetched. Technically, it is easy to accomplish. Section 5.4 on page 101 in Part II introduced the RFC1006 method, which allows OSI applications to run in a TCP/IP-based network.

Thus, rather than re-introducing the technical aspects, consider this possibility from the user perspective. Users, per se, are not interested in which actual protocols they use. They are interested only in the services that those protocols offer. Most of the application protocols in the Internet suite are over a decade old, whereas the OSI applications are the products of intense, recent development. It should not be surprising, therefore, that the OSI applications are significantly richer than their counterparts in the Internet suite: users will be attracted by the additional functionality of the OSI applications. Hence, if it were technically feasible to run OSI applications in a TCP/IP-based network, many users would opt to do so.

Furthermore, the claim can also be made that many developers of OSI applications would prefer to experiment using their OSI applications over TCP/IP-based networks.

There are two reasons to support this:

- the ability to utilize the more mature "administrative" protocols in the Internet suite (e.g., network management and routing protocols); and,

- the ability to utilize the more widespread "connectivity" protocols in the TCP/IP suite (e.g., the TCP and the IP).

In short, given the maturity of the technology and the already existing connectivity of today's TCP/IP-based networks, OSI developers can test applications in larger, potentially more demanding environments.

Given the *D-day conjecture*, we note that parts of both the Internet and OSI communities will be using the same (OSI) applications and only the underlying TS-stack will differ between the two. For example,

- in an OSI-based network, the TS-stack will consist perhaps of the TP4 over the CLNP over some set of subnetwork technologies; whilst

- in a TCP/IP-based network, the TS-stack will consist of the RFC1006 method, which is a thin transport service convergence protocol running over the TCP, running over the IP over some set of subnetwork technologies. (Part II discusses this technology in detail.)

This leads to an interesting approach to coexistence: perhaps end-to-end OSI applications can be run between the two networks. It has been observed that this approach is a hybrid of dual-stack and application-gateway approaches: the same application protocol is used over different transport and underlying protocols.

In order to achieve interworking between the two communities, a transport service bridge is used as described in Section 5.6.4 on page 114. The concept is simple: the TS-bridge resides on top of two more more TS-stacks. When a connection indication is received, it ascertains the actual destination and initiates a new connection request. After the second connection is established, it simply copies data back and forth between the two connections. Thus, for our particular problem of transition, the coexistence solution is shown in Figure 14.1.

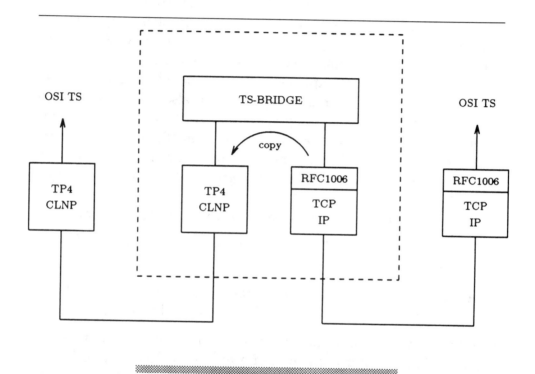

TS-BRIDGE NODE

Figure 14.1: The Transport-service Bridge approach

14.1.1   An Implementation

The TS-bridge notion is a relatively new one. Stephen E. Kille of University College London and Christian Huitema of INRIA discussed such an entity in late 1987. The first implementation (to the author's knowledge) was done at The Wollongong Group, Inc., in early 1988 and demonstrated in February of that year. The particular TS-stacks connected were those shown in Figure 5.4.[1] Shortly thereafter, the TS-stacks shown in Figure 14.2 were demonstrated as well. This particular configuration may well become the most heavily used TS-bridge in Europe. Consider the widespread availability of X.25–based public data networks coupled with the ever increasing introduction of local area networks. OSI applications will probably be running over TCP/IP in the local environment. They will also need to communicate with OSI applications running in other local area networks, using a public data network as "long-haul hop." The TS-bridge configuration shown in Figure 14.2 solves this problem quite handily. This particular scenario will be discussed in greater detail in *Scenarios for Transition*.

The particular sequences of events were due to two factors:

- the transport-switch that was already present in the ISODE; and,

- experience with a TP0–based transport-gateway built by Julian P. Onions of the University of Nottingham [JOnio88].

The transport-switch, an integral part of the ISODE since its inception, provides an interesting level of abstraction. Recall from Part II that the transport-switch provides a uniform transport service, the OSI transport service, over different TS-stacks. In order to accomplish this, it supports both native OSI TS-stacks, e.g., TP4/CLNP and TP0/X.25, and non-OSI stacks, e.g., RFC1006/TCP/IP.

From this point, it is easy to ignore the details of TS-stack implementation and simply imagine copying the service primitives from

---

[1]There are reports of ICL in the UK having developed a transport-service bridge for the ROSE project in 1985. This clearly predates the Wollongong implementation. However, the author has been unable to verify that it was in fact a transport bridge as opposed to a transport gateway. The difference is key: a bridge relies on the OSI transport service to provide commonality, regardless of the underlying TS-stacks, whereas a gateway is intimately familiar with the mechanisms of each TS-stack.

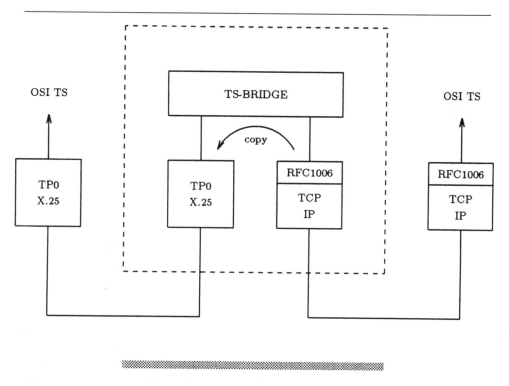

Figure 14.2: TS-bridge between TCP and X.25

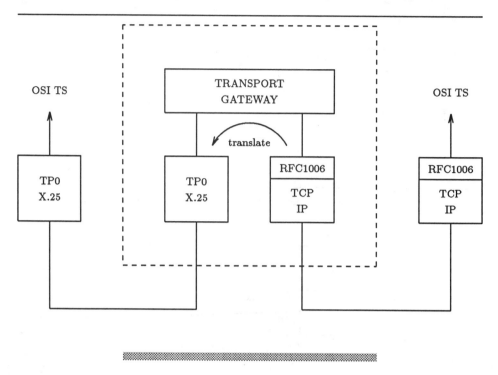

GATEWAY NODE

Figure 14.3: TP0–based Transport-Gateway

one connection to another. However, this wasn't realized back in 1986 when the transport-switch was first built. It wasn't considered until two years later. It happened in this way: Julian Onions wanted to solve the problem, described above, of internetworking LAN-based OSI applications over a PDN. The LAN-based applications were using the RFC1006 method (which is mostly TP0 over TCP), whilst the PDN support applications were running TP0 over X.25. To solve the problem, Julian built a TP0–based transport gateway shown in Figure 14.3. To construct such a gateway, he started using several of the routines used by the transport-switch. Within a few hours, Julian had solved his internetworking problem and was back to working merrily on MHS. It should be noted that the TP0–based transport gateway is still a level-4 relay; as such, it shares the same problems as the TS-bridge.

This spurred discussion between Kille and Huitema in late 1987 as to the possibilities of constructing a slightly more generic technology that could also accommodate TP4 (the possibility of having $n * m$ transport-gateways was a frightening management possibility). Shortly thereafter, the first TS-bridge was written by the author on top of the ISODE transport-switch in early 1988 for The Wollongong Group, Inc. At the end of 1988, Huitema at INRIA independently implemented a TS-bridge containing the TS-stacks shown in Figure 14.2. Finally, Julian, convinced of the errors of his ways, independently implemented the third known TS-bridge in March, 1989. This implementation was donated to the ISODE a few months later.

14.1.2 Scorecard

Performance: Fair, the only degradation being that the user data is subjected to two checksums (one end-to-bridge, the other bridge-to-end), which introduces some additional processing delay in the TS-bridge.

Flexibility: High, as the TS-bridge is independent of any application that ultimately uses the OSI session protocol.

Transparency: Total, given special algorithms in the transport-switch. However, the TS-bridge is a single point of failure, as discussed earlier.

Amenability: All end-systems must run the same set of application protocols. To achieve this before they transition to an OSI TS-stack, TCP-based users must be prepared to transition to the newer OSI applications in the interim. Note that support of the OSI applications should not require any "kernel" modifications on systems, such as UNIX, that have such a concept.

14.2   Network-service Tunnels

*"Encapsulation complies with the layering concept, but
violates the notion of absolute levels."*
  – Danny Cohen and Jonathan B. Postel, The ISO
  Reference Model and Other Protocol Architectures
                                             (1983)

The final approach we examine is termed a network-service tunnel or
NS-tunnel.

Figure 14.4 introduces the notion of tunnel: several OSI subnetworks are connected via CLNP-routers. Between two of the routers,
a tunnel exists. Conceptually, the tunnel appears as an ordinary subnetwork to both of the attached routers.

Figure 14.5 shows the NS-tunnel in greater detail. The idea is
simple: the CLNP is encapsulated inside of the IP, treating IP as
simply a data-link protocol. In this figure, there are only three CLNP-
hops. One of those hops consists of two IP hops.

This approach will require common protocols at the transport
layer and above on both end-systems. However, it does not require
all intervening routers to use the same network protocol. Just as the
TS-bridge might be viewed as a refinement of the application-gateway
approach, the NS-tunnel can be seen as a refinement of the dual-stack
approach, as it focuses on one particular OSI service boundary for
emulation. In comparing Figure 5.4 to Figure 14.5, note that the NS-
tunnel passes traffic regardless of the transport service being carried
on the traffic, whereas the TS-bridge only passes traffic for the OSI
transport service.

14.2.1   Advantages of Level-3 Relays

The NS-tunnel has two key advantages when compared to either the
transport-gateway or the TS-bridge. It is a stateless approach and,
as such, failure of an NS-tunnel need not result in the end-to-end
connection being lost. Routing can also occur dynamically (rather
than being fixed as with the TS-bridge). Further, a true end-to-end
checksum can be employed to ensure data integrity. However, if a
TCP-based host is directly attached to the NS-tunnel, then there is
one disadvantage that it shares with the dual-stack approach: implementing a second transport protocol (TP4) on that host may well

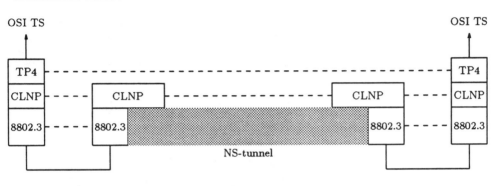

Figure 14.4: Tunneling

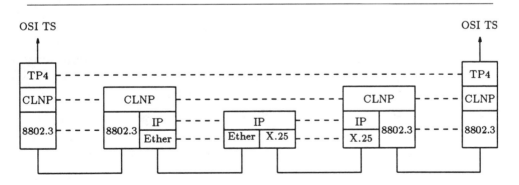

Figure 14.5: The Network-service Tunnel approach

be problematic. Routers participating in the NS-tunnel have no such limitations.

14.2.2 An Implementation

Although tunneling has been in use for quite some time, The particular tunnel described in the discussion, one in which the CLNP is encapsulated inside of the IP, is not yet in use. The reasons for this are twofold:

- few TP4/CLNP-based systems able to participate in such an environment; and,

- lack of a standardized method for performing the encapsulation.

First, there are few TP4/CLNP-based systems connected to networks that are based on the Internet suite of protocols. This is partly because of the general lack of CLNP-based intermediate-systems. As TP4/CLNP-based systems proliferate, then the technology required for this approach will also become more common.

Second, although the procedures for encapsulation are conceptually quite simple, there are still a few choices possible as to how the encapsulation is performed. It would not be productive to have two incompatible encapsulation schemes come into widespread existence! Hence, one delay has been the preparation of an agreed-upon method for performing the encapsulation. Fortunately, one such proposal, known as EON, is undergoing final review at this writing. The discussion next considers this proposal in modest detail.

The proposal for an *Experimental OSI-based Network* presented in [RHage89] defines a technique for building an NS-tunnel. EON is motivated by an interesting phenomena. The OSI connectionless-mode network layer (CLNL) is very much in its infancy: some parts of the layer are defined in International Standards, whilst other parts are "contributions" (not having even progressed to draft proposal stage). Despite this lack of maturity and experience, there is a massive push being made for use of the protocols. For example, use of the CLNL is mandated by the U.S. Government OSI Profile. A concern of many researchers and practitioners is that the CLNL has not yet received adequate testing and experimentation. (Indeed, Part II describes many problems in the OSI end-to-end services, of which the lack of maturity of the CLNL is only one!) EON's goal is to foster testing and implementation of the protocols concurrently with the progression of the protocols to ISO standards. As such, it is imperative that an adequate laboratory for the CLNL be built immediately.

Unfortunately, physical construction of a CLNL-based backbone is impractical. The cost alone of such a laboratory would be prohibitive. One alternative has been the OSINET, an OSI testing network managed by the U.S. National Institute of Standards and Technology. Members of OSINET subscribe to an X.25 service (AT&T's ACCUNET), usually attaching an end-system. In some cases, an intermediate-system is attached, and other subnetworks, such as a local area network are connected.

Although one might suggest that the OSINET might be adequate for these purposes, it is not, for two reasons:

- the primary backbone is an X.25–based subnetwork; and,

- it is far too small with a relatively simple topology.

These reasons highlight an important point: in order to test the robustness of OSI end-to-end services, it is important to use a connectionless-mode network service over a network of diverse topology. OSINET has a relatively simple topology, consisting of relatively few nodes (less than 35 as of this writing), most of which are directly connected to an X.25 subnetwork. Although OSINET runs TP4 over CLNP over X.25, thereby using the connectionless-mode network layer, the reliability of the X.25 subnetwork "smooths over" the network service considerably. As such, the "exceptional" aspects of TP4, which might be invoked due to packet loss at the network layer, are rarely exercised. In defense of the OSINET effort, note that for interoperability testing of OSI applications, these limitations are largely unimportant. (The aspects of interoperability that are not tested deal with mutually acceptable recovery from network related failures.)

What is needed then, is a large, complex, CLNL-based backbone, which regularly loses packets, re-orders them, corrupts them, and so on. Preferably, this backbone should also have widely varying throughput and latency. In other words, the laboratory should be *packet-hostile*.

Fortunately, there is such a network in use today. It's called the
Internet, and it's what the largest TCP/IP-based community uses in
order to get its day-to-day work done.[2]

The argument now comes full-circle: in order to fulfill the EON
mandate, it will be necessary to use the Internet, an IP-based network,
as the backbone for the EON. Naturally, this sounds like a job for an
NS-tunnel.

To build an NS-tunnel, three issues must be addressed:

- the method for encapsulating CLNL PDUs into IP datagrams;

- the format used for NSAP-addresses used in the network, along
  with the method used for mapping between NSAP-addresses
  and media addresses; and,

- the method for providing the multicasting services required by
  some components of the CLNL.

All of these are straightforward to accomplish.

Encapsulation is easy. A new value for the IP protocol field (the
mechanism used by the IP to identify its client, such as the TCP), is
assigned. All CLNL PDUs, such as routing PDUs, CLNP PDUs, etc.,
are placed in the user-data portion of an IP datagram with protocol
number 80. Although the IP, like the CLNP, can provide fragmentation, it is preferable to avoid fragmentation in the IP, so that this
mechanism can be exercised in the CLNP.

The format of NSAP-addresses is defined in a companion RFC
[RCall89]. A fixed-format address is used, of length 13 octets:

AFI	ICD	vrsn	Global Area	Routing Domain	pad	IP address	sel
1	2	3	4	5	6	7	8	9-15	16	17	18	19	20

The components of this address are:

AFI: The *Authority and Format Identifier* for the address. In
EON, this always takes the value decimal 47, which means
that the address consists of two parts:

- an *Initial Domain Identifier* (IDI); and,

---

[2]It is a testament to the TCP and the IP that they can actually function in such
a perverse environment!

- a *Domain Specific Part* (DSP).

Further, an AFI of value 47 indicates that the address is binary-encoded.

ICD: The *International Country Designator* for the address, which forms the Initial Domain Identifier (the remainder of the address is the Domain Specific Part). In EON, the IDI always takes the value 6, which designates the Internet. (More precisely, values 5 and 6 under AFI 47 were delegated from the ISO to the U.S. National Institute of Standards and Technology; the U.S. NIST then designated value 6 for use by the U.S. DoD.)

vrsn: A *Version Identifier.* This field is used for extensibility purposes. The current value is 2 (an earlier proposal used the value 1).

Global Area/Routing Domain: Reserved for use by OSI routing protocols. In EON, these fields are zero-filled until more experience is gained.

pad: A field of zero-valued octets used to force the address to be exactly 20 octets in length.

IP address: The *Subnetwork Point of Attachment* (SNPA) address of a node in the subnetwork. This corresponds to the Internet Protocol address used by the IP-based subnetwork.

sel: The *Network Selector* of the attached entity. This identifies the desired entity at a given point of attachment. As such, the routing protocols ignore this field. When a datagram reaches its final destination however, the network entity is concerned with this field. The most commonly used value, hexadecimal fe, denotes the entity providing the OSI transport service. Other values exist for a "ping" facility, which can be used either to test reachability or to measure performance at the network layer.

Hence, the actual addresses used look something like:

47	00	06	02	00	00	00	00	...	IP address	fe
1	2	3	4	5	6	7	8	9-15	16 | 17 | 18 | 19	20

Mapping between addresses of the format and SNPA-addresses is simple, given that there is a one-to-one mapping between an NSAP-address in EON and its corresponding IP address: the SNPA is the IP address.

Now all that remains is how to provide multicasting facilities in the IP-based subnetwork. The end-system to intermediate-system (ES-IS) and the intermediate-system to intermediate-system (IS-IS) protocols both assume that underlying subnetworks provide a multicasting facility in order to reach all attached intermediate-systems or end-systems. In order to foster testing of implementations that operate over multicasting media (e.g., most LAN technologies), EON provides a simple emulation of this capability. It is important to understand that the Internet (or any IP-based network, for that matter) consists of several media, some of which are broadcast oriented, and others that are point-to-point in nature. Although research in IP-based multicasting is progressing (e.g., [SDeer88]), IP-based multicasting is not yet widespread. Thus, EON must use some other technique.

EON emulates the multicasting facilities that might be provided by a "real" OSI subnetwork, by providing a *Subnetwork Access sub-layer* between the OSI CLNL and the IP subnetwork. The purpose of this sub-layer is to take the point-to-point datagram service offered by the IP, and augment this slightly to provide the desired multicasting facility. The actions of the access sub-layer are simple: it internally maintains a list of the IP-based nodes that are to be considered reachable in one hop (in the CLNL sense). Logically, all IP-based nodes are one hop away. However, for experimentation, it is useful to enforce a more restrictive logical topology. Thus, some nodes will consider themselves OSI end-systems, whilst others will consider themselves OSI intermediate-systems. Each will maintain a list, usually quite small, that defines the logical topology in use. In the case of end-systems, usually only IP-based nodes on the same physical cable will be considered reachable in one hop. Intermediate-systems are a bit more complex: in addition to IP-based nodes on the same cable, other intermediate-systems will need to be included. This list may be static, e.g., read in at initialization time; or (more likely), it will be dynamic, undergoing modification as the OSI routing protocols are used.

In order to provide the actual multicasting facility, it will be necessary for the access sub-layer to prefix a small amount of control information to each CLNL PDU given to the IP. This will be removed by the access sub-layer at the receiving end. The format of the control information is simple, containing only 4 octets:

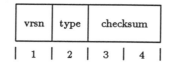

The components are:

vrsn: A *Version Identifier*. In EON, this takes the value 1. Based on experience, the format of the control information might be variable-length.

type: The *Address Semantics* of this PDU. Currently, only four values are defined:

00: Unicast;

01: Multicast to all end-systems;

02: Multicast to all intermediate-systems; and

03: Broadcast to all systems.

checksum: Since the IP does not checksum user data (this is a responsibility for end-to-end protocols such as the TCP and the UDP), the access sub-layer must perform check-summing of the two preceding octets.

When the CLNL passes a PDU to the access sub-layer, an indication of the desired recipient is included. The access sub-layer prefixes the control information, selecting the correct address type and calculating the checksum. If multicasting is selected, then the list of one-hop distant peers is consulted and IP is called repeatedly, once for each peer. For peers that are on the same physical cable, if that media supports IP-broadcasting, then IP-broadcasting is used. If multicasting is not selected, then the IP is called exactly once to send the resulting user data.

On the receiving end, if the length is at least 4 octets and the checksum is satisfied, then the address type is consulted. If either the unicast or broadcast semantics is present, then the control information for the access sub-layer is stripped off the IP user data and the remainder is given to the CLNL. Otherwise, the user data will be passed up only if the logical configuration of IP-based node matches that of the desired address semantics present in the control information.

This is hardly an efficient approach to multi-casting. However, it optimizes flexibility, which is good for the purposes of experimentation.

14.2.3 Scorecard

Performance: No worse than a typical CLNP-based router.

Flexibility: High, as the NS-tunnel is independent of any application that ultimately uses the CLNP.

Transparency: Total, given adequate routing protocols.

Amenability: If directly attached to an NS-tunnel, participating TCP-based end-systems must now run transport protocols from both suites (usually requiring "kernel" modifications on systems, such as UNIX, that have such a concept).

14.3   Summary and Comparisons

With the *Service-based Approaches* drawing to a close, the discussion now turns to a comparison between the approaches examined thus far.

    Service-based approaches are approaches to *coexistence*, not tran- | soap... | sition. As such, service-based approaches are extremely unpopular with the "lunatic fringe" of networking, those few individuals who promote purity of the protocol stacks at all costs. For those at one extreme, any effort that prolongs the existence of the Internet suite of protocols, by allowing it to coexist well with the OSI suite, is at best, a waste of time, and at worst, heretical. Similar judgements are made by those at the other extreme, who view with disdain any effort that introduces OSI protocols into an Internet environment. | ...soap |

    To understand why service-based approaches are more effective at coexistence, return one last time to the two protocol entities, E_1 and E_2. Both protocol-based and service-based approaches are based on mappings: they differ in the orientations of the mappings they require. Recall that difficulty in constructing such a mapping is either

$$|P_2 - P_1|$$

or

$$|O_2 - O_1|.$$

("how hard it is to map between one protocol to another" and "how hard it is to map between one service to another").

    The question becomes "is it harder to map services or protocols"? The answer depends on the particular layer in the protocol hierarchy.

    Both the OSI transport service and the TCP-based transport service are simple. In contrast, both protocols are quite complex. This suggests, at the transport layer, that:

$$|P_2 - P_1| \; > \; |O_2 - O_1|.$$

The modest empirical evidence known to the author bears this out: the complexity of building a transport-gateway described in [IGroe86] is easily an order of magnitude larger than building Onions' TP0–based gateway. This in turn was still much more complex than the first TS-bridge. In other words, it is more difficult to build a gateway between two transport protocols offering dissimilar transport services than it is to build a bridge between two protocols offering the same service.

Chapter 15

Scenarios for Transition

None of the strategies presented have received uniformly high scores across the metrics chosen for comparison. However, against a subset of the metrics, each strategy can be seen to have advantages over the others: one must view the particular environment in which the goal is one of transition or coexistence, when deciding which strategy or combination of strategies is optimal.

As *Transition to OSI* draws to a close, this final chapter looks at two scenarios that apply the approaches previously discussed.

15.1   Example: U.S. DoD Strategy

It should not be surprising that the U.S. Department of Defense, which sponsored and heavily uses the Internet protocol suite, will have a tremendous problem when it tries to transition to OSI. In order to provide for an orderly and effective transition, an OSI Implementation Strategy[DDN88] was prepared and is being acted upon. Although quite detailed and extensive, the plan focuses on two areas:

- implementation of OSI in the DoD internetwork environment; and,

- provision of interoperation between the Internet and OSI protocol suites.

The discussion now examines each of these in turn.

15.1.1   OSI-POSIX Project

Standards play an important part in the operations of the DoD internetwork environment. In addition to standardized networking protocols, standardized interfaces to operating systems also are of interest.

One such standardization effort is POSIX, which is an IEEE proposed standard for an interface to a UNIX-like portable operating system. Currently, POSIX specifies only the kernel interface, but does not specify a standard method for accessing network services from the kernel interface. Work on a shell and tools standard for POSIX is also advancing. A U.S. Federal Information Processing Standard (FIPS) was also developed for POSIX. It is meant to be the initial set of guidelines for procurement of operating systems for U.S. Government users.

As noted in *Introduction to Open Systems*, After consensus is reached on a standard, it is often the case that functional profiles are required before the standard can be widely implemented by a variety of vendors. The U.S. Government OSI Profile (GOSIP) [USGOS88] provides this focus for Federal users of OSI. The aims of the GOSIP are actually quite simple: it seeks to enable users to specify and procure OSI products that are interoperable, multi-vendor, and "off-the-shelf." Technically, the GOSIP is aligned with the NIST OSI Implementor's Agreements[NIST88]. The Implementor's Agreements, which specify functional profiles of existing OSI standards, are the results of an ongoing, cooperative, multi-vendor effort. In addition, the GOSIP Advanced Requirements Group provides an emphasis on those parts of OSI that are still lagging behind the needs of Federal users (e.g., security).

GOSIP became a FIPS in August of 1988. In doing so, it started a "countdown for opportunity" (i.e., timebomb) for the U.S. Department of Defense. DoD policy states that approximately two years after GOSIP became a FIPS, networking procurements must reference GOSIP. Given that the clock is running, how might the U.S. Department of Defense achieve its goals?

Many have noted that the widespread use of the Internet suite was dramatically accelerated by the inclusion of these protocols in Berkeley UNIX. This observation leads to several questions:

- Can a reference version of the OSI protocols be put into Berkeley UNIX?

- Can the Berkeley UNIX kernel be made POSIX compliant?

- Can POSIX be extended to define an interface for network services?

- Can these three goals be made openly available and ready for inclusion for the next major release of Berkeley UNIX?

The answer to all four questions is... *yes!* If successful, then it is entirely possible that such a project may vastly accelerate the process of OSI becoming ubiquitous. Of course, it should be noted that one factor contributing to the widespread acceptance of the Internet suite of protocols was the lack of widespread networking software. Hence, at the conclusion of this project, the results may not be so dramatic. It will probably be too early to judge the success of this project until a few years after completion.

From a distance these four goals seem somewhat ambitious: Implement a complete OSI stack. Add the POSIX interface to Berkeley UNIX. Define a networking interface from scratch. And have all of this ready for a release of Berkeley UNIX. However, it turns out that a large number of the pieces are already openly available. As such, the work consists mainly of filling in the gaps, integrating the components, and then testing the system.

An openly available implementation of the OSI upper layers already exists: the ISODE. Other organizations have also developed or are planning to develop the lower layers, such as ISO transport class 4 (TP4), along with some OSI applications, such as X.400 message handling.

Figure 15.1 shows the contributions to the OSI-POSIX project. Each box in this figure represents an OSI module. Most of the modules are already present in the ISODE. For those modules that weren't a part of the ISODE when the project began, the name of a contributing organization is found in the corresponding box. To summarize:

- X.400 Message Handling System (MHS) — University College London and the University of Nottingham

- MHS/822 gateway — the U.S. National Institute of Standards and Technology, using the gateway supplied by University College London

- Virtual Terminal Protocol (VT) — the MITRE Corporation

- FTAM/FTP gateway — the U.S. National Institute of Standards and Technology, using the gateway supplied by the MITRE Corporation

- Directory Services — the U.S. National Institute of Standards and Technology,

- Transport Layer — joint project between the University of Wisconsin, Madison, and the IBM Corporation

- Network Layer — joint project between the University of Wisconsin, Madison, and the IBM Corporation

- Subnetwork support — joint project between the University of Wisconsin, Madison, and the IBM Corporation

The University of California, Berkeley is charged with the overall integration of the software into UNIX.

Hence, the work plan is straightforward: a few OSI applications will be integrated into the ISODE (most are already in place); the OSINET facility will be used to perform interoperability testing; and, ultimately, conformance testing with the Corporation for Open Systems (COS) will be performed.

As it turns out, the actual kernel interface specified by POSIX is very close to some of the services provided by the Berkeley UNIX kernel. Hence, only minor work will be required to provide a POSIX compliant interface in Berkeley UNIX. The U.S. National Institute of Standards and Technology is developing a conformance test suite for POSIX, and once both (independent) tasks are complete, conformance testing will be performed. Finally, as the POSIX interface becomes available in Berkeley UNIX, the ISODE and the other OSI applications will be converted to use the relevant facilities.

Finally, the various parties contributing to this effort are participating in the emerging POSIX effort to produce a network interface.

15.1.2 Application-Gateways

The U.S. Department of Defense has been active in supporting the development of application-gateways between the Internet protocol suite and the OSI suite. In fact, under DoD sponsorship, two application-gateways for file service have been built:

- a staging gateway, built by the U.S. National Institute of Standards and Technology; and,

- an in-situ gateway, built by the MITRE Corporation.

In addition, the NIST has also built a prototype application-gateway for mail service.

As a part of the OSI-POSIX plan, these gateways, or their descendants, will be made widely available throughout the DoD internetwork environment.

MHS/822 GW [NIST]		FTAM/FTP GW [NIST]	
MHS [UCL]	VT [MITRE]	FTAM	
RELIABLE TRANSFER	REMOTE OPERATIONS	ASSOCIATION CONTROL	DIRECTORY SERVICES [NIST]	ASN.1 TOOLS
PRESENTATION SERVICES			
SESSION SERVICES			
TRANSPORT SERVICES [U. Wisconsin]			
NETWORK SERVICES (CLNP AND ES-IS) [U. Wisconsin]			
SUBNETWORK SUPPORT (8802.x AND X.25) [U. Wisconsin]			

Figure 15.1: Contributors to the OSI-POSIX Project

15.2 Generic Example

Now discussion turns to an alternative strategy that focuses on mixing several approaches. This strategy focuses on two policies in the short-term:

- favor use of OSI applications operating on top of TCP on local area networks; and,

- locate application-gateways and a TS-bridge on all nodes with attachments to wide area networks.

Then, wait for the OSI lower layers to become competitive with TCP, both in terms of local area network performance and LAN/WAN internetworking and robustness. At this time, switch over to the OSI lower layers on the LANs, and use NS-tunnels for internetworking over the WAN. Continue this until all WAN attachments support CLNP. This entire process might take as long as 10 years or more!

The configuration of a local area network with two wide area network attachments is shown in Figure 15.2. Basically, each attachment to the "outside world" should support coexistence services. In practice, this attachment consists of a dual-stack node containing a TS-bridge, an application-gateway for file service, and an application-gateway for mail service. If resources permit, one other dual-stack node is selected to support these services for use by local uni-stack hosts. A modestly capable directory mechanism would be helpful in making sure that the intermediary node is chosen when coexistence services are needed. This arrangement has the advantage of isolating coexistence traffic at the "edges" of the local environment.

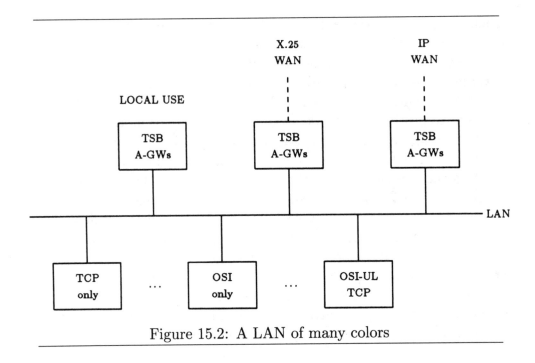

Figure 15.2: A LAN of many colors

15.3 Conclusions

"Optimality differs according to context."
– Michael A. Padlipsky, The Elements of Networking
Style, Prentice-hall (1985)

Given the *D-day conjecture* as the basis for our environment, we argue for an emphasis on coexistence: in the short-term, the TS-bridge can be used to minimize software investment whilst retaining full application layer functionality between the two communities; in the long-term, the NS-tunnel can be used to maximize performance. To supplement this approach, application-gateways are employed for those hosts that will always remain uni-stack. Presumably the prevalence of these hosts will dwindle rapidly as the installed base moves towards the newer protocol stack. Hence, our reliance on application-gateways for coexistence will shrink to insignificance.

This leads us to speculate that, if one can coexist well, then transition, per se, is a non-issue. In short, we let the market decide how long the Internet suite remains useful, and then when no more TCP/IP-based hosts exist in a community, the coexistence period is over and transition is complete. In other words, if we handle coexistence correctly, transition will occur naturally. The danger, of course, is that users will become so accustomed to running OSI applications on top of TCP/IP-based networks, that they may not be motivated to move to complete OSI environments. This is unlikely: with technology such as the TS-bridge, transition from TCP/IP-based end-to-end services to an OSI-based backbone can be done transparently.

It is interesting to note that this strategy is directly contrary to the transition scheme proposed by many proponents of OSI. They suggest that transition should be accomplished first in the network by standardizing first on the OSI end-to-end services on an enterprise-wide basis and then by standardizing on the OSI application services and applications. Some proponents of this scheme are so brazen as to call this an *evolutionary* rather than *revolutionary* approach.

In general, this strategy lacks coherence. Once again, recall that network users are productive in today's environments. As such, any change that occurs must be minimally disruptive on existing facilities. To convert the network backbone to the OSI lower-layer protocols would also require changing the user's applications to make use of these protocols. Even if this change could be accomplished without disruption, the fact still remains that the users do not perceive any benefit from this change.

There are notable exceptions however. The U.K. Academic community, for example, has long anticipated the emergence of International Standards. They developed a set of "coloured books" defining the interim protocols that they would use until OSI was widely available. Their transition strategy is described in the *White Book* [JNT87].

The end-to-end service provided in the JANET (U.K. Joint Academic Network) is very similar to the OSI end-to-end services. In particular, the 1980 CCITT X.25 Recommendation is used to provide this service along with the transport protocol defined in *Yellow Book*. Thus, in terms of end-to-end services, transition consists primarily of upgrading the backbone to the 1984 CCITT X.25 Recommendation. The latter X.25 supports the OSI Connection-oriented Network Service (CONS) directly, so the Yellow book will no longer be needed.

Hence, by embracing OSI early on, the U.K. Academic Community has a substantial leg up on the transition problem. Unfortunately, their interim application protocols are not closely aligned with the OSI applications. As such, they face many of the same transition problems as other communities.

In contrast, return to the alternative described earlier where transition occurs from the outside towards the network:

- users are motivated to change because they want the more functional OSI applications; then,

- end-systems slowly change to support the OSI lower-layers; and then,

- intermediate-systems change to support the OSI lower-layers as well.

By introducing new services, rather than replacing old ones, this approach seeks to minimizes disruption.

Finally, consider: all of the approaches examined in Part IV are expensive: the techniques differ in where the cost is placed. This has led some to note that perhaps it is simply too expensive either to transit or to coexist. Perhaps it is best to keep the two protocol suites separated as much as possible. In considering such a strategy, one must also consider how much it costs "just to do nothing." Although hard to quantify, intuitively, one might suspect that the costs of this will be even higher! Unless some cross-over takes place, either through transition or coexistence, then the installed bases of both systems will only become more entrenched. Some users are likely to continue buying systems supporting the current set of protocols (the Internet suite), simply because they can continue to leverage their existing investment. Similarly, other users, with a smaller investment of TCP/IP-based systems may start investing in OSI. This scenario will lead only to more and more problems as the two large installed bases find that they are unable to leverage their combined resources when necessary. Thus, regardless of whether one favors transition or coexistence, it is clear that some approach must be taken!

Part V

The Final Soapbox

Chapter 16

The Politics of Open Systems

Considering the potential leverage that OSI offers, it shouldn't be ⟨soap...⟩ surprising that technical issues, per se, take a back seat to political and market pressures. Only recently has the Internet suite come under these non-technical pressures. With OSI, these pressures have been permeative. Pressures are not necessarily evil by design, they just appears that way most of the time.

To make it clear that the following is entirely of a non-technical nature, this entire chapter appears inside a soapbox. The author makes no claim that he actually supports any of the conflicting views that follow. He is merely reporting on commonly held non-technical beliefs from various camps.

16.1 Problems with the Standards Process

The fundamental failure of the OSI standards process is that it is detached from practicality. Democracy might be a fine way to run a government, but it is no way to produce rational technology.

16.1.1 Standards Organizations

The standards process is designed so that no one vendor achieves a competitive advantage over any other. This works well in areas where there is an already a single *de facto* standard, since the standards process essentially does no more than formalize existing technology.

When there is no de facto standard, or where there are several competing technologies, it is up to the standards process to create something in order to avoid the appearance of favoritism. The result is often inferior technology. To gain consensus, the standards committee must take the bells-and-whistles from each existing technology. The result often is a set of bloated, fundamentally inconsistent protocols. For example,

- the OSI network layer, and in particular its internal organization [ISO87a], is the result of two competing, incompatible, technologies that got merged into one layer by the standards process; and,

- the OSI application layer structure [ISO87n] is what happens when there is nothing pre-existing before the standards process gears up.

In the former case, the result is something that is hardly implementable, let alone comprehensible. In the latter case, the result merely lacks comprehensibility. (Some of the members of the committee that defined the OSI application layer structure actually giggle audibly whenever they contemplate an outsider trying to read their document.)

Another problem with the standards process is that there is simply *tremendous* market pressure to have standards produced as soon as possible. Vendors are often put into a strange dilemma as to when to begin implementation. Because a DIS is supposed to be technically stable, one would naturally expect that, once a document reaches DIS status, vendors could begin implementation. However, throughout 1988 it was not uncommon for a document to undergo significant technical change from DIS to IS. For example, in the case of one minimal implementation of the OSI file service, approximately 50% of the implementation was replaced or, worse yet, subtly changed when upgraded from DIS to IS. Of course, this merely encourages vendors to wait until the last possible moment before implementing. However, unless OSI implementors begin prototyping during the standards process, then there is very little confidence that the resulting IS will be workable.

This example points out something very critical: just because a document becomes a standard, there is little guarantee that the technology is workable or even well understood. A famous remark overheard at a standards meeting that reenforces this view:

> *Let's hope it's not a problem, because it certainly is getting larger.*

This pretty much underscores the comprehensibility argument.

Consider who actually gets sent to standards meetings. When a technology enters the standards process, vendors send their best and brightest to safeguard proprietary interests. Once the course is set, the *Doers* are called back to the office where they can perform more productive tasks for their employers. To finish off the process, the vendors then send persons they can *afford* to have out of the office, the professional standards *Goers*. The Goers have likely never implemented anything in their professional careers (if they have, it was so long ago as to be unworthy of mention, e.g., when vacuum tubes were the rule). There is a propensity among the Goers not even to use computers, the very technology they are working to enhance. A Goer attends meetings to deal with weighty political issues, travel, and have many fine lunches and dinners.

The caricature of the Goer is someone who pops into the office Monday morning to pick up mail, and then jets off to a standards meeting, liaison session, workshop, or symposium. On the airplane, the Goer reviews the numerous written contributions and gets ready for the next meeting, all around the in-flight movie.

In 1988, the Goers were commonly referred to as *nitwits* (genus *nitwitus vulgaris*). A nitwit, in the standards sense, is someone who thinks that just because you write something down that it is implementable and workable.

There are notable exceptions. The landmark standards on message handling are the result of a few key persons, combination Doer/Goers, who were able to come to the table with savvy technology and then keep the discussion focused, regardless of the political influences. This is but a stellar exception, not the rule.

A large number of Doers boycott standards meetings because they are afraid of being tainted by nitwits. Instead, Doers are sending their colleagues, who in turn report back, thereby letting *them* ruin *their* careers. Nevertheless, without the few combination Doer/Goers in attendance, OSI would be simply unimplementable, as opposed to being mostly unimplementable.

What happens when a Doer meets a Goer makes for an interesting vignette. When one of the OSI subcommittees invited experts from the Internet suite of protocols to attend a meeting, the result was:

> *You OSI guys really need a sanity check.*

The "OSI sanity check" could probably be a very popular gift. It would probably be a lapel pin containing a very loud, obnoxious buzzer. Whenever a Goer utters nonsense, the buzzer emits an ear-shattering sound until a Doer resets it. This is a superb example of a self-correcting system: if the ratio of Doers to Goers is high enough, then lots of productive work occurs. If the reverse is true, especially if there are no Doers on the committee, then eventually the Goers will be rendered completely incoherent and no documents will ever be produced. Considering some of the OSI standards that do exist, it is clearly better to have no standards than to have bad ones.

It is important to appreciate that even the Doers who attend don't always agree on the correct technical approach. An illustrative quote from Stephen E. Kille, a Doer who also attends standards meetings:

> *I am here to put my hand on the OSI bible and imple-*
> *ment everything. Except, of course, for the bits that aren't*
> *sensible!*

This illustrates why functional profiles are necessary.

16.1.2   Functional Profiles

The unfortunate problem with the organizations producing functional profiles is that they have a heavy population of Goers and marketeers. The implementors are now actually in the *minority*.

It is useful to have a few committee members attend the profiling meetings, so as to provide clarifying information. But, there is no legally acceptable way of keeping all the Goers out and once again, pragmatism takes a back seat to politics.

The marketeers are there to protect the proprietary interests of their employers. Whilst this is correct in the competitive sense, these are probably the wrong skill sets to apply towards pragmatic issues.

It is wise for Doers to refuse, on general principles, to attend profiling meetings, for fear of being tainted by nitwits. If only the term *Implementors' Workshop* meant *Implementors Only*, then a Doer would find it more worthwhile to attend. For example, one industry expert, responsible for much of the stellar work done in Message Handling, has noted that one of the organizations producing functional profiles is largely "the blind leading the blind." Interestingly enough, many other Doer/Goers share this viewpoint: they view functional profiles and the organizations that produce them with contempt.

Another problem of the standards process are the various parties who may try to subvert the process by having the functional profiles reference documents that are not produced by the standards community. These parties seek to hang on OSI's coat-tails in order to further their own agendas; it is the functional profile, and not international standards, per se, which receive force of law. Great diligence is required to circumvent this kind of unfortunate manipulation.

It is interesting to note that the Internet suite of protocols has quite easily out-achieved OSI in terms of workable technology, without the benefit of functional profiles or today's style of implementors' workshops.

16.2 The Myths of Formalism

A particularly disturbing trend fostered by OSI has been the use of so-called formal methods in the specification of standards and the testing of implementations.

It is clear that a common "language" must be used when describing technology so as to achieve universal understanding. In the OSI case however, the terminology is somewhat different from the notation used by other protocol suites. Severe culture shock results when experts from another protocol suite (e.g., the Internet suite of protocols) try to read OSI documents. The term *osified* is used to refer to such documents. This means to obscure or to make unclear, usually for no good reason other than for the sake of formality. Any relationship to the word ossified is purely intentional (the two words are pronounced identically).

Once one learns OSI terminology, it is surprisingly effective. It does, however, require a great deal of energy and dedication to become proficient.

16.2.1   Conformance Testing

There is one school of thought which believes that in order to have
true interoperability it is necessary to test each OSI implementation
to ensure compliance to the appropriate standards and profiles. Such
an activity is termed a *conformance test*. In a nutshell, conformance
testing is an argument for program verification, where the input specification to the program is the standards and profiles, and the implementation under test is the program to be verified. Several organizations have been formed with the goal of providing conformance
testing systems for the most common standards and profiles.

Many feel that conformance testing is not very effective. There
are two reasons for this. From a theoretical perspective, program verification is an unsolved problem, and it is simply beyond the state of
the art to produce programs that can guarantee that other programs
are correct. There are plenty of instances of two implementations,
each able to pass a conformance test, but not being able to interoperate with each other. Conformance testing therefore inspires little
confidence in the user community. In contrast, conformance testing
potentially provides benefits to an implementor during the early stages
of development — as a simple check.

From a practical perspective, conformance testing is probably the
wrong approach. Consider: when an implementation is put under
test, in effect it must interoperate with the test system. A conformance test is *nothing more* than an interoperability test with another
implementation, the test system. The test system isn't placed in the
user's environment — it isn't end-user equipment. The user doesn't
buy test systems, the user buys systems to get work done. Interoperability testing against equipment the user will never buy — what's
the point?

If conformance testing is a myth, what can be learned from interoperability testing?

16.2.2   The Lessons of Interoperability Testing

Experience shows that there is simply no substitute for interoperability testing. The goal of OSI is to make interoperability between

different vendors a non-issue. Hence, pair-wise interoperability testing is the litmus test of OSI.

As of the end of 1988, only one organization had sponsored an interoperability testing forum, and that was an experimental, pilot project.

In practice, the only way interoperability testing occurs is when an OSI trade show is announced. For example, in March, 1989, the EurOSInet organization sponsored a multi-vendor OSI booth at the CeBIT '89 show in Hannover, FRG. A few months before the show, the technical representatives began coordination for interoperability testing, which is held in complete secrecy.

The interactions can, without loss of generality, be broken down into two categories: testing between systems which had already been tested at previous shows, and testing between systems that had never tested with each other. In the first case, testing was largely a formality. In the latter case, testing was an absolute disaster for the technical personnel involved.

At of the end of 1988, while hundreds of vendors have announced OSI capabilities of one form or another, there were probably less than ten independent implementations. Whenever a new implementation arrived on the scene, the technical parties got a first hand look at how *fragile* OSI software really is.

Here is the common example: testing begins with a new OSI implementation. The vendor of the implementation knows there will be some bugs found during testing. Given the complexity of OSI and a relatively new implementation, this is unavoidable. The vendor commits their top technical resources to perform the testing and resolve any problems as quickly as possible. The vendor of the "established" implementation, probably having tested with twenty or so other implementations, is confident that they will not find any problems in their code. What the second vendor has forgotten is that of those twenty implementations, perhaps only six come from different sources. It can be a very rude awakening when an implementation from the seventh source begins testing.

The most complicated aspects of an OSI protocol are the negotiations at the beginning of a communication. There are many options to be negotiated, and many facilities to be proposed, and then either enabled or disabled. The most telling indication of the state of an OSI implementation is how well it handles negotiations, particularly those negotiations with options and parameters that it has not seen in prior testing.

When a new implementation begins testing, on the first try it is almost certain unintentionally to crash each and every one of the different implementations it tests against! The new implementation will likely have some minor bugs in the options it proposes. However, in the majority of cases it will probably be the case that the more established implementations simply don't handle option negotiation well.

The lack of hardening on the part of OSI implementations is more widespread than any would care to admit. For example, after much testing between an established implementation and a newer one, the established implementation would mysteriously crash in the middle of a transaction, without any meaningful diagnostics. After more than a man-month of investigation, a bug in the newer implementation was found: during negotiation it did not propose a mandatory parameter. Once this was fixed, communications occurred without any further problems. This points to a larger problem in the established implementation: it simply isn't robust. The lack of a mandatory parameter should have set off alarm bells in the established implementation. At the very least the established implementation could say *why* it had crashed. Interestingly enough, none of the other "established" implementations neither detected the missing parameter, nor did they crash: they were robust.

Interoperability testing is painful, but it is necessary. It is the *only* guarantee of working open systems.

16.3   The Internet Community

Based on the preceding discussion of how International Standards and Internet Standards are produced, it can be seen that there are two entirely different models. The International model favors widespread consensus. The Internet model favors technical focus. It should not be surprising that the OSI community and the Internet community are the most fanatical of combatants.

16.3.1   An Amusing Anecdote

To appreciate better the Internet tradition, consider this now famous story: in the early days of the Internet suite of protocols, an inter-operability "bake-off" was hosted at the USC/Information Sciences Institute. Ten different implementations were represented. The test began by having all implementations connected to the same network with the *checksumming* algorithm disabled. This algorithm ensures data reliability by computing an arithmetic sum, the checksum, over the data sent. The receiver looks at the data and the checksum and determines if either has been corrupted during transmission.

With the checksumming algorithm disabled, all ten implementations could interoperate. Another round of tests were run, this time with the checksum algorithm enabled. Only two implementations could interoperate! The two implementors were asked to explain their interpretation of the checksum algorithm. The document describing the checksumming algorithm was then modified to contain these explanations, and the other eight implementors changed their code. The result became the standard way in the Internet for calculating checksums.

This illustrates an important point: *all* Internet technology is based on things which are known to work before standardization occurs.[1]

16.3.2   Internet versus OSI

The Internet community tries its very best to ignore the OSI community. By and large, OSI technology is *ugly* in comparison to Internet

---

[1]Sadly, this is no longer true; see Section 16.3.3 below.

technology. Unfortunately, there are often disastrous consequences of OSI ignorance on the part of the Internet community.

The *nitwits* of the OSI community have colleagues of a sort in the Internet community, the *Fabergé Egghead* (genus *cranius favrius*).

A Fabergé Egg is an extraordinary, valuable, piece of jewelry, a rare bauble that is nonetheless non-functional [ASolo88,ASolo89]. The term Fabergé Egghead is commonly used when referring to the senior members of the Internet community, and in particular to the IAB! These researchers have made tremendous contributions to the networking field. They proved their value. Unfortunately, they refuse to have anything to do with OSI, whether it be direct influence or subtle technology transfer. Thus, they have ceased to be functional in the new world of networking.

There are two other types of Internet Fabergé Eggheads, the Aspiring and the Would-Be. The Aspiring Fabergé Egghead *thinks* they are contributing substantially to the advancement of Science and Technology by writing papers and jetting off to conferences and symposia (international locations are favored). The Aspiring Egghead does not really implement or produce a tangible that changes the world into a better place. If an Aspiring Fabergé Egghead eventually manages a seminal contribution to The Greater Good of networking, they are accorded full Egghead status, and proceed to retire in place. The Would-Be Egghead is likened to an OSI Goer. They contribute to the impedance of progress by not doing much of anything and making sure others don't either.

Most Fabergé Eggheads are often found as fixtures in ivory tower institutions. Collectively these institutions compose *The National Jewel Collection*. As with all highly desired collectables, to prove worth, it is periodically necessary to display the valuables. Show-and-tell for the networking faction of The National Jewel Collection is usually at the Internet Engineering Task Force (IETF) meetings. The IETF provides Eggheads the opportunity to parade their many accomplishments past colleagues. These colleagues are primarily composed of young turks in their mid-20's who favor scheduling the quarterly meetings in central locations known for high productivity, e.g., Hawaii and Florida. In early 1989, a Beachcomber Working Group was chartered to help with these weighty issues. As might be imagined, not much is really engineered at IETF sessions, although many fine lunches and dinners are enjoyed. After attending a few IETF meetings an industry professional was heard to have remarked:

The IETF is in need of adult supervision.

This is a particularly sad state of affairs as the IETF is charged with solving the short-term engineering needs of the Internet community.

Between the terms nitwit and egghead it is easy to see the extent to which animosity exists between the two camps.

16.3.3   The Network Management Shibboleth

With the growth of the Internet community, network management became a much needed technology. In 1987, the IAB directed a promising scientist to begin a research project in network mangement. The project began in the typical Internet tradition: senior technical direction and brilliant engineering. The result was HEMS, the High-Level Entity Management System [CPart87]. Unfortunately, there were two things not counted on.

First, the explosive growth of the Internet community in 1987, meant that a solution was needed immediately. A group of engineers, responsible for network line-management in the Internet community, specified the Simple Gateway Management Protocol (SGMP) [JDavi87]. The SGMP was neither as powerful or as elegant as HEMS, but it was simple to implement and it got the job done.

Second, network management had become a "hot" topic in OSI. Naturally documents for OSI network management began creeping their way through the standards process. Another group, consisting primarily of professionals from the fringe of the Internet community, proposed using the OSI network management protocol and framework to manage networks based on the Internet suite of protocols.

Throughout 1987, much controversy reigned, until the IAB called an ad hoc meeting to resolve the issue. At this meeting, held in February, 1988, HEMS was, by and large, judged to be the superior technical solution. There was, however, a problem for HEMS: it did not have the widespread deployment of the SGMP, nor the inevitability of OSI behind it.

When the lead researcher on the HEMS project threw in the towel a *modus vivendi* emerged:

- The SGMP would be slightly upgraded to reflect (then) recently gained experience. The resulting protocol would become the short-term solution for network management in the Internet community.

- The OSI-based approach would receive extensive scrutiny and experimentation, in the hopes of one day becoming the long-term solution.

Such statesmanship is rarely seen these days. Of course, it wasn't the HEMS researchers who lost that day. It was the Internet community. This unfortunate situation caused some cutting edge research to be prematurely terminated. All because it wasn't yet deployed and it wasn't OSI.

After the HEMS accord, the SGMP evolved into the *Simple Network Management Protocol* [JCase89b]. The SNMP was declared a Draft Internet Standard in the fall of 1988. The SNMP quickly became the de facto standard for management of TCP/IP-based networks. The SNMP was being supported by several vendors, having at least two reference implementations publically available, and receiving widespread use.

Meanwhile, work continued on the OSI-based approach, ultimately resulting in an RFC describing OSI Common Management Information Services and Protocol over TCP/IP (CMOT) [UWarr89].

In April of 1989, the IAB made the CMOT a co-standard with the SNMP. Although the reasons for this action are not clear, it established an interesting precedent: there were no implementations of the CMOT when standard status was declared. There was no *experience* in either the laboratory or operationally. In contrast, the SNMP, and all protocols bearing the term (Draft) Internet Standard, were promoted only after extensive implementation, experimentation, and revision. By promoting the CMOT as a co-standard, the valued Internet tradition of "basing standards on things that are known to work" was discarded.[2]

---

[2]It is interesting to note that the IAB cited no technical reasons for advancing the CMOT as a co-standard.

16.4   Where to Now?

Work began on OSI in 1978. In 1989 the market is still waiting for OSI's promise. The Internet protocols have provided the user community with many of the technical benefits of Open Systems with few of the political problems. Nevertheless, the days of the Internet suite are numbered — perhaps they are numbered in years, but they *are* numbered. To rephrase a popular witicism about computer languages:

> *I don't know what the computer-communication protocols of the 90's will consist of, but they will be called OSI.*

How can the history of the last ten years be interpreted?

Does the success of working Open Systems consist of holding committee meetings or forming organizations with the term "Open" in their name? Is an organization's commitment to Open Systems well demonstrated with advertisements in The Wall Street Journal and trade publications? The unprecedented success of the Internet experience has eloquently argued that Open Systems can be achieved *only* through implementation and experimentation.

Nonetheless, the committees continue to meet; "Open" organizations continue to be formed; and, organizations continue to jockey to win the hearts and minds (and presumably pocketbooks) of the market by praising OSI through Madison Avenue tactics.

Unfortunately, there continues to be a dearth of OSI implementations. In fairness it can probably be stated that by mid-1989 there still weren't any *workable* implementations of OSI.

The ISODE, described throughout Part III, is intended only as a tool to study OSI. Nevertheless it emerged as the de facto reference implementation of the OSI upper-layers, as a platform for deploying OSI services, and as a means for transitioning from TCP/IP to OSI protocols. The ISODE was meant to make these things possible to *study*. It was never intended as the basis for production software or services. Regardless of this, the ISODE has been pressed into production service for all these roles, if for no other reason than the utter lack of any reasonable alternatives. For example, by mid-1989, the author knew of at least three major computer hardware vendors who had, or were planning to announce, OSI products based primarily on the ISODE. As the principal implementor of the ISODE, it is gratifying, perhaps even enviable, to see the ISODE receive such wide use on an international basis. As a proponent of Open Systems, it is embarrassing. If the ISODE is a leading implementation of OSI, then the market is in a lot of trouble!

In the meantime, the Internet community has become highly politicized. This has resulted in a lack of technical direction and the usual emphasis on trench-fighting and damage-control. Politics is the death of technology, regardless of the community.

Well, that's the theory and practice of Open Systems. This soapbox may seem either pessimistic or hostile. In fact, the author believes it is pretty well balanced. It is necessarily painful for an industry and profession when someone cuts through the veil of respectability to expose the inner workings, along with the requisite excesses and the excuses. Fortunately, the reviewers of *The Open Book* approved of this soapbox by a margin of nearly two to one. And, since OSI is based on the notion that democracy is fine for technology, this final soapbox was included.

So, with the publication of this soapbox, its time to take on a new role, that of the *Pariah of Networking*!

`...soap`

Appendix A

Ordering the ISODE

For those interested in ordering the *ISO Development Environment*, reproduced here is the announcement for the ISODE 6.0 release. Note that information such as this is always out of date. It is best to call one of the phone numbers listed below to determine current ordering information:

ANNOUNCEMENT

The next release of *The ISO Development Environment* will be available on 24 January 1990. This release is called

ISODE 6.0

This software supports the development of certain kinds of OSI protocols and applications. Here are the details:

- The ISODE is not proprietary, but it is not in the public domain. This was necessary to include a "hold harmless" clause in the release. The upshot of all this is that anyone can get a copy of the release and do anything they want with it, but no one takes any responsibility whatsoever for any (mis)use.

- The ISODE runs on native Berkeley (4.2, 4.3) and AT&T (SVR2, SVR3) systems, in addition to various other UNIX-like operating systems. No kernel modifications are required.

- Current modules include:

    - OSI transport service (TP0 on top of TCP and X.25; TP4 for SunLink OSI)

    - OSI session, presentation, and association control services

    - ASN.1 abstract syntax/transfer notation tools, including:

        * remote operations stub-generator (front-end for remote operations)

        * structure-generator (ASN.1 to C)

        * element-parser (basic encoding rules)

    - OSI reliable transfer and remote operations services

    - OSI file transfer, access and management

    - FTAM/FTP gateway

    - OSI directory services

    - OSI virtual terminal (basic class, TELNET profile)

- ISODE 6.0 consists of final "IS" level implementations with a few exceptions: ROSE and RTSE are current to the last circulated drafts (March, 1988); VT is a DIS implementation. ISODE also contains implementations of the 1984 X.400 versions of ROS and RTS. ISODE is aligned with the U.S. Government OSI Profile (GOSIP).

- Modules planned for future releases include:

    - OSI message handling system

    - MHS/SMTP gateway

- Although the ISODE is not "supported" per se, it does have an address to which problems may be reported:

    `Bug-ISODE@NISC.NYSER.NET`

    Bug reports (and fixes) are welcome, by the way.

- The discussion group `ISODE@NIC.DDN.MIL` is used as an open forum on ISODE. Contact `ISODE-Request@NIC.DDN.MIL` to be added to this list.

- The primary documentation for this release consists of a five volume User's Manual (approx. 1000 pages) and a set of UNIX manual pages. The sources to the User's Manual are in LaTeX format. In addition, there are a number of notes, papers, and presentations included in the documentation set, again in either LaTeX or SLiTeX format.

For more information, contact:

> PSI, Inc.
> PSI California Office
> Attn: Marshall T. Rose
> 420 Whisman Court
> Mountain View, CA 94043–2112
> USA
>
> +1–415–961–3380

Information on getting a distribution follows on the next page.

DISTRIBUTION SITES

- NORTH AMERICA
  For mailings in NORTH AMERICA, send a check for 375 US Dollars to:

  Postal: University of Pennsylvania
                Department of Computer and Information Science
                Moore School
                Attn: David J. Farber (ISODE Distribution)
                200 South 33rd Street
                Philadelphia, PA 19104-6314
                USA

  Telephone: +1–215–898–8560

  The tape will be written in *tar*(1) format at 1600bpi, and returned with a documentation set. Do not send tapes or envelopes. Documentation only is the same price.

- EUROPE
  For mailings in EUROPE, send a cheque or bankers draft and a purchase order for 200 Pounds Sterling to:

  Postal address: Department of Computer Science
                        Attn: Natalie May/Dawn Bailey
                        University College London
                        Gower Street
                        London, WC1E 6BT
                        UK

  For information only:

  Telephone: +44–1–380–7214
  Fax: +44–1–387–1397
  Telex: 28722
  Internet: `natalie@cs.ucl.ac.uk`
             `dawn@cs.ucl.ac.uk`

  Specify one of:

  1. 1600bpi 1/2–inch tape, or

2. Sun 1/4–inch cartridge tape.

The tape will be written in *tar* format and returned with a documentation set. Do not send tapes or envelopes. Documentation only is the same price.

- EUROPE (tape only)
  Tapes without hardcopy documentation can be obtained via the European UNIX User Group (EUUG). The ISODE 6.0 distribution is called EUUGD14.

> Postal: EUUG Distributions
> c/o Frank Kuiper
> Centrum voor Wiskunde en Informatica
> Kruislann 413
> 1098 SJ Amsterdam
> The Netherlands

For information only:

> Telephone: +31–20–5924121
> (or +31–20–5929333)
> Telex: 12571 mactr nl
> Telefax: +31–20–5924199
> Internet: `euug-tapes@cwi.nl`

Specify one of:

1. 1600bpi 1/2–inch tape: 130 Dutch Guilders

2. 800bpi 1/2–inch tape: 130 Dutch Guilders

3. Sun 1/4–inch cartridge tape (QIC-24 format): 190 Dutch Guilders

4. 1600 1/2–inch tape (QIC-11 format): 190 Dutch Guilders

If you require DHL, this is possible and will be billed through. Note that if you are not a member of EUUG, then there is an additional handling fee of 300 Dutch Guilders (please enclose a copy of your membership or contribution payment form when ordering). Do not send money, cheques, tapes or envelopes; you will be invoiced.

- AUSTRALIA and NEW ZEALAND
  For mailings in AUSTRALIA and NEW ZEALAND, send a
  cheque for 250 Dollars Australian to:

  > Postal: CSIRO DIT
  >   Attn: Andrew Waugh (ISODE Distribution)
  >   55 Barry Street
  >   Carlton, 3053
  >   Australia

  For information only:

  > Telephone: +61-3-347-8644
  > Fax: +61-3-347-8987
  > Internet: ajw@ditmela.oz.au

  Specify one of:

  1. 1600/3200/6250bpi 1/2-inch tape, or

  2. Sun 1/4—inch cartridge tape in either QIC-11 or QIC-24
     format.

  The tape will be written in tar format and returned with a documentation set. Do not send tapes or envelopes. Documentation only is the same price.

- Internet
  If you can FTP to the Internet, then use anonymous FTP to the host `nisc.nyser.net` residing at [192.33.4.10] to retrieve `isode-6.tar.Z` in BINARY mode from the `pub/isode/` directory. This file is the *tar* image after being run through the compress program and is approximately 4.5MB in size.

- NIFTP
  If you run NIFTP over the public X.25 or over JANET, and are registered in the NRS at Salford, you can use NIFTP with username "guest" and your own name as password, to access `UK.AC.UCL.CS` to retrieve the file `<SRC>isode-6.tar`. This is a 14MB *tar* image. The file `<SRC>isode-6.tar.Z` is the *tar* image after being run through the compress program (4.5MB).

- FTAM on the JANET or PSS
  The source code is available by FTAM at the University College London over X.25 using JANET (DTE 00000511160013) or PSS (DTE 23421920030013) with TSEL 259 (ascii encoding). Use the "anon" user-identity and retrieve the file `<SRC>isode-6.tar`. This is a 14MB *tar* image. The file `<SRC>isode-6.tar.Z` is the *tar* image after being run through the compress program (4.5MB).

- FTAM on the Internet
  The source code is available by FTAM over the Internet at host `osi.nyser.net` residing at [192.33.4.10] (TCP port 102 selects the OSI transport service) with TSEL 259 (numeric encoding). Use the "anon" user-identity, supply any password, and retrieve `isode-6.tar.Z` from the `pub/isode/` directory. This file is the *tar* image after being run through the compress program and is approximately 4.5MB in size.

For distributions via FTAM, the file service is provided by the FTAM implementation in ISODE 5.0 or later (IS FTAM).

For distributions via either FTAM or FTP, there is an additional file available for retrieval, called `isode-ps.tar.Z` which is a compressed tar image (7MB) containing the entire documentation set in PostScript format.

SUPPORT

A UK company has been set up to provide support for the ISODE and associated packages - X-Tel Services Ltd. This company provides an update service, general assistance and site specific support. Although inclusion of this information should not be considered an endorsement, it should be noted that one of the primary ISODE developers now works at X-Tel Services Ltd.

Postal address: ISODE Distribution
X-Tel Services Ltd.
13–03 Tower Block
Nottingham University
Nottingham, NG7 2RD
UK

Telephone:	+44–602–412648
Fax:	+44–602–588138
Telex:	37346
Internet:	`xtel@cs.nott.ac.uk`

If other organizations offering formal support for the ISODE wish to be included in future announcements, a suitable index will be organized.

Glossary

abstract syntax: a description of a data type that is independent of machine-oriented structures and restrictions.

Abstract Syntax Notation One: the OSI language for describing abstract syntax.

ACPM: *association control protocol machine*

ACSE: see *Association Control Service Element.*

acceptor: a user that receives the .INDICATION primitive associated with a service. See *requestor.*

AD: an *addendum* to an International Standard. For example, ISO/IEC 8473 AD1 refers to the first Addendum of International Standard 8473.

ADDMD: see *Administrative Directory Management Domain.*

address: a location; when used in the context of a particular layer (e.g., session address), it refers an instances of a service access point at that layer (e.g., a session service access point).

ADMD: see *Administrative Management Domain.*

Administrative Directory Management Domain: a Directory management domain run by a PTT authority. See *DMD* and *PRDMD.*

Administrative Management Domain: an MHS management domain run by a PTT authority. Each ADMD must contain MHS routing information to all other ADMDs.

AE: see *application entity.*

American National Standards Institute: the U.S. national standardization body. The ANSI is a member of the ISO.

ANSI: see *American National Standards Institute.*

AP: see *application process.*

APDU: *application protocol data unit*

application context: the collection of application service elements (ASEs) which comprises an application entity (AE) along with the rules defining the interactions between the ASEs.

application entity: the OSI portion of an application process (AP).

application layer: that portion of an OSI system ultimately responsible for managing communication between application processes (APs).

application process: an object executing in a real system.

application protocol: see *application context.*

application services: the services collectively offered by the upper four layers of the OSI model.

application service element: the building block of an application entity (AE). Each AE consists of one or more of these service elements, as defined by its application context.

ARPA: see *Defense Advanced Research Projects Agency.*

ASDU: *application service data unit*

ASE: see *application service element.*

ASN.1: see *Abstract Syntax Notation One.*

association: a presentation layer connection augmented with application layer semantics (e.g., application layer naming).

Association Control Service Element: The application service element responsible for association establishment and release.

Basic Encoding Rules: the OSI language for describing transfer syntax.

BDT: *bulk data transfer*

BER: see *Basic Encoding Rules.*

bridge: (imprecise usage) an entity responsible for simple mappings at a single layer.

British Standards Institute: the U.K. national standardization body. The BSI is a member of the ISO.

BSI: see *British Standards Institute.*

C: the *C programming language*

CCITT: see *International Telephone and Telegraph Consultative Committee.*

CL-mode: see *connection-less mode.*

CLNS: *connectionless-mode network service*

CLTS: *connectionless-mode transport service*

CMIP: see *Common Management Information Protocol.*

CMIP over TCP: a mapping of the OSI network management framework to management networks based on the Internet suite of protocols.

CMISE: see *Common Management Information Service Element.*

CMOT: see *CMIP over TCP*

CO-mode: see *connection-oriented mode.*

Common Management Information Protocol: the OSI protocol for network management.

Common Management Information Service Element: the application service element responsible for carrying network management semantics.

connection: a logical binding between two or more users of a service.

connection-less mode: a service that has a single phase involving control mechanisms such as addressing in addition to data transfer.

connection-oriented mode: a service that has three distinct phases: *establishment*, in which two or more users are bound to a connection; *data transfer*, in which data is exchanged between the users; and, *release*, in which the binding is terminated.

CONS: *connection-oriented network service*

COR: a *confirmation of receipt* in the network service.

COTS: *connection-oriented transport service*

DAD: a *draft addendum* to an International Standard. If ratified, the draft addendum advances to Addendum (AD) status.

DAP: see *Directory Access Protocol.*

DARPA: see *Defense Advanced Research Projects Agency.*

DARPA Internet: see *Internet.*

data: (slang) see *user-data.*

data link layer: that portion of an OSI system responsible for transmission, framing, and error control over a single communications link.

DCS: see *defined context set.*

Defense Advanced Research Projects Agency: an agency of the U.S. Department of Defense that sponsors high-risk, high-payoff research. The Internet suite of protocols was developed under DARPA auspices. DARPA was previously known as ARPA, the Advanced Research Projects Agency, when the ARPANET was built.

defined context set: the set of defined presentation contexts for a presentation connection.

DIB: see *Directory Information Base.*

Directory Access Protocol: the protocol used between a Directory User Agent (DUA) and a Directory System Agent (DSA).

Directory Information Base: the collection of information objects in the Directory.

Directory Information Tree: the global tree of entries corresponding to information objects in the Directory.

Directory Management Domain: a collection of DSAs that holds a portion of the DIT. For political reasons, there are two kinds of DMDs: ADDMDs and PRDMDs. This distinction is largely artificial.

Directory System Agent: an application entity that offers the Directory service.

Directory System Protocol: the protocol used between two Directory System Agents (DSAs).

Directory User Agent: an application entity that makes the Directory service available to the user.

DIS: a *draft* International Standard. If ratified, the draft advances to International Standard (IS) status.

Distinguished Name: the global, authoritative name of an entry in the OSI Directory.

DIT: see *Directory Information Tree.*

DMD: see *Directory Management Domain*

DN: see *Distinguished Name.*

DP: a *draft* proposal. If ratified, the draft proposal advances to Draft International Status (DIS) status.

DSA: see *Directory System Agent.*

DSP: see *Directory System Protocol.*

DU: see *Data Unit.*

DUA: see *Directory User Agent.*

ECMA: see *European Computer Manufacturers Association.*

end-system: a real system performing functions from all layers of the OSI model. End-systems are commonly thought of as hosting applications.

end-to-end services: the services collectively offered by the lower three layers of the OSI model.

ENSDU: *expedited network service data unit*

ES: see *end-system.*

ETSDU: *expedited transport service data unit*

European Computer Manufacturers Association: a group of computer vendors that have performed substantive pre-standardization work for OSI.

External Data Representation: a transfer syntax defined by Sun Microsystems, Inc.

FADU: see *File Access Data Unit.*

Federal Research Internet: see *Internet.*

File Access Data Unit: a portion of a file in FTAM's virtual filestore, consisting of one or more data units structured in a hierarchical tree.

File Transfer, Access and Management: the OSI file service.

File Transfer Protocol: the application protocol offering file service in the Internet suite of protocols.

FTAM: see *File Transfer, Access and Management.*

FTP: see *File Transfer Protocol.*

FU: see *Functional Unit.*

Functional Unit: a grouping of one or more elements of a service that are functionally related. The elements of this group can be enabled or disabled as a unit, by enabling or disabling use of the corresponding functional unit.

gateway: (imprecise usage) an entity responsible for complex mappings, usually at the application layer; also, (Internet usage) a router.

header: (slang) see *protocol control information.*

host: (Internet usage) an end-system.

IAB: see *Internet Activities Board.*

IEEE: see *Institute of Electrical and Electronics Engineers.*

IETF: see *Internet Engineering Task Force.*

IFIP: see *International Federation of Information Processing.*

initiator: a service user that initiates a connection or association. See *responder.*

Institute of Electrical and Electronics Engineers: a profession organization, which, as a part of its services to the community, performs some pre-standardization work for OSI.

intermediate-system: a real system performing functions from the three lower-layers of the OSI model. Intermediate-systems are commonly thought of as routing data for end-systems.

International Federation of Information Processing: a research organization that performs substantive pre-standardization work for OSI. IFIP is noted for having formalized the original MHS model.

International Organization for Standardization: the organization that produces much of the world's standards. OSI is only one of many areas standardized by the ISO/IEC.

International Standards Organization: there is no such thing. See the *International Organization for Standardization.*

International Telephone and Telegraph Consultative Committee: a body comprising the national Post, Telephone, and Telegraph (PTT) administrations.

Internet: a large collection of connected networks, primarily in the United States, running the Internet suite of protocols. Sometimes referred to as the *DARPA Internet, NSF/DARPA Internet,* or the *Federal Research Internet.*

Internet Activities Board: the technical body overseeing the development of the Internet suite of protocols. The IAB consists of several task forces, each charged with investigating a particular area.

Internet Engineering Task Force: a task force of the Internet Activities Board charged with solving the short-term needs of the Internet.

Internet Protocol: the network protocol offering a connectionless-mode network service in the Internet suite of protocols.

Internet suite of protocols: a collection of computer-communication protocols originally developed under DARPA. The Internet suite of protocols is currently the de facto solution for open networking.

internet: (Internet usage) a network in the OSI sense; historically termed a *catenet.*

interpersonal message: a structured message exchanged between two MHS user agents, consisting of a well-defined heading and one or more arbitrary body parts.

IP: see *Internet Protocol.*

IPM: see *interpersonal message.*

IS: either *intermediate-system* or *International Standard*, depending on context.

ISO Development Environment: A research tool developed to study the upper-layers of OSI. It is an unfortunate historical coincidence that the first three letters of the ISODE are "ISO". This is not an acronym for the International Organization for Standardization, but rather three letters which, when pronounced in English, produce a pleasing sound.

ISO/IEC: see *International Organization for Standardization.*

ISODE: see the *ISO Development Environment.*

LAN: see *local area network.*

length indicator: in the session protocol, a field indicating the length of a parameter in the session protocol control information (PCI).

LI: see *length indicator.*

local area network: any one of a number of technologies providing high-speed, low-latency transfer.

Management Information Base: a collection of objects that can be accessed via a network management protocol. See *Structure of Management Information.*

Message Handling System: a store-and-forward third-party system for deliverying arbitrarily structured messages.

Message Store: an entity acting as an intermediary between an MHS user agent and its local message transfer agent.

Message Transfer Agent: an application entity that offers the Message Transfer service.

Message Transfer System: a collection of connected Message Transfer Agents (MTAs).

MHS: see *Message Handling System.*

MIB: see *Management Information Base.*

MMDF: see *Multi-channel Memorandum Distribution Facility.*

MS: see *Message Store.*

MTA: see *Message Transfer Agent.*

MTS: see *Message Transfer System*.

Multi-channel Memorandum Distribution Facility: a   pioneering software package developed for memo-based message handling under the Internet suite of protocols.

National Bureau of Standards: see *National Institute of Standards and Technology*.

National Institute of Standards and Technology: the branch of the U.S Department of Commerce charged with keeping track of standardization. Previously known as the *National Bureau of Standards*.

NBS: see *National Bureau of Standards*.

network: a collection of subnetworks connected by intermediate-systems and populated by end-systems; also, (Internet usage) a single subnetwork in the OSI sense.

Network File System: a file service defined by Sun Microsystems, Inc.

network layer: that portion of an OSI system responsible for data transfer across the network, independent of both the media comprising the underlying subnetworks and the topology of those subnetworks.

NFS: see *Network File System*.

NIST: see *National Institute of Standards and Technology*.

NS: *network service*

NSAP: *network service access point*

NSDU: *network service data unit*

NSF/DARPA Internet: see *Internet*.

NSSDU: *normal data session service data unit*

NPSDU: *normal data presentation service data unit*

OSI: see *Open Systems Interconnection*.

Open Systems Interconnection: an international effort to facilitate communications among computers of different manufacture and technology.

parameter group identifier: in the session protocol, a field indicating the identity of a group of parameters in the session protocol control information (PCI).

parameter identifier: in the session protocol, a field indicating the identity of a parameter in the session protocol control information (PCI).

parameter value: in the session protocol, a field indicating the value of a parameter in the session protocol control information (PCI).

PCI: either *presentation context identifier* or *protocol control information*, depending on context.

PDAD: a *proposed draft addendum* to an International Standard. If ratified, the proposed draft addendum advances to Draft Addendum (DAD) status.

PDU: see *protocol data unit.*

PE: see *presentation element.*

pepy: the *Presentation Element Parser (YACC-based)*, a tool of the ISODE serving as an ASN.1 parser.

PGI: see *parameter group identifier.*

PI: see *parameter identifier.*

physical layer: that portion of an OSI system responsible for the electro-mechanical interface to the communications media.

posy: the *Pepy Optional Structure-generator (YACC-based)*, a tool of the ISODE that defines structures in the *C* programming language that correspond to structures defined using ASN.1.

PPDU: *presentation protocol data unit*

PPM: *presentation protocol machine*

PRDMD: see *Private Directory Management Domain.*

presentation context: a binding between an abstract syntax and a transfer syntax.

presentation context identifier: an integer identifying a particular presentation context active on a presentation connection.

presentation element: in the ISODE, a C data structure capable of representating any ASN.1 object in a machine-independent form.

presentation layer: that portion of an OSI system responsible for adding structure to the units of data that are exchanged.

presentation stream: in the ISODE, a set of routines providing an abstraction to provide transformations on presentation elements.

Private Directory Management Domain: a Directory management domain *not* run by a PTT authority. See *DMD* and *ADDMD*.

Private Management Domain: a MHS management domain run by a private organization. Each PRMD must contain MHS routing information to its parent ADMD. In addition, by bilateral agreement, a PRMD may have MHS routing information to other ADMDs and PRMDs.

PRMD: see *Private Management Domain.*

protocol control information: (conceptually) the first part of a protocol data unit used by a protocol machine to communicate information to its peer.

protocol data unit: a data object exchanged by protocol machines, usually containing both protocol control information and user data.

protocol machine: a finite state machine (FSM) that implements a particular protocol. When a particular input (e.g., service request or network activity) occurs in a particular state, the FSM potentially generates a particular output (e.g., service indication or network activity) and possibly moves to another state.

PS: either *presentation service* or *presentation stream*, depending on context.

PSAP: *presentation service access point*

PSDU: *presentation service data unit*

PTT: a *post, telephone, and telegraph* authority

PV: see *parameter value.*

QOS: see *quality of service.*

quality of service: the desired or actual characteristics of a service; typically, but not always, those of the network service.

RDN: see *Relative Distinguished Name.*

requestor: a user that initiates a service by invoking the .REQUEST primitive associated with that service. See *acceptor.*

Relative Distinguished Name: a component of an entry's Distinguished Name, usually consisting of an attribute/value pair.

Reliable Transfer Service Element: the application service element responsible for transfer of bulk-mode objects.

remote operation: an action invoked by one application entity but performed by another.

Remote Operations Service Element: the application service element responsible for managing request/reply interactions.

remote protocol call: a synchronous remote operation.

Request for Comments: the document series describing the Internet suite of protocols and related experiments.

responder: a service user that responds to a connection or association. See *initiator.*

RFC: see *Request for Comments.*

RO: see *remote operation.*

RO-notation: an set of extensions to ASN.1, defined using ASN.1's macro facility, that convey the semantics of remote operations.

ROPM: *remote operations protocol machine*

ROSE: see *Remote Operations Service Element.*

rosy: the *remote operations stub-generate (yacc-based)* a tool of the ISODE that defines stub procedures in .the *C* programming language that correspond to remote operations defined using the RO-notation.

router: a level-3 (network layer) relay.

RPC: see *remote protocol call.*

RTPM: *reliable transfer protocol machine*

RTSE: see *Reliable Transfer Service Element.*

SAP: see *service access point.*

SDU: see *service data unit.*

selector: a portion of an address identifying a particular entity at an address (e.g., a session selector identifies a user of the session service residing at a particular session address).

service access point: an artifact modeling how a service is made available to a user.

service data unit: user-data passed through a service access point.

service primitive: an artifact modeling how a service is requested or accepted by a user.

session layer: that portion of an OSI system responsible for adding control mechanisms to the data exchange.

SGMP: see the *Simple Gateway Monitoring Protocol.*

Simple Gateway Monitoring Protocol: the predecessor of the Simple Network Management Protocol.

Simple Mail Transfer Protocol: the application protocol offering message handling service in the Internet suite of protocols.

Simple Network Management Protocol: the application protocol offering network management service in the Internet suite of Protocols.

SMI: see *Structure of Management Information.*

SMTP: see the *Simple Mail Transfer Protocol.*

SNAcP: see *subnetwork access protocol.*

SNDCP: see *subnetwork dependent convergence protocol.*

SNICP: see *subnetwork independent convergence protocol.*

SNMP: see the *Simple Network Management Protocol.*

SNPA: *subnetwork point of attachment*

SPDU: *session protocol data unit*

SPM: *session protocol machine*

SSAP: *session service access point*

SSDU: *session service data unit*

Structure of Management Information: the rules used to define the objects that can be accessed via a network mangement protocol. See *Management Information Base.*

subnetwork: a single network connecting several nodes on a single (virtual) transmission medium.

subnetwork access protocol: a protocol used to access a particular subnetwork technology.

subnetwork dependent convergence protocol: a protocol used to augment the service offered by a particular subnetwork technology to the OSI network service.

subnetwork independent convergence protocol: a protocol used to provide the network service between two end-systems.

TCP: see the *Transmission Control Protocol.*

TCP/IP: see the *Internet suite of protocols.*

TELNET: the application protocol offering virtual terminal service in the Internet suite of protocols.

TLV: *tag, length, and value*

token: a object whose ownership conveys permission to request the service associated with the token.

transfer syntax: a description of an instance of a data type that is expressed as string of bits.

Transmission Control Protocol: the transport protocol offering a connection-oriented transport service in the Internet suite of protocols.

TPDU: *transport protocol data unit*

TPM: *transport protocol machine*

transport layer: that portion of an OSI system responsible for reliability and multiplexing of data transfer across the network (over and above that provided by the network layer) to the level required by the application.

TSAP: *transport service access point*

TSDU: *transport service data unit*

TSSDU· *typed data session service data unit*

TWA: *two-way alternate*

TWS: *two-way simultaneous*

UA: see *User Agent.*

UDP: see the *User Datagram Protocol.*

User Agent: an application entity that makes the message transfer service available to the user.

User Datagram Protocol: the transport protocol offering a connection-less-mode transport service in the Internet suite of protocols.

user-data: conceptually, the part of a protocol data unit used to transparently communicate information between the users of the protocol.

virtual filestore: the abstraction provided by FTAM to model a system-independent file service.

Virtual Terminal: the OSI virtual terminal service.

VT: see *Virtual Terminal.*

WAN: see *wide area network.*

WD: a *working draft.* If ratified, the working draft advances to Draft Proposal (DP) status.

wide area network: any one of a number of technologies providing geographically distant transfer.

X.121: the addressing format used by X.25–based networks.

X.25: a connection-oriented network facility.

X.409: the predecessor to Abstract Syntax Notation One.

XDR: see *External Data Representation.*

XPSDU: *expedited presentation service data unit*

XSSDU: *expedited session service data unit*

yacc: *yet another compiler compiler*, a UNIX-based compiler generation tool.

Bibliography

[ANaka88]   Anastase Nakassis. Fletcher's Error Detection Algorithm: How to implement it efficiently and how to avoid the most common pitfalls. *Computer Communication Review*, 18(5):63–68, October, 1988.

[ASolo88]   Alexander von Solodkoff. *The Art of Carl Fabergé*. Crown Publishers, Inc., New York, 1988. ISBN 0–517–571242.

[ASolo89]   Alexander von Solodkoff. *Masterpieces from the House of Fabergé*. Harry N. Abrams, Inc., New York, 1989. ISBN 0–8109–8089–4.

[ATane88]   Andrew S. Tanenbaum. *Computer Networks. Prentice Hall Software Series*, Prentice-Hall, 1988. ISBN 0–13–162959–X.

[ATT88a]   *Network Programmer's Guide*. AT&T, 1988. UNIX System V/386.

[ATT88b]   *STREAMS Programmer's Guide*. AT&T, 1988. UNIX System V/386.

[BKern78]   Brian W. Kernighan and Dennis M. Ritchie. *The C Programming Language. Software Series*, Prentice-Hall, Inc., Englewood Cliffs, New Jersey, 1978.

[CCarg89]   Carl F. Cargill. *Information Technology Standardization: Theory, Process, and Organizations*. Digital Press, Maynard, Massachusetts, 1989. ISBN 1–55558–022–X.

[CCITT84a] Message Handling Systems: Presentation Transfer Syntax and Notation. International Telegraph and Telephone Consultative Committee, October, 1984. Recommendation X.409.

[CCITT84b] Message Handling Systems: Remote Operations and Reliable Transfer Server. International Telegraph and Telephone Consultative Committee, October, 1984. Recommendation X.410.

[CCITT84c] Message Handling Systems: System Model-Service Elements. October, 1984. International Telegraph and Telephone Consultative Committee.

[CCITT84d] Session Protocol Specification for Open Systems Interconnection (OSI) for CCITT Applications. International Telegraph and Telephone Consultative Committee, October, 1984. Recommendation X.225.

[CCITT84e] Session Service Definition for Open Systems Interconnection (OSI) for CCITT Applications. International Telegraph and Telephone Consultative Committee, October, 1984. Recommendation X.224.

[CCITT88a] Association Control Protocol Specification for CCITT Applications. International Telegraph and Telephone Consultative Committee, December, 1988. Recommendation X.227.

[CCITT88b] Association Control Service Definition for CCITT Applications. International Telegraph and Telephone Consultative Committee, December, 1988. Recommendation X.217.

[CCITT88c] Message Handling: System and Service Overview. International Telegraph and Telephone Consultative Committee, 1988. Recommendation X.400.

[CCITT88d] Presentation Protocol Specification for Open Systems Interconnection (OSI) for CCITT Applications. International Telegraph and Telephone Consultative Committee, 1988. Recommendation X.226.

[CCITT88e] Presentation Service Definition for Open Systems Interconnection (OSI) for CCITT Applications. International Telegraph and Telephone Consultative Committee, 1988. Recommendation X.216.

[CCITT88f] Reliable Transfer: Model and Service Definition. International Telegraph and Telephone Consultative Committee, March, 1988. Recommendation X.218.

[CCITT88g] Reliable Transfer: Protocol Specification. International Telegraph and Telephone Consultative Committee, March, 1988. Recommendation X.228.

[CCITT88h] Remote Operations: Model, Notation and Service Definition. International Telegraph and Telephone Consultative Committee, March, 1988. Recommendation X.219.

[CCITT88i] Remote Operations: Protocol Specification. International Telegraph and Telephone Consultative Committee, March, 1988. Recommendation X.229.

[CCITT88j] The Directory — Overview of Concepts, Models, and Service. International Telegraph and Telephone Consultative Committee, December, 1988. Recommendation X.500.

[CPart86] Craig Partridge. Mail Routing using Domain Names: An Informal Tour. In *Proceedings, Summer Usenix Conference and Exhibition*, pages 366–376, June, 1986. Atlanta, Georgia.

[CPart87] Craig Partridge and Glenn Trewit. *The High-Level Entity Management System.* Request for Comments 1021–1024, DDN Network Information Center, SRI International, October, 1987.

[CPart88] Craig Partridge and Marshall T. Rose. A Comparison of External Data Formats. In *Proceedings, Fourth International Symposium on Computer Message Systems*, Einar Stefferud, editor, pages 233–245, September, 1988. Costa Mesa, California.

[DClar85]   David D. Clark. The Structuring of systems using Up-
             calls. In *Proceedings, Ninth Symposium on Operating
             System Principles*, pages 171–180, December, 1985. Or-
             cas Island, Washington.

[DCohe83]   Danny Cohen and Jon B. Postel. The ISO Reference
             Model and Other Protocol Architectures. In *Proceedings
             of the IFIP Congress*, 1983. Paris, France.

[DCroc79]   David H. Crocker, E.S. Szurkowski, and David J. Far-
             ber. An Internetwork Memo Distribution Facility —
             MMDF. In *Proceedings, Sixth Data Communications
             Symposium*, pages 18–25, November, 1979. Asilomar.

[DCroc82]   David H. Crocker. *Standard for the Format of ARPA
             Internet Text Messages*. Request for Comments 822,
             DDN Network Information Center, SRI International,
             August, 1982.

[DDN88]   The Department of Defense Open Systems Interconnec-
             tion (OSI) Implementation Strategy. May, 1988. The
             MITRE Corporation.

[DMill87]   David L. Mills and Hans-Werner Braun. The NSFNET
             Backbone Network. *Computer Communication Review*,
             17(5):191–196, August, 1987.

[DPlum82]   David C. Plummer. *An Ethernet Address Resolution
             Protocol*. Request for Comments 825, DDN Network In-
             formation Center, SRI International, September, 1982.

[ECMA85]   Remote   Operations: Concepts,   Notation
             and Connection-Oriented Mappings. December, 1985.
             ECMA TR/31.

[FCane86]   Fausto Caneschi. Hints for the Interpretation of the
             ISO Session Layer. *Computer Communication Review*,
             16(4):34–72, August, 1986.

[GMars89]   George Marshall. The NetMan Demonstration at IN-
             TEROP '88. *ConneXions*, 3(3):20, March, 1989.

[IAB89]   IAB. *IAB Official Protocol Standards.* Request for
              Comments 1100, DDN Network Information Center,
              SRI International, April, 1989.   Internet Activities
              Board.

[IGroe86]   Inge Groenbaek. Conversion Between the TCP and ISO
              Transport Protocols as a Method of Achieving Interop-
              erability Between Data Communication Systems. *IEEE
              Journal on Selected Areas in Communications,* SAC-
              4(2):288–296, March, 1986.

[ISO86a]   Information Processing Systems — Open Systems Inter-
              connection — Transport Protocol Specification. Inter-
              national Organization for Standardization and Interna-
              tional Electrotechnical Committee, 1986. International
              Standard 8073.

[ISO86b]   Information Processing Systems — Open Systems In-
              terconnection — Transport Service Definition — Ad-
              dendum 1: Connectionless-mode Transmission. Inter-
              national Organization for Standardization and Interna-
              tional Electrotechnical Committee, 1986. International
              Standard 8072/AD 1.

[ISO86c]   Information Processing Systems — Open Systems In-
              terconnection — Transport Service Definition. Inter-
              national Organization for Standardization and Interna-
              tional Electrotechnical Committee, 1986. International
              Standard 8072.

[ISO87a]   Information Processing Systems — Data Communica-
              tions — Internal Organization of the Network Layer.
              International Organization for Standardization and In-
              ternational Electrotechnical Committee, May, 1987. In-
              ternational Standard 8648.

[ISO87b]   Information Processing Systems — Data Communica-
              tions — Network Service Definition. International Or-
              ganization for Standardization and International Elec-
              trotechnical Committee, April, 1987.   International
              Standard 8348.

[ISO87c]   Information Processing Systems — Data Communica-
             tions — Network Service Definition — Addendum 2:
             Network Layer Addresisng.   International Organiza-
             tion for Standardization and International Electrotech-
             nical Committee, April, 1987. International Standard
             8348/AD 2.

[ISO87d]   Information Processing Systems — Data Communica-
             tions — Network Service Definition — Addendum 1:
             Connectionless-mode Transmission. International Or-
             ganization for Standardization and International Elec-
             trotechnical Committee, April, 1987.   International
             Standard 8348/AD 1.

[ISO87e]   Information Processing Systems — Data Communica-
             tions — Protocol Combinations to Provide and Support
             the OSI Network Service — Part 3: Provision and Sup-
             port of the connectionless-mode network service. Inter-
             national Organization for Standardization and Interna-
             tional Electrotechnical Committee, June, 1987. Draft
             International Standard 8880–3.

[ISO87f]   Information Processing Systems — Data Communica-
             tions — Protocol Combinations to Provide and Sup-
             port the OSI Network Service — Part 1: General Prin-
             ciples. International Organization for Standardization
             and International Electrotechnical Committee, June,
             1987. Draft International Standard 8880–1.

[ISO87g]   Information Processing Systems — Data Communica-
             tions — Protocol Combinations to Provide and Sup-
             port the OSI Network Service — Part 2: Provision and
             Support of the connection-mode network service. Inter-
             national Organization for Standardization and Interna-
             tional Electrotechnical Committee, June, 1987. Draft
             International Standard 8880–2.

[ISO87h]   Information Processing Systems — Data Communica-
             tions — Protocol for providing the Connectionless-mode
             Network Service and Provision of Underlying Service.

International Organization for Standardization and International Electrotechnical Committee, May, 1987. Consolidated Final Text of Draft International Standard 8473.

[ISO87i]   Information Processing Systems — Data Communications — Use of X.25 over Local Area Networks to Provide the OSI Connection-mode Network Service. International Organization for Standardization and International Electrotechnical Committee, May, 1987. International Standard 8881.

[ISO87j]   Information Processing Systems — Data Communications — Use of X.25 to Provide the OSI Connection-mode Network Service. International Organization for Standardization and International Electrotechnical Committee, September, 1987. International Standard 8878.

[ISO87k]   Information Processing Systems — Data Communications — X.25 Packet Level Protocol. International Organization for Standardization and International Electrotechnical Committee, September, 1987. International Standard 8208.

[ISO87l]   Information Processing Systems — Local Area Networks. International Organization for Standardization and International Electrotechnical Committee, May, 1987. International Standard 8802.

[ISO87m]   Information Processing Systems — Local Area Networks — Logical Link Control. International Organization for Standardization and International Electrotechnical Committee, May, 1987. International Standard 8802–2.

[ISO87n]   Information Processing Systems — Open Systems Interconnection — Application Layer Structure. International Organization for Standardization and International Electrotechnical Committee, March, 1987. Draft Proposal 9534.

[ISO87o]   Information Processing Systems — Open Systems Inter-
                connection — Basic Connection Oriented Session Pro-
                tocol Specification — Addendum 1: Session Symmet-
                ric Synchronization for the Session Protocol. Interna-
                tional Organization for Standardization and Interna-
                tional Electrotechnical Committee, July, 1987. Draft
                Addendum 8327/DAD 1.

[ISO87p]   Information Processing Systems — Open Systems Inter-
                connection — Basic Connection Oriented Session Ser-
                vice Definition — Addendum 2: Incorporation of Un-
                limited User Data. International Organization for Stan-
                dardization and International Electrotechnical Commit-
                tee, August, 1987. Draft Addendum 8326/DAD 2.

[ISO87q]   Information Processing Systems — Open Systems In-
                terconnection — Basic Connection Oriented Session Ser-
                vice Definition — Addendum 1: Session Symmetric Syn-
                chronization for the Session Service. International Or-
                ganization for Standardization and International Elec-
                trotechnical Committee, July, 1987. Draft Addendum
                8326/DAD 1.

[ISO87r]   Information Processing Systems — Open Systems Inter-
                connection — Basic Connection Oriented Session Proto-
                col Specification — Addendum 2: Incorporation of Un-
                limited User Data. International Organization for Stan-
                dardization and International Electrotechnical Commit-
                tee, August, 1987. Draft Addendum 8327/DAD 2.

[ISO87s]   Information Processing Systems — Open Systems Inter-
                connection — Basic Connection Oriented Session Proto-
                col Specification. International Organization for Stan-
                dardization and International Electrotechnical Commit-
                tee, August, 1987. International Standard 8327.

[ISO87t]   Information Processing Systems — Open Systems Inter-
                connection — Basic Connection Oriented Session Ser-
                vice Definition. International Organization for Stan-
                dardization and International Electrotechnical Commit-
                tee, August, 1987. International Standard 8326.

[ISO87u]   Information Processing Systems — Open Systems Interconnection — Data Link Service Definition. International Organization for Standardization and International Electrotechnical Committee, December, 1987. Final Text of Draft International Standard 8886–2.

[ISO87v]   Information Processing Systems — Virtual Terminal Service: Basic Class. International Organization for Standardization and International Electrotechnical Committee, August, 1987. Draft International Standard 9040.

[ISO87w]   Information Processing — Open Systems Interconnection — Abstract Syntax Notation One (ASN.1) — Draft Addendum 1: Extensions to ASN.1. International Organization for Standardization and International Electrotechnical Committee, 1987. Draft Addendum 8824/DAD 1.

[ISO87x]   Information Processing — Open Systems Interconnection — Abstract Syntax Notation One (ASN.1) — Draft Addendum 1: Extensions to ASN.1 Basic Encoding Rules. International Organization for Standardization and International Electrotechnical Committee, 1987. Draft Addendum 8825/DAD 1.

[ISO87y]   Information Processing — Open Systems Interconnection — Specification of Abstract Syntax Notation One (ASN.1). International Organization for Standardization and International Electrotechnical Committee, 1987. International Standard 8824.

[ISO87z]   Information Processing — Open Systems Interconnection — Specification of Basic Encoding Rules for Abstract Syntax Notation One (ASN.1). International Organization for Standardization and International Electrotechnical Committee, 1987. International Standard 8825.

[ISO88a]   Information Processing Systems — File Transfer, Access, and Management. International Organization

for Standardization and International Electrotechnical
Committee, April, 1988. Final Text of Draft International Standard 8571.

[ISO88b]   Information Processing Systems — Open Systems Interconnection — Connection Oriented Presentation Service
Definition. International Organization for Standardization and International Electrotechnical Committee,
April, 1988. Final Text of Draft International Standard
8822.

[ISO88c]   Information Processing Systems — Open Systems Interconnection — Connection Oriented Presentation Protocol Specification. International Organization for Standardization and International Electrotechnical Committee, April, 1988. Final Text of Draft International Standard 8823.

[ISO88d]   Information Processing Systems — Open Systems Interconnection – Protocol Specification for the Association Control Service Element. International Organization for Standardization and International Electrotechnical Committee, April, 1988. Revised Final Text of
Draft International Standard 8650.

[ISO88e]   Information Processing Systems — Open Systems In-
terconnection — Service Definition for the Association
Control Service Element. International Organization
for Standardization and International Electrotechnical
Committee, April, 1988. Revised Final Text of Draft
International Standard 8649.

[ISO88f]   Information Processing Systems — Open Systems Interconnection — The Directory — Overview of Concepts, Models, and Service. International Organization
for Standardization and International Electrotechnical
Committee, December, 1988. International Standard
9594-1.

[ISO88g]   Information Processing Systems — Text Communication — MOTIS — Message Handling: System and Ser-

vice Overview. International Organization for Standardization and International Electrotechnical Committee, December, 1988. International Standard 10021-1.

[ISO88h]   Information Processing Systems — Text Communication — Reliable Transfer Part 1: Model and Service Definition. International Organization for Standardization and International Electrotechnical Committee, March, 1988. Working Document for International Standard 9066-1.

[ISO88i]   Information Processing Systems — Text Communication — Reliable Transfer Part 2: Protocol Specification. International Organization for Standardization and International Electrotechnical Committee, March, 1988. Working Document for International Standard 9066-2.

[ISO88j]   Information Processing Systems — Text Communication — Remote Operations Part 1: Model, Notation and Service Definition. International Organization for Standardization and International Electrotechnical Committee, March, 1988. Working Document for International Standard 9072-1.

[ISO88k]   Information Processing Systems — Text Communication — Remote Operations Part 2: Protocol Specification. International Organization for Standardization and International Electrotechnical Committee, March, 1988. Working Document for International Standard 9072-2.

[JCase89a] Jeffrey D. Case, James R. Davin, Mark S. Fedor, and Martin L. Schoffstall. Network Management and the Design of SNMP. *ConneXions*, 3(3):22–26, March, 1989.

[JCase89b] Jeffrey D. Case, Mark S. Fedor, Martin L. Schoffstall, and James R. Davin. *A Simple Network Management Protocol*. Request for Comments 1098, DDN Network Information Center, SRI International, April, 1989.

[JDavi87]   James R. Davin, Jeffrey D. Case, Mark S. Fedor, and Martin L. Schoffstall. *A Simple Gateway Monitoring*

Protocol. Request for Comments 1028, DDN Network Information Center, SRI International, November, 1987.

[JDelg88]   Jaime Delgado and Manuel Medina. Use of the Abstract Service Definition Conventions for Distributed Information Processing Systems Specification. In *Proceedings, Fourth International Symposium on Computer Message Systems*, Einar Stefferud, editor, pages 217–231, September, 1988. Costa Mesa, California.

[JFlet82]   John G. Fletcher. An Arithmetic Checksum for Serial Transmissions. *IEEE Transactions on Communications*, COM–30(1), January, 1982.

[JNT87]   JNT. Transition to OSI Standards. U.K. Joint Network Team, July, 1987. Final Report of the Academic Community OSI Transition Group.

[JOnio88]   Julian P. Onions and Marshall T. Rose. *ISO-TP0 bridge between TCP and X.25.* Request for Comments 1086, DDN Network Information Center, SRI International, December, 1988.

[JPost80]   Jon B. Postel. *User Datagram Protocol.* Request for Comments 768, DDN Network Information Center, SRI International, August, 1980.

[JPost81a] Jon B. Postel. *Internet Protocol.* Request for Comments 791, DDN Network Information Center, SRI International, September, 1981. See also MIL-STD 1777.

[JPost81b] Jon B. Postel. *Transmission Control Protocol.* Request for Comments 793, DDN Network Information Center, SRI International, September, 1981. See also MIL-STD 1778.

[JPost82]   Jon B. Postel. *Simple Mail Transfer Protocol.* Request for Comments 821, DDN Network Information Center, SRI International, August, 1982. See also MIL-STD 1781.

[JPost83]   Jon B. Postel. *TELNET Protocol Specification.* Request
             for Comments 854, DDN Network Information Center,
             SRI International, May, 1983. See also MIL-STD 1782.

[JPost85]   Jon B. Postel. *File Transfer Protocol.* Request for Com-
             ments 959, DDN Network Information Center, SRI In-
             ternational, October, 1985. See also MIL-STD 1780.

[JQuar89]   John S. Quarterman. *The Matrix: Computer Networks
             and Conferencing Systems Worldwide.* Digital Press,
             Bedford, MA, 1989.

[JReyn87]   Joyce K. Reynolds. *Assigned Numbers.* Request for
             Comments 1010, DDN Network Information Center,
             SRI International, May, 1987.

[KMcCl88]   Keith McCloghrie and Marshall T. Rose. *Management
             Information Base Network Management of TCP/IP
             based internets.* Request for Comments 1066, DDN Net-
             work Information Center, SRI International, August,
             1988.

[MRose85]   Marshall T. Rose and John L. Romine. MH.5: How
             to process 200 messages a day and still get some real
             work done. In *Proceedings, Summer Usenix Conference
             and Exhibition*, pages 455–487, June, 1985. Portland,
             Oregon.

[MRose86]   Marshall T. Rose and Dwight E. Cass. OSI Transport
             Services on top of the TCP. *Computer Networks and
             ISDN Systems*, 12(3), 1986. Also available as NRTC
             Technical Paper #700.

[MRose87]   Marshall T. Rose and Dwight E. Cass. *ISO Trans-
             port Services on top of the TCP.* Request for Com-
             ments 1006, DDN Network Information Center, SRI In-
             ternational, May, 1987.

[MRose88a]   Marshall T. Rose. *ISO Presentation Services on top of
             TCP/IP-based internets.* Request for Comments 1085,
             DDN Network Information Center, SRI International,
             December, 1988.

[MRose88b]   Marshall T. Rose and Keith McCloghrie. *Structure and Identification of Management Information for TCP/IP based internets*. Request for Comments 1065, DDN Network Information Center, SRI International, August, 1988.

[MRose89]   Marshall T. Rose. *The ISO Development Environment: User's Manual*. The Wollongong Group, 5.0 edition, March, 1989.

[NIST88]   Stable Implementation Agreements for Open Systems Interconnection Protocols. December, 1988. Version 1, Edition 4.

[NRC85]   Transport Protocols for Department of Defense Data Networks. National Academy Press, February, 1985. Report to the Department of Defense and the National Bureau of Standards by the Committee on Computer-Computer Communication Protocols, Board on Telecommunications and Computer Applications Commission on Engineering and Technical Systems, National Research Council, C. Chaplin Cutler, chair (Executive Summary available as ARPA Internet Request for Comments 939).

[OSI84]   Information Processing Systems — Open Systems Interconnection: Basic Reference Model. International Organization for Standardization and International Electrotechnical Committee, 1984. Interational Standard 7498.

[OSI87a]   Information Processing Systems — Open Systems Interconnection: Basic Reference Model — Addendum 1: Connectionless-mode Transmission. International Organization for Standardization and International Electrotechnical Committee, 1987. Interational Standard 7498/AD 1.

[OSI87b]   Information Processing Systems — Open Systems Interconnection: Service Conventions. International Or-

ganization for Standardization and International Electrotechnical Committee, 1987. Technical Report 8509.

[PGree86]   Paul E. Green, Jr. Protocol Conversion. *IEEE Transac-
             tions on Communications*, COM–34(3):257–268, March,
             1986.

[PKarn87]   Phil Karn and Craig Partridge. Improving Round-Trip
             Time Estimates in Reliable Transport Protocols. In *Pro-
             ceedings, SIGCOMM '87 Workshop*, pages 2–7, ACM
             SIGCOMM, ACM Press, August, 1987. Stowe, Ver-
             mont.

[PMock87]   Paul V. Mockapetris. *Domain Names — Concepts and
             Facilities*. Request for Comments 1033, DDN Network
             Information Center, SRI International, November, 1987.

[RCall89]   Ross Callon and Hans-Werner Braun. *Guidelines for the
             use of Internet-IP addresses in the ISO Connectionless-
             Mode Network Protocol*. Request for Comments 1069,
             DDN Network Information Center, SRI International,
             February, 1989.

[RHage89]   Robert A. Hagens, Nancy E. Hall, and Marshall T. Rose.
             *Use of the DARPA/NSF Internet as a Subnet for Ex-
             perimentation with the OSI Network Layer*. Request
             for Comments 1070, DDN Network Information Center,
             SRI International, February, 1989.

[SDeer88]   Stephen E. Deering. Multicast Routing in Internetworks
             and Extended LANs. *Computer Communication Re-
             view*, 18(4):55–64, August, 1988.

[SKill86]   Stephen E. Kille. *Mapping between X.400 and RFC822*.
             Request for Comments 987, DDN Network Information
             Center, SRI International, June, 1986. Also available as
             UCL Technical Report number 120 and Mailgroup Note
             number 19.

[SKill88]   Stephen E. Kille. The QUIPU Directory Service.
             In *Proceedings, Fourth International Symposium on
             Computer Message Systems*, Einar Stefferud, editor,

                      pages 173–185, September, 1988. Costa Mesa, Califor-
                      nia.

[SKill89a]   Stephen E. Kille. *A string encoding of Presentation Ad-
                      dress.* Research Note RN/89/14, Department of Com-
                      puter Science, University College London, February,
                      1989.

[SKill89b]   Stephen E. Kille. *An interim approach to use of Net-
                      work Addresses.* Research Note RN/89/14, Department
                      of Computer Science, University College London, Febru-
                      ary, 1989.

[SMI86a]   *External Data Representation Protocol Specification.*
                      Sun Microsystems, Inc., Mountain View, California,
                      February, 1986. Part Number 800-1324-03.

[SMI86b]   *Network File System Protocol Specification.* Sun Mi-
                      crosystems, Inc., Mountain View, California, February,
                      1986. Part Number 800-1324-03.

[UKGOS88]   U.K. Government OSI Profile. January, 1988. Ver-
                      sion 3.0.

[USGOS88]   U.S. Government Open Systems Interconnection Profile
                      (GOSIP). August, 1988. U.S. Federal Information Pro-
                      cessing Standards Publication 146.

[UWarr89]   Unni Warrier and Larry Besaw. *Common Manage-
                      ment Information Services and Protocol over TCP/IP
                      (CMOT).* Request for Comments 1095, DDN Network
                      Information Center, SRI International, April, 1989.

[VCerf83]   Vinton G. Cerf and Edward A. Cain. The DoD Inter-
                      net Architecture Model. *Computer Networks and ISDN
                      Systems*, 7(10):307–318, October, 1983.

[VCerf88]   Vinton G. Cerf. *IAB Recommendations for the Develop-
                      ment of Internet Network Management Standards.* Re-
                      quest for Comments 1052, DDN Network Information
                      Center, SRI International, April, 1988.

[VJaco88]   Van Jacobson. Congestion Avoidance and Control. In *Proceedings, SIGCOMM '88 Workshop*, pages 314–329, ACM SIGCOMM, ACM Press, August, 1988. Stanford, CA.

Index